GOVERNMENT DEBTS AND FINANCIAL MARKETS IN EUROPE

T0330926

FINANCIAL HISTORY

Series Editor: Robert E. Wright

GOVERNMENT DEBTS AND FINANCIAL MARKETS IN EUROPE

EDITED BY

Fausto Piola Caselli

LONDON AND NEW YORK

First published 2008 by Pickering & Chatto (Publishers) Limited

Published 2016 by Routledge
2 Park Square, Milton Park, Abingdon, Oxfordshire OX14 4RN
711 Third Avenue, New York, NY 10017, USA

First issued in paperback 2015

Routledge is an imprint of the Taylor & Francis Group, an informa business

BRITISH LIBRARY CATALOGUING IN PUBLICATION DATA

Government debts and financial markets in Europe. – (Financial history)
1. Debts, Public – Europe – History 2. Finance – Europe – History
I. Piola Caselli, Fausto
336.3'4'094

ISBN-13: 978-1-138-66371-8 (pbk)
ISBN-13: 978-1-85196-962-3 (hbk)

Typeset by Pickering & Chatto (Publishers) Limited

CONTENTS

CONTRIBUTORS

Carlos Álvarez-Nogal, University Carlos III de Madrid.

Christophe Chamley, Boston University, Paris School of Economics and HEC.

Giuseppe Conti, Università di Pisa.

Giuseppe De Luca, University of Milan.

Anne Dubet, University Blaise Pascal, Clermont-Ferrand, France.

David Alonso García, Universidad Complutense (Madrid).

Patrick Karl O'Brien, London School of Economics.

Luciano Pezzolo, School of Advanced Studies, University Ca'Foscari, Venice.

Fausto Piola Caselli, Dipartimento di Studi Economici, University of Cassino.

Andreas Ranft, Institut für Geschichte, Martin-Luther-Universität, Halle-Wittenburg.

Gaetano Sabatini, University of Rome III.

David Stasavage, New York University.

José Ignacio Andrés Ucendo, Department of Economic History, University of the Basque Country.

Hans-Peter Ullmann, Department of Modern History, University of Cologne.

François R. Velde, Federal Reserve Bank of Chicago.

LIST OF CHARTS AND TABLES

INTRODUCTION

Fausto Piola Caselli

Government debts and financial markets in Europe, from the sixteenth to the twentieth century, were the subject of discussion at the XIVth Congress of the International Economic History Association in Helsinki in August 2006. In particular, the relationship between government indebtedness and the creation of enduring financial markets provided a focus of the discussions. Scholars from different academic backgrounds looked at the subject from a comparative perspective and from different angles. This collection publishes the essence of this research, but the articles provide for a more in-depth discussion than what was presented at Helsinki. All contributions draw on original research and discuss some of the most important aspects of public finance history.

Throughout history and until the present day, public debt service has signified a basic problem within European state finances. From the late middle ages onwards – if not earlier – urban and central governments began to raise money through long- and short-term loans. Initially, indebtedness was intended to finance war budgets, but gradually money was channelled towards civil purposes such as public works or food supply. Municipal and state authorities could either approach prominent bankers, merchants and money lenders, or they could apply directly for the savings of private citizens. On occasion, both methods were pursued in parallel in some local areas. Monarchs largely preferred to negotiate with high-level financiers, in exchange for profitable fiscal revenues from the crown, whereas urban governments preferred to launch forced or free loans, involving citizens in the debt business along the way. However, it is very difficult to categorize or locate the various debt systems across Europe from the late medieval and early modern period onwards.

The growth of a public debt service is closely linked with the most important aspects of state-building processes and forms of government. Raising money through debts strongly depends, where representative assemblies are in place, on the consensus won by government or the power held by the ruling morarch. Public debt service also represents a responsive tool of political economy that needs to be continuously balanced with the global sustainable fiscal burden, as huge debt increases enforce bankruptcies or new taxes. Expenses resulting from indebtedness practically trigger the circulation of new monetary flows within a territory, having an impact on price levels, production costs and consumption. The amount of debt is conditioned by the economic wealth of a territory, which ultimately is the sole guarantee of any advantageous return. On a different but no less important level, public debt management is linked to other variables, such as the general level of interest rates, the efficiency of institutions and central bureaucracy, and even the accuracy of an accounting system.

The existing literature predominantly looks at the history of public debt from the perspective of city and territorial states as borrowers. More focus still needs to be given to investors and the markets they enlivened. Monarchs and rulers preferred to approach wealthy bankers, who in turn relied on their own lenders' network. Free markets, however, even welcomed the purchase of single one-off bonds. Government bonds with only a few formal constraints attached soon became marketable. They were therefore traded wherever capital was in search of good investments. As a result, investors became aware that their savings were no longer frozen in government coffers but could actually be made available as liquid assets. Investments underwent changes, with capital being diverted from uncertain traditional investments such as land. Procedures, guarantees and techniques were well known to lenders at a national and international level. The demand for information transparency grew. The increasing efficiency of financial markets eventually allowed governments to raise money at less cost. More significantly, it is worth noting that a wider financial market encouraged governments to realize their debt obligations.

Public debt markets were thus widely accessible through stock exchanges, banking network services or even ad hoc bureaux. Private institutions and local authorities also entered the market, building up their assets with public bonds rather than real estate. Underlying these considerations was the assumption that, in an emergency, bonds could be used more easily as a credit pledge. Financial markets became the best place to expect returns and compare private and public loans in terms of safety, interest and refunds.

The contributions to this collection are invaluable in shedding new light on this subject. However, they do not comprehensively exhaust the immense and fascinating subject of public debt in modern European history. A lot of work still needs to be done, focusing, for example, on town and local debt paralleling the national debt, or on the whole subject of government debts and financial markets in Eastern Europe.

This volume has been accomplished thanks to the efforts of many people and institutions working in close cooperation. To name only a few, I wish to express my sincere gratitude to Pierre-Cyrille Hautcoeur, Michael North and José Ignacio Andrés Ucendo. All three organized and co-chaired with me the session on debt at the said International Economic History Association meeting in Helsinki.

Many thanks also to David Stasavage, who rounded up the discussions with some brilliant final remarks. I am also grateful for the very important contribution made by the economics departments of the universities of Palermo and Cassino in helping to realize this collection. Finally, the steering role of CIRSFI (Inter-University Centre for the History of Italian Finance), under the chairmanship of Angelo Moioli, must be highlighted. From the very beginning CIRSFI carried out wide-ranging national research – aimed at comparative historical studies – that was to culminate in the preparation of the Helsinki Congress. The volume received support out of a research project from the 2003 Italian PRIN (Research Programmes of National Interest)

1 THE FINANCIAL ADMINISTRATION OF NORTH HANSEATIC CITIES IN THE LATE MIDDLE AGES: DEVELOPMENT, ORGANIZATION AND POLITICS

Andreas Ranft[1]

Introduction

The particular character of the material culture of North Hanseatic medieval cities suggests impressive urban structures with their own law.[2] Behind these are complex institutions with 'public' services deriving from them, which is what make it possible for a highly-differentiated township to function.[3]

The written *monumenta*, in particular the town and invoice books (as well as documents like privileges, files of jurisdiction or business acts, wills, public and private chronicles, parish registers, etc.), help to decipher that administrative core, the workings behind the protection and control of that complex community. The reason for this is that the budget system in general played a key role in the organization of all aspects of urban life.[4] The complex structures of urban society were unthinkable without finances and without the 'rationality' of a 'specific management'.

The formation and maintenance of a city are only conceivable in connection with the development of a public cash system. Its structure, along with the development of urban law,[5] determined the level of understanding of local administration, and its efficiency defined the scope of material mobility vis-à-vis the town authority and the surrounding powers.[6] As this demonstrates, money is power. Examples to be borne in mind are the acquisition of privileges by purchase (e.g. wall construction), financing of military potential (e.g. mercenary force), purchase of profitable jurisdiction (e.g. tolls, mills), and investment in public infrastructure (e.g. harbours, cranes, department stores, canals).[7]

General Observations

The genesis of urban finances and their administration in Braunschweig, Bremen, Hamburg, Lübeck and Lüneburg could be interpreted as an entirely synchronous process. Lüneberg's position as a salt-town made it something of a special case, which I will return to later. If we look at the oldest documents in each case –fragments of the finance departments' calculations (*Kämmereirechnungen*) from the early fourteenth century – and also bear in mind that no other systematically organized accounting tradition was established until some decades later, it is possible to arrive at some initial general observations.

After the constitution of an independent council, the medieval town budget consisted of an ordinary budget and an extraordinary budget.[8] The 'ordinary' part involved the acquisition and use of budgetary means for managing the town's normal business operations. These were the regular current expenses, without which the administration of the urban community could not function and the cities' various outside debts could not be serviced. The 'extraordinary' part can be described as one-off or very irregular payments and transactions and as the 'debt service' of the city.[9] For this a separate debt register (*registrum creditorum*) was started each time that the debenture bonds, by which the cities financed their structural expansion and their increasingly wide-ranging trade policy (protection of privileges, military protection of the trade routes, communication systems, etc.), could no longer be paid from the current tax revenue.[10]

In this context it can also be seen that the late medieval town budget grew from one core, containing the framework and instruments with which the total budget (the amount of all financial activities transacted by the council) was run. Its size, construction and functioning were indicators of the economic and budgetary dimensions of urban council policy, to the extent that this core provided the apparatus for internal services and was also used for handling the extraordinary budget.[11]

A core budget of this sort also gives some insight into a town's specific role in its region – for example within North Germany – and within the Hanseatic network around the Baltic Sea and from there to West Europe and England. The first was primarily concerned with each town's policy of close alliances and militia (*Landwehr*) for the protection of the surrounding traffic network. The latter concerned, for example, day journeys (*Tagfahrten*), the system of embassy missions and messenger communication networks. The expenditure from a core budget of this sort has very often been preserved and passed down, as it was mostly recorded in cash books maintained for many years. Due to their size these were not so easily lost as the single sheets or separate books in which the credit and bond transactions in the sphere of the extraordinary budget were recorded. Even a partially-preserved book from a city treasury shows in its structure and dimensions clear signs of previous accounts, revealing layers of different accounting and administrative practice.

Sources

The treasury accounts – systematically established as books or handed down as single fascicles – are the oldest evidence of fiscal activity we have for North Hanseatic medieval cities. They were initiated by the council and had official documentary value like all other entries in a town book, be they legal transactions of a public or private nature (here the council also acted as a notary's office) or legal decisions of the jurisdiction. In fact, the whole range and diversity of urban duties can be found in them – even if only in note form – as indeed would be the case today.[12] They are mainly reflected in the expenses, which included material costs of administration, wages and salaries; entertainment costs (expenses, gifts, wine and spices for the business service of the council); messengers and guard costs; costs for building and city cleaning; the purchase of arms; and finally, the net debt service at the bond market, in which the city participated right from the beginning. This shows an amazing diversity that appears modern, as far as the apparently systematic and exhaustive registration of the duties of an urban or – as it was often claimed – state administration is concerned.

The revenues reveal that in addition to the *vorschoß* (input tax)[13] and the urban businesses that yielded profit (e.g. brickyards, wine and beer cellars),[14] there were also rents for houses and gardens (outside of the city) that belonged to the municipality, and fees for wells and markets. They show that along with the *schoß* (property tax) the expenses system was rapidly differentiated, thereby providing regular incomes.

It is quite remarkable that even now the list of expenses (and with that the area of urban responsibility) is not exhausted. For each of the cities analysed, more can be found regarding expenses for local needs. Thus the number of individual transactions could more than double and the volume of the budget multiply many times. On average the costs of a medium-sized city (about 10,000 to 15,000 inhabitants) with approximately 1,000 transactions reached between 15,000 and 20,000 Mark lübisch.

At the end of the fourteenth century more cashbooks are found, which began one after the other in quick succession at the initiative of the council and under its supervision.[15] First of all so-called *Baubücher* (construction books) are found in archives.[16] As one might expect – even though this sphere was already mentioned extensively in the accounts of the finance department – these reveal more about the construction work that was under urban responsibility: notes about repairs to the urban fortification, organization of urban hygiene (irrigation and drainage), carts, and again wages. Incomes were also recorded. These were fees collected for raw materials (e.g. quicklime and wood) on which the city had a monopoly, also a brothel tax, pram and cart fees, wedding fees and fines. But large donations for extremely high constructions costs are also revealed (e.g. for building walls and churches). So, looking at the revenues, it can already be assumed that the current needs were helping to create new additional rates and taxes. The fact that a specific matter (construction and security affairs) is being dealt with in these books, which in a systematic respect had already appeared in different cashbooks, leads us to question – as will often be the case – the overarching system, the rationality or at least the genesis of such a system. Payments to various craftsmen and servants (e.g. farm-labourers) make it clear that behind the master builder's office, for which the accounts were kept, a large economic enterprise was hidden, which tried to work in a profit-orientated way.

Two more books – produced around the same time as the construction books – deal largely, though not exclusively, with foodstuffs. One is the documentation of a cash account, which was sustained by the profit from the trade of imported beer (this was in the council's hands).[17] Here again are familiar expenses: construction and repairs, travelling expenses, beer money, as well as wages and salaries. What is new, however, are supplies for the defence system (*Landwehr*). Here again servants were regularly employed: loading staff (*Verladeknechte*), caretakers and administrators (for the beer cellars), as well as special equipment to calibrate the measures. The other is the so called *Czsiebook*,[18] which refers in general to a rate or rather tax on foodstuffs and luxury goods, and which, in the cities being looked at here, was levied on all beer sold and drunk and on wine. Here, once again, are familiar expenses: travelling costs for mayors and councillors, payment of town hall wages, soldiers' pay, costs for materials and carriage, food and fodder, as well as beer donations. Worth noting here are oats and straw for the mayor's horses, stable expenses (for the armoury), annuity payments (debt services) and boot-money (*Stiefelgeld*) for the marksmen.

Additional cash accounts, devoted only to enterprises that acquired raw materials, such as salt-works and silver mines, are exceptional and only comparable with those of other salt-towns like Halle/Saale or cities with a similar structure like the mining towns in the Harz (for example Goslar). In Lüneburg there are the so-called *Sotmeisterrechnungen*, which account for the proceeds from the salt-works and also create expenses for the city out of percentage rates.[19] The *Sotmeister*, a member of the town council who was elected to office as the highest salt-works administrator, made a meticulous note of the expenses incurred for the urban administration. Along with wages for the guards and mercenaries involved in the permanent defence of the town, these included the purchase of ammunition and arms, gifts, anonymous transfers by the mayors (higher amounts), as well as donations to the councillors and finally the financing of expensive day journeys by the councillors.

Systematic Observations

The outward schema of these invoice books more or less follows that of the finance department books mentioned earlier.[20] They begin with the appointment of the accountant and/or the treasurer – two members of the council were regularly elected or confirmed in these offices. Then follow the expenses, written one under the other, with a subtotal on each page. The calculation of the total amount of all expenses forms an extra section. After that, generally on one page, the revenues are listed, with a sum total. The annual balance is not always at the end, sometimes – as in Hamburg – the income is recorded first. In such cases this is usually more extensive because the surplus from other cash accounts generally had to be transferred to the finance department (*Kämmerei*), and noted accordingly.

This somewhat condensed schematization already reveals the important rank of these sources – although in the books the editor has the sobering and somewhat dreary task of dealing mainly with numbers, mostly monotonous data, and checking that the basic arithmetic is without error. In order to explain how these invoice books could help to create a detailed picture of the regime of a late medieval town, the organization and functions of this kind of municipality, I should briefly describe what has been done in this direction so far, and where the methodological problems lie.

Methodology

At the turn of the twentieth century researchers were already becoming aware of the marked, and increasing, information available in these sources, as well as the extent of what they (taken as a whole) registered and documented of urban activity. At that time it was the so-called historically orientated *Staatswissenschaften* (political sciences) that recognized the late medieval city as a precursor of the modern political system and sought after elements of modern state-building.[21] On the one hand researchers were generally interested in discovering the existence of various parallel cashbooks: these were seen as independent units of administration with a well-coordinated distribution of responsibilities, as was required by an efficient administrative structure rationally orientated towards urban duties in their entirety. This impression was reinforced by the fact that every invoice book was basically kept according to the same scheme (as already mentioned), i.e. there was a standardized bookkeeping system. In addition, the cashbooks were directly linked to the central management (council) via their bookkeepers. At the same time, however, it should be noted that there was no central (main) cashbook that would – as we would say today – allow for budgeting.

On the other hand these researchers unearthed a differentiated arsenal of financial-technical institutions, which the cities – in different forms and dimensions according to their financial requirements[22] – used to maintain and improve the essential business of expenditure and income, and taking and giving credit. Apart from direct taxes (*schoß* and *vorschoß*) there was also a system of indirect taxation, which was a burden on food consumption, and the fiscal use of trade and business (*Accisen* on wine, beer, corn, salt and meat, etc., as well as on raw materials, for example iron, lead, tin and wax), depending on the economic structure of the city. In addition there were fees for the use of the urban infrastructure (roads, waterways/canals, department stores, market stalls, etc.) and income from owning real estate. Finally, the charges also included the citizen-fee (*Bürgergeld*), taxes arising from, for example, wills and death duties. Apart from that the urban enterprises like wine cellars, brickyards and hop markets also brought in a fairly regular income.

In modern research, an attempt is being made to see the urban budget not just as a sort of static structure formed by acquired administrative norms, pointing only to a community's system of classification. Budgets are instead being viewed in their developmental processes – propelled by the general dynamics of urban economic and social development. One could say that the budget is the seismograph of urban development. This has sometimes led to the formal combination of single invoice and cash books that indicated specific administrative authorities. This in turn has made it possible to construct – through the book covers – seemingly uniform statistical series as the basis for computerized measurement of the economic system of that time, and indeed to pursue, for example, the development of investment, indebtedness and cash value.[23]

Results

If the analytical image of every single cashbook is put together to form a general impression, and coordinated with the prosopographical material of the town council and office-holder, it is possible to formulate some initial conclusions about the development of urban budgets in the late Middle Ages. At the start of urban accounting, it was not the practice to establish several cashbooks. In the oldest treasury accounts the expenses still include transactions that were booked separately in the later urban invoice books, for example beer donations or costs of the quicklime mines.[24] In the case of revenue too, transactions that were later booked separately were all recorded in one book, i.e. there was only one cashbook.

It was not, however, expenditure, which in course of the fourteenth century became more comprehensive and voluminous, that led to the establishment of additional cashbooks. What seems more likely is that it was the revenues, whose structure was more complicated, and which mainly consisted of the organization and control of consumer taxes and the income from donations, that made a more extensive bookkeeping system necessary. This is why additional cashbooks were set up. It is also clear, however, that this process did not consist of just one single act. Fairly lengthy transitional phases can be seen, initiated by the establishment of a construction cashbook at a time when defence construction in the cities, as well as the construction of churches and town halls, was especially demanding in terms of financing and bookkeeping. Eventually, by the first half of the fifteenth century, the urban budget consisted of five or six cashbooks.

Finally, let me just address two points briefly – the allocation of offices and the structure of the budget and/or cashbook. First of all it is consistently clear that by setting up different cashbooks the burden of running the budget was divided between several members of the council. If we look at how offices were allocated – every year when the council was reformed ten new treasurers had to be elected, apart from the other offices, because there had to be two in each post – it becomes clear that the councillors named in the invoice books were only recruited from a small elite group of the council. They were all elected in turn, so that in the course of fifteen years on average only about fifteen councillors were elected to these offices. Thus each councillor was a council treasurer for about eight to ten years. Every treasurer changed his department at least once, and about half of them had been in charge of at least three cashbooks. Here we can see a balance between the continuity of bookkeeping already seen in each cashbook and the opportunity to acquire qualified councillors, who knew the internal workings of several of these cashbooks and their specific duties. In this way it was possible to develop and maintain the necessary analytical expertise for the requirements of the budget as a whole, which then made it easy to check the bookkeeping of each cashbook at the annual rendering of accounts. There was no hierarchy between these offices; it was possible to switch from one to the other without losing esteem. The exception was bookkeeping for the finance department, the office of which was very often a stepping-stone to the mayor's office; nearly one-third of the mayors were former treasurers of the finance department. None of them changed back to a different cashbook.[25] It is interesting to note that analysis of the individual calculations shows that the keepers of the cashbooks did not communicate with one another, nor was there any common system of assignment for fields of expenses that sometimes overlapped.

Second, in order to describe the budgetary system in such a way that the part played by each cashbook in the various fields of expenditure is recognizable, it is necessary to redefine overarching and also specific areas of expenses – considering all expenses – only some of which can be found in all cashbooks, but which nonetheless constitute the budget. There are about thirty spheres that are to be found in each of the cities analysed. The order they are placed on the list is not determined by any particular system, but rather by their volume. A comparison between the expenditure fields dealt with in each cashbook shows that the budgetary structure – measured against the budget of the city treasury as a yardstick

– was developed early on, but that proportional variations were caused when additional cashbooks were set up.

To summarize, it can be seen that the late medieval town budget did not correspond at all to the criteria of a modern rational administration, as some researchers claim today. There are neither instructions nor regulations, be they oaths or other written notes, that really define the tasks of the office. Nor was there any unified system, which might have had the same effect. On the other hand it is clear that – even measured against present-day municipal responsibilities – individuals were skilfully chosen for specific duties, even though such elements as the fiscal cash unit, budgeting, raising income and trade taxes were completely alien to them.

Such an assessment, however, does not really do justice to the budgetary situation. This would be to underrate the efficiency of budget-keeping, even though some of the accounts are rendered in a very ponderous way. The pragmatism of the councillors in questions concerning the budget as well as the 'rule of thumb' approach taken by various office-holders, given the lack of formal instructions, allowed a flexible budget policy, which could respond both efficiently and quickly to daily problems, to one-off issues and to given circumstances. Although the late medieval budget was essentially needs-driven, it includes forward-looking elements, without which the efficient and rapid planning of public buildings would not have been possible, nor indeed the smoothly coordinated trade and alliance policy of these North German Hanseatic cities.

Public Debt

The second point, however, is not covered by an analysis of the accounting system of public cashbooks and still shows us today that urban finances – like state finances – were, and remain, one of the best-kept secrets of political activity in the Middle Ages and the early modern period. Admittedly, the urban councils communicated their public accounting to the citizens to show their concern for the *bonum commune*, and the purpose of the annual rendering of accounts by the treasurers, apart from checking on one another, was a political demonstration, an attempt to engender trust, that would create legitimacy and help to secure their domination. Yet the public only kept a critical eye on the outward signs and perceptible handling of the finances, particularly dissatisfied groups who felt they had been short-changed in the distribution of benefits and power, while the poorer classes simply regarded it with suspicion. At this time finances and their administration provided good conspiracy theories and accusations of corruption, which the 'common man' was quick to believe. Complaints and arguments of this sort run like a thread through the urban unrest from the thirteenth to the sixteenth century.

The impetus for public demands for improvement of councils, or even their resignation and the establishment of new councils, came from the debts arising from commitments in the so-called extraordinary budget, which came at the expense of the municipality. Only very rarely, however, if a *registrum creditorum* was brought to the public's attention, did it actually reveal very much. Rather it was impatient creditors or simply tax increases that caused urban opposition. As regards the handling of the extraordinary budget debt, it was more a question of concealing actual transactions and taking up credit or debts as the ruling classes weighed up their own interests from both the inside and the outside. The practice of mixing public and private together in this budgetary sphere largely dominated the financial administration. We should not be deceived by the mass of account books that have been handed down, since many financial files, even in cities like Basel that are richly documented, have not been preserved. How great the danger of mixing interests was is revealed inter alia by the condition in the Wismar council constitution which strictly forbade councillors from selling the town's money privately as annuities.

The urban annuities markets were, indeed, a well-tested way of taking up public credit and were used by councillors who, as businessmen themselves, set up in the private annuities trade. They very often sat on the supervisory boards, or were trustees and represented the town's interests in foundations (hospitals and urban monasteries) whose wealth played a part in the annuities market. Unfortunately even the most minute examination of the annuities markets in Hamburg, Lübeck, Braunschweig and Stade does not reveal a great deal about the proportion of the municipality's funds involved in the urban annuities market and its instrumentalization in terms of finance policy for the urban budget.[26] It is only the regulations of privileges for recipients of urban rents (frequently *Leibrenten*, payment of which ceased at the death of the creditor), such as the guaranteed *Schoßfreiheit* (exemption from taxes on wealth) and/or higher interest rates (up to 10 per cent instead of the average 5 to 7 per cent),[27] which indicate that the towns were perfectly capable of using the annuities markets as instruments for generating urgently-needed capital. What is striking here is that there was an above-average involvement of the councillors as lenders. They were the ones who profited most from such special conditions and, as the decision-making authority, were most readily in a position to offer the most appropriate credits.[28] The sometimes fierce competition with other entrepreneurs in the face of the public demand which this caused gave a measure of balance, due to the formation of a network of rent markets in North Germany.[29] At the same time, the financial involvement of the respective urban elites led to acts of solidarity in the course of urban revolts which, as has been mentioned, were triggered by problems of excessive debt or massive rises in expenditure. It is mostly circumstances of this kind that led to the production of written sources giving evidence regarding the loans raised by communes to finance their defence enterprises (e.g. fortifications, militias and mercenaries), to keep open their political and diplomatic options, and to meet their frequently very costly commitments as allies which, in turn, helped to protect their merchants and markets and allowed the towns to resist external pressures.[30] It is difficult to give exact figures for this time, but it can be safely assumed that in the period around 1500 approximately 30 per cent (as interest) of the overall urban budget of the towns considered here went into contraction due to debt.[31] In the case of Hamburg, this meant that the state debt was in the region of 66,000 Mark lübisch.[32] Considering that the average tax burden was around 3,000 Mark lübisch, the severity of the strain that extraordinary financial commitments put on public authorities becomes evident. No amount of economic prosperity could ever prevent the steady growth of public debt; it was only reliability in the field of interest payment and the occasional restructuring of debt on the rent market which shifted the burden and created political leeway in struggles for power within the town.

Public Debt and Participation in Economic Monopolies

The budget of the town of Lüneburg shows a unique structure of organizing public finances and, by extension, of handling debt.[33] One of the most important locations of salt production during the Middle Ages was located within the geographical area of legal authority (*Weichbild*) of this commune, and the council formed by the families of leading salt-producers (*Sülfmeister*) could claim special rights to the fruits of this lucrative monopoly. Despite the complexity of ownership rights the *Sülfmeister* alone possessed the *Siederecht* (the right to produce salt) and, together with the town, made the technological infrastructure available. In this sense, the interested parties in this trade, who were scattered all over North Germany, were involved in a conflict-laden but ultimately indissoluble symbiosis with the town of Lüneburg and its council regarding the production and sale of salt, and became natural givers of credit.[34] In the wake of the town's ill-fated involvement in a local war of succession, which resulted in crippling debt and the ultimately catastrophic overburdening of its budget,[35] the council achieved ever greater success in its long drawn-out efforts, during the 1480s, to force its powerful creditors (for the most part, ecclesiastical institutions frequently scorned as 'salt prelates' by contemporaries) to hand over shares in the salt water (*Sole*) produced in the vicinity and to fix additional dates for manufacturing salt for the town's benefit. It was at this time that the *registrum creditorum* mentioned above was compiled. It aimed to help to maintain transparency in the distribution of the profits of salt production. In this way it became possible to achieve tangible debt reduction in several waves; however, no long-term legal solution to the problem of financial contribution was found. Only at the end of this process, which was not always a peaceful one, was the so-called fund of the *Sotmeister*[36] introduced. It complemented the occasional fixed-term credits granted by the notorious 'salt prelates'. This fund continuously collected the profits from the shares conceded to the council, which could be spent at the mayor's behest. Whereas hitherto the expenses of Lüneburg's network of treaties and alliances and of extending and maintaining the transport infrastructure had been jointly responsible for the growth of the town's debt burden, the opportunity now arose to cover those costs on a regular basis. In this respect, it can be said that the regular budget of Lüneburg and other salt-towns of the fifteenth century rested on two pillars, which gave lasting support to the commune in coping with considerable parts of the financial commitments which would otherwise have incurred more debt. However, fortunate as these circumstances may have been, they were not enough to prevent Lüneburg from sharing the sometimes dangerous practice of contracting debt followed by other late medieval towns.

2 GOVERNMENT DEBTS AND CREDIT MARKETS IN RENAISSANCE ITALY

Luciano Pezzolo

The Financing System of Governments

At first sight a marked difference between the Italian governments of the early Renaissance can be seen: the means of financing their deficit. There were, on the one hand, communal cities and republics raising money from citizens through the system of forced or voluntary loans; and, on the other, princes and lords who exploited the services of bankers and merchants. These two different systems of borrowing bring about significant financial and political variations. In this paper I will examine the main features characterizing the two mechanisms of indebtedness and the implications concerning the emergence of a true financial market connected with state bonds.

As far as we know, the first loans in cities were made on a voluntary basis. Pressed by urgent – usually military – needs, the commune requested the wealthiest citizens to lend a given sum and committed itself to pay it back in a short time. The social group of lenders was composed of merchants, bankers, Jews and sometimes foreigners. The government usually granted tax proceeds or domain revenues as guaranty. This practice took place from the beginning of the twelfth century, as the cities seized control of taxing rights from feudal lords and ecclesiastical institutions.[1]

The availability of loans, however, was not adequate for the growing financial needs of city governments engaged in an expensive territorial expansion. Governments thus requested both forced and voluntary loans. The system relied on fiscal documents (*estimi* and *catasti*) that assessed all citizens for the amount of their wealth or income. According to these documents, the government assigned the amount each citizen had to lend. In this case loans usually were short term and with a modest interest rate. This system considerably enlarged the social sector of lenders; all the citizens, apart from the poorest ranks, were requested to put money into the commune's coffers. Likewise, the Jewish community was obliged to lend to the government. Although the government debt was characterized first

17

and foremost by the participation of city dwellers, it is nevertheless worth noting that in some cases subject communities were involved in the system. In 1287 in Siena, for example, the *presta generalis* (general loan) was imposed on both the capital city and the rural communities. In 1371, the same occurred in Lucca. During the second half of the fifteenth century, Venice also, albeit seldom, collected forced loans from the subject cities. Like the voluntary loans, the forced loans were conceived as short-term loans, guaranteed on fiscal revenues that also assured interest payments.[2]

As far as the *signorie*, the Papal States and the Kingdom of Naples were concerned, the picture was very different. The mechanism of borrowing first relied on the money provided more or less freely from merchants, bankers, courtesans and foreigners. As a consequence, one might paradoxically argue that a primary market existed in the princely states, whereas on the other hand a 'public' debt similar to that of the city-states did not exist. It was a very peculiar primary market, however, which should be defined more correctly as a personal market. The lenders to princes were usually merchants and bankers whose business in the country was conspicuous. Thus, it is no surprise to see the Strozzi bank heavily involved in managing state finance in Aragonese Naples; or the Medici lending to the Duke of Milan. Loans to rulers and commercial activities intertwined, constituting a mechanism extremely advantageous to lenders as long as the debtor kept his promises.[3] Along with these people, who can be considered credit specialists, there were also nobles and officers around the prince, who wished to get or to enhance a political role through their lending activity. They willingly lent, sometimes even at no interest, counting on princely benevolence in order to get privileges, offices and advantages, as in late medieval Turin.[4] Such a mechanism in some ways recalls the cronyism evoked by Hilton Root with regard to Ancien Régime France.[5] The king stood at the centre of a system of relations that, if well exploited, allowed him to achieve enormous political and economic advantages, but at the same time encouraged rent-seeking behaviour. This system, however, called for high costs, due to the great uncertainty pervading the interaction between creditors and king. The latter, in fact, was not bound to any rule and could repudiate his commitments almost with no consequences. This sharp asymmetry of course brought about costly loans. Therefore it was usual that loans for princes were much dearer than those obtained by urban governments. In the mid-fifteenth century, the Aragonese Crown in Naples, for example, paid interest rates as high as 40 per cent, while in Florence interest on short-term loans usually did not exceed 12–14 per cent.[6] This difference showed, among other things, the different degree of risk in government borrowing.

Funding Debt and the Emergence of the Financial Market

Beginning from the second half of the thirteenth century, some urban governments recognized it was impossible to return the principal being borrowed, and decided to change some elements of their debt. Short-term loans were transformed into long-term loans; the receipts of some tax revenues were assigned for paying interest (5 per cent in Florence and Venice, 7 per cent in Genoa, from two to six times a year); all the debts were unified in a *Monte* (or *compera*, in Genoa) and managed by a specific office; furthermore, negotiability of state credits was allowed. Venice in 1262 and Genoa in 1274 led the way; by the mid-fourteenth century they were followed by Florence, Pisa, Siena and Lucca.[7] It was not indeed a true consolidation, since reimbursements were still undertaken; but undoubtedly government creditors had abandoned hope of getting their money back. The institutionalization of the debt also brought about an important process of socialization of the debt. By means of middlemen and speculators bonds circulated throughout almost all social environments, from the great merchants to the humble artisans. It is also worth noting that the resort to forced loans pushed governments to improve the tax records. Citizens thus became true lender-taxpayers rather than lender-investors. It is useful to stress this aspect, which sheds a particular light on the indebtedness mechanism of Italian Renaissance cities. A structural change actually occurred. As long as state finance was not under severe and extended pressure, the system represented a 'moneylender's paradise'.[8] Principal was paid back in a relatively short time and interest was also paid regularly. But growing and endless expenses provoked huge holes in the budget: so indebtedness became a regular tool, which led almost naturally to funding. The pace of indebtedness of the main cities can be seen in Table 2.1, showing the performances of Italian cities in comparison with data concerning the great European powers, the latter available only for the mid-seventeenth century.

Table 2.1: Estimate of Per Capita Indebtedness, 1350–1650 (in kg of silver).[9]

Year	Venice	Genoa	Florence	Holland	Castile	France
1350	0.2		0.2			
1400	1.7	2.1	2.8			
1450		3				
1500	4.1	2.7	3.0			
1600	0.1	5.4				
1650	1.7	3.6	0.5	1.7	0.6	0.4

These figures confirm how the political and above all the economic power of major Italian city-states relied on the exploitation of capital-intensive resources, according to the well-known definition of Charles Tilly.[10] It is also worth noting that the amount of indebtedness considerably increased, despite the demographic crisis of the mid-fourteenth century, due to a long period of interstate conflicts.

Still, it is surprising that by the mid-seventeenth century the per capita burden was not lower than the Dutch figure, which represented the most developed area in Europe at that time and furthermore had been a recent theatre of a long and costly war against the Spanish Crown. One has, however, to consider that in Italy the debt was concentrated within the single cities, while in other countries it was spread throughout a wider area.

Undoubtedly the consolidation triggered the development of the secondary market of state credits, yet it did not create it. Credits had sometimes been circulating before consolidation. In the thirteenth century in Treviso and Vicenza credits were, albeit not often, negotiated; but it is likely that this operation was quite exceptional.[11] There are Milanese examples of transferring credits of the commune, but these were IOUs, which did not seem very popular among citizens.[12] The secondary market, however, developed as the government demand for loans grew and the institutionalization of the debt took place.[13] The formation of a wide secondary market made government bankruptcy expectations a matter of public discussion.[14] A system, on the one hand, based mainly on personal relations between creditors and government allowed the latter to decree a selective suspension of payment; a system, on the other hand, based on a large secondary market presented the government with few choices and stronger constraints, for a wider public had to be taken into account. This does not mean that urban governments did not make any distinction between creditors. In 1316, as the Venetian government decided to extinguish a part of its debt, creditors of amounts below 10 lire were repaid with 70 per cent of their principal, whereas 80 per cent was returned to the bondholders of amounts from 10 to 15 lire. In Genoa the *partecipes grossiores* (most important shareholders) exercised a certain influence on the government's financial policy.[15] In principalities, however, major financiers – who managed the mechanism of taxation – enjoyed more advantages than small lenders. The former purchased from the latter their devaluated credits and then, counting on their influence at court and the treasury, were more successful in getting back money.[16]

Venice and Genoa present the emergence of a precocious financial market of state credits. Some decades later, Florence followed the example of the two maritime cities, when in 1345 it allowed the transferability of rights on Monte bonds in order to face creditors' protest.[17] As far as the working of market is concerned, some common elements are shown. The bond trade was vivid and involved large sections of the population; middlemen took on an essential role to meet sellers and buyers, fixing the current price and thus leading the market movements; transactions had to be registered at the offices managing the debt.

But differences were indeed significant. Especially in the fifteenth century, the Florentine government appointed prominent people – bankers and merchants – as Monte officers who were expected to collect short-term loans, mostly from their network of relatives and friends. The principal was to be returned through the receipt of successive forced loans.[18] Although it seems that the Genoese and Venetian governments did not use intermediaries between lenders and the treasury, Venetian bankers were called to anticipate money and pay on behalf of the government, but there is no evidence of their involvement in finding lenders.[19] It is, however, not surprising that in these two cities there were no influential intermediaries. Particularly in Venice, the need to maintain equilibrium within the patriciate prevented the formation of powerful positions and, at least up to the fifteenth century, the wealth of individuals (and of their families) did not exert that influence which was to be found later. In fifteenth-century Venice, the ruling group was still constituted largely of merchants; the assignment to a few of them of the function of fundraisers would have been very risky, both in financial and political terms. In Florence, on the other hand, the ruling group was economically less homogeneous and, mainly during the Medici period, was not very concerned with maintaining an apparent egalitarian structure. Likewise, in princely states the lord could count on some individuals to construct close relationships of reciprocal interest that linked the financial needs of the government to merchant lenders' prospect of profit. Personal relations therefore prevailed in principalities, whereas in cities run by oligarchies the debt relied on a sort of impersonal market, where as a rule all creditors enjoyed the same rights and suffered the same damages.

It would, therefore, seem reasonable to consider the urban means of indebtedness more dynamic and flexible than those of seigniorial and monarchic regimes, unable to develop financial innovations. This is true, but only partially. Beginning from the mid-fifteenth century, in fact, in both Naples and Rome the government attempted, although cautiously, to promote innovations. Alfonso V, in order to fund the war for the conquest of Naples, not only resorted to usual means (e.g. mortgages and bills of exchange) but also sought new ways of raising money. The liquidation of consistent loans was scheduled over quite a long period, so transforming short- into long-term loans. The royal treasury, moreover, issued certificates of credit guaranteed on tax receipts; such credits could be transferred to creditors of merchants, who in turn had to get money from the treasury.[20] However, the continuous financial needs of the Aragonese foreign policy did not allow the establishment of the system and the emergence of a broad capital market.

On the contrary in Rome some financial innovations took on a firm feature and represented the base for further developments. Along with the traditional role of bankers, the popes had exploited the venality of offices, but from the pontificate of Sixtus IV (1471–84) the system began to show new characteristics, becoming a true financial device that released the office from any administrative duty. In 1486, for the first time this new charge was sold, setting up the so-called offices of third category. The purchaser of the office was to pay a given amount (the principal) and the government was to pay him a life-term 'salary' (the interest).

Later the transfer of the right to the 'salary' was allowed even upon the nominee's death. In 1514, furthermore, the first *societas officiurum* was founded, that is a company constituted of people willing to invest in life-term ('vacable') offices, but who individually could not purchase them.[21] The diffusion of government loans through offices brought about, according to Bauer, the 'democratization of the papal state credit'.[22] The vacable offices actually enjoyed a large success. By 1520 the selling of third category offices had provided the papal coffers with an amount of 2.5 million ducats.[23] The success of the vacable offices over the sixteenth century is shown by their growing market price.

Table 2.2: Prices of Offices of Third Category at Rome, 1514–90. Constant price index (1514 = 100). The silver content of currency has been used as a deflator.[24]

Offices	1514	1525	1531	1565	1590
Cubicolari	100	120	116	122	196
Scudieri	100	103	105	151	256
Collettori	100	103	95	57	70
Giannizzeri	100	94	93	73	89
Archivio	100	103	102	139	158
Presidenti	100	92	99	108	104
Porzionari	100	94	70	121	121

Up to the middle of the century, prices did not significantly grow while later the market received offices warmly. The success of these investments, however, declined as the *monti camerali* appeared. The *monti camerali* were true bonds, sold by the Apostolic Chamber, which since the mid-sixteenth century broadly spread out and constituted the pillar of the papal debt up to the arrival of the Napoleonic troops. Over the seventeenth century, however, offices continued to play an important role as a means of credit among individuals.[25]

In the early sixteenth century the interest rate of offices was around 12 per cent, in line with returns in other markets. It is worth noting that the papal choice to sell annuities – as was happening in early sixteenth-century Venice – was against the trend of other cases. In Bâle, for example, the city government gave up resorting to annuities because they proved very expensive.[26]

How the Market Works

In the cities, creditors were above all the inhabitants registered in the *estimo* and, particularly, those assessed above a given threshold of taxable wealth. Lending to the commune was considered a duty as much as servicing the urban militia. The option of borrowing therefore was not, at least initially, criticized; it reflected the choice to limit the use of direct taxation. The continuous resort to forced loans, however, raised criticism and unrest. It was not by chance that in Florence during the revolt of the Ciompi, the rebels aimed to abolish loans carrying high interest rates as well as to resort to direct taxation.[27] In 1339, during one of the numerous riots that occurred in Genoa, the records of creditors were burnt; and in 1408 the same fate occurred to the first documents of the Casa di San Giorgio.[28] At the same time, the registers were important as proof of ownership of credits and served to support trust in the Monte, *compere*, and served to minimize fraud.

In many cases the duty to lend to the city government was, as already said, closely linked to the citizenship right. In the urban world of northern Italy, to be a citizen took on different aspects and involved different categories according to places and periods.[29] Not all the inhabitants of the city were considered citizens *pleno iure*, there were *cives comitatenses*, not to speak of the 'originals', who distinguished themselves from the 'foreigners'. Citizenship created a specific interaction between the inhabitants falling in the definition and the ruling elite. It was a sort of contract that was, on the one hand, to protect the citizens from government abuse and, on the other hand, to guarantee a wide consent to the fiscal demand of authorities.[30] It is thus interesting to wonder whether the growing fiscal demand brought about a reconsideration of citizenship within the urban fabric. The authorities' major concern was to identify the taxable citizens, without considering their local status. It was the payment of the taxes which actually sustained the legitimacy of applications for citizenship. If to defend the homeland, as much with arms as money, was considered the primary duty of a citizen, then the restless financial needs of the government pushed it to widen the urban structure to provide it with some rights.

As far as foreigners were concerned, the statutes generally raised constraints to their purchase of state bonds. They could buy credits only upon the commune's authorization. In Florence, for example, the law did not allow Florentines to sell their credits to foreigners, but in case of need the government also called for foreigners' purses, though with caution.[31] In 1415 the government opened the door to non-Florentine subscribers, but at the same time raised a tax of 10 per cent on the amount being purchased. The tax was on the face value, usually much higher than the market price. This rule – which was sometimes flexible – however does not seem to have limited foreign capital supply. It is interesting to note that the government granted citizenship in order to draw foreign investors, who sometimes enjoyed a higher interest rate than the usual one.[32]

Borrowing from foreigners was not a matter to be trifled with. In exchange for an inflow of fresh money there might be the danger of creating too strong a connection with the creditor, especially if the latter was a powerful person. In 1446, Florence, not having paid interest to Pope Eugenio IV's Monte credits, had to face a reprisal, which was carried out by seizing the goods of Florentine merchants in Rome and even imprisoning the ambassador Bernardino of Antonio de Medici.[33] It is not surprising, therefore, that in 1470, when the government reduced the interest rate on the Monte credits, the king of Portugal and several Genoese were excluded, to avoid the threat of reprisals.[34]

The institutionalization of the state debt brought about an important process of socialization of debt. The move from voluntary loans, addressed to a restricted group of people, to forced loans based on tax records and *estimi* represented a true innovation, not only in financial but also political and to some extent social terms.[35] Almost all the social groups in the main central-northern cities held or dealt with government bonds. The wide diffusion – particularly among artisans – of the Florentine debt, for example, during the revolt of the Ciompi prevented the government from significantly reforming the system of borrowing.[36] The registers of the Genoese debt witnessed a significant increase of the number of bondholders, from 1,773 in 1392 to 11,315 in 1460 and a slight decline in 1500 with 9,997 nominees.[37] One can argue that in the second half of the fifteenth century one-quarter or one-fifth of the urban population held credits of their commune.[38] It must, however, be considered that if in the early phases the amount of subscribers increased, later it was to shrink.[39] The picture provided by the Florentine catasto of 1427 is eloquent.

Table 2.3: The Distribution of Monte Credits in Florence, 1427.[40]

% of households	% of Monte credits
100	100.00
99	56.97
98	42.91
97	35.34
96	30.22
95	25.42
90	13.85
80	5.71
70	2.18
60	0.91
50	0.30
40	0.07
30	0.01
20	0.00
10	0.00

It is worth noting that in 1427 the Gini index of wealth concentration was 78.75, while that of Monte credits was 89.67. Still, data of the catasto of 1480 stress the close relation between wealth and Monte investments.[41]

Bonds were used in many ways, as the social base of citizens involved in the system enlarged and the size of government indebtedness grew. Buying and selling was extremely important on the local credit market, favouring diffused speculative behavior. This conduct involved mainly medium and large creditors, whereas small bondholders tended to be quite passive.[42] Credits were used to pay taxes, so as to allow governments to withdraw a share of the debt by means of taxes. Because in many cases tax farmers could pay a part of their lease through bonds and overdue interest, they helped to maintain the lively market.[43] Bonds, furthermore, were widely used as a surrogate for cash, to buy goods, to form dowries and to provide guarantees for further loans.[44]

The return provided by state credits depended of course on both the capacity of governments to pay interest charges regularly and the general economic atmosphere. Between the late fourteenth and the early fifteenth century, governments proved more and more unable to maintain their promises. As difficulties came up, market prices of bonds steadily declined, and the path to speculation was opened up.

Chart 2.1: Market Prices of Government Bonds in Italy, 1285–1590.[45]

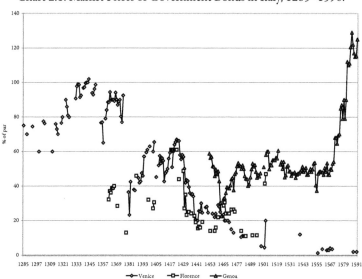

The restless devaluation of securities, however, forced Florence and Venice to launch a new series of bonds, which had the aim of renewing the relationship between state and taxpayers, who had to get cash, possibly by selling their state credits, to pay for new obligatory loans.

The market witnessed remarkable variations according to the typology of bonds. If it is obvious that before the consolidation of the debt several credits were traded, characterized by the date of maturity and the taxes on which they relied, a relative heterogeneity persisted even after the unification of the series. In fifteenth-century Florence, along with the Monte commune bonds, those of the *Monte dei depositi* (since the early part of the century), the *Monte di Pisa* (since 1406), the *Monte dei cinque interi* (since 1424), the *Monte dei Prestanzoni* (since 1425), the *Monte delle doti* (since 1425) and the *Monte comune nuovis-*

simo (since 1446) were negotiated.[46] In early sixteenth-century Venice, people could invest in bonds of the *Monte vecchio*, the *Monte nuovo* (1482), the *Monte nuovissimo* (1509), the *Monte sussidio* (1526) and the *Depositi in zecca* (since the 1520s).[47] So the choice was very wide, although destined to be reduced, for bonds tended to adjust around one interest rate. Nevertheless one wonders whether such menu was a feature of a developed credit market. According to Larry Neal, a wide supply of bonds would restrain the development of financial markets, in that it would bring about a limited homogeneity of conditions.[48] This would cause insufficient transparency and high transaction costs. In the Italian case, despite several issues, the market did not present a wide heterogeneity. Investors had few choices and these were mostly linked to government credits. One could even argue that, within the context of both modest demand and restricted market, the position of the government was that of a monopolist, with the attached advantages.

A peculiar aspect of the market concerned the negotiability of overdue interest (the so-called *paghe*). When claims upon *paghe* fell due, they were negotiable, as much as the state securities. From the mid-fifteenth century, the Genoese government used to pay interest charges only after at least four years from their maturity; in the meanwhile, creditors' arrears were registered in special accounts of *lire di paghe* until they were paid.[49] The creation of the *lire di paghe*, whose value progressively increased as the maturity date got closer, institutionalized the system of arrears. A market, therefore, was created, which counted annually as much as 10,000 transactions,[50] based upon an intense speculation extremely sensitive to events. It is noteworthy that in 1506 a riot in Genoa was said to be provoked by those whose investment fell short of their anticipation.

As far as the credit market in principalities goes, it is not surprising that information is very scarce. As we have already seen, most indebtedness of princes relied on financial means related to trade, whose negotiability at least up to and throughout the fifteenth century was socially limited. A partial exception is represented by Roman vacable offices, which were to some extent traded.

The purchase and sale of credits was generally made before a notary or a scribe of the office managing the debt, and registered in the books of the same office. Transaction costs were quite modest and of course were lower depending on the amount negotiated. In Genoa the shares (*luoghi*) sold were taxed with 20 soldi each, split equally between the buyer and the seller. To these taxes one has to add the intermediation costs. Some operations of Paolo Guinigi, Lord of Lucca from 1400 to 1430, on the Venetian market provide a good picture of the costs. The total transaction costs proved to be 1.5 per cent of the total amount, but most of the expenses were due to bills of exchange in order to get cash.[51] It is interesting to compare this percentage with those relating to other dealings. During the second half of the fourteenth century, only the tax on selling land in Florence withdrew 5 per cent. Toward the middle of the fifteenth century, in Siena a similar tax was 3.3–3 .5 per cent of the declared value; while one had to pay 1.5 per cent of the total amount on dowries.[52] In the 1760s, on the highly-developed financial market of Amsterdam, brokering costs accounted for 0.25 per cent of the nominal value of obligations.[53] Such a comparison shows that state credits trading in Italy did not therefore present high transaction costs, as a proof of the efficiency of the financial market. The role of middlemen (*sensali*) was crucial: intermediaries between demand and supply, they fixed the price according to news that diffused throughout a marked that was presumably restricted. In Venice everything occurred within an area circumscribed between Rialto, the financial heart of the city, and San Marco square. It is nevertheless worth stressing that the big limit of the Italian market – as elsewhere – was due to the fact that there were not bearer bonds.[54] There were actually several difficulties, both legal and practical, to protect the last creditor in case of the default of his own debtor. A true large-scale innovation emerged during the second half of the sixteenth century in Antwerp, where in the local stock exchange several securities were negotiated, including state bonds.[55] The negotiability, however, of state bonds was only allowed in Holland from the mid-seventeenth century.[56] In a restricted market such as the urban one, evidently, the ability to transfer bearer bonds was not an urgent need. Governments were concerned more with identifying and finding effective bondholders than allowing a full and uncontrolled portability.

Credible Commitments?

The forced loans system de facto circumvented a crucial point, namely the need for robust constraints which compelled governments to fulfill their creditors. It is therefore inopportune to define such a system as a true public debt because, among other things, the voluntary character of investment was lacking.[57] For foreign investors, however, the picture is different. Their investments were voluntary and their amount reflected on the one hand the degree of reliability governments enjoyed in markets and on the other the capability of ensuring high returns to investors on the secondary market.

As far as citizens were concerned, the announcement that given tax receipts were earmarked for paying interest represented an important, if not crucial, consideration. Credibility probably depended on the government's reputation and, above all, the heavy involvement of the ruling group as state creditors. This was the case in Venice, where several members of the patriciate held wide shares of debt.[58] Genoese investors relied on guarantees which were much more effectively than elsewhere. Beginning from 1407 the foundation of the Casa di San Giorgio – that is a consortium of creditors of the government – allowed a close control over state finance and debt management. This semi-private institution played a central role in state financing, heavily influencing the government's policy. The collaboration between the powerful representatives of the Casa and the government provides a excellent example of how the whole power of proxy to the Casa for managing the state finance allowed the commune to collect enormous amounts of money at low cost. The same principle (the responsibility of a group in creditors for paying their interest from tax receipts) was be found in sixteenth-century Rome and, with much more modest results, in the Paris of King Francis I.[59]

The key feature that underpinned the system and above all supported a vivid and large market – which in turn called for a certain degree of credibility – laid in the close link between major bondholders and the powerful elite. As long as this identity subsisted it was unlikely that the government would default. The success and efficiency of government debt in the Italian city-states would not be so much the natural outcome of the republican institutional structure (as opposed to princely states) as the result of a power system that took advantage of the mechanism of state indebtedness in a rather limited context. If this hypothesis is plausible, it is then necessary to reconsider the classic model put forward by North and Weingast.[60]

It is well known that these two scholars argued a close relationship between the institutional dynamics in early eighteenth-century England and the emergence of a modern and advanced financial market. In short, as the parliament took on the whole political power after the Glorious Revolution the road would have been paved for funding the debt, with the resulting decline of the interest rate and the development of the financial market. This was due to the credibility of the parliament as a debtor and above all as a unique body responsible for a fiscal policy as well as the more effective enforcement of property rights. The thesis of North and Weingast had a large impact and prompted researchers to put institutions, the financial sector and the legal context at the heart of the debate on economic development.[61] Recent critics, however, have stressed that the Glorious Revolution did not represent a turning point concerning property rights, nor did it determin such a dramatic change in the trend of interest rates.[62] It was furthermore argued that interest rate variations show on the contrary a significant interaction with the turnover of parties (Tory and Whig) in power.[63] The link between efficiency of public debt and constitutional power would therefore seem quite weak. It would instead be important to look at the fiscal system: it seems in fact that there is a positive relationship between the width of representative institutions and tax efficiency.[64] Some scholars argue that the power of the English state lay first of all in its capability to borrow thanks to its tax resources. A similar model has been put forward for Holland.[65] Let us try to apply, though briefly, this hypothesis to the Italian case.

In order to compare the different cases interest rates will be examined, which can after due consideration be thought of as 'the most evident quantitative dimension of the efficiency of the institutional framework'.[66] It is manifest that republican governments paid for fewer loans than kings and princes. It is necessary to ask why.[67] First of all, lords seemed to be scarcely reliable debtors and consequently they had to pay a high-risk premium. Monarchs did not actually present credible commitments to lenders. The only risk was due to the eventual bad reputation that had been formed in the past. It is not simple to compare interest paid by republics with that of principalities. Market conditions were different. Princes, on the one hand, negotiated loans according to certain elements (power relations, patronage, guarantees, capital availability), republics on the other hand resorted mainly to forced loans, at lower interest rates than that of the market. It is therefore necessary to examine voluntary loans raised by republican governments. When Florence's treasury needed cash it resorted to professional financiers' services. In the Arno city bankers were, as was well known, not short and it is not surprising to find them within the mechanism of state financing.[68] But that means that public borrowing was expensive, and sometimes more expensive than in the private market. Some data, although scanty, are worth considering.

Chart 2.2: Interest Rates in Florence, 1290–1380.[69]

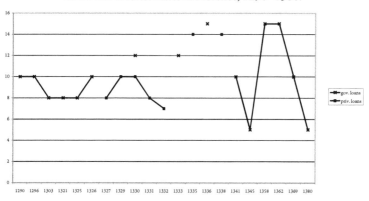

Of course one has to consider that high government rates correspond to periods of severe need, due to political and military factors. Let us, however, take some things into consideration, albeit necessarily provisional. The consolidation of the mid-1340s did not provide great relief to communal coffers. In the 1350s and 1360s the high interest rate promised (a nominal 5 per cent on a nominal principal twice or three times as much of that effectively paid) shows how it was hard to collect money from voluntary lenders. The spread, however, which could be considered as the risk premium paid by the government, was not usually large. This meant that a certain confidence, difficulties notwithstanding, was widespread among investors. It cannot be denied that in Florence money was largely diffused and that sophisticated financial techniques and skill helped maintain the cost of money in a moderate way. A further element worth stressing concerns the interest rate trend. In this case it seems that government interest rate drove the market movement, also increasing rates between individuals. Therefore it remains to account for the influence of declining government yield on the private credit market.[70]

It is worth stressing a further crucial element. Beginning from the mid-fourteenth century, tax pressure increased, just as the funded debt system was created and the aggressive expansion of the Florentine state took place. The growth of indebtedness was actually backed by tax receipts: both sustained each other to provide the commune with the resources necessary for political expansion and to fulfill creditors' interests.[71]

Conclusions

In late medieval western Europe some differences came to light, characterizing the system of indebtedness of urban communities. There were, on the one hand, Mediterranean cities, which resorted to forced loans mainly through fiscal records and, on the other hand, there were cities in northern France and Flanders that from the thirteenth century sold annuities to finance their deficit. These annuities were bought also in other markets and had the character of life annuities.[72] It is worth stressing this element. In northern Europe, from France to Switzerland, life annuities enjoyed great success, at least up to the early sixteenth century, but in Italy they were not widely used. It is very likely that Italian governments were aware of such financial devices: several merchants acted in French and Flemish cities and so it would be easy to get information. Issuing annuities was not a mere trifle. In order to take the profit, the government had to exploit statistical and actuarial knowledge, which were not simple and were to develop starting from the seventeenth century.[73] The advantage that these annuities were self-liquidating was probably not offset by the great uncertainty stirring over life annuities. By the late fifteenth and particularly the early sixteenth century, some Italian governments began to issue life annuities, perhaps because of their severe financial needs. In some cases it was these very annuities that paved the way to a true primary state bonds market, as in Rome and Venice.

One can argue that the indebtedness mechanisms of western Mediterranean cities were not very different. Loans issued by Valencia or Barcelona had much in common with Florentine or Venetian loans. Yet, it appears that in the Aragonese territories the strongly forcible character which was found in Italy was missing. In the Peninsula, lending to governments was not as much an investment choice as a duty of taxpayers. Accordingly, the problem of credibility of institutions did not play a significant role. It would, however, be wrong to deny some innovations which occurred in northern Italy, namely the emergence of a vivid secondary market of state bonds. The turnover of bonds was quite fast, suggesting an annual rate of exchange of 5 per cent of the nominal amount.[74] The secondary market allowed for liquidating credits in case of need; furthermore it offered attractive chances for speculation on both bonds themselves and overdue interest. These speculations nevertheless did not seem to characterize the practice in the main Italian market – with the exception of Genoa – due to the tiny size of commercial credit and the conservative behaviour of bondholders.[75] The presence of state credits became more and more consistent in the assets of noble families and of religious and charitable institutions. These were categories that by definition did not follow speculative patterns of behaviour. A dynamic secondary market was the product of at least two elements: on the one hand, creditor-taxpayers, and particularly the less well off, were compelled to sell their credits to face the government's growing demand for further loans and, on the other hand, buyers were attracted by the high profitability of credits and the belief that the government would keep its promises. The credibility of government institutions therefore dealt with speculators in the secondary market. But who were they, if not the members themselves of the ruling groups?

3 GOVERNMENT DEBTS AND FINANCIAL MARKETS IN CASTILE BETWEEN THE FIFTEENTH AND SIXTEENTH CENTURIES

David Alonso García

One of the most remarkable developments of modern finance was the emergence of a public debt. Governments of different kingdoms – including papal kingdoms – were able to increase their resources due to credit and, more importantly, these governments were able to make payments abroad through bankers who had previously lent the funds. These bankers lent money in order to finance armies or wars, and their loans constituted short-term debt. The development of this system in Castile began at the end of the fifteenth century, when the Catholic kings needed loans in order to conquer the Muslim city of Granada.[1] Scholars have highlighted this event as the origin of Charles V's loans; so, the fiscal and financial system of the Habsburg dynasty had precedents before 1516.

Charles V's fiscal system took its influences from Castile and the Low Countries. The administration was built in a previous period (the *Contadurías* of Castile)[2] and the reforms of 1523–5 were influenced by the model of Flanders. But, if there is an area in which tradition and innovation went together, it was debt. Castile had several types of debt and credit systems in place dating from the fourteenth and fifteenth centuries, while the Catholic kings continued with a new type of *juros* with more modern elements.[3] Why did public credit arrive? Traditionally, scholars have always recognized that there was the need to increase expenses to build a new model of army, and this would include a process of authority centralization and fiscal increases. In this paper, we argue about the importance of financial markets in attracting more resources to Castile in the first decades of the sixteenth century. The increase of expenditure was very important, of course; this increase, however, would not have been possible without a new context. Money, credit, merchant networks and, in general, a very good economic situation characterized this context. Moreover, production growth and merchant profits were a reliable source of potential income for the monarchy. We cannot forget that the fiscal system was a way to earn money as well.

In which regard were they modern? Public debt had been very common indeed in Europe in the Middle Ages during the previous centuries. Furthermore, countries such as England were developing their public credit before the modern age.[4] The financial system of Castile was no exception from that of other countries. Consolidated debt was known in Castile and Europe before the financial revolution, and because of that we will examine medieval aspects in order to understand the system.[5] Finally, we will attempt to analyse this first public debt (both consolidated and short term) in both the traditional and modern systems.

Short Term Debt and Financial Markets at the Beginning of the Early Modern Period

During the first years of the sixteenth century, a short-term debt was consolidated in the form of annual credits to maintain the court and war campaigns, especially in Italy and North Africa. By the 1500s the named *obligados a guardas* began loaning money every year. We can see that these credits were usual and were not a consequence of any unbalance between income and expenses. The Catholic kings first, then Philip I – King Fernando of Aragon's son-in-law – and, lastly, Charles V (until 1523 especially) needed money from *obligados a guardas*, who lent between 80 and 100 million *maravedíes* each year, that is, more or less 30 per cent of the total ordinary revenues.[6] It was not a very expensive credit; the tax rate was about 3–4 per cent per annum. With these loans, financiers, rather than seeking economic profit, were able to control the largest percentage of *encabezamientos* on the cities, which the Crown gave as a guarantee of their credits.

Chart 3.1: Castilian Income and *Obligados a Guardas*, 1501–25 (1501 = 100).[7]

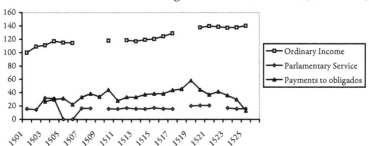

This system of loans was managed by businessmen. Some of these financiers were also important tax farmers. For instance, with his brother Juan and other members of his family, Diego de la Fuente controlled the silk tax for several decades.[8] Pedro de Santa Cruz and his group were tax farmers of *Tres Obispados* in 1505.[9]

In fact, a lot of taxes depended on private merchants, who linked credit, loans, farm taxes and collection in their own businesses. It is therefore very difficult to understand government debts without examining the financiers.

Table 3.1: *Obligados a Guardas*, 1505.[10]

Name	Neighbourhood	Amount of Loan (in *maravedíes*)	Fiscal Jurisdictions (Headed Taxes)	Regions
Juan de Figueroa	Valladolid	16,000,000	Maderuelos, Cerrato, Soria, Astorga, León, Señoríos de Plasencia, Cangas y Tineo, Peñaranda, Monzón, Asturias, Provincia de Castilla	Asturias, Castilla y León
Diego de la Fuente	Toledo	9,000,000	Marquesado de Villena, Villanueva de Gómez Dávila, Cartagena, Arévalo, Murcia, Provincia de Castilla	Murcia, Castilla La Mancha, Castilla y León
Gonzalo Arias Juan de Lerena	Valladolid	8,000,000	Carrión, Saldaña, Tordesillas, Villarejo de Fuentes, Villanueva de Santa Cruz, Cuenca y Huete, Salamanca	Castilla y León, Castilla la Mancha
Juan de Vozmediano Alonso de Vozmediano	Madrid	8,000,000	Calatrava del Andalucía, Andújar, Bézmar, Madrid	Madrid, Andalucía
Alonso de la Torre	Toledo	15,210,000	Zorita, Baeza, Arzobispado de Talavera, Condado de Niebla, Término Realengo, Talavera de la Reina, San Román, Jerez de la Frontera, Sierras de Sevilla	Castilla La Mancha, Andalucía
Alonso de la Torre Fernando de la Higuera	Toledo	total of previous	Uceda, Toledo, Illescas, Campo de Calatrava, Yepes, Ciudad Real	Castilla La Mancha
Alonso del Castillo	Burgos	6,000,000	Burgos, Candemuño, Villadiego, Burueva, Miranda del Ebro, Olmillos, Valderrama, Pernía, Castrojeriz, Segovia, Rioja, Campoo	Castilla y León, La Rioja
Jorge de Vitoria	Alcaraz	2,920,000	Alcaraz	Castilla La Macha

Name	Neighbourhood	Amount of Loan (in *maravedíes*)	Fiscal Jurisdictions (Headed Taxes)	Regions
Alonso Núñez de Madrid	Granada	2,000,000	Adelantamiento de Cazorla	Andalucía
Pedro de la Rúa	Zamora	–	Zamora	Castilla y León
Pedro de Santa Cruz	Aranda del Duero	5,160,000	Santo Domingo de Silos, Sepúlveda, Merindad de Logroño, Utrilla, Sigüenza	Castilla y León, Castilla La Mancha, La Rioja
Diego de Cazalla Pedro de Cazalla	Palma (Sevilla)	1,096,000	Cáceres, Badajoz, Iglejuela, Casar de Palomero	Extremadura
Total		73,386,000		

The growth of tax income and, especially, the support of a wealthy 'Castilian capitalism' in this period was not possible without the development of financial markets. It is not incidental that the payback of loans coincided with the months when financiers could collect taxes (March, June, August and December).[11] Loans to the army revealed an interesting financial market. For example, Juan de Figueroa and Lope de Urueña – two of the most important financiers of the period – offered almost forty million *maravedíes* in 1523 to support the war against France.[12] The tax rate was 2.4 per cent (very low for this financial period). In the contract, Figueroa and Urueña received loan repayment extensions in order to recover their credit. They had anticipated problems with collecting taxes within the original repayment period.

More importantly, one of the conditions of this loan outlined a possible plan for the financiers to find other participants for the operation, which enabled Figueroa and Urueña to find other businessmen with money and credit. This loan, in turn, was a way to interlink the financial world with the monarchy, where Figueroa and Urueña were heads of the operation. This business could then be opened to a financial market. For Figueroa and Urueña, the loans to the government were a good opportunity to increase their credit through repayments and direct control of taxes. The Crown supported what Figueroa and Urueña were doing in order to engage other financiers. Because of this support, both would receive 150,000 *maravedíes* if they were able to bring in other creditors to finance the operation. As a consequence, loans to the army were a way to increasingly finance the monarchy and a means of strengthening financial markets as well. The more loans made to finance the king, the greater the potential profits for financiers. So a particular type of economic and political order emerged.

The fairs of Medina del Campo were ideal platforms on which to transfer money or letters of exchange. We can see the importance of the financial market in a list of payments to Dr Beltrán, who worked for Francisco de Vargas, the general exchequer at the time:

Table 3.2: Payment Letters from Dr Beltrán's Records, 1519.[13]

Financier	Amount of Loan (in *maravedíes*)	Broker in the Fair	Mechanism
Almansa, Juan de	1,125,000		1) Letter of exchange to Seville for Juan López de Recalde (1,000 *ducados*); 2) In Juan Bautista de Grimaldo (2,000 *ducados*)
Álvarez de Madrid, Rodrigo	937,000	Palma, Fernando de	Paid by Fernando de Palma through banker Bernardino de Santa María
Ávila, Rodrigo de	1,012,500	Torre, Juan de la	Paid by Juan de la Torre on behalf of Pedro de Cazalla into Juan Álvarez de Seville's account 'que los ovo de aver por Rodrigo de Ávila en Alonso de Castro'
Bruselas, Diego de	2,000,000	Bruselas, Diego de	Paid to Francisco de San Pedro (1,600,000) and García Cocón (400,000)
Campo, Francisco del	475,000	Campo, Francisco del	Paid to Bernardino de Santa María
Chaves de Bañuelos, Juan	200,000	Chaves de Bañuelos, Juan	Paid to Bernardino de Santa María
Coca, Alonso de	500,000	Coca, Alonso de	
Cuenca, Fernando de	1,125,000	Berlanga, Francisco de	Paid to Francisco de San Pedro
Cuenca, Fernando de	1,125,000	Gumiel, Juan de	Paid to Francisco de San Pedro
Cuenca, Fernando de	4,500,000	Vivaldo, Agustín de	1,500,000 paid to Bernardino de Santa María
Fernández de Parada, Alonso	1,700,000	Fernández de Parada, Alonso	Paid to García Cocón
Fernández Arias, Diego	375,000	Pedrarias [Davila?]	Paid to García Cocón
Figueroa, Juan de	1,000,000	Angulo, Fernando de	
Madrid, Francisco de	1,500,000	Castro, Alonso de	
Madrid, Francisco de	500,000	Castro, Alonso de	
Miño, Pedro de	1,500,000	Vivaldo, Agustín de	Vivaldo paid to Andrés de Frías
Morejón, Francisco	1,500,000	Morejón, Francisco	

Financier	Amount of Loan (in *maravedíes*)	Broker in the Fair	Mechanism
Niño de Castro, Alonso	2,850,000	Niño de Castro, Alonso	Paid to Bernardino de Santa María
Núñez de Andujar, Luis	375,000	Núñez de Andujar, Luis	
Pérez del Castillo, Juan	3,375,000	Santa María, Bernardino de	
Suárez de Lara, Fernando	1,500,000	Suárez de Lara, Fernando	
Gutiérrez, Fernando		Gutiérrez, Fernando	
Urueña, Lope de	4,000,000	Vilafana, Francisco de y Ochoa de Urtasabel	Paid to Bernardino de Santa María and Andrés de Frías
Total	31,674,000		

There were different levels of financial world participation. The fiscal system worked thanks to groups of businessmen. This financial community took advantage of the king's debt. As previously mentioned, there were people linked to the financial market who were in a position to channel funds to the monarchy by means of tax collection. Some of these individuals became remarkable lenders during the reign of Charles V.[14] These financiers used different methods of payment. There were those who paid themselves – direct payment in other words. Included in this group were Diego de Bruselas, Francisco del Campo, Chaves de Bañuelos, Alonso de Coca, Francisco de Morejón, Alonso Fernández Parada, Alonso Niño de Castro, Núñez de Andújar and Suárez de Lara with Fernando Gutiérrez. Most of them – except Núñez de Andújar's group – were citizens of Medina del Campo, Valladolid, Burgos and, even, Huete (Cuenca).

Other financiers employed brokers to make their transactions at the fair. Some of these agents were servants of the main financier. For instance, Ochoa de Urtasabel had been Lope de Urueña's servant since 1515.[15] Rodrigo Álvarez de Madrid and Fernando de Palma, both citizens of Málaga, worked together. However other brokers were independent financiers: Francisco de Berlanga was an important tax farmer of Aranda de Duero[16] and, a few years before, had had a company with Juan de Gumiel and Sevillian Pedro del Alcázar. It is very significant that Juan de Gumiel was the son of Nuño de Gumiel, exchequer of Philip I. Juan Pérez del Castillo made use of Bernardino de Santa María, banker of Burgos, a city where Castillo's family was well known.[17] Furthermore, Genoese bankers were implicated: Agustín de Vivaldo worked for Pedro de Miño and Fernando de Cuenca. Pedro de Miño – a citizen of Llerena – had cooperated with Lope de Urueña in loaning money to the monarchy in 1518.[18] Fernando de Cuenca was one of the most important Castilian financiers because of tax farming as well as loans.

The Crown also used intermediaries. The general exchequer, Francisco de Vargas, saw to it that Diego Beltrán was an operative at the fair. Beltrán was an adviser of the emperor who was given funds which he could bargain with either directly or indirectly.[19] The general exchequer's servant used bankers such as Juan Bautista Grimaldo, Bernardino de Santa María or García Cocón (banker of Valladolid),[20] who were in charge of receiving the money from financiers – or other brokers – to keep securely for the king to use when necessary.

Long-Term Debt and the Financial System

In Castile, like in other countries, a long-term debt had been developing over the latter decades of the medieval era. The cost of *juros* had started to increase more and more by the end of the fifteenth century and this tendency continued during subsequent reigns.[21] Between 1501 and 1525, the sum of long-term debt grew from 36.89 per cent to 44.31 per cent of the total income of ordinary taxes.[22] What was the role played by financiers during this period of debt increase? The administration needed people with the ability to sell bonds and for this reason asked specific individuals to sell a certain amount of long-term debt at a determined price and interest rate. During the first decades of fifteenth century, the general exchequer (Francisco de Vargas and later Alonso Gutiérrez de Madrid) sold titles.[23] However, the king's officials were not the only ones who could sell bonds; Juan de Figueroa was ordered by Philip I to sell 500,000 *maravedíes* of *juros* at an interest rate of 7.14 per cent.[24] In 1523, Figueroa sold bonds again during the time he was employed by Francisco de Vargas.[25] The Fugger's firm bargained with bonds as well.[26] Bernardino de Santa María was the other financier who participated in these transactions.[27] It is important to note that Santa María was one of the primary bankers of Burgos.

Parts of the titles sold by Santa María were seized by other merchants. Men like Diego de Gamarra, Juan Vázquez del Campillo, Pedro Ruiz de la Torre, Juan Chaves de Bañuelos, Diego de San Pedro and, particularly, Nicolás de Grimaldo and Alonso Gutiérrez de Madrid were among the buyers.[28] Financiers and exchequers have contacts with people capable of selling these bonds, deeming money and information necessary for ensuring that *juros* were out there in the market. Italian bankers used public debt as a means to spread their personal contacts' networks within society:

Table 3.3: Examples of Consolidated Debt Sold by Italian Bankers, 1523.[29]

Main Seller	Principal Amount (in maravedíes)	Price (in maravedíes)	Italian Intermediate	Amount of Principal Transfer (in maravedíes)	Price (in maravedíes)	Beneficiary
Francisco de Vargas	227,640	3,166,.900	Mafeo de Tarsis	77,640	1,086,960	Ana Barrientos from Bonilla de la Sierra (Ávila)
Francisco de Vargas	268,600	3,760,607	Nicolás de Grimaldo	100,000	1,400,000	Alonso Niño de Castro (Valladolid)

Where was the benefit to financiers? In legal terms, these titles were similar in price and tax rate (7.14 per cent). From a theoretical perspective, Mafeo de Tarsis and Nicolás de Grimaldo did not earn money with this operation. The prime interest for Italian bankers was simply that the banker who sold bonds could collect liquid money, an element that was very important when the same financiers had significant loans with the Crown. In 1523 Mafeo de Tarsis lent more than 27 million *maravedíes*; Nicolás de Grimaldo had lent 42,827 *ducados* and the loans of his combined family surpassed 23 million.[30] The same can be said in relation to Juan de Figueroa: for the same year he sold *juros*, he also made huge loans.[31] Furthermore, financiers had other types of contacts with the Crown. Tarsis, for instance, was *correo mayor*. From Philip II's reign, there were different types of long-term debts which guaranteed loans;[32] but during the first decades of the sixteenth century, the international bank was involved in selling long-term debt even in the secondary market. All these elements were of a financial world that was actively involved in long-term debt development.

Juros became more influential in the Castilian fiscal system and this tendency increased during the sixteenth century. Everybody with credit and reputation had bonds in Castile. Aristocrats, merchants, monasteries, local elites and royal councillors all invested, not just for profit but also because it was considered prestigious and denoted social success. However, interest rates fell from 10 per cent in 1504 to 5.79 per cent in 1598 (maximum prices).[33] Historians have accurately recorded titles and ownership and how these were distributed, as well as payment methods right down to who owned bonds. But the secondary market requires considerably more research. Often, *juros* were bought to sell on as opposed to being retained as cash. So, there was a financial market around consolidated debt that depended on several elements: genre of title, collection location, guaranteed tax, economic contexts, etc. For this reason, secondary market *juros* helped to develop the financial system in Castile. In fact, at the start of the sixteenth century there were offices which specialized in buying and selling bonds.[34] On the other hand, the public debt secondary market took advantage of the development of the financial system. In addition, the collection of the principal of bonds required bankers, merchants, and others involved in the financial field to be conveniently located for ease of business.[35] It is clear that the increased number of *juros* would not have been possible without a developed financial market which permitted transactions with the reigning monarch's agents and other merchants.

Financing Embassies: Money Transfer from Castile to other Countries

So far we have dealt with the tax system and financiers in Castile. But they had international links. In fact, the connection between the king's finance and the financiers' market was common with regard to the payment of embassies. During the Renaissance a new model of diplomacy with representatives of the Crown in different kingdoms of Europe was developed.[36] However, this process would have been impossible without a system of financial sustenance. The ambassadors in Rome, the empire or London needed people who presented a variety of methods in which money was exchanged. The usual instrument of relations between Castile and other countries was the bill of exchange, which meant a loan and a currency exchange service. Ambassadors could negotiate with financiers to receive money in this way, as A. Pacini has proved regarding Charles V's reign.[37] During the first two decades of the sixteenth century, ambassadors negotiated directly with bankers and, only after this bargaining was completed, Francisco de Vargas – as general exchequer – would send the agreed amount plus taxes.

Genoese bankers were the main protagonists of this system.[38] Surnames like Grimaldo, Vivaldo or Lomelini financed Jerónimo de Vich (ambassador in Rome), who received an annual payment of around 2,200 *ducados*.[39] In 1514, the interest rate was about 5–6 per cent. These financiers used also paid Vich through other financiers in Rome.[40] Genoese bankers worked with other countries; Agustín de Grimaldo and Agustín de Vivaldo both sent 187 *ducados* to Flanders for several payments during the first decades of the sixteenth century.[41] Andrea Belluti also used the fairs of Medina del Campo in order to move money between Castile and the ancient territories of the Duke of Burgundy. Belluti took part in financing Don Pedro de Urrea, Aragon Ambassador to Maximilian I.[42] Lastly, Belluti loaned 20,000 *ducados* to Gómez de Fuensalida, Castilian Ambassador to London.[43]

Italian bankers were not the only financiers with the ability to move money around Europe. Castilian merchants invested their money in the monarchy, collaborating with Genoese bankers in some operations. Some merchants from Burgos were heavily involved in such dealings. Families such as López de Calatayud or Salinas made good use of their important links in the Low Countries. They provided the funds for the ambassador in Bruges which would be repaid by Andrea

Belluti on behalf of Castile.[44] Finally, we have to mention the Sánchez family from Aragon, not Castile, who also sent money to Italy and the empire.[45] Significantly, Luis Sánchez was the exchequer of Aragon. The growing relationship between financial markets, bankers, taxes and the particular families therefore developed a new type of financial system.

The Role of Institutions

In 1503, Pedro del Alcázar – one of the most important Sevilian financiers and merchants – filed a lawsuit against Diego de la Muela, lieutenant of the chief accountant (*contador mayor*) at the time.[46] One witness presented by Pedro del Alcázar said that 'Every tax farmer would do what Diego de la Muela wanted them to do even though they suffered as a result, as every one was afraid of Diego de la Muela'.[47] These words show the narrow relationship between officials and financiers during the first decades of the sixteenth century. Pedro del Alcázar was afraid of Diego de la Muela because his financial dealings with the tax system depended on their relationship. Diego de la Muela took advantage of this situation and asked Pedro del Alcázar for a personal loan. The personal loan was then charged to public finance,[48] an incident which demonstrates the difficulties facing those embroiled in the fiscal system.

Fiscal institutions have been analyzed from legal and political angles, but social connections and implications have not been covered at all.[49] Institutions could only be effective through social links with agents who collected taxes and received payments and orders. The purposes of fiscal institutions were first to activate all financial systems to create a permanent bargain with bankers, tax farmers and cities, and second to gain as much information as possible in order to win a better position in negotiations. Financiers, on the other hand, needed the fiscal system to improve their connections in their own business. Cities needed headed taxes (*encabezamientos*) in order to better support local policy. Both officials and financiers or cities used institutions as intermediaries since government officials did not only have their king's interests at heart.[50]

Spanish fiscal institutions strengthened during the early sixteenth century. After Isabella I's death (November 1504), the chief accountants (*contadurías*) affirmed their positions against other institutions controlling public finance. There were two *contadurías*: the chief accountants of the tax system (*contaduría mayor de hacienda*) managed every aspect of tax collecting, credits and making of payments in Castile; the chief accountant of accounts (*contaduría mayor de cuentas*) observed the management of the tax system and uncovered cases of corruption.

Dealing with the process of strengthening royal institutions would be beyond this paper's aim. Interestingly, that process took place in the context of the political and monarchical crisis after the death of Elizabeth I. How was this paradox possible? Officials of both royal institutions had important links with merchants, tax farmers, bankers and collecting agents. Servants of officials were financiers or brokers bargaining and collecting taxes. Such officials included Cristóbal Suárez, who often financed payments for the royal house.[51] On the other hand, financiers could finance the tax system by interacting with officials.

The efficiency of institutions depended on the financial world. Ambrosio Spínola – from a Genoese family of merchants – was appointed general captain in the Low Countries early in the seventeenth century. Curiously, the efficiency of the payment system in Holland was improved.[52] Bartolomé Spínola was later appointed general factor in Castile with the purpose of implementing a payments system in the cities.[53] There were other examples of efforts to improve and refine systems within the fiscal institutions and various families were involved. There were also foreign families in Castilian institutions and Spanish merchants acting as officials in other countries during the first decades of the sixteenth century. For example, the Salinas family worked for Ferdinand I[54] and Gabriel de Salamanca took de role of master of finances to the emperor's brother.[55] In this position Salamanca was unhindered to negotiate loans for Ferdinand I. Both the Salinas family and Gabriel de Salamanca were merchants and bankers of Burgos. On the other hand, the Argüello brothers (Alonso and Rodrigo) worked for Antonio Fonseca, one of the chief accountants in Castile. Alonso was also appointed finance accountant for Princess Margaret, regent in Flanders. Because of their positions, Alonso and Rodrigo Argüello partly secured the financing of the Castilian embassy in Flanders. Diego Flores, Margaret's treasurer, worked with the Argüello brothers abroad. These personal relations enabled payments for the Flemings in Castile and for the Castilians in Flanders.[56]

Conclusion

Up until a few decades ago historians perceived the building of the tax system in terms of modernization and centralization. New taxes, higher expenses and the growth of royal control were elements of the 'fiscal state'. But centralization and bureaucracy grew with financial markets and this kind of situation was difficult for the reigning monarch to control. In addition, as Professor Thompson has shown, increased expenses do not necessarily lead to a higher control of all fiscal and financial systems.[57] With regard to government debts, the theory of financial revolution developed by historians like J. Tracy offered new perspectives of study.[58] However, government debts were increasing for centuries, suggesting that this was a case of 'evolution' before 'revolution'.[59]

If war expenses were not the only cause of tax system transformation, how are the increased resources of the reigning monarch to be explained? The answer obviously lies with the financial markets. Importantly, bankers and merchants had enough money to make loans in different countries and their success rate depended on markets, exchange centres and investments. The financial success of the current monarch also depended on these elements. By 1522, the problems of Charles V's finances in Flanders coincided with an exchange crisis in Antwerp.[60] Interestingly, the Spanish fiscal system was in crisis as well. Everything moved around the same economic world. Though requiring further research in Spain, there also seemed to be a close connection between institutions and financiers. In Castile, fiscal officials acted as financiers or brokers of other financiers; without this connection, the financial administration could not have worked. On the other hand, the financial world needed institutions as an access channel to the monarchy. The evolution of all these systems had started several decades before Emperor Charles V. His financial system therefore contained important influences from the Trastamara dynasty.

4 GOVERNMENT DEBT AND FINANCIAL MARKETS: EXPLORING PRO-CYCLE EFFECTS IN NORTHERN ITALY DURING THE SIXTEENTH AND THE SEVENTEENTH CENTURIES

Giuseppe De Luca[1]

Beginning with the first decades of the sixteenth century, the principal states of northern Italy (along with other states, leaders in the 'financial revolution', both on and off the peninsula) faced the problem of long-term public financing by introducing innovations that notably increased collection of monies and tied financial capital to the state organization. These were – even with some differences – the progressive substitution of the emission of bonds for compulsory loans. These securities were freely subscribed, the interest was guaranteed by a fixed fiscal source, there was no set time for the return of capital, they were marketable, they could be inherited and they were exempt from confiscation and taxes. This kind of debt did not constitute the only method used by these states to obtain money. The difficulties of sorting out the stratified typologies are well known; beside the short-term loan or floating debt, there was the sale of offices, pensions, forced advance payments and even rewards, but quite soon all these types of short-term debt began to be converted into the new solution. The earmarking of future tax income for interest payment on the bonds issued, connected to their transferability, set up a public funded debt, thus long-term arrangements in this form became prevalent.

If the governments of Milan, Venice, Turin, Genoa and the Farnese Duchy were pushed in this direction by the extraordinary expansion of their balances due to war costs and the limits of their own fiscal systems (see section 1, below), the notable growth of this new form of financing came about because of its acceptance by a large segment of subjects, who found this type of investment suitable to their own needs (see section 2, below). In some periods a real push-pull mechanism occurred during which the buyers' response was very quick; in 1559 the sale of 600,000 lire of securities at 12 per cent by the Ferrata della Loggia dei mercanti of Milan was completed in only ten days,[2] while in 1639 in Venice, a series of deposits at 5 per cent was sold out in six days; in Turin in 1703 some purchasers, coming late at the Treasury Office, offered to subscribe bonds at 5 per cent of interest rate instead of 6 per cent.[3]

At the same time the spread of this genotype of public debt and its tumultuous increase did not seem to cause a sterile drain of private wealth to cover war expenses, nor did it have a negative effect on the real economy. We have clues, especially for Lombardy, that this form of long-term public indebtedness, acting in a situation of expansion of circulating currency, did not cause a decrease in productive investments and neither did it bring private capital cost increases; on the contrary it had a pro-cycle effect from the second half of the sixteenth century until 1620 and in the economic reorganization of the second half of the seventeenth century. In fact, in the former the public bonds turned into an attractive collateral for loans and increased the possibilities of private financing, acting as a credit matrix (i.e. it was the guarantee of the stipulation of personal loans, the *censi consegnativi*) for merchants and entrepreneurs; in the latter, when the economic centre of gravity moved towards a less dynamic agricultural-mercantile equilibrium, the debt allowed the state to sustain the public demand and the upper classes – who had in these securities a good income not subject to taxation – to enjoy a remarkable level of conspicuous consumption (palaces, art, clothing, but also country villas that were efficient agricultural farms; see section 3, below).

Furthermore, investments in public debt constituted a means of redistribution and strengthening of assets that implicated the subscribers in the decision-making processes of their governments and helped to maintain political stability throughout the seventeenth century, as is the case of the Duchy of Milan (see section 4, below).

1

The data in Chart 4.1 and Tables 4.1 show – even if with different analytical detail and reflecting studies of uneven depth – how movement of this type of debt substantially mirrors the phases of greater governmental financial need in the five regional states we are considering, marked by military expenses for wars past or in preparation, costs of neutrality or territorial expansion. The differences between these countries were notable with regard both to their unequal size and the varying degrees of political independence, but each of them provides us with a different variation on the same theme.

Chart 4.1: Funded Debt of the State of Milan during the Sixteenth and Seventeenth Centuries (current value in lire).[4]

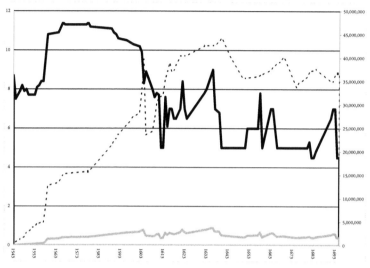

Table 4.1: Funded Debt of the States of Venice, Genoa and Piedmont during the Sixteenth and the Seventeenth Centuries.[5]

a. Venice Public Bonds – Depositi in Zecca – (current value in ducats).

Year	Ducats	Nominal Interest Rate %
1537	424,000	–
1538	655,000	7.5
1539*	525,000	8.0
1540	207,110	7.5
1541	45,000	6.0
1544	25,000	6.0
1545	24,600	–
1546	20,200	5.0
1547	90,000	–
1548	25,000	4.0
1551	60,000	–
1567	40,000	3.0
1569	40,000	–
1570*	700,000	7.0
1571	1,172,219	8.0
1573	925,000	8.0
1574	531,000	7.5
1607	180,933	4.0
1616	900,000	5.0

* Incomplete data

b. Venice Funded Debt (current value in ducats).

Year	Nominal Funded Debt	Interest	Nominal Interest Rate %
1554	10,181,000	584,000	5.74
1609	611,000	19,000	3.11
1641	8,435,000	492,000	5.83
1670	46,082,000	2,378,000	5.16
1679	46,300,000	1,537,000	3.32

c. Genoa Funded Debt (current value in lire).

Year	Nominal Funded Debt	Interest	Nominal Interest Rate %
1450	8,687,000	390,000	4.48
1500	14,744,000	379,000	2.56
1550	37,957,000	997,000	2.62
1600	43,992,000	1,636,000	3.71
1650	102,191,000	3,301,000	3.23
1700	119,158,000	2,845,000	2.38

d. Piemontese Funded Debt (current value in lire).

Year	Nominal Funded Debt	Interest	Nominal Interest Rate %
1684	15,526,734	690,676	4.4
1702	17,441,246	1,003,716	5.7

In the Milanese state, at the time of Francesco Sforza, there had already been recourse to the sale – for the most part compulsory – of state taxes with the anticipation of a sum equal to the capitalized value, at a given interest rate (between 5.7 per cent and 10 per cent), of the annual tax revenue, of which the authorities reserved the right of redemption; with the inheritance of the Duchy of Milan, Spain come into a public debt whose nominal capital accounted for 2,394,041 lire and whose interest meant 11.3 per cent of the total revenues (the estimate was 1,208,364 lire in 1536).[6]

It is with the Spanish domination of Milan, starting in 1535, that the sale of fiscal revenues of the Milanese state stopped being compulsory subscription and became the keystone of a consolidated debt destined to assume much greater dimensions. The universalistic strategy of Charles V exacted an active participation in the imperial plan that translated into an economic solidarity sub-specie financial trust. As Castile, Flanders and Naples, so also Milan was pushed towards the anticipated sale of fiscal revenues by the constantly worsening conditions of their balances, tied to the increasing political-military tensions of the empire using a model typical of the Austrian domain (the Spanish *juros*).[7]

From the early 1540s, when other types of financing – such as the sale of jurisdictions, anticipations on future balances and short-term loans – were no longer able to cover the growing needs, the sale of revenues became systematic for the Milanese

Hacienda. This funded debt, whose interest payment was guaranteed by the tax revenue, was immediately well received by the subscribers (reassured also by Charles V's recognition of the bonds sold by his predecessors) and it soon put down solid roots, given the fact that it was simpler and less risky to collect customs or other fiscal sources – effectively paid regularly and in full in this early phase – than to be paid interest by the central government and trust in its promises of payment. For the rest, after the degree of confusion that years of warfare, destruction, and plague had brought to the Milanese domain, beginning in the 1540s the economic and demographic recovery started to produce a decided increase in ordinary revenues, besides offering the possibility of increasing taxes, imposing new ones and broadening the tax base (towards the end of the century).[8] By means of the 'multiplier effect' of the tax alienation system, the treasury finally took in large quantities of money in exchange for cessions of relatively modest revenues. In this way the increase of taxes and/or income, which in itself may not have been very significant, became a much more important amount of money for the state's treasury, as for example the increase by 20 *soldi* of the salt Ferma in 1556, equal to 136,211 lire and sold at 12 per cent, providing a sum of 1,135,096 lire.[9]

The evaluation of the progress (Figure 4.1) of this massive recourse to debt and its principal must obviously include the inflationary processes that largely characterized the second half of the Cinquecento. But if from 1555 to 1601 the silver content of the Milanese lira diminished from 5.88 grams to 5.48 grams, in the course of the seventeenth century its stability was second only to Tuscany's, in all the peninsula, and was accompanied by a prolonged stagnation of prices.[10]

In 1542–3 war returned to all the frontiers and help from the Spanish arrived only with difficulty: the first sales of revenues, from those of 1543 to those of 1555, reflect the treasury's continuous need under these conditions, that did not diminish even after the peace of 1544; the sales of 1548 (at 5 per cent and 10 per cent) mirror the beginning of the more tragic period, from the financial point of view, of the Milanese state under Charles V, while the sales of 1551 and 1553 (effected at 12 per cent) are testament to the needs brought by the humiliation at Innsbruck.[11] If in the earlier alienations the greater part was made up of the taxes collected in the *contadi* (rural administrative unit) (like the salt and Tassa dei Cavalli, which could be called direct taxes), from the Milanese *gabelles* and from some minor levies, beginning at the end of the 1540s the revenues relative to the cities (and in any case pertinent to the Chamber) and the indirect taxes began playing a pre-eminent role in funding securities. At the end of the reign of the first Habsburg sovereign the nominal capital of the public long-term redeemable debt of the Duchy reached 7,300,407 lire and its interest was 548,835 lire (equal to 52 per cent of ordinary revenue and 21 per cent of total revenues).[12]

After the peace of Cateau-Cambresis, the Milanese state became 'definitively' Spanish and the 'new' loyalty of the Lombardy was expressed in new emissions of redeemable debt: before 1559 Philip II had sold income of the Milanese state worth 1,163,833 lire, making the debt service increase to 58 per cent of ordinary revenue.[13] In 1560, in line with the Spanish decree of suspension of payment, there was a compulsory reduction of all securities to 5 per cent.[14] Starting with the end of that decade, the strategic importance of Lombardy in the core of the European theatre was further increased as the Flemish revolt developed and the state of Milan became the logistic centre for the Habsburgs. At this point Lombard finances began a rapid and noteworthy decline that was reflected directly on those of the citizens and communities, and the alienation of revenues increased dramatically. The positive economic movement of the Duchy from the mid-sixteenth century was producing a socialization of wealth that broadened both the fiscal base by increasing the flow of income (and so also the revenues available for sale) and the number of possible subscribers; in order to further expand income there was a parallel initiation of new indirect taxation and increase of those already existing (the most important of these, the *dazio della mercanzia*, a trade duty, was increased by 50 per cent), which is to say, those levies that least involved the dominant groups. The last decade of the century saw an increase in the monarchy's financial difficulties: the Castilian Hacienda was no longer able to guarantee the delivery of the enormous sums (*socorros*) indispensable to the Milanese Chamber and so the sale of revenues, at rates that were very unfavourable to the treasury, again increased. Attempts at redemption in order to lower the interest rates either failed or had little effect.[15] Between 1570 and 1610 the relative amount of sold revenues to the total of ordinary income (notwithstanding the fact that these were constantly growing, and actually tripled during the second half of the sixteenth century) reached 52–6 per cent, with prevailing remuneration rates of 8–10 per cent.[16]

With the second decade of seventeenth century and the beginning of Mantua's first War of Succession, military expenses spiked further, and the deficit left no choice other than the sale of more than 900,000 *scudi* of bonds backed by *gabelles* by 1619, at 7 per cent.[17] But from this moment, with the exceptionally grave situation of the Milanese Hacienda (the deficit in 1625 was almost 1.4 million *scudi* while the *atrasado*, or the sum of precedent deficits, was 11.5) and the progressive exhaustion of the quotas of annuities still available, functional behaviour took on more consistency. The administration of bonds itself was reorganized within a process that touched the entire function of the Royal Exchequer: an effective policy of redemption of the annuities at a higher interest; after the reduction to 5 per cent of all the sales made after 1565, the Redemption Cassa was established (in Naples it was the Military Cassa) and given the deposits made by the tax farmers.[18]

The difficulties due to the plague of 1630 and worsening of the military situation from 1636 brought further complications both in the sense of a reduction in interests and in the regularity of payments on state annuities. In 1647 the Chamber, copying modalities of the pontifical banks, had begun the voluntary collection of 100,000 *ducatoni* by putting out *luoghi*, which finally would be placed only through coercion. Five years later this issuing of *luoghi* was suppressed and its capital transferred to the Monte di San Carlo, established in 1638 to consolidate the debts of the state with the Genoese Stefano Balbi.[19] The local governments, as well as the public, were fully aware that state and urban revenues were almost exhausted. Therefore, in the manner of the Spanish *arbitrios*, several proposals were devised to restore the government debt. Such was the case of a plan by the Milanese noble Carlo Girolamo Cavazzi della Somaglia that aimed at redeeming all the alienated revenues within forty-eight years by lowering the interest rate the bondholders would accept in exchange for *donativo* (donation in monies) and the assured restitution of the principal.[20]

In the second half of the seventeenth century, the low income from the bonds backed by revenues (after the legal reduction of interest to 4 per cent in 1640 and to 2 per cent in 1648; to 5 per cent on the part of the Redemption Cassa in 1643) as from all the consolidated Milanese debts (those of the Banco di Sant'Ambrogio, consolidated in 1662, of the Monte di San Francesco and of San Carlo)[21] strongly compromised the earnings from these investments, and their quotations dropped. Only between 1691 and 1694, during the crisis of public finance due to heavy military expenditures for the war of the League of Augsburg, would annuities again be sold at 7 per cent, to return immediately afterwards to the more usual 4.5 per cent.[22] At the end of the Spanish era, the consolidated public debt constituted by the total of the annuities was equal to 36,782,000 lire (7.5 times the total of a year's revenue) and the relative interest accounted for 39 per cent of total revenues.[23]

The system of public debt in the Republic of San Marco was founded on compulsory loans from the fourteenth century to the early decades of the following century: based on assessments, the taxpayer would have had to pay a certain quota of his earnings (in large part real estate) as a loan, at 5 per cent yearly interest. In the first decades of the sixteenth century this type of financial instrument showed its limits: late interest payments, non-payment and a lack of trust on the part of the taxpayer.[24]

The patriciate replied by appealing to the free marketplace through the emission of new loans – called 'Depositi in Zecca' (mint deposits) – emitted by the state and freely subscribed. The deposits were successful because of their favourable earnings, the prospect of redeemable capital, the rapid formalities of redemption, and because the bonds could circulate. Their large-scale use began during the Turkish war of 1537–40 and their absolute fiscal immunity and exemption from any sequestration reinforced their attractiveness. The interest rate climbed from 6 to 7 per cent.

The way to satisfy the state's demand was by now decidedly the way of the free credit market. With the return of peace in 1540 the emissions were moderated and interest fell as far as 3 per cent on the eve of the war with Cyprus, indicating the ample supply of money in the market, which attracted conspicuous sums also from foreign countries (for example from Genoa).[25]

On the lagoon as well, the trend of emissions of Depositi in Zecca between the sixteenth and seventeenth centuries reflects the moments of major war needs and their real progress is compared with an inflationary process that made the content of fine silver in the Venetian ducat pass from 31.18 grams in 1562 to 26.61 ten years later, and to 16.88 in 1704.[26]

Taking advantage of a period of relative peace, between 1577 and 1584, more than 5 million ducats (almost twice the revenues of a year) were returned from the Depositi in Zecca and towards 1615 the Republic could consider itself free of public debt. The war against the Archdukes of 1615–17 and the involvement in the Thirty Years War put Venetian finances to a severe test, which was passed by the collection of capital both in Venice and from Genoese investors. From 1609 to 1641 the annual average of capital collected in Zecca was 244,500 ducats, with moments of 900,000 in 1616. The years following the plague showed an alternation between moments of hard need and periods of relative tranquillity. In 1637 the favourable conditions of the public finances induced the government to decree a new release of capital in the Zecca. A part of the capital was returned and the rest kept at an interest rate that was lowered from 7 to 6 per cent and then to 5 per cent.

The war of Candia began in 1645 and by its end in 1669 the public debt had risen to 35 million ducats (eight times yearly revenue) and its service absorbed 54 per cent of revenues. But recovery was rapid: in 1672 the government put all its various deposits into a single fund and reduced the interest rate to 3 per cent, beginning to liquidate the principal.[27]

In Genoa the issues of public debt, due to the provisions for political expansion and reform, followed one another frequently from the thirteenth century, accelerating financial innovation and making its bankers leaders in this sector.[28] Beginning in the last decades of the thirteenth century the Genoese public debt grew through alternating phases of dilation and reinforcement which in the modern era are marked above all by defence, repression, and contributions to wars imposed by enemy forces. In 1407 the government had gathered all its debts into a single fund managed by the Casa of San Giorgio, a consortium of public creditors to which the state ceded a large number of tax revenues assigned for the payment of interest.[29]

At the middle of the sixteenth century the authorities formally admitted that they were unable to redeem the principal, and this marked the beginning of a lively debt market. In the course of the seventeenth century the Republic of Genoa created ever greater spaces of autonomous manoeuvring by opening numerous public loans directly (or through the lower judiciary): in 1650, of the 102 million in consolidated debt, 74 was in purchases of San Giorgio and 28 of the state, while fifty years later 78 was in purchases and 34 in state bonds.[30]

The case in the Duchy of Savoy is just the opposite, in that the public debt was formed later and more slowly because the governors were almost always able to fulfil their own needs by introducing extraordinary taxes on the community and from help given by their powerful allies: for example, this aid from allies accounted for 22 per cent (equal to 15,700,000 lire) of the military expenses from 1690 to 1696 and 49.3 per cent from 1700 to 1713 (equal to 49,276,000 lire).[31] But even here the prime bonds backed by the yield of tax income appeared just at the middle of the sixteenth century: this was the sale of the principal direct land tax, the *tasso*, that began to constitute the nucleus of consolidated long-term public debt. Although we do not have detailed information, the scarce data give us sales equal to 165,000 lire for 1638, for 1651 equal to 271,000 and for 1666 equal to 520,000, figures that are to be judged keeping in mind that the silver content of the Piedmont lira passed from 10.81 grams of 1632 to 5.63 at the end of the century. Simultaneously in 1653 and 1681 the Monte della Fede and that of San Giovanni Battista were funded and emitted bonds guaranteed by the revenues on the sovereign's behalf.[32] In 1684 the consolidated public debt totalled more than 15 million lire and in 1702, following the war of 1690–6, it rose to 17,441,246 (1.8 times the annual revenues of the state, which were equal to about 9 million lire) and paid an average interest of 5.7 per cent.[33]

As for the Piedmontese state, so also for the small Duchy of Parma and Piacenza, created in 1545 by a nepotistic act of Paolo III Farnese, the recourse to indebtedness was slow and dictated by the inability to cope with extraordinary expenses. Here too the turning point occurred close to 1590 and was concentrated in some exceptional events (the costs of Alessandro Farnese's military campaigns in Flanders and those determined by the famine of 1590–3): the total debt rose to around twice the ordinary revenue (circa 155,000 lire).

In the mid-seventeenth century the situation became more difficult and the Farnese debts with Roman bankers brought the definitive loss of their fiefs in Lazio. At the time of restitution of the debts, in 1644, the Duke had sworn to repay the creditors who had subscribed the *luoghi* of the Monte Farnese, but these payments soon ceased for lack of funds. Called on by the creditors, Pope Innocent X occupied Castro and Ronciglione. This caused the second war of Castro, at the end of which the Farnese lost all their property in Lazio, confiscated by the Apostolic Chamber to satisfy the creditors.[34]

2

We can see that in the states of northern Italy military needs and urgencies mainly determined the trend of this kind of debt, which took very different proportions (from 31.5 times the revenues for the Republic of Genoa, to 2.2 times for the Duchy of Savoy) and variable costs (from the interest rate of 3.23 per cent for Genoa to that of 4.5 per cent for the Milanese state, see Table 4.2). The spread of funded debt represented a turning point since, for the countries, the cost of indebtedness was lowered, but its diffusion and success were due to the dynamic response found among the buyers, although with different features.

Table 4.2: Funded Debt and Revenues in the States of Northen Italy in the Second Half of the Seventeenth Century.[35]

	Year	Funded Debt	Interest Rate %	Interest/ Revenues (%)	Funded Debt/ Revenues	Funded Debt in Silver (kg)
Duchy of Milan	1695	36,782,000 lire	4.5	39.0	7.5	142,346
Republic of Venice	1679	46,300,000 ducats	3.32	35.9	10.8	894,748
Duchy of Savoy	1684	15,526,734 ducats	4.4	22.5	2.2	87,508
Republic of Genoa	1650	102,191,000 lire	3.23	97.9	31.5	555,919

If compared to the traditional image for this period of a range of purchasers of public bonds belonging to the political and economic elites, or to ecclesiastical and charitable institutions, one is struck, in the state of Milan, by the plurality and variety of subjects who, at least in the initial phase of Spanish domination, subscribed to these issues. The amount of 1,753,724 lire of revenues, alienated between 1542 and 1573, was subscribed by 2,196 different subjects and, while the larger sums were purchased by local and Genoese bankers, nobles and members of the patriciate, the lowest share, 66 lire of the *dazio del prestino* of Milan, ended up in the hands of a tailor of Porta Vercellina, Giovanni Piccardini.[36] Also for revenues sold between 1574 and 1611 for 2,191,302 lire, there was a large number of buyers, 2,640 (the average share went from 800 to 830 lire; see Chart 4.2).

Chart 4.2: First Buyers of Public Bonds of the State of Milan, 1543–73 and 1574–1611.[37]

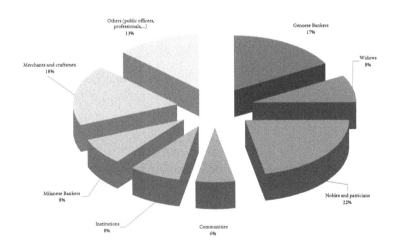

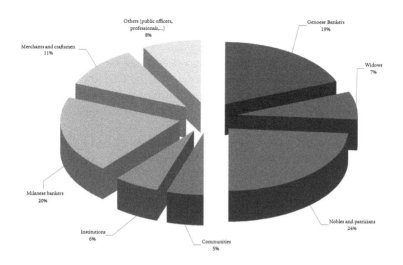

The intense economic recovery that started in the 1540s, after the end of wars and famines, determined, especially in the capital city, a significant distribution of wealth: a resident of Ferrara witnessed that Milan was 'very wealthy; but of riches shared by many; although there are only three or four families with an income of 25–30,000 *scudi*, and very few with 10,000 *scudi*, there is an infinite number of families with 2, 3 and 4,000 *scudi*'.[38] The fact that the payment of interest was guaranteed (collected directly from the taxpayers thereby reassuring more than any government promise), the alienation rate and the easy tradability all represented persuasive elements for a large number of craftsmen, bureaucrats, merchants, bankers, professionals, nobles, patricians, religious institutions and single women, who saw the purchase of revenues as safe as regular, non-taxable income.

To mention just a few names, in the second half of the sixteenth century we find high-level financial Genoese operators (not only the 'naturalized' Marino brothers but also the Centuriones, the Spinolas, the Grimaldis and the Balbis), remarkable figures of the economic and aristocratic spheres such as Agostino Foppa; the D'Adda brothers (Agostino, Pagano, Lodovico and Erasmo); the Carcassolas (Antonio and Giacomo Filippo, wool merchants); the Fagnanos (who were also active in Antwerp and among the leading Milanese money traders), such as Earls Camillo and Vitaliano Borromeo; Giovanni Battista Lodrone; Bartolomeo Arese; Girolamo Sala; Gattinara di Sartirana or Giovanni Giacomo Medici (the renowned 'Medeghino'), marquis of Melegnano; Simone de Tassi, the Imperial Post Master; Pietro Paolo Arrigone, President of the Senate; Castellano Maggi and Francesco Taverna. We also have religious, pious and municipal institutions (such as the Certosa of Pavia, the Grangia of Chiaravalle, the Certosa of Garegnano, the Ospedale Maggiore in Milan and the Friars of San Giovanni in Conca), civil and military institutions (such as the Collegio dei causidici in Milan and the Military Hospital in Asti), and several women, primarily from the aristocracy, such as the Duchess of Lorena, Violanta Lampugnani Visconti, Anna Carcassola, Isabella Borromeo Trivulzio and the Countess Pada Torrella Barbiana; but also middle-class females, such as the widow Caterina Porta, who invested her dowry and life savings to secure an annual income for her young children.[39]

Even though many bonds sold on the same day of the same month of the same year often yielded different interest rates – depending on the kind of tax revenue funding them (for example, the *censo del sale* of a small community rather than the *dazio della mercanzia*), and on the proximity to the centres of power – the returns, however, were in many cases higher than the ones offered in the Duchy of Milan by other kinds of investment (a witness tells us that land rent was 2–3 per cent during the 1560s)[40] and their range (5–12 per cent in this phase) was in line with that of public debt in other countries.[41] However, since such annuities satisfied a need for fungible securities in commercial and manufacturing activity (see section 3, below), they were bought even when the yield was not competitive because it was compensated by the other uses given to them. Government securities lost the older patrimonial aspect and appeared more clearly as investments, hence becoming extremely popular.

Many communities of the state were pushed to subscribe to this debt because of fiscal reasons: their many purchases of the two direct taxes (*censo del sale* – one third of which was imposed on goods – and *tassa dei cavalli e perticato su teste morte*) that burdened their own territory can be interpreted as an attempt to shift this taxation (that was supposed to hit their population individual by individual according to a precise sharing, also in proportion to their wealth) into an indirect form, gaining the tax revenue through additional duties (whose payment was shared by everybody to the advantage of the families with higher incomes)[42] or in other ways, as shown by the cases of Casalmaggiore, Cerano, Pizzighettone, Voghera and Vimodrone, where inhabitants reported that 'the wealthier families had purchased the revenues in order to pay less out of their pockets'.[43]

It was this varied typology of purchasers that responded to some sales so quickly that they exhausted them within a few days; it was their demand that pushed Milanese *sensale* (broker) Bernardo Molina, during the last decades of the sixteenth century, to write repeatedly to the Royal Chamber that he had 'buyers available', he was searching for good securities to sell.[44] In addition, precisely in the middle of the 1570s, taking advantage of the temporary coolness of Philip II towards the Genoese and of the related downturn of short-term loans, Milanese banker-cambists – who asserted themselves also because of the macro-impulse provided by the government debt, above all in relationship with the trend of economic growth, in order to respond to the demand for credit and services – structured an articulate financial system, which also contributed to the organization in a functional way of the primary bond market.[45]

These dealers – who participated in the distribution of *asientos* – played a fundamental role in the market of alienated revenues (they purchased 46 per cent of the total of alienated revenues in 1579, versus 21 per cent of the Genoese)[46] and in the system of farming of duties, which represented the obvious guarantee and indemnity for that market. Through a network of local mediators and brokers, they contributed to extending the geography of demand for bonds to all parts of the state. They are the protagonists, along with the Genoese bankers, of a secondary market of Milanese alienations that appeared particularly lively in this phase. It was a technically efficient market, which offered lower transaction costs than those available in other centres: the commission of Milanese brokers (0.5 per cent of the security) was less than that charged by their Roman and Bolognese colleagues;[47] the procedure of transfer provided for free registration at the Chamber registry office, while the change of ownership was not taxable (unlike the same process in the Papal States); also the norms protecting the renters and regulating their right to collect interest were detailed and carefully applied.[48] Although rules entitled only Milanese citizens to hold these revenues, foreigners, mainly from Genoa, were also included as purchasers both under exceptions and, in the case of major operators, acquiring *civilitas mediolanensis*, involving a number of fiscal exemptions.[49] On the informative efficiency of the market, that is, on the extent prices circulated, our sources only allow us to point out the common asymmetry in favour of the issuer and the main bankers. One of the main references for the smaller buyers seems to be the behaviour of the ruling class and of the richest layers of society that boosted official confidence in the stability and profitabilty of the debt.[50]

Our sources do not tell us at which quotation the revenues were traded in; they allow us, however, to reconstruct the percentage of the value of the ones that changed holders: within five years from their first sale, 42 per cent of more than 600,000 lire alienated in 1559, 53 per cent of 410,000 in 1581, and 22 per cent of 310,000 in 1603 found a new owner. The first two percentages, already significant, increased even more if we take into account a few single taxes that were composed of the different alienations (87 per cent of the *dazio della mercanzia* of Milan alienated in 1559, and 76 per cent of the *gabella grossa* of Cremona in 1581 changed holders), showing that the most profitable and safest state revenues enjoyed a strong demand.[51] In 1599, in Madrid, Leonardo Torriano, engineer in the kingdoms of Portugal from Cremona, sold to Juan de Herrrera a security on the *dazio della mercanzia* of the state of Milan for 1,700 lire and 18 *soldi*.[52]

In the 1620s, the typology of buyers changed drastically in favour of great Genoese and Milanese bankers, who in some cases also controlled the later trading of the alienations. The needs of the state, particularly pressing in this phase, made it more convenient to alienate large sums at once to those operators instead of waiting for a direct sale to a wider public. However, the reduction of interest rates that began in those years, and the uncertainty on the general conditions of the Hacienda, which, beginning in 1630, suspended several times, partially or entirely, the payment of securities,[53] reduced the attractiveness and liveliness of the state securities market, which had also to compete with the city bonds issued by the Banco di Sant'Ambrogio.[54]

In addition, the structural reorganization of Lombard economy, against the background of European macro-structural transformation, moved its centre of gravity towards the export of semi-finished products and caused a strong polarization of both the wealth and the size of operators. In this phase, the sales of government bonds became problematic and it is very difficult to find evidence of later sales. In these decades, besides the Genoese (headed by Balbi and Durazzo), we find a group of great native bankers allowed to manage state revenues as compensation for the *asientos* they had stipulated. The trend towards a concentration of revenues through the redemption or diversion of shares is also clear. In 1641, Carlo Francesco Ceva, representative of a pool of Genoese renters, bought the revenues of all Milanese bakers, the Chamber grindstone, the calcine and others, to allow the Royal Chamber to redeem the revenues held by the family Omodei.[55] Still in an operation of sale and return, five years later Gerolamo Turconi from Como carried out a fraud that yielded 131,000 lire.[56] In 1685, a taxation on the revenues of foreigners was imposed on the subjects of Genoa, and these people, also because of other heavy impositions, began to reduce their old presence in the Duchy's public debt.[57]

For the state natives, however, in a century characterized by a substantial stability of prices, government bonds continued to play an important role in assuring some of the most profitable returns and protecting one's income from a constantly growing taxation. This aspect is well highlighted in the second half of the century by Francesco Bigatti, author of a project of tax reform, who noticed how subscribers of securities cashed their yields and 'laughed, while everybody else cried under the burden of taxation'.[58]

It was only from the first decades of the seventeenth century that, instead of considering the different patterns of bond emissions and the contraction of investment opportunities in maritime trades, Venetians looked at state securities as an attractive destination for their money.[59] Between the second and the third decade of the century, Genoese investors strengthened the money supply, subscribing to 46.3 per cent of 2,177,905 *ducati*, collected in lifetime deposits from 1617 to 1625. In the second decade, the government made sure to expand the base of potential buyers, declaring its availability to accept money both from Venetian subjects and foreigners. This measure was not introduced as a way to make up for a scarcity of currency, but rather as an attempt to weave a web that tied the different spheres of the state, the capital city and the subject territories.[60]

In actuality, attracted by the reliability of the deposits, Genoese bankers purchased them in a massive way and contributed to enlivening the market: whereas in 1641 14.3 per cent of funded debt in the mint deposits belonged to non-Venetians, in 1673 30.3 per cent of these redeemable securities was in the hands of Genoese bankers.[61]

The increasing tax burden, caused by the war of Candia, together with the related economic difficulties, had the effect of animating the financial market, which recorded a remarkable movement of capital in the form of government bonds; between 1645 and 1671 an annual average of 236,388 *ducati* of credits was negotiated on the secondary market, and more than a quarter of the securities changed holders (rather elevated figures that would exceed the average value – compared by silver content – of the transactions operated on the London market by the joint-stocks of the East India Company in the years 1661–72). The available data indicates that high-yield deposits record a good circulation, whose general speed was certainly favoured by easy and cheap transaction procedures.[62]

Therefore, the Venetian demand of public credit grew remarkably during the seventeenth century, attracting capital that otherwise would have been difficult to employ safely and with the same returns: the growing costs and the risks of trade discouraged people from investing in that sector – agriculture did not offer good rents, and returns over the fairs of exchange had been declining. The actual yield, that is the yield calculated on the security market price, was, on the contrary, quite favourable: in 1646, the Ottoboni sold some deposits on the secondary market for 70 out of 100 and that meant for the buyer an actual interest rate of 7 per cent on a security that yielded 5 per cent; in 1687, securities at 3 per cent were sold at 80, with a 3.75 per cent yield for the buyer.[63]

In Genoa, we can identify a non-forced securities primary market from the first decades of sixteenth century; however there is evidence of a public bond secondary market from the Renaissance.[64] We know there were brokers who had desks to manage the purchase and sale of shares, and who fixed the prices as well. Since government bonds were not bearer bonds, every transaction had to be registered at that state agency. The Genoese government took 1 lira for each share negotiated.[65] Object of trade was not only the principal, but also the interest claims. Public credits could be sold, used as collateral, or given as dowries. We know that foreign merchants, whose presence became more visible in the fifteenth century, held credits of San Giorgio that were used as guarantees for their business. At any rate, the foreign presence among bondholders was rather limited and, in 1629, 92 percent of the principal of San Giorgio belonged to Genoese citizen and institutions.[66]

The structure and dynamics of the securities market in the Duchy of Savoy have not been fully explored yet. From the analysis of the social distribution of the first buyers, however, we can deduce that altogether the most significant participants were people who were building their wealth through a *cursus* – that is an activity as merchants, bankers or officials – rather than landowners or aristocrats, as previously suggested by S. J. Woolf.[67] Now we have evidence that out of the total issues of the Monte della Fede (1635–68) and San Giovanni Battista (1681–1708), and in the alienation of the Tasso (1622–90), the old aristocracy purchased around 25 per cent of capital, while the nobility of office, magistrates and bourgeois bought more than 68 per cent.[68] Several factors accounted for such a high percentage. Mostly, Savoy resorted to bourgeois families who held judiciary and financial offices, and also the most prestigious posts of the Camera dei Conti because the dukes were able to pay them back in inexpensive ways, for example, in personal and inherited nobility and concessions of feudal privileges. Moreover, buying government bonds meant not only getting a secure yield but also having the possibility to climb the social ladder.

Among the Piedmontese subscribers there were bankers like the Quaglias; the Barbarossas, Bistort and Giovanetti; the Martinis; the Spadas or the widow Giulia Papona, both from Racconigi; the businessman Ubertalo of Biella, wool merchant; and the Bormioli brothers from Altare, famous representatives of one of the most important dynasties of the glass industry. Moreover, there were representatives of a rising well-off bourgeoisie such as the Marchisios; the Agliaudis; the Berlias, who operated in the silk market; or the banker Marcello Gamba, who managed several tax farming contracts and advanced part of the subsidies coming from England or the Netherlands to the Duke. There were other families, too, such as the Biancos, the Amorettis, the Oliveros, the Dentis, the Buniattos and the Chioatteros, who moved from financial activities and fiscal contracts to aristocracy. Along with them artisan families arose: tailors, shoemakers, blacksmiths and carpenters whose guilds had achieved a relevant role in Turin between the seventeenth and eighteenth centuries.[69]

Furthermore, while the sale by the Savoy state of the *tasso* could help the landowners who subscribed to that alienation to redeem the tax burdening their estates (as was the case in the Milanese state), many alienations of this tax after 1622 were fixed in the stable gold *scudo*, sheltering from inflation the investments of subscribers throughout the seventeenth century.[70]

Although not constant, because of the permanent hostility between the Duchy and the Republic of Genoa, the presence of Genoese operators in the Savoy public debt dated back to the sixteenth century and found its proper institutional instrument in the creation of the Monte della Fede and Monte of San Giovanni, to whose securities the Savoy king granted exemption from retaliations and confiscations – even when the security holders belonged to belligerent enemy states – a perpetual tax exemption, free negotiability and other privileges.[71]

Genoese bankers found in public bonds of these countries both good investment opportunities to place revenues coming from their wide capital networks, and, as in the case of Milanese debt, long-for-short-term swaps which the Spanish

Crown realized at the conclusion of each bankruptcy. During the long reign of Philip II, the Genoese *hombres de negocios* had in fact strengthened their hegemony in the 'international republic of money' through their control of the fairs of Piacenza; those were periodical credit markets (organized every three months) through which both large short-term state loans (the *asientos*), in particular to the Austrians, and more modest private and commercial transactions were negotiated. These fairs represented the *trait d'union* between private finance and state economic institutions and were based on the multilateral settlement of bills of exchange, at the origin, together with public bonds, of the financial dynamism of European capitalism in the sixteenth and seventeenth centuries. In 1622, in order to have larger operational autonomy at these fairs, Genoese bankers moved their meetings to Novi, on their territory, but their fading from the top level management of international finance after the Austrians' bankruptcy in 1627, and the refusal to recognize this move by the other Italian bankers, would mark the gradual loss of centrality of this negotiation system.[72]

3

Considering the good response received by this type of government bond and the dynamic influx of investors in the securities market, it is natural to wonder whether the significant amount of money that ended in the alienation of revenues, in deposits in Zecca and in purchases meant a subtraction of capital to private long-term investments destined for the economy and/or increased their cost. On this issue, there are no available studies that allow us to delineate a homogeneous picture of northern Italy, but we do have some empirical findings that permit us to suggest some ideas regarding the most advanced economic regions in the area.

It has been possible to reconstruct the long-term demand of capital by entrepreneurs in the state of Milan, assuming that it can be represented by the totality of *censi consegnativi* stipulated by the group of local bankers for the years 1575–1611, which certainly display the most intense economic expansion in the sixteenth and seventeenth centuries.[73] In 1569, a bull by Pius V had ratified the final approval of this loan contract, based on real guarantees and on the structure *emptio cum locatione*, confirming its redeemability; in the *censi* ownership of the borrower's property would be transferred to the lender in return for the loan; interest was then paid as if it were rent for the continued use of the property by the borrower.[74] In this timeframe we have identified 241 *censi* for a total of 2,116,000 lire (see Chart 4.3), with an interest of 7 per cent for the twenty-year loans and 9 per cent for the ten-year loans. Until the early 1590s, borrowers were almost exclusively metal industry entrepreneurs who used the capital to start mines and blast furnaces in Valsassina, while in the following two decades they were mainly merchants who used them to establish silk manufactures (after 1610 the use of this instrument seems to fade among merchants, where it is replaced by limited partnership, while it grows in popularity among communities).

Chart 4.3: Public Bonds and *Censi Consegnativi* in the State of Milan, 1575–1611 (current value in lire).[75]

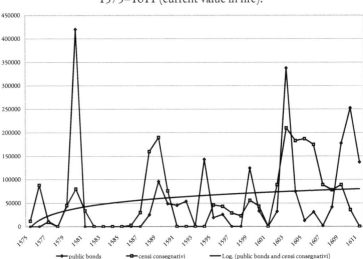

On the basis of these data, the curve of capitals destined for productive activities presents a rising logarithmic trend, like the one of capitals for public credit in the same phase (as shown in Chart 4.3). Both demands, therefore, seem to increase at the same time. This was allowed by the soaring amount of circulating currency, not limiting the loanable funds. We presume the expansion of currency for three reasons. First, even though it is extremely complex to calculate the real adding effect of new coinages because it is impossible to know how much currency was withdrawn, and summing up the value of money minted in different times is not precise, there is no doubt that the trend for new monetary emissions was growing; in 1542–54 it is already possible to record an expansive trend that reaches its peak in 1580–91, when almost thirty million lire were minted, and in the following decade, when twenty million more were coined.[76] Second, several testimonies tell us that there was a strong balance of payments surplus as a consequence of substantial export flows that lasted until the end of the second decade of the seventeenth century.[77] Third, between the end of the sixteenth century and the beginning of the following one, the circulation of trade credit bills, 'which are issued by any indebted merchant in favour of the creditor either on the forms that are currently printed or also with simple notes' and that 'pass from one hand to the other as they were real money',[78] rose, dispensing with the use of metallic money for commercial matters and increasing the global circulating currency.

In one of the most prosperous Milanese economic cycles in the early modern period, centred around an articulate urban and extra-urban productive structure and fuelled by a strong export flow of gold and silk cloths, private and public demands of capital were not depleting each other and met the supply curve in different points, with an advantage in terms of interest rates in favour of the first (7–9 per cent versus 8–10 per cent). The cost of money was slightly lower for private customers because of both the shorter temporal commitment and the real guarantee (in the *censi* the contractual ownership of the property represented a good security). Moreover, during this phase, the interest rate offered by state revenues tended to conform essentially to the political and military needs and paid a premium on a risk of which Milanese bankers were very aware, especially after the first crisis of Spanish finances. The circuit that ran the meeting between the collection of capital and supply was in fact in the hands of a group of banker-cambists. These businessmen received the money collected by money-changers, with whom they formed partnerships, by widows who invested in the bills of exchange market, and by landowners, nobles and patricians, and invested this capital in loans to private customers or in both funded and floating debt.[79]

In this phase, public bonds represented a large part, or the entirety, of the goods that *censi consegnativi* borrowers sold to the lenders (as a security) in exchange for the loan (and that is rented in exchange for another rent that represents the interest). In the *censi* stipulated by our merchant-entrepreneurs from 1575 to 1611, the total of revenues which were 'temporarily' transferred with this function summed up to 379,580 lire (see Chart 4.3). For granting lenders the financial risks were considerably reduced. Therefore state securities not only represented an additional, non-taxable income, but were also used as a collateral of credit by the productive world and contributed to increase its chances to obtain more funds, playing a pro-cycle effect on private investments. The diffusion of this use of government bonds is also witnessed by the ordination of the Milanese merchant guild, dated 7 July 1572, in which it is specified that in order to constitute a *censo* on the 'state revenues from which a yield is received',[80] it is necessary to present a copy of Chamber records testifying how the borrower acquired them. Later developments in other countries do corroborate the potential benefits of securities and their market.[81]

Extending the spectrum of the interrelations between public debt and economy, we have to consider the possible effects that the significant deficit spending, carried out by the Milanese government and made possible by the debt (and the aid provided by the other Spanish provinces), had on the regional economy. Between the two possible alternatives – that deficit spending acted in an economy characterized by full employment subtracting factors of production from civilian uses and triggering an inflation process, or that it managed to mobilize idle factors, utilizing them in the war expense – the fact that prices and wages remained stable throughout the seventeenth century (and actually tended to decrease after 1620) makes us privilege the second hypothesis. In Lombardy, the huge public expenditure destined for the military (clothes, arms and fortification) created supplementary employment and new flows of income that in their turn contributed to keeping elevated the civil demand for goods and services, especially in urban contexts.[82] In the same way, the policy of deficit spending carried out by the Savoy dynasty in the second half of the seventeenth century had important consequences in the building industry and in the field of military architecture, fostering a more general recovery of regional economy.[83]

In the state of Milan, with the reversal of the economic trend from the end of 1620s – related to a new macroeconomic equilibrium in the European context and certainly not to a lack of capital for the productive and distributive sector – the articulate structure of the urban economic system entered a phase in which, although at a disadvantage with the manufactures in the traditional major sectors, found a new equilibrium in its commercial vocation that saw the exploitation of imports balanced through the sale of semi-manufactured products ('*seta filata*' spun silk above all). The core of the economic interests of the higher classes and the ruling circles turned in this direction.[84] Opportunities for social mobility decreased in favour of a gradual polarization. In this context, public debt, together with land rent, would offer good returns and safeguard them from the growing tax burden. It would protect the property and dowries (both secular and religious) of the ruling class, supporting both its social role and its more productive investments in agriculture.

The seventeenth-century Venetian economy displayed the same process. The productive and distributive system of the Republic had to be restructured because of the strong northern European competition and the structural transformation that was affecting the economy of the continent. In the streamlining of traditional activities and the shrinking of the economic space under control, the importance of financial capital increased and, together with land rent, assured a high standard of living to the wealthy strata and allowed a widespread luxury consumption which, keeping demand elevated, encouraged specific activities.[85]

4

This genotype of government debt emerges with a branched functionality, offering multiple perspectives, settling it at the centre of complex interrelationships that tied the administration of power to the stratified local society, the tax system to the economic structures and conjunctures, military needs to the interests of the native local groups and to the means of their success or preservation.

The cost of state credit was, in economic terms, rather moderate. In the second half of the sixteenth and seventeenth centuries, these governments were enabled to collect money at interest rates raging from 2.3 to 12 per cent, whereas many other European countries had to borrow at higher price. Furthermore, the trade of bonds and interest claims initiated sophisticated forms of speculation and were the springboard for financial innovation all over the continent.

It would be unwise, however, in a financial market strongly affected by extra-economic elements, by rulers and operators inspired more by distributive than commutative justice, by interest rates which responded more to reasons of urgency and reciprocity than to availability of capital, to limit our analysis of public debt to a search for features of presumed economic and administrative rationality and elements of modern efficiency. The credibility itself, the trust itself (although well guaranteed) that Milanese lenders – as well as their Venetian, Genoese and Piedmontese counterparts – granted to their governments, that helped to determine the success of this new type of public debt, was rooted precisely in the kind of oligarchic societies in which, despite the diverse constitutional organizations, the ruling class and economic élite basically coincided.

In the state of Milan itself, subject to the Spanish Crown, the rule of the foreign dynasty was based on a substantial alliance with the local élites and on the respect of their economic interests and choices. Still, the sense of the precariousness of the destiny of the Duchy following the extinction of the Sforza dynasty was widespread, and one of the first successful demands of the Milanese subjects to Charles V was that all the past sales of public revenues were to be confirmed and honoured.[86] In the administration of the Duchy, the members of the local ruling élites – descending from merchant families – adopted a style of government based above all on negotiation and mediation with other centres of power and different social groups.

In addition, despite the concentration of bonds in the hands of a few holders that had started in the early decades of the seventeenth century, small and middling investors were an important part of the Milanese securities market in the middle of the century, especially compared to the different example offered by the Kingdom of Naples.[87] In Milan in 1639, 24 per cent of the funded debt was made up of bonds which were worth less than 150 lire and were in the hands of more than 4,350 local holders from 77 communities.[88] As is well known, the Duchy of Milan was the only Italian domain of the Spanish monarchy that did not undergo either a political or a social insurrection against the Crown, nor were there any significant cases of anti-Habsburg conspiracies in the mid-seventeenth century, although strains and conflicts were not absent.[89] The majority of the low and middle classes, the cities, the boroughs and the communities[90] – drawing yields from the public debt along with the patriciate, the merchants, the bankers and the religious institutions – had nothing to gain from rebelling against a government from whom they claimed such huge credits. They therefore played a crucial role in the peculiar and uninterrupted quietude of the Milanesado. Public debt represented one of the most important bonding agents of social and political stability.

Like Venice, which through the powerful instrument of public debt tried to tie the different spheres of the state and the subject territories to the central politics, Madrid involved the local ruling élites and the territorial bodies in a mechanism of redistribution of income aimed at their gradual integration, participation and sharing of central governmental policy.

5 GOVERNMENT POLICIES AND THE DEVELOPMENT OF FINANCIAL MARKETS: THE CASE OF MADRID IN THE SEVENTEENTH CENTURY

José Ignacio Andrés Ucendo[1]

The rise of the modern state during the early modern period could hardly been explained without taking into account the development of the first national fiscal systems. To achieve their political objectives the European kings had to increase their revenues, introducing new taxes, promoting all kind of reforms to improve the efficiency of their fiscal systems and curtailing the social and regional privileges enjoyed by certain social groups and territories.[2] Yet in most cases this was not enough. As expenditures were usually well above revenues, most European monarchies and republics had to borrow, and this paved the way for the expansion of the first public debt systems which, in the cases of the Dutch Republic and England, led to the development of advanced financial markets.[3]

In the Spanish and, particularly, Castilian cases, during the sixteenth and seventeenth centuries the Crown's fiscal revenues experienced a substantial rise, especially in the last quarter of the sixteenth century and the central decades of the seventeenth. This was not enough, however, to finance the Habsburg fight for European hegemony and the Spanish kings had to rely on all kinds of measures to provide them with the funds needed.[4] Among them, borrowing had a prominent place, but the importance of public debt should not hide the fact that there were other ways of supplying the Crown's needs, and this paper tries to analyse one of them: the alienation to Madrid of a significant part of the Crown's fiscal ordinary revenues in return for monetary subsidies.

The process began in 1653 and lasted until 1679. At its end, the Crown had transferred to its capital most of the *servicio de millones* collected in Madrid and its fiscal district in return for substantial monetary subsidies, which could be described as forced loans (*donativos*). To raise the amount of money involved in such *donativos*, the government allowed the capital to issue bonds (*efectos de villa*) so, as it will be seen in section 1, below, the whole operation should best be described as an effort to funnel the considerable wealth of the capital into the service of the monarchy through the expansion of Madrid's debt, which rose in the years between 1653 and 1680, when, after a group of fiscal and monetary reforms, its amount stabilized around the levels reached at the end of the seventies (see section 2, below).

The growth of the city's debt had deep social, economic and financial consequences, analysed in section 3, below. Particularly important, from the financial point of view, is the fact that the *efectos* were welcomed by the public during the first years of their existence. The profitability of these financial assets was high, particularly during the years 1653–79, and there are even hints to suggest that something like a secondary market of *efectos* was developing in the city, although it is impossible to know where this would have led because it seems that after the delays and discounts in the payment of the interests of the *efectos* of the first decades of the eighteenth century, these assets lost most of their former appeal to investors. If, as is commonly believed, there is a close connection between governmental policies and the growth of financial markets, then the case of Madrid would be an example of the negative consequences political interference may have on the development of such markets.[5]

1

Pressed by its urgent needs, during the central years of the seventeenth century the Castilian government introduced new taxes, as two new *servicios de millones* in 1656 and 1657 and two *unos por ciento* (the third and fourth) in 1656 and 1663. Thanks to them, the revenues of the most profitable ordinary taxes collected in the kingdom (*millones*, *alcabalas* and *cientos*) increased nearly 30 per cent (in nominal terms) between 1657 and 1664, reaching the highest level of the sixteenth and seventeenth centuries.[6] Remarkable as it was, the growth of the ordinary fiscal revenues did not solve the inadequacy between the fiscal incomes and the expenses of the imperial policy which constituted the main structural problem of the Castilian fiscality, and after the arrival of Carlos II to the throne the idea that the fiscal burden had reached a ceiling was so widespread in governmental circles that it prompted the adoption of a policy of fiscal relief which culminated in the famous *Encabezamiento General del Reino*.[7] The constraints of the fiscal policy were compounded by the problems experienced in the traditional financial system of the country in the central decades of the century, which coincided with a simultaneous fall in the arrival of American silver.[8] After that period, most of the traditional lenders to the monarchy (mainly the well-known Portuguese and Genoese bank houses) left the country. Although some foreign bankers kept their deals with the Crown and during the last decades of the century a group of Castilian and Spanish merchant houses achieved some relevance, it seems undeniable that they could not fill the gap left by the departure of the Portuguese and Genoese bankers.[9]

The difficulties experienced by the traditional fiscal and financial systems of the country during the central decades of the seventeenth century prompted the adoption of a vast array of devices in order to provide the government with the funds needed and, not surprisingly, the Crown turned its attention to the main Castilian cities in search of monetary subsidies. This policy offered some advantages. First, the possibility of obtaining substantial amounts of money straight from the cities, sidelining the complex and long political negotiations with the assembly of the kingdom (the Cortes) which had presided over the political life of the country in the first decades of the century, would have sounded particularly attractive to the ears of the Crown ministers. Second, the inclination of Madrid (and other Castilian cities) to grant substantial *donativos* to the government reflected the close cooperation between the urban oligarchies and the monarchy prevailing in Castile after the departure of Olivares, and offered the Castilian government the welcome possibility of reducing the risks of an excessive dependence on foreign bankers and *asentistas*, always prone to developing a common front in their financial dealings with the Crown.[10] Third and last, it should be added that the Crown's ministers were acquainted with the new policy. In fact, since 1621 (if not before) the monarchy had obtained various forced loans from the most important cities. To quote an example, Madrid had awarded nearly 2 million ducats in various *donativos* in the years 1629–52, so the continuous request of new *donativos* by the Crown to its capital after 1653 could be interpreted as the continuation, on a longer scale, of a policy previously followed.[11]

Of course, there were also disadvantages. Particularly important among them is the fact that, given the deep crisis suffered by the previously flourishing Castilian urban world, it was clear from the beginning that the main burden of the new policy was going to fall on the capital of the country, Madrid, which could be considered as the most remarkable exception to the decadence we have just outlined, especially when we remember how the other big Castilian city, Seville, had entered the last stage of its decadence after the plague of 1649 which killed nearly 50 per cent of its population.[12]

In November 1653 Madrid granted a *donativo* of 220,000 ducats to the government and the Crown decided in return to transfer to the city the 'servicio de los 8,000 soldados' collected in the capital and its fiscal district.[13] This marked the beginning of nearly three decades during which Madrid obtained the control of most part of the *servicios de millones* collected in the city and its province in return for substantial *donativos*, so, according to our estimates, in the last decades of the seventeenth century Madrid controlled 82 per cent of the total value of the *servicios de millones* paid by the city and its fiscal district.

Originally, the *millones*, introduced in the last years of the sixteenth century, were a temporary aid granted by the Castilian Cortes to the king, although in the years around 1653 they should be considered as an ordinary and permanent tax of the royal treasury. It should also be emphasized that the term *servicio de millones* encompasses, in fact, a group of different *servicios* collected through monetary charges and excises on the consumption of wine, meat, vegetable oil and vinegar (the so called *cuatro especies*). A good measure of the importance of this fiscal income for the royal treasury can be gauged from the fact that from 1635 the *millones* were the Crown's most important source of ordinary tax revenue, leaving the *alcabala* (a sales tax) in second place.[14]

The 1653 *donativo* set the model followed by Madrid for its awards to the Crown in the years to come. To raise the 220,000 ducats offered in this *donativo*, the government licensed Madrid to issue bonds yielding a yearly interest of 10 per cent, the *efectos de villa*. The *efectos* could be considered as a kind of *censo consignativo* which, in legal terms was a contract involving a credit operation widely used in Castile and in other European areas. In return for the granting of an amount of money, the lender (*censualista*) received an interest regularly paid by the borrower (*censuatario*) on the pledge of real estate. Although in an initial period the *censos consignativos* were irredeemable, the *censuatarios* were later given the right to repay the principal.

The transfer of the 'servicio de los 8,000 soldados' to Madrid was thought to provide the city with a safe source of income to guarantee both the payment of their interest to the owners of the *efectos* (*efectistas*) and the repayment of the capital lent by them to the city, although, as it will be seen in section 2, at least since the beginning of the 1660s it was clear that in the best case only a small fraction of the debt was ever going to be repaid. This meant that what had originally been conceived as temporary debt became, in practical terms, permanent and had two lasting consequences. First, as long as Madrid did not amortize its debt, the owners of the *efectos* would enjoy the payment of the interest, and this helps to explain why during the first years of its existence many groups of the local society saw in the *efectos de villa* a safe and attractive investment. Second, if at the beginning the transfer of the *servicios de millones* to the capital was transitory, limited to the time needed by the city to repay its debt, at the end it became permanent and this was reflected in the change of the legal position of the *servicios* alienated to the town, which were included in the list of its ordinary fiscal incomes, being part of its municipal taxes.

2

As has been indicated in section 1, to raise the amounts offered in the *donativos* the Crown allowed its capital to issue *efectos de villa* and transferred to the city most of the *servicios de millones* collected in the province. The *servicios* were invested by the city in the payment of the interest owed to the *efectistas* and, to a lesser extent, in the repayment of the capital, and the second column of Table 5.1 shows the value of the *donativos* granted by Madrid in this way. It should be noted here that these *servicios* obtained by Madrid were considered, in legal terms, municipal taxes, at the same level as those taxes usually collected by the town council, which monitored the collection of the *servicios* transferred without any interference by the Crown until the last decades of the seventeenth century.

Apart from the *servicios de millones*, the Crown had other important fiscal revenues, such as the tobacco monopoly (*estanco del tabaco*). Introduced in 1634,[15] its value experienced an important rise, from 106,666 ducats in its first year to 152,000 in 1655 and nearly 700,000 in 1674 and, not surprisingly, the monarchy decided to use this monopoly as pledge to obtain substantial *donativos* in the the years 1673–8 (see Table 5.1).[16] Unlike what had been the norm in other cases, this time Madrid did not obtain control of this tax. The *estanco del tabaco* was farmed out, and the Crown ordered the farmer of this tax in Madrid to transfer the value of the collection every year to the city to allow the capital to pay its interest to the *efectistas*.[17]

In its unending search for new sources of revenue, the Crown developed the idea of obtaining *donativos* without surrendering the control of any royal tax. Obviously, this was the most advantageous scenario for the royal treasury, and in 1657 the city obtained the right to introduce a new municipal tax, after a *donativo* of 200,000 ducats, to pay the expenses of the war against Portugal, and the third column of Table 5.1 shows the value of the *donativos* awarded by the capital to the Crown on the pledge of new municipal taxes created to pay their interests to the *efectistas*.

The fourth column of Table 5.1 lists those *donativos* that Madrid granted simultaneously on the guarantee of the *servicios* transferred and the municipal taxes. Finally, it should not be forgotten that there are cases in which our documentary sources do not explain whether a *donativo* had been introduced in return for the alienation of the *servicios* or in exchange for the introduction of a municipal tax and the fifth column of Table 5.1 lists their global value.

Table 5.1: *Donativos* Awarded by Madrid to the Crown, 1653–79 (in Castilian ducats).[18]

Year	Millones Transferred	Municipal Taxes	Millones Pledged	Unspecified	Tobacco	Total
1653	220,000			75,000		295,000
1654				75,000		75,000
1655	125,333					125,333
1656	400,000					400,000
1657	272,000	200,000				472,000
1658	226,666			136,266		362,932
1659	300,000			360,000		660,000
1660		200,000		300,000		500,000

Year	Millones Transferred	Municipal Taxes	Millones Pledged	Unspecified	Tobacco	Total
1661	200,000			116,000		316,000
1662		7,533	200,000	438,000		645,533
1663		453,333		240,000		693,333
1664		200,000		630,000		830,000
1665	544,000			100,000		644,000
1666	550,000	276,613	100,000			926,613
1667	569,333	550,000		39,000		1,158,333
1668		150,000	20,000			70,000
1669	200,000					200,000
1670	415,630		40,000			455,630
1671	300,000					300,000
1672	400,000		46,165			446,165
1673	400,000				700,000	1,100,000
1674	140,000	22,000			600,000	760,000
1675	70,000	270,000		112,272	400,000	852,272
1676	50,000	711,583	49,090	99,000		909,673
1677		45,000		114,000	520,000	679,000
1678	1,413,666	464,045	15,454	70,000	540,000	2,502,965
1679	300,000	66,000	165,000	1,680		532,680
Total	7,096,428	3,662,272	589,544	2,906,218	2,760,000	17,014,462

Table 5.1 shows how during the years 1653–79 the Crown obtained 17.01 million ducats from its capital, in addition to the amount of the *donativos* of 1661–70 (6.5 million ducats) and 1671–80 (8.45 million). Thanks to the alienation of most part of the *servicios* collected in the province and to the transfer of the value of the *renta del tabaco* in the district to its capital, the Crown had obtained nearly 10 million ducats. Simultaneously, the city had given another 3.6 million ducats in exchange for the right to impose new municipal taxes, but this sum should have been higher when we consider that part of the *donativos* listed in the fourth and fifth columns were probably granted in return for the right to sell *efectos* on municipal taxes. Thanks to other sources it is possible to suggest that the global value of these *donativos* would have amounted to around 6.3 million ducats; slightly less than that of the *donativos* granted on the pledge of the *servicios* transferred to the city by the Crown.[19] As for the destination of these sums, most of the money (91 per cent) was invested by the Crown to pay its expenses, as would be expected, although a small amount (9 per cent) was used by the city to finance the improvement of some urban services and public works.

It can be assumed that Table 5.1 reflects the main trends in the evolution of Madrid's indebtedness, which should have experienced a fast growth during the years 1653–79, especially in the years 1660–79. Between 1629 and 1679 the city had granted nearly 18.87 million ducats to the Crown. In 1680 the amount the city invested in the *efectos* was 18.79 million, so it seems clear that Madrid had decided to follow a strategy focused on the payment of the interest of the *efectos*, leaving in second place the redemption of the capital it had borrowed.[20]

This confirmed the fears expressed by the city's officials as early as 1660 and later in 1679, when they warned the city authorities of their increasing difficulties to repay the sums borrowed by the *efectistas* for two main reasons.[21] First, the global value of the *donativos* granted by the city council to the Crown was always much higher than originally expected. To quote an example, in November 1653 the city obtained the 'servicio de los 8,000 soldados' in exchange for a *donativo* of 220,000 ducats, but after new *donativos* in later years this amount grew to 0.542 million ducats (0.31 million ducats more than originally planned).[22]

Second, the interest rate of the *efectos* during the 1660s and 70s was high by Castilian standards. Until 1670 the interest rate had been 10 per cent, and that same year it was lowered to 8 per cent, being reduced at the beginning of 1680 to a more tolerable (for the stability of urban finances) 5 per cent.[23] As has been remarked before, the transfer of both the *servicios* and the value of the *renta del tabaco* collected in Madrid together with the introduction of new municipal taxes were devised to provide the city with the income needed to pay the interest of its debt and to redeem the capital. Not surprisingly, then, the years 1653–79 saw a marked increase in the revenues collected by the town council which, according to our estimates, rose from 0.4 million ducats in 1653 to 1.4 in 1679.[24] This was a remarkable expansion, but the problem was that the city's debt should have risen even faster, so the overwhelming majority of the sum collected by Madrid from its municipal taxes (including the *servicios* transferred by the Crown) was invested in the payment of the interest of the *efectos* (83 per cent in 1669 and nearly 94 per cent in 1679), leaving virtually no room for the redemption of the funds borrowed by the *efectistas*.[25]

What we have mentioned so far may be considered as proof that at the beginning of 1680 the burden of the city's debt had become its most pressing financial problem. From a comparative perspective it is interesting to remark here that the percentage of urban fiscal revenues used to service Madrid's debt seems particularly high, especially when we compare it with other examples, such as sixteenth-century Venice or the province of Holland in the seventeenth century.[26] Simultaneously, given the demographic stagnation of the capital during the years between 1653 and 1679, the burden of the city debt in per capita terms increased, so it is no surprise to find that in 1680 the per capita value of the funds borrowed by city through the *efectos* was nearly 147 ducats.[27] The relevance of this sum can be best appreciated when we take into account that in the same year the per capita value of the main ordinary taxes of the the royal treasury (*millones, alcabalas* and *cientos*), the *servicios* transferred to the city and the municipal taxes collected in Madrid was 14 ducats. Of course, it could be argued that the inflationary trend of Castilian prices in the years 1653–79 should have lessened the burden of this debt, but then it should be acknowledged that the deflationary period inaugurated in 1680 ought to have had the opposite effect.[28]

The deflationary monetary policy introduced with the *Pragmática* of 10 February 1680, which marked the beginning of a period of deep fiscal and monetary reforms whose objective was to put an end to the monetary disorder, symbolizes the arrival of a new phase in Castilian economic and social history and, in Madrid's case, the end of the expansion of the city's debt and the beginning of a new period, marked by the interference of the Crown in the urban finances.[29]

The fall in the prices of basic foodstuffs, such as vegetable oil, fish and, especially, meat and ordinary wine, the price of which dropped nearly 10 per cent (from 56 *maravedíes* per *azumbre* to 48 *maravedíes* per *azumbre*) after a royal order of 13 April, and the simultaneous reduction in the interest rate of the *efectos* were two important consequences of the *Pragmática*.[30] Our estimates suggest that ordinary wine, together with meat, was the cornerstone of the city's fiscal system. In the last two decades of the century 45 per cent of the revenues collected by the city from its ordinary taxes and from the *servicios* transferred came from the excises and monetary charges levied on this product (while meat provided an important 35 per cent), so any reduction of its price threatened fiscal revenues, whose value had peaked at 1.71 million ducats in 1679.[31] In the same year Madrid had to invest nearly 90 per cent of these revenues to pay the interest of its debt, so it was clear that any fall in such revenues undermined the capacity of the city to keep servicing its debt. Because of this, the another royal order also dated 13 April 1680 lowered the interest rate of the *efectos* from 8 per cent to 5 per cent, and to this it should also be added that the Crown had decided to introduce from the beginning of 1680 a royal committee (*Junta de Refacciones*), which took the control of the municipal taxes and servicios previously in Madrid's hands.[32]

The new committee worked for only a short period of time, but long enough to adopt two important measures which heavily conditioned the course of financial history of the city in the years to come, so its importance should not be overlooked. First, on 16 January 1680 the excises and monetary charges levied on ordinary wine had been farmed out by the Publicans' Guild, which offered 0.837 million ducats annually. After the reduction of the price of wine on 13 April 1680, the guild gave up the farm, and the committee began to collect all taxes levied on this product, while negotiating a new contract which was signed on July of the same year, when the Publicans' Guild obtained the farm again, this time in return for an amount of 0.648 million ducats annually. Second, in order to lessen the fiscal burden which fell on the inhabitants of the city after the deflationary 10 February *Pragmática*, the committee also decided to withdraw the municipal tax on coal.[33] Taken together, the measures caused a substantial drop in the revenues collected from Madrid's municipal taxes and the *servicios* transferred, which fell from 1.71 million ducats in 1679 to around 1.32 million in 1681.[34]

The measures adopted by the committee and the cuts in the interest rates of the *efectos* awakened a strong opposition in the ranks of the city oligarchy, although it is possible to judge the whole operation from a slightly different perspective.

After the deflationary *Pragmática* of February 1680 a fall in the fiscal incomes of the city was predictable. Simultaneously, when we consider that until April 1680 Madrid had to devote around 1.5 million ducats every year to pay the interest of its debt, it becomes clear that the objective was to lower the interest rate of the *efectos* in April 1680 and later in 1684 (when the interest rate fell from 5 to 4 per cent).[35] Thanks to these cuts the sums devoted by the city to servicing its debt fell from 1.51 to 0.75 million ducats annually in 1686. If it had not been for such reductions, it is difficult to see how the city could have serviced its debt in a phase when its fiscal incomes had fallen nearly 25 per cent, as result of the withdrawal of the tax on coal and the reductions in the farm on wine ordered by the committee as an answer to the new circumstances created by the deflationary policy adopted by the Crown from the beginning of 1680.

3

The transfer of portions of their fiscal revenues in return for monetary subsidies has been well known to monarchies and republics since the Middle Ages.[36] Thanks to such operations, governments could obtain substantial funds in the short term, but at the obvious cost of reducing their capacity to increase their fiscal revenues in the medium and longer term, and Madrid's case may be considered as a convincing illustration of this. Around 1679, 25 per cent of the global value of the *servicios de millones* collected in the whole kingdom was in Madrid's hands. It could be argued that in return for this the Castilian Crown had obtained more than 7 million ducats, as indicated in section 2 above, yet the importance of this amount decreases when we bear in mind that during the years 1653–1700 the city collected 21.2 million ducats from the *servicios* transferred and that those taxes were controlled by the capital until their disappearance during the liberal reforms of the nineteenth century.

The advantages that the *donativos* described in section 2 brought to Madrid, and especially to the members of the city's oligarchy which monitored the town finances, were more important than what the rough estimates of the previous paragraph seem to suggest. During the second half of the sixteenth century and the first years of the seventeenth the Castilian public debt bonds (*juros*) had been one of the favourite investments of the well-to-do sections of Castilian society, yet in the seventeenth century this changed for at least two reasons. First, in 1608 the interest rate of the *juros* was reduced to 5 per cent.[37] Being a fixed source of income, the profitability of these assets could not escape from the consequences of the inflationary trend prevailing in the Castilian prices for most of the century. To this it should be added that after the introduction of the *media annata* in 1634 the Crown adopted a policy of continuous and arbitrary cuts in the sums received by the owners of the *juros* (*juristas*), so, in fact, the profitability of such assets would have fallen well below the nominal 5 per cent fixed in 1608.[38] Second, the *juristas* had to face rising transaction costs over the whole period. Traditionally, the Crown took care to indicate the taxes earmarked for payment of the interest of the *juros* to their owners. When the Castilian public debt system began to show signs of strain, however, the *juristas* had to compete between themselves to obtain the most profitable taxes, such as, for examle, the Seville or Madrid *alcabalas*, which were allocated by the royal treasury to pay the interest of their bonds.[39] This forced to those *juristas* living outside those districts to hire the services of intermediaries to supervise the payment of their interest and the transfer of the money, something which would have affected the profitability of the *juros*.[40]

What we have mentioned so far helps to explain why the *juros* lost large part of their former appeal as a safe investment. When we also consider the simultaneous difficulties of the Castilian agriculture and manufacture, then it becomes clear that around the central decades of the seventeenth century the Castilian investors had to face the problem of finding safe places to invest their capital.[41] The expansion of the municipal debt after the granting of *donativos* by the Castilian cities to the Crown, which led to the birth of Madrid's *efectos*, would have been seen by many of them as a good opportunity to solve the problem. The interest yielded by these bonds during the first decades of their existence (10 per cent annually between 1653 and 1669 and 8 per cent from 1670 to 1680) was higher than that of the *juros*, and this advantage was reinforced by the fact that these assets did not suffer cuts in the interest paid to their owners until the last decades of the seventeenth century. As has been indicated earlier, the *servicios* transferred to Madrid were monitored by the town, which took good care to keep the payment of interest to the *efectistas* regular. According to our estimates, the service of the municipal debt was by far the most important expenditure of the municipal budget during the second half of the century, and this did not change during the eighteenth century.[42] Given that the *efectistas* were usually religious institutions and members of the city oligarchy, very often linked with the town councillors (*regidores*) who monitored the *servicios* transferred and the disposal of the sums collected, it is easy to understand why the buying of *efectos* should have seemed to them, at least during the first stages, a good investment, and why the assets received such a warm welcome.

Recent research on financial history has emphasized the pivotal role played by the credible commitment of the authorities to the property rights of the owners of public debt titles in the development of financial markets.[43] Such commitment helps to generate and to spread confidence in the profitability and soundness of such assets (although in favourable cases private joint stocks can play the same role), something seen as a basic condition for the development of secondary markets, which leads, through the reduction in transaction costs, to the growth of more complex and advanced financial markets. Although the case of Madrid deserves a more detailed analysis, our sources seem to suggest that for some decades after 1653 the *efectos de villa* were at the centre of a process which resembles that developed in Amsterdam around Dutch East India Company shares during the first decades of the seventeenth century and in England around the shares of the Bank of England, the United East India Company and the South Sea Company in the last years of the same century.[44] Given the careful attention paid by the town council to the payment of interest to the *efectistas*, the confidence of the public in these assets grew and an active traffic of *efectos* in which such assets were sold above par developed.[45] This suggests that the transaction costs of the *efectos* were low. Their liquidity was high and, not surprisingly, our sources also indicate that they were actively used as collateral in loans and in market transactions, apart from other more traditional and well-known uses.[46]

Yet the splendour of the *efectos* was short-lived. At first sight it would seem reasonable to consider that the reduction in the interest rate of these bonds from 8 per cent to 5 per cent at the beginning of 1680 (and later to 4 per cent in 1684) would have been the main cause of this, yet when we remember that, as it has been indicated in the previous section, the reduction was prompted by the deflationary 10 February *Pragmática* and the subsequent fall of Madrid's fiscal revenues, it seems more appropriate to consider that with these measures Madrid kept its capacity to pay its interest to the *efectistas*. When we also consider that i prices fell nearly 40 per cent between 1671–1680 and 1691–1700 and that the interest rates of the *efectos* fell in roughly the same measure (50 per cent after the cuts of 1680 and 1684), then it becomes clear that the profitability of these assets suffered probably much less than what the town authorities were ready to accept.[47]

More relevant for the capacity of the *efectos* to be the basis for the development of a secondary market in Madrid and even in Castile seems to have been the measures adopted in the first years of the eighteenth century. Pressed by the need to obtain enough funds to finance the war of sucession, in 1703 the Crown ordered the reduction of the interest rate of the *efectos* to 3 per cent.[48] In the following years the monarchy introduced continuous discounts in the sums paid to the *efectistas* as a first step to obtaining new *donativos* to pay for the quartering and the supplying of troops and the welcome of the royal family to the city. Particularly important was the introduction by the Crown in 1709 of a 50 per cent cut in the interest rate of the *efectos* (*valimiento*), which, in practical terms, halved the interest rate established in 1703 to 1.5 per cent, prompting a storm of protests which allows us to understand the financial problems of the city.[49]

According to the town authorities, in 1713 Madrid owed to its *efectistas* 2.97 million ducats. This amount was equal to the value of the interest of the *efectos* during a 5.5 year period (at the 3 per cent interest rate established in 1703). As the cuts in the sums paid to the *efectistas* since 1703, together with the 1709 *valimiento*, had yielded 2.57 million ducats, it seems clear that the bulk of the city's debt to its *efectistas* came from those discounts.[50] Not surprisingly, then, the confidence of the public in the *efectos* plummeted during this period, and these assets lost most of their former appeal for investors, being sold in the market at 50–60 per cent below par. While in the previous phase the investors had shown a marked preference for buying *efectos*, which, being a safe and liquid asset, had a privileged place in their investment portfolios, in the new phase the *efectos* were replaced by other assets and traffics. Although more research on this issue is clearly necessary, all this indicates that after the first years of the eighteenth century the development of a secondary market centred in the traffic of the *efectos* suffered a serious blow, as was suggested by the memorials sent by the town to the Castilian authorities.

4

The transfer of royal taxes in return for the *donativos* awarded by Madrid (and other Castilian cities) during the second half of the seventeenth century was one of the measures adopted by the Crown to raise its revenues. Thanks to this, the monarchy obtained substantial amounts of money, yet, as it has been indicated in section 2, at the cost of reducing its capacity to raise fiscal revenues in the medium and long term. In Madrid, this process led to the expansion of its municipal debt through the issue of *efectos*. This was the origin of the problem of Madrid's indebtedness which lasted during the eighteenth century and well into the nineteenth and whose burden fell on the shoulders of the poor and middle sorts of the city population, who paid the municipal taxes whose revenues were mainly invested in the payment of interest to the *efectistas*.[51]

The growth of the city's debt had deep and lasting financial consequences. As could be expected, the town's commitment to the property rights of the *efectistas* was strong. Thanks to the careful payment of the interest of the *efectos* during the first decades after 1653, public confidence in these assets grew. As it has been indicated in section 3, the *efectos* had advantages compared to the more traditional public debt titles (*juros*). Their interest rate was higher (10 per cent until 1669 and 8 per cent after that until 1679 against 5 per cent for the *juros*) and they did not suffer reductions and discounts in the payment of their interests until the last decades of the seventeenth century. Bearing this in mind, the success of the *efectos* during the period 1653–79 is easy to explain. The members of the city oligarchy invested large sums of money in such assets and, according to the evidence showed in section 3, it seems clear that something akin to a secondary market centred in the *efectos* was developing in Madrid during this period. It seems equally clear, however, that this did not last after the progresive interference of the Crown in the city's finances during the first years of the eighteenth century.

Together with other well-known episodes, Madrid's case provides a good example of the importance of governmental policies in the development of Castilian finances during the early modern period. Broadly speaking, it could be argued that the problems which hampered the development of the country financial system did not lie in the lack of technical expertise. Madrid (and the Castilian Crown) always employed a set of procedures (mainly the issue of public debt bonds whose interests and principal were paid and redeemed through revenues coming from taxation) which originated in Italian cities during the Middle Ages and then disseminated to the rest of continent, so the roots of the difficulties of Spanish finances during the period should be found in another direction. Recent historiography has demonstrated the critical importance of credible governmental commitment to property rights as a basic condition for the development of financial markets.[52] It seems clear that this commitment, subordinated to the short-term consideration of obtaining revenues, always had a secondary role in government considerations, and the example of Madrid described here illustrates this. The success of the *efectos* during the years 1653–79 was to a great extent the unplanned result of the policy of transferring portions of the Crown fiscal revenues to Madrid in return for *donativos* and could be explained by the fact that during those years the city's finances were monitored by the town authorities, without serious Crown interference. The measures of 1680 described in section 2 affected the *efectos* less than what Madrid was ready to accept, yet it is doubtful whether this could be considered the result of a conscious policy. It seems more plausible to argue that these measures should be interpreted as part of the programme implemented during those years by a group of reformist ministers to restore some measure of stability to the monetary and fiscal systems of the country after the problems of the central decades of the seventeenth century. Finally, when the new Bourbon dynasty needed revenues to fund the War of Succession, the government did not hesitate in promoting substantial cuts in the sums paid to the *efectistas* without taking into account the point of view of the city. Although this area needs more reserch, it seems clear that these cuts lessened public confidence in the *efectos*, whose price fell well below par, so the potential of these assets in the development of a secondary market suffered a serious blow.

6 THE ROLE PLAYED BY SHORT-TERM CREDIT IN THE SPANISH MONARCHY'S FINANCES

Carlos Álvarez-Nogal[1]

It is widely known that the Spanish monarchy borrowed large quantities of money from foreign bankers during the sixteenth and seventeenth centuries. Many foreign companies, especially Italian, provided money and financial services to the Spanish kings. Scholars have described the financial system of Castile and the important role played by short-term credit in maintaining imperial policy.[2]

The Spanish monarchy, like other medieval and early modern European sovereigns, had problems making credible commitments to honour its financial agreements.[3] Periodically, bankers faced suspension of payments and defaults in the contracts signed by the Crown. A traditional interpretation of these crises maintains that they damaged the relationship between the monarchy and its bankers, increasing the price of short-term credit compared with other borrowing alternatives.

The history of Spanish sovereign debt in this period poses a puzzle: why did bankers continue to lend money to the kings of Spain when they repeatedly suspended their payments? As might be expected, the king could cancel his obligations whenever he wanted to after the lender had risked his money. One could argue that reputation and future borrowing needs would prevent the monarchy from cheating the banker. However, both bankers and the king knew their relationship had a finite life, so bankers in the later period could anticipate that the king would default. Carrying this logic further back would lead to an outcome in which lending would not have been provided in any period.

Historical evidence proves, however, that despite the finite horizon and repeated cheating on the part of the king, lenders and the Spanish monarchy continued to cooperate and maintain a strong credit relationship over time. It also shows that it did not make this kind of credit more expensive than others. The system worked in such a way that many small investors around Europe helped bankers to lend their money to the Spanish kings.

Did bankers make 'irrational' economic decisions? The situation is especially noteworthy given the fact that bankers did not coordinate their actions. In the absence of a tough penalty from the whole group of lenders, why would the king pay when he could expropriate the funds? The institutional literature predicts that without credible institutions for protecting property rights, such credit would not have been provided. Sovereign debt theory analyses the reputation arising from repeated interaction, which generates equilibrium with self-enforcing lending agreements.

Theory and evidence concentrate on the ability of organized bankers to punish kings who renege on their debts. Sovereign debt theory shows that the principal constraint on sovereign behaviour is a penalty which lenders can impose on the sovereign.[4] This penalty also provides a ceiling on the level of sustainable debt. Bulow and Rogoff assume that lenders can impose additional and more costly penalties beyond cutting the sovereign off from credit in the future. The debt ceiling increases with the severity of the punishment, but lenders do not lend as much if they are not able to coordinate a boycott because this represents their best penalty. Grossman and Van Huyck, and also Atkeson, derive a positive lending equilibrium when partial defaults and debt rescheduling are not violations of the agreement between sovereigns and lenders, but an unexpected fiscal shock suffered by the sovereign. In this case, lenders do not implement any penalty[5].

Conklin applied some of these debt models to the study of loans provided by a group of Genoese bankers to Philip II of Spain (1556–98).[6] He considers this group of bankers as a cartel and identifies a boycott as the penalty imposed by the group to enforce their loans.[7] This explanation raises two problems. First, there was no cartel during the reign of Philip II, nor in any other period; the reality was that of a competitive group of bankers.[8] Second, the incentives for such a penalty are unclear and it would be difficult to enforce as some bankers would suffer more than others as a consequence.

The problem with 'penalty' models is that lenders must be in a strong position to punish the sovereign in the event of default. Moreover, for the penalty to be credible, bankers need to coordinate their actions. Otherwise, the inability to punish the sovereign harshly implies an absence of lending.[9] From the declining marginal productivity of capital it could be derived that the king would be indifferent to whether he could obtain the last loan or not, which would be an incentive to cheat the last lender.

This paper shows that the Spanish monarchy, despite being an absolutist government, did not need help from any other institution to provide credible commitments to its bankers and obtain access to important amounts of credit for more than 150 years.[10] In order to explain the Spanish monarchy's case, this paper focuses on the sovereign's incentives to extend cooperation over time rather than on the lenders' power to punish him. Here we consider a very important element: the powerful self-enforcing nature of the value that a stable cooperation over time had for the sovereign and his bankers which did not depend on the lender's penalty but on the 'belief' that cooperation was essential for the king.

Asientos and Foreign Bankers

An important issue explored by the literature of sovereign debt is the limit of the credit available for the sovereign. Models imply that any increase in the penalty that can be imposed on the sovereign will increase the amount of credit available. This is not so good for the king because if the bankers were so powerful that they could control the king's actions, they would also be able to increase the price of their loans. The king would be a price-taker with a horizontal demand curve of credit, while the bankers would be price-searchers with a negatively sloped demand curve, reflecting their market power. They could control the price and quantity of credit, maximizing their profits by choosing the amount of credit where marginal revenue is equal to marginal cost. This amount might be not enough for the king.

This situation had two consequences. First, the amount of credit would be less than that supplied at the intersection of the price of the marginal cost curve with the demand curve. Second, whatever the amount of credit finally offered, the king would pay the highest possible price. A coordinated group of bankers would offer less credit than several lenders in competition facing identical cost functions and the same demand curve from the king.

Traditionally, historians have explained the credit of the Spanish monarchy by a high-risk premium paid by the king on the loan contracts, also called *asientos*.[11] However, historical evidence does not corroborate this claim. It needs an explanation. The interest charged on the *asientos* experienced a decline between the reigns of Carlos I (1516–58) and Philip IV (1621–65), as was also the case with the interest on public debt. For example, the interest rate of the *asientos* stood at 14 per cent a year during the sixteenth century.[12] After 1609, with the truce in the Low Countries, the rate dropped to 12 per cent for the first year of the contract and 8 per cent thereafter. The base rate paid by the Crown on borrowing in Castile was 8 per cent, whenever foreign exchange and foreign remittance costs were not involved.[13] This rate was comparable to short-term interest rates available anywhere, including places like Amsterdam. Furthermore, high interest charged on credit contracts did not resolve the risk problem involved in the negotiation. The king could revoke his promise of repayment at any time after the banker had advanced the money, no matter what interest rate had been agreed in the contract.

The total cost of an *asiento* included several services. Credit cost is one, but there were others, not necessarily explicit in the contract. In an *asiento* contract the cost of the loan was specified separately but the total cost included additional payments, for example bonuses (*adehala*), the cost of collecting and transporting money and exchange rates, which were not always described. Consequently, the total cost of the *asiento* was greater than that of a short-term loan. The most expensive aspect of this type of debt compared with public debt was not so much the cost of the money itself, but rather the cost of obtaining large amounts of different currencies quickly in different parts of Europe.[14]

Why did Spanish Kings Borrow Short-Term Credit from Foreign Bankers?

The Spanish monarchy needed large amounts of money every year to pay its armies and other expenses. Taxes were collected throughout the fiscal year while expenses had to be met on a monthly basis. Surpluses from the fiscal system of Castile made it possible to maintain this situation during the sixteenth and seventeenth centuries, but the Crown had to transfer its money from Castile to different parts of Europe in order to pay its army regularly in Antwerp, Germany and Italy, far from the centres where the main revenues were collected.

If the king wanted credit and different currencies in several parts of Europe, access to a vast financial network of agents able to borrow from other people in those places was essential. The monarchy did not have the administrative efficiency that merchant bankers could provide. A good example of the lender's interest in controlling Spanish silver was the crisis suffered by the Genoese bankers when Philip II ended his cooperation with this group temporarily in the 1570s. For months, the Council of Finance sent money to Flanders using other methods, far from the markets controlled by Genoese bankers.[15] The experience was not a success; it was very expensive and inefficient, suffering from delays and problems with agents.

The ideal scenario for the Crown would have been an extended and healthy credit market with many lenders able to offer all the credit that was needed. Trade fairs could not play this role because they had been created to support trade, not to lend and transfer large amounts of precious metals around Europe on the behalf of monarchies. Moreover, risk and the urgency of these credit demands increased the price that the king had to pay. A good example of this situation was the high prices that the monarchy paid in Catalonia when it borrowed from local merchants in 1575. Many of the bills of exchange issued in Barcelona payable in Lyon had interest rates between 5 and 11 per cent for periods as short as two or three months.[16] This was three or four times the regular price of a normal credit contract (*asiento*) signed with the king's bankers in Madrid.

The Crown solved this problem by creating its own private credit market, setting up stable, bilateral relationships with the most important merchant bankers of Europe. The Crown signed loan contracts, formulating and scheduling the whole compensation scheme, including interest, with the bankers. The debt was usually paid between one and three years after the lender had advanced the funds. Repayment included other non-monetary rewards, such as honours, protection in the territories of the monarchy, licences to trade in America, and social prestige, among others. An important characteristic of the credit negotiations was that most bankers or their agents stayed in the court, living close to the king.

Solving Problems in Credit Negotiations: Competition and Cooperation

How did the monarchy create confidence in its creditors and collect the amount of credit needed? The monarchy required a certain amount of credit to be able to finance its annual budget. No banker was able to raise the full amount required, so the king needed to borrow from several bankers at the same time.

However, the situation of several bankers lending at the same time without coordination leads to a problem related to the decreasing marginal productivity of capital for the sovereign.[17] If the Crown has funds available at an interest rate of i, then the optimal sized loan is M, where the marginal productivity of the last gold coin is exactly equal to the sovereign's cost of borrowing the gold coin, i. Raising funds to the optimal limit, M, implies that the first loans are very valuable to the sovereign, but the last loans are not. This is because at M, the sovereign's marginal value of the last loan is exactly equal to its costs and hence has a net value of zero (Chart 6.1).

Chart 6.1: The Marginal Value of Loans.

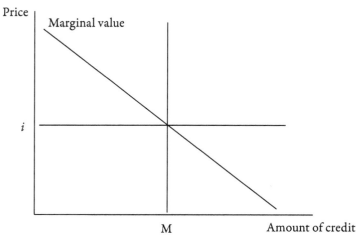

If the king were able to get all the credit he needed from the first banker, the value of borrowing from the second would be zero. The king's only concern would be to repay the debt to the first banker at the end of the period established in the contract in order to borrow again the next time. In this case, the second banker is unnecessary for the Crown and, if the lender had provided a loan, the sovereign could cheat him without suffering any cost. Because the second banker could expect this behaviour, he would realize that his value to the king was zero, so he would not lend his money. The crucial question in this game for all the king's bankers was: who was the last, the unnecessary banker?

It is important to remember that bankers were not only offering money, but also financial services. In fact, the main problem for the monarchy was not obtaining money but transferring its revenues from Spain to Europe. Without the help of bankers this was problematic and expensive. Furthermore, the sovereign was aware that not every lender could offer the same services to the same places in Europe as easily every year. On the other hand, no one banker had enough money and personal contacts to cover all the Crown's requirements each year. What is more, a banker could die and then had to be replaced as soon as possible.[18] The sovereign also tried to keep all of the bankers because it was the only way to avoid critical situations in which one banker could force the king to make expensive concessions.

Bargaining with a single banker was dangerous for the king because of the problem of market power (monopoly) that a unique lender might enjoy. However, to open the door to many bankers was a bad strategy because it could decrease the confidence of the lenders in the cooperative behaviour of the sovereign. The probability of being the unnecessary banker increased. The outcome could be that nobody would want to cooperate. The solution was an unwritten rule, but one which was explicit and clear to everybody. The Spanish monarchy borrowed from many lenders at the same time each year, but treated each banker as if he was the only one. The king would divide the total amount of credit that he needed each year into portions. He offered a portion to each banker, giving guarantees that the rest, until the whole amount was raised, would be obtained from others. Although there could be many bankers in the negotiations, the king made it clear that each lender was unique and had no substitute because he was required to complete the whole amount of credit, M. To show lenders that this situation was true, the Crown committed itself to treat all bankers in the same way, avoiding even the slightest hint of preferential treatment in credit negotiations.

This rule had an important consequence. If one banker was very valuable for the king, this value was extended to the rest, independent of how important they really were or the amount of credit they were able to provide. Although some bankers were clearly more important than others, they all received the same treatment from the king.

On the other hand, the behaviour of any one banker was a reference for the others. When an important lender was willing to sign an *asiento*, the other bankers received a clear signal to bargain with the king. The actions of others could be a source of information about the situation of the king in credit negotiations. If a banker knew that nobody wanted to lend, it would also be difficult to convince him. Treating everybody in the same way meant that even though the value of one banker could be very low for the monarchy, the king was obliged to honour his agreements if he decided to cooperate with the rest of the bankers. The king would honour the contract because his payoff from choosing cooperation now would be higher in the long run, not only with him, but with all bankers.

Credit Without a Collective Penalty from Lenders

Sovereign debt theory traditionally considers that cooperation is possible because the lender is able to impose a penalty on the sovereign when he decides to renege. This punishment would be the largest credible penalty available to the lender and it could be applied by the lender himself or by an external institution. The sovereign will honour his loan agreement if, and only if, the cost of honouring the contract is less than or equal to that of the penalty.[19] If the maximum credible penalty that can be imposed on the sovereign depends on several variables, then any change in them will affect the maximum credible loan to the sovereign.

The theory of sovereign debt identifies two problems in the credibility of the penalty. First, Bulow and Rogoff show that in some cases the lender's capacity to impose a penalty is limited because the penalty hurts him as well as the sovereign.[20] Second, there is a problem of penalty credibility when there are multiple or potential lenders. In a situation with many lenders, a boycott after a default is potentially difficult to enforce.[21] Lenders must coordinate their actions and prevent defection from a credit boycott.[22] Without coordination the penalty will not be credible because the lenders will not cooperate to provide credit.

The Spanish monarchy was able to create confidence among potential lenders without the existence of a penalty or a formal mechanism of coordination between them. This situation was successful because several lenders agreed to lend money over a period of decades. The key element of their relationship was not a penalty but three crucial conditions: the existence of enough revenues to repay the loan, the king's belief in the high value that the bankers had for him and the bankers' belief in the king's cooperation. Defaults occurred when the first condition failed, but the second and third remained firm and allowed credit negotiations to continue over time.

The Crown was not indifferent to the potential threat from a powerful cartel of bankers. To avoid this threat, the Council of Finance was always looking for new bankers and trying to open negotiations with more lenders. The Genoese bankers were the biggest and most efficient group, but not the only one. In a situation of cooperation without the credible threat of a penalty from the lender, as explained earlier, the king is free to create competition in credit negotiations by inviting more bankers to participate in order to obtain more credit at a lower price without the threat that this increased number of financiers might discourage some bankers from taking part in negotiations.

Competitors but No Cartel

Even though several authors consider that the Spanish monarchy's bankers were a compact and highly coordinated group, the evidence does not support this theory. Coordination between bankers was possible in the wake of a bankruptcy in order to renegotiate their debts, but not before the bankruptcy.

Sometimes, in order to reinforce their position vis-à-vis the king, bankers bargained with the Crown and signed an *asiento* together, but each one had absolute and individual liability for his own part of the contract. This meant that when a banker was not able to provide the amount promised, other bankers were not responsible for it. In fact, they were under no obligation to increase their quota to cover their colleague's failure. Signing together was a way of making all conditions in the contract explicit and clear to everybody. It provided more information about the conditions offered by the king to other bankers and about what was going on in credit negotiations. In this sense, it is possible to observe signals of temporary cooperation between bankers. This coordination was much easier when they were from the same city or had cultural roots in common, for example the Genoese, but even in such cases they were always competitors.[23]

German bankers were the most important financiers during the reign of Charles I. After the first bankruptcy in 1557, many of them withdrew from negotiations, permitting the arrival of more Genoese bankers,[24] but the Fugger continued to work with the Crown in Spain until the 1640s. The Genoese and Germans were not alone – Italians, Portuguese and Castilians were also involved in these negotiations.

Many bankers came from the same city or country but they were always rivals. The lack of collective action against the Crown was clear before and after each bankruptcy. An example of non-cooperative behaviour within the Genoese group was documented in 1586. Stefano Doria found that Lorenzo Spínola had been falsifying accounting books with the aid of a royal official. He did so because he had accepted a secret agreement with the Council of Finance to reduce the Crown's debt in exchange for being paid with good currency. It was against the interests of the rest of the Genoese bankers because in the wake of the previous bankruptcy they had decided to join forces in their dealings with the Council in order to achieve the best possible agreement. The Crown had recognized the total amount of its old debt because financers had accepted compensation with poor quality payments. However, some of the Genoese bankers, including Lorenzo, broke their agreement.[25] Another example of this independent behaviour was the lack of collective reaction among the Portuguese bankers against the king when the Inquisition arrested some of them during the 1630s.

There were two major obstacles to coordination: ambiguous contracts and asymmetric information between lenders. Cultural and geographical diversity made association almost impossible. Furthermore, even bankers in the same group had different incentives. Players had personal economic goals and they were in permanent competition between themselves. The free-rider problem was always present. Information asymmetry, slow communication, and different networks and kinds of business implied very different interpretations of facts between financiers. Without an organization that coordinated responses, it was not likely that all the bankers would have responded together against the king after the abuse of any one banker. However, this did not mean that the king's actions did not influence their beliefs about negotiations with the monarchy. Any action on the part of the king against one of the bankers could modify the willingness of the lender to risk his money, as described earlier.

Philip II was convinced of the benefits of competition when he invited some Castilian bankers to come to the court to lend money in 1575.[26] Spanish bankers, including Pedro de Maluenda, Simón Ruiz and Diego Vitoria among many others, were interested in participating in credit negotiations. However, they could not offer the same amounts of money lent by the Italians, even when the monarchy offered them very good conditions. Moreover, their connections were available only in a small number of European cities.[27] In spite of these drawbacks, the monarchy supported them in the negotiations with the objective of limiting the power of the Genoese group.

Another example was Philip IV's attempt to increase competition by inviting Portuguese bankers into credit negotiations. Since 1621 it had been difficult to persuade Genoese bankers to accept *asientos*. The Council had to accept many of their expensive demands and the reputation of the Crown suffered when royal officials had problems in meeting these conditions. In 1626 a group of Portuguese bankers, Manuel Rodríguez de Elvas, Nuño Díaz de Brito, Manuel de Paz, Simón Suárez and Juan Núñez Saravia, were invited to sign an *asiento* in Madrid to lend 400,000 *escudos*.[28] Philip IV recognized that this contract had been signed 'in order to increase the number of bankers, and also to encourage my subjects from Portugal to participate in this kind of *asientos*'.[29]

Often, the new bankers did not lend money more cheaply than the veterans because the most efficient agents were already working for the Crown. The higher cost for the same or lower quality financial services was justified by the attempt to reduce the demand for expensive conditions in new *asientos* from former bankers. If they saw that a number of non-monetary benefits of *asientos* were given to others, it may have provided a strong incentive to reduce their demands. The Council of Finance preferred to pay a higher cost in the *asiento* of 400,000 *escudos* because: 'the value of having Portuguese in the Court to deal with them is higher than the price of this *asiento*'.[30]

Although the Portuguese were important in the financial system of Spain, they were not the only group used by the Crown to increase the number of bankers during the reign of Philip IV. In 1633, the Council of Finance was worried about the consequences of losing businessmen like Simón Suárez and Marcos Fernández. In its opinion, 'it would be convenient to cheer up the bankers that we have while we look for new ones. This is the way to have enough bankers available to borrow and also compete among each other, with the outcome that we will get better *asientos*'.[31] In 1638 the Crown, with a great deal of exasperation, was looking for lenders in several European cities. The goal was 'shutting out the necessity of the Genoese bankers for *asientos* in all places'.[32] The Crown looked for new bankers in Antwerp in the 1630s. The Portuguese had the best contacts there, but royal officials also found people from Milan, Naples and Florence willing to lend.[33]

Bankruptcies and Borrowing or Lending

Bankruptcies were mechanisms used by the king to recover part of his income blocked by old credit negotiations when new credit negotiations became impossible. All agents in this bargaining process knew that it would happen sooner or later. The Council of Finance declared bankruptcy several times: in 1557, 1560, 1575, 1596, 1607, 1627, 1647, 1652 and 1662. These were not wholesale repudiations of obligations, simply the rescheduling of debts.[34]

Bankruptcies reduced the Crown's debts in the short run, converting the short-term debt into a long-term debt, which took the form of public debt (*juros*). The *juros* delayed the payments for longer than had been agreed in the *asientos*, and provided other kinds of compensations which were more convenient for the king.[35] The agreement reached with the bankers after each bankruptcy was called the *Medio General*. Many bankers had strong reasons to accept these agreements because they needed to recover as much money as they could as quickly as possible in order to save their reputation in the eyes of their other clients, but they were unable to embark on new negotiations with the Spanish monarchy.

Following a bankruptcy, the threat of default disappeared from credit negotiations for an indeterminate period. After a suspension of payments, everybody knew that the Spanish Crown had huge incentives to borrow again and to respect its credit contracts. Cooperation seemed very safe once more because revenues were available again. Despite the frequency of bankruptcies, the Crown always reached an agreement with its creditors very quickly and financial services were resumed immediately. The trend shown by the annual amount of the *asientos* contracted during the period 1598–1650 shows the success of the Crown in bargaining with bankers even when there were regular defaults (Table 6.1). An example of how bankers' beliefs about profits in the credit negotiation changed after a bankruptcy is shown by what happened after the suspension of payments in 1596. The monarchy was able to borrow again from the group of bankers trapped in the default after the *Medio General* had been signed. They provided 4.5 million *escudos* starting in January 1598 in Antwerp, Dunkirk, Lille and Namur.[36]

A bankruptcy served to reduce uncertainty, but it came at a cost. This mechanism pushed some bankers out of the credit negotiations because they received public debt instead of cash. They were not out of business, but they were not able to lend to the Crown again. This was not a positive outcome for the monarchy. If the king suspended payments too often, he could lose all his bankers, a situation which was clearly undesirable. Therefore the king only used bankruptcies in very extreme cases. Bankruptcies also had a positive outcome, however. This mechanism allowed the Crown and its bankers to start negotiations once again. It required that some new bankers and extra cash become available, at least during the arrangement of old debts.[37] The king's American silver played this role when negotiations were blocked. For example, in 1626 the bankers did not want to lend more money before receiving the American precious metals they had been promised, but the king had secretly decided to use this revenue to bargain for new *asientos* in the coming months. He did not have other funds available at that time.[38] For this reason the Crown used to wait for the arrival of the American fleets before declaring a bankruptcy.[39]

Other examples show how new bankers were invited in after each bankruptcy. The 1557 bankruptcy marked the real entry of the Genoese. In 1575 the monarchy invited some Castilian bankers to the negotiations and attempted to create its own network of financial agents in Europe; the bankruptcy of 1627 was the moment when the Portuguese began to play a part in the finances of Castile. In 1647 the king introduced a new group of Genoese financiers and Portuguese merchants into the proceedings.

Table 6.1: Amount of Money Lent by Bankers to the Spanish Monarchy, 1600–50.[40]

Years	Ducats	Years	Ducats	Years	Ducats
1600	2,822,000	1617	5,496,830	1634	6,536,116
1601	2,341,932	1618	4,818,194	1635	8,925,000
1602	3,890,036	1619	8,621,099	1636	4,842,313
1603	5,197,943	1620	3,545,000	1637	7,314,000
1604	3,983,829	1621	7,735,615	1638	7,360,273
1605	7,233,816	1622	7,999,000	1639	8,358,100
1606	4,119,432	1623	12,442,764	1640	10,079,400
1607	2,515,361	1624	6,539,973	1641	8,472,141
1608	3,990,535	1625	8,646,000	1642	10,697,439

Years	Ducats	Years	Ducats	Years	Ducats
1609	4,174,692	1626	8,013,998	1643	5,973,393
1610	2,561,332	1627	5,823,999	1644	5,183,161
1611	3,078,147	1628	7,713,308	1645	5,969,984
1612	5,987,781	1629	5,946,460	1646	5,453,600
1613	1,505,000	1630	4,761,971	1647	3,168,706
1614	1,450,498	1631	5,787,500	1648	4,795,705
1615	not available	1632	4,371,182	1649	4,284,055
1616	4,404,170	1633	8,254,978	1650	3,219,768

Table 6.1 suggests that bankruptcies did not negatively affect the ability of the monarchy to borrow; on the contrary, they improved it. The amount of credit available after these episodes was always higher than before. Bankruptcies did not break the rules of negotiations, they were part of them. On the other hand, bankers did not make irrational decisions when they decided to restore their credit lines. As history shows, they were able to cooperate with the king in a stable way for many years before the next suspension of payments took place. The 'willingness-to-pay' of the Spanish king was a sufficiently credible belief so that both parties were able to cooperate and make it profitable.

Treating Many Bankers as One

The king negotiated with many bankers at the same time because no one was able to provide all the credit that the monarchy needed. This implies that the king had to create confidence in his behaviour in the credit negotiations with each banker. It was very important for the Spanish king to convince each and every banker that he was as important as the others. If a banker had even a tiny reason to suspect that he was superfluous in the credit negotiation, he would conclude that he could be cheated by the king and would not lend his money. This fear could extend between bankers and, in the end, credit would not be available. For this reason, the sovereign allowed information about credit negotiations to become public knowledge for all bankers. The king also invited several bankers to credit negotiations at the same time, discussing the amount of credit needed with them as a group, and dividing the total amount between them. Each would provide his portion individually, knowing that the others were doing the same.

There is much evidence of this behaviour. The most important credit negotiations in Madrid were the *Provisiones Generales* which took place in the royal palace at the end of each year. All bankers were invited by the Council of Finance to know the amount of money that the king needed. Negotiations could be held individually or in groups, but everybody was aware of the conditions and the success of others. This information was often provided by the Council of Finance itself. The king was always keen to celebrate in public that a banker or a group of bankers had decided to sign the *asientos*.

If the king bargained with many lenders and there were serious problems of coordination between them, the monarchy would not suffer any repercussions from cheating some of them because there would be other bankers available. However, this behaviour would spread the belief that the sovereign was only interested in collaborating with the most important bankers. Difficulties among the bankers themselves in identifying who was important would have spread a more dangerous belief: everybody could be cheated. The greater the number of lenders, the greater the competition, a situation which was desirable for the king, but bad for the negotiations because it created more uncertainty. Each banker was less valuable for the monarchy. Thus, the probability of being cheated increased and bankers would be less willing to offer credit. To avoid this undesirable outcome, the Spanish monarchy was responsible for maintaining the correct beliefs in the negotiation process. It behaved with each banker as if each banker was the only one lending to the Crown at that moment. There is much historical evidence of this kind of behaviour in the actions of the Council of Finance. Consequently, the amount of credit lent by a banker was not related to his importance in the game of credit.

A good example of this is how bankruptcies took place. When there were no revenues and the king had to renege on his contracts, there was frequently enough money to pay some bankers at least. The king could have maintained his cooperation with the most important group and simply not paid the rest. However, this strategy would have changed the expectations of all lenders about the Spanish king's willingness to respect credit contracts. It was very difficult for the king to pay some bankers only and default with the rest without affecting the belief of all lenders. Such behaviour would mean that the king was distinguishing between 'friends' and 'enemies', 'good agents' and 'bad agents'. As explained above, in order to avoid uncertainty among the bankers, it was very important that cooperation was a credible outcome for all of them.

For this reason, the first step in each bankruptcy was always to default on all payments to all bankers. Subsequently, the Crown and lenders negotiated an agreement, called the *Medio General*, to resolve differences regarding debts. The agreement fixed the amount that the king would pay in the future and the way the debt would be paid.

Another example of how the monarchy treated all bankers in the same way was the mechanism used to pay debts when the king had problems of liquidity in specific areas. In such cases, everybody received the same proportion according to the amount initially lent, irrespective of geographical location. The Casa de la Contratación in Seville was one of the royal offices with most outstanding debts during the seventeenth century. American treasure arrived there every year and all bankers wanted a share, but the problem was that the Crown promised more payments than the amount of money which arrived with the fleets. Each time this happened, the Council of Finance ordered each banker to be paid the same proportion of money with respect to the amount promised in the contract by the king. The smallest banker received the same proportion as the most important financier.

One of the many examples of this behaviour was the distribution of the silver that arrived with General Larraspuru's fleet in April 1629 (Table 6.2). In the *asientos* the king had promised to give 714,500 ducats to the bankers, but the Crown only had 291,100 ducats available. Instead of only paying the most important bankers, Gerónimo Fugger and Octavio Centurione, the monarchy divided the money among all the bankers, paying each one the same proportion, 41 per cent, of the amount initially promised.

Table 6.2: *Asientos*: Amount Promised and Real Payments, 1629 (in ducats).[41]

Bankers	Date of the Asiento	*Asiento*	Amount Promised	Payment	%
Gerónimo Fugger	8 February	780,000	150,000	61,500	41
Herederos Marcos y Cristóbal	24 January	743,492	50,000	20,500	41
Octavio Centurione	8 February	450,000	100,000	41,000	41
Lelio Imvrea	8 February	390,000	80,000	32,800	41
Agustín Giustiniani	19 February	390,000	80,000	32,800	41
Nuño Díaz Méndez	8 February	253,418	50,000	20,500	41
Simón Suárez[42]	23 March	218,333	50,000	19,885	39.77
Duarte Fernández	23 March	218,333	50,000	19,885	39.77
Manuel de Paz	23 March	218,333	50,000	19,885	39.77
Juan Núñez Saravia	23 March	240,000	52,000	21,320	41
Juan Gerónimo Spinola	5 April	61,000	2,500	1,025	41
Total		3,962,909	714,500	291,100	40

Conclusions

Short-term credit borrowing from bankers has been used as a paradigm of the worst financial strategy for some new states in the early modern age. It provided huge benefits for a privileged group of financiers and politics, but damaged the financial situation of any government and the country. On the contrary, the case of the Spanish monarchy is a good example of how short-term credit was not an expensive and dangerous financial strategy as many scholars have previously believed. It was an important way of obtaining credit in different parts of Europe, paying a very competitive price compared with alternatives such as public debt. However, it was not an easy system to operate.

A cartel of bankers able to penalize the king would provide enough confidence to lenders and credit to the king, but it would be very expensive given their monopolistic power in negotiations. A group of uncoordinated bankers competing between themselves would provide cheaper loans and more credit, but the danger of being cheated by the king would be so high that no banker would lend.

Some models of sovereign debt predict that if there is no penalty, there is no lending.[43] How can this dilemma be solved?

The solution applied by the Spanish monarchy was to increase lenders' confidence in the negotiations and to reinforce bankers' belief in the monarchy's willingness to cooperate. These unwritten rules brought about a situation which was stable enough to guarantee the amount of credit the Spanish monarchy needed for decades. Bankruptcies were not a problem, simply an emergency mechanism to solve some problems which formed part of the negotiations.

Spanish kings and bankers worked together for decades because both knew that they would be worse off if they could not establish cooperation. Bankers were looking for silver, a good rate of interest and different non-monetary compensation that they could only find in Castile, while Spanish kings needed financial services to fund their wars in Europe which only bankers could provide. Without cooperation, the king would not have credit to pay the army and bankers would not have access to Spanish silver. They would lose their privileged position controlling the financial markets in Europe.

Another commonly-held idea was that the outcome of non-cooperation affected bankers' payoffs differently. Non-cooperation was a more damaging outcome for the king than for bankers. Bankers had many varied ways of doing business and investing their money. Lending to the Spanish monarchy was not their only activity, indeed for many of them it was not even the most important. However, the king did not have better options for paying his armies in Europe safely and quickly. The king really needed to borrow money every year. This situation was very well known by all lenders and was an important shared belief of this business.

A banker could avoid lending when there was competition because it increased uncertainty about his relationship with the king. The Spanish monarchy, however, was able to convince its bankers that competition was not bad for negotiations because no distinction between 'good' and 'bad' bankers would be made. Treating each banker as if he was the only one maintained his confidence in negotiations because the bankers knew that the value their loans had for the king was not negligible. Spreading this belief among lenders was good for the king because it increased the confidence of each banker in negotiations and created 'competition' among lenders, which avoided any kind of market power resulting from a possible strong cartel. This allowed the sovereign to increase the amount of credit that he could borrow and keep its price low.

7 FROM SUBORDINATION TO AUTONOMY: PUBLIC DEBT POLICIES AND THE CREATION OF A SELF-RULED FINANCIAL MARKET IN THE KINGDOM OF NAPLES IN THE LONG RUN (1500–1800)

Gaetano Sabatini[1]

In this paper I have tried to determine some essential points regarding the evolution of the Neapolitan public debt in the early modern age. In brief, these are:

1. The Kingdom of Naples had recourse to the public debt from the beginning of the early modern age, in line with the development of the public debt in the most economically dynamic areas of Europe;
2. Until the beginning of the eighteenth century, recourse to the public debt was closely connected to the political and financial demands of the Spanish monarchy of which Naples was part; at the same time, the public debt, especially that part ascribable to the communities, not only fed a flourishing domestic financial market, but was also an important point of contact and equilibrium between the classes that were most active economically and between these classes and the state;
3. The recovery of the Kingdom of Naples' political independence in the eighteenth century can be seen in the adoption of an independent financial policy regarding both the public debt and the regulation of the financial market;
4. The changes which took place during the eighteenth century, and especially from the beginning of the nineteenth century with the vast operation of consolidating the public debt during the decade of French rule, mark important moments in the modernization of the Neapolitan financial market, in its links with the network of big European finance and in the emergence of new operators.

In the Spanish Imperial System

The concept of the 'Spanish Imperial' system – a definition used more by early modern historians than by economic historians – embodies the idea that between the sixteenth and the eighteenth centuries a multiplicity of institutional, political, military, religious and economic-financial ties united the lands of the Spanish monarchy, surmounting its inherent differences and giving rise to a single body with a fair degree of cohesion. However, historians interpret this concept in very different ways, ranging from the classical interpretations of the *polisinodiale* monarchy by Jaime Vicens Vives and the composite monarchy by John Elliot to other more recent publications.[2]

In the context of Italian historiography, this concept has been accepted, in particular, by Giuseppe Galasso and Aurelio Musi.[3] In this paper, the reference to the imperial dimension aims to show that the characteristics, dynamics and ways of managing the Neapolitan public debt in the early modern age, together with its interactions with the broader socio-productive context and with the general situation of the Kingdom's public finances, can be fully understood and interpreted only in the light of the incorporation of mainland Southern Italy in the Spanish system between 1503 and 1707 and in view of the fact that models of controlling the economy were transferred from Castile to the other territories of the Spanish monarchy.

Highlighting this aspect, however, means something much more complex than merely referring to the fact that the relationship with the Spanish Crown bound the Kingdom of Naples to sharing the monarchy's defence costs, and that public debt was the main instrument for finding resources – both financial and other – to send beyond the borders of the Kingdom.[4] Furthermore, with reference to this specific aspect, it is necessary to determine more precisely the period when there was a closer connection between the increase in the military expenses of the Spanish monarchy, with which Neapolitan finances were saddled, and recourse to the public debt. It is our opinion that this connection should be limited on the whole to the period from Philip II's accession to the fall of the Count-Duke di Olivares as *valido* of Philip IV, i.e. from 1556 to 1643, with considerable acceleration in the first twenty years of the reign of the fourth Spanish Hapsburg.[5]

To understand the connection with the Spanish imperial system we must first of all point out that, especially in the above-mentioned years, the decisions regarding Neapolitan public finance reflected policies that originated at the centre of the monarchy and were put into effect, in different contexts and in different ways, in other territories of the empire, and sometimes throughout the whole empire; these policies concerned the extent to which taxation and the public debt should be increased or how to combine both these measures in view of the form of public debt undertaken.[6]

As in other areas of the Spanish monarchy, in Naples resort to the public debt involved capitalization and the transfer of tax or property revenue – often created expressly for this purpose – to private individuals for life, or with the obligation to redeem it, if the Crown reserved the future right to recover the asset, paying back the capital it had received. During the sixteenth and the seventeenth centuries, the transfer of revenue occurred with increasing frequency and on such a large scale that the value of the assets sold was further and further reduced and the difference between the nominal value and the market value of the public debt's assets became increasingly higher.[7]

Second, bearing in mind how widely spread the Neapolitan public debt was among very different social strata, the other area in which the close geopolitical connection with Spain is seen is that of the management decisions which could affect the Kingdom's stability and social cohesion: the methods of floating, funding, consolidating and redeemting the Neapolitan public debt were always decided, or revoked, according to their effects in terms of strengthening or weakening domestic approval of the monarchy's political strategies.[8]

Some Historiographical Precedents

The point of view put forward here has, of course, no claim to be original: it has been stated explicitly by Giovanni Muto, if not by others. In particular in two papers published in 1994 and 1995,[9] Muto drew attention to the need to consider the financial management of the Neapolitan public debt in the context of similar situations in other territories of the Spanish monarchy, at least with reference to common characteristics, the processes of reform and the attempts to make the financial machinery in the Spanish Hapsburgs' three largest Italian possessions converge: the Kingdom of Naples, the Kingdom of Sicily and the Duchy of Milan, in other words, in the Spanish monarchy's 'Italian area'.[10]

As far as the management of the public debt during the reign of Philip II is concerned, Muto considers particularly significant the 1556 attempt to introduce a new figure, that of the royal agent, who would assist with the work of the Crown's *factor general* in the Italian territories. His function was to transfer funds between the various areas of the monarchy and to negotiate terms for loans with the *hombres de negocios* from a stronger position. The attempt did not succeed, and in 1557 Philip II was obliged to proclaim the first of the suspensions of payments which marked his reign.[11] Every suspension was followed by a *Medio General*, the agreement reached to renegotiate the size of the debt and the methods of payment, and the tax revenue from the Italian territories was used to guarantee the new *juros* issued. On the occasion of the *Medio General* in 1598, a few months before the death of Philip II, the total sum of the debt recognized by the Crown was 14 million ducats. Two-thirds of this debt was covered by issuing *juros* at 5 per cent, and the remaining third by *juros* at 7.14 per cent, half of which were issued on revenue from Naples and Milan.[12]

Luigi De Rosa and Roberto Mantelli have published research on the evolution of the Neapolitan public debt in connection with the financial affairs of the Castilian Crown in the context of a more general reconstruction of the overall credit system in mainland Southern Italy in the modern age. De Rosa has carried out research on the operators involved in the management of credit and in the credit market, and on the role of public and private banks. Mantelli has examined and reclassified – according to capitalized revenue sources and social groups – all the alienations of public revenue in Naples between 1556 and 1583.[13]

Antonio Calabria has published a book which, although not specifically about public debt, deals with it in the reconstruction of the evolution of Neapolitan public finances between the mid-sixteenth century and the 1630s.[14] He identifies the elaborate technical characteristics of recourse to the public debt, retraces its stages of rapid expansion, in particular between 1563 and 1596, and emphasizes the great vitality of the financial market, pointing out, among other things, that in Naples, unlike in Holland, the revenue market was completely free: in other words, it did not issue compulsory loans.[15] Thus Calabria's interpretation places Naples in the 'financial revolution', but, unlike the situation in the United Provinces, the contribution the public debt in Italy made to the development of a highly sophisticated credit market did not assist a process of growth; on the contrary, it encouraged a period of stagnation in the economy.[16] Calabria finds confirmation of his theory by observing the different social status of those who bought the revenue. He shows – beyond the ever massive presence of the Genoese merchant bankers – the greater participation of small investors as proof of the growing uncertainty of the general economic climate and the impossibility of finding alternative forms of investment.[17] However, the data regarding the distribution of public debt purchasers according to their social group and to the sum they invested suggests that a more complex process of accumulation and redistribution of wealth was underway, set in motion by the public debt.[18] In other words, in Calabria's synthesis, the analysis of the Neapolitan public debt sways between the progressive model of the financial revolution and an interpretation of the role of the credit market which is contradictory to any form of growth.[19] Is it possible to reunite these two different models?

Alienation and the Recovery of Neapolitan Revenue between the Seventeenth and the Eighteenth Centuries

In seventeenth-century Naples, the signs of a slackening in economic growth should not be sought in the social distribution of the public debt nor in the technical ways in which revenue was issued or, more generally, in which the credit market was structured, which were very modern. The fundamental difference between Naples and the United Provinces lies not in the means but in the ends. The Neapolitan public debt did not develop to increase credit for international trade, but to contribute to funding the Spanish monarchy's war efforts, to pay off the trade deficit, to pay in Genoa, Florence and Venice the yields their respective merchants and financiers earned from investments they had made in the Kingdom of Naples, and to send to Rome the revenue that the Church earned from its property in Southern Italy.[20]

Reconstructing the network of connections which link Southern Italy to the international finance system means, therefore, drawing attention to the fact that the Neapolitan public debt was managed as a complex whole of interdependencies with its hub in the Spanish monarchy and with an exceptional ability to mobilize capital, men, goods and services.[21] But this ability to mobilize resources was put into practice continually, and Naples paid a high price, not least in terms of the effective control of public finances.

From the beginning of the sixteenth century, the Spanish government in Naples constantly resorted to the system of *arrendamenti* – farming out to private citizens the contract for the collection of customs duties, both external (which were paid on goods which arrived in the port of Naples) and internal (such as the *ius fondaci*), and for the collection of taxes on the production and consumption of goods, as well as of other smaller taxes; thus the royal treasury obtained at first a little less than it would have done by means of direct taxation, but it had the great advantage of collecting a definite sum immediately, leaving the responsibility of actually collecting the taxes to the contractor, who had a margin of net profit guaranteed. The revenue from the *arrendamenti*, duly capitalized, formed the basis for floating the public debt.[22]

In 1649, after the risings of the previous two years, the Spanish government, burdened with not only the financial but also the administrative responsibility of paying private citizens the interests of the public debt which had been created by capitalizing the *arrendamenti*, resolved to hand over completely the management of each *arrendamento* to its creditors, meeting the demands *in solutum et pro soluto*.[23] The tax authorities kept only 300,000 ducats per year from the entire revenue of tax farming, and this sum was used for the needs of the *Cassa militare*, i.e. that sector of the state budget which covered the Kingdom's defence costs.[24] And so, at least from the mid-seventeenth century, part of the Neapolitan public debt was totally outside the control of the state administration, to such an extent that its size and its interest were no longer recorded in the public bookkeeping entries.[25]

The Spanish government saw this as an extreme and temporary measure and, from its promulgation in 1649, had asserted its right to regain possession of the *arrendamenti* by repurchasing the alienated sources of income.[26] Various attempts were made in the last years of the seventeenth century[27] and again during the short-lived Austrian rule in the Kingdom of Naples (1707–34),[28] but a turning point was not reached until Naples regained political independence and the reign of Charles Bourbon began. The Bourbon administration tried to regain control of some alienated sources of revenue in the 1730s and the 1740s, but such measures aroused strong opposition on the part of those who held the rights on the *arrendamenti,* and this led to the abandoning of the project. It was not until 1751 that it was taken up again with renewed vigour in a political climate which encouraged more energetic action on the part of the Bourbon government, and so a special financial body, the *Giunta delle ricompre,* was founded.[29]

The *Giunta* began its activity by dealing with the important salt *arrendamento.* The retrieval of the salt *arrendamento* and its return to the royal coffers was a particularly significant episode in the history of the Neapolitan public debt. This measure resembles a very modern way of refunding revenue: those who had invested sums in the *arrendamento* were faced with two alternatives: they could accept either the reimbursement of the capital originally paid out or a reduction in the interest rate from 7 per cent to 5 per cent, but even with this second option they lost their status as agents of a state revenue source and became subscribers to public revenue.[30] This policy of bringing the *arrendamenti* back to the public treasury continued with some regularity until 1768 and then began again in 1782, in a period when the Bourbon administration's reforming activity resumed and continued to the end of the century.[31]

The holders of this form of revenue always bitterly opposed the state's attempts to repurchase the alienated sources of revenue, especially when, in the second half of the 1780s, refunding was offered at a rate of 3 per cent: the lack of real alternatives as far as investment was concerned, however, induced the beneficiaries of this income to prefer investment in the public debt, while trying to keep it at the most advantageous rate possible.[32] It was not only among those social classes – the aristocracy and ecclesiastical bodies[33] – which had traditionally preferred the public debt in the sixteenth and seventeenth centuries that the preference for this investment area continued to remain high: a middle-class group, made up of professional people, merchants and public officials, showed markedly increased preference for the public debt.[34]

The fact that preference for the public debt persisted and increased should not be understood solely in terms of stagnation in Neapolitan economic life, and hence the absence of other possible investment alternatives. In fact, in Naples, as in other areas of Europe, income securities were generally fully negotiable, and from the seventeenth century had begun to perform the function of coinage. Accepted by the state and by the communities with full redeeming power, and used in every kind of commercial transaction, the shares of the public debt enjoyed the same function of coinage as the certificates for deposits made at the Neapolitan public banks.[35] In this respect too, the characteristics of the Neapolitan public debt changed profoundly when the French arrived in the Kingdom of Naples.

The Napoleonic Reforms

One of the first actions of the new Napoleonic administration in 1806 was to regain public control over income which for various reasons had been alienated over the course of the previous centuries, repeating what had happened in France. The loss of revenue was to be recognized by a life annuity registered in a ledger called the *Gran Libro* (Great Ledger) of the public debt and calculated on the basis of the original capital deposited. To complement the compiling of the Great Book, the *Cassa delle rendite* (Income Fund) and the *Cassa di ammortizzazione* (Redemption Fund) were founded. The *Cassa delle rendite* was in charge of paying consolidated revenue, whereas the *Cassa di ammortizzazione* was to deal with the gradual repayment of the debt.[36]

Although the revenues' actual rate was some 3 or 4 per cent, capital was calculated at a rate of 5 per cent, thereby achieving a considerable reduction as far as the state's costs were concerned. Furthermore, about 35 million of the 100 million ducats of the public debt recorded in the *Gran Libro* were deleted, in that they were ascribed to monasteries belonging to religious orders which the Napoleonic government suppressed and whose personal property and real estate had gone to the state. Lastly, the size of the new consolidated public debt was further reduced by a rapid devaluation in the value of stock issued for the debt.

In the liquidation transactions, carried out between 1806 and 1812 (the results of which were publicized in 1814), more than 57 million ducats of credit owed by the state to private individuals was acknowledged in the form of public debt stock.[37] Whoever owned such stock had the right to the registration of a life annuity of 5 per cent (later reduced to 3 per cent) in the *Gran Libro*, to free negotiation on the market, to purchase state-owned property or to pay off debts to banks or to the state. The government tried to urge as many creditors as possible to purchase state-owned property instead of being registered in the *Gran Libro*, in order to avoid paying service on the debt, but in fact only very few creditors chose this option: there was no doubt that people preferred the public debt to investments in real estate.[38]

At the closing of the liquidation transactions, 30 per cent of the revenue was registered in the *Cassa di ammortizzazione*, 10 per cent went to organizations of various kinds and 60 per cent went to individuals; within this latter category, 46 per cent of the public debt was owned by non-aristocratic investors, 37 per cent by nobles and 17 per cent by foreigners.[39]

The group of non-aristocratic and foreign investors was made up of lawyers, public notaries, doctors, engineers, magistrates and, in general, representatives of the bureaucracy, together with numerous merchants, many of whom were to become part of the entrepreneurial class which began to take shape during the decade of French rule and then went on to develop throughout the nineteenth century, showing that in Naples the world of manufacturing and the world of finance had finally come together.

8 PUBLIC DEBT IN THE PAPAL STATES: FINANCIAL MARKET AND GOVERNMENT STRATEGIES IN THE LONG RUN (SEVENTEENTH–NINETEENTH CENTURIES)

Fausto Piola Caselli[1]

Origin and Growth of Papal Debt

Regular public debt in the Papal States lagged far behind the main Italian city states. Except the well-known venality of offices,[2] it started officially in 1526 with the first issue at a 10 per cent yearly rate (*Monte Fede*) and expanded markedly only after the second half of the sixteenth century.[3]

Papal debt increased at a rapid pace throughout the seventeenth century until the large 1684 and 1687 concentrations of a jumble of different issues into the St Peter *Monti*, reduced at 3 per cent. In little more than a century and a half the *Camera Apostolica* – the central treasury – had authorized 187 separate issues: 71 to provide funds to the treasury itself; 55 to bail out the Roman nobility; 23 to benefit the Capital city; and 38 to underwrite the debts the communities had accumulated with the Apostolic Chamber.[4]

After the end of the seventeenth century nearly all new emissions were issued to replace older ones, at the nominal value of 100 silver *scudi* for each *luogo*, or bond. The total stock of debt stabilized around 50 million *scudi*. Interest rates remained stable at 3 per cent, but bonds were always highly appreciated in the secondary market, fetching prices well above par until the end of the eighteenth century, when the Napoleonic Wars shattered the whole system.

From the available documentation,[5] Chart 8.1 shows the debt growth (interest paid on yearly balance sheet expenditures from 1599) for two hundred years.

Chart 8.1: Nominal Yearly Expenditures and Interests in the Papal States, 1599–1769.

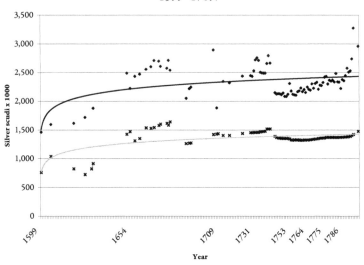

* Expenditures/1000   ⁕ Interests/1000   — Log. (Expenditures/1000)   — Log. (Interests/1000)

The two logarithmic curves apparently show a continuous increase, with a clear parallelism between expenditures and interests paid. However, nominal values in the long run do not describe correctly the real dimension of public debt. From a demographic point of view, the Papal State population gained a good 25 per cent from the late sixteenth to late eighteenth century, mainly due to the annexation of the Ferrara territories (1598) and the conquest of the Farnese Castro duchy (1649). In term of money, the silver *giulio* was debased about 17 per cent in two hundred years. Therefore, on the basis of figures thus indexed in grams of silver per capita, both yearly exits and interests show in Chart 8.2 a quieter trend, and even a clear decrease.

It can be thus proved that papal debt, considered in terms of indexed figures, sloped down progressively from the first decades of seventeenth to the end of the eighteenth century. Its global amount was not so high in comparison with the usual level of indebtedness of other European countries: anyway, its total weight was compatible with the inflow of tax revenues.

The per capita debt burden for interests peaked at 25 grams of silver in 1678, but it decreased to 20 grams in the first half of the eighteenth century. It contracted further to 15 grams and even less in the second half of the eighteenth century. Considering that the daily salary of a bricklayer amounted to 4–5 grams of silver, the per capita cumulated debt for interests ranged from a minimum of three working days to a maximum of six days. In the early modern age, papal debt

Chart 8.2: Indexed Yearly Expenditures and Interests in the Papal States, 1599–1796.

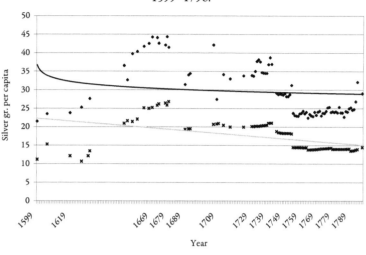

was always kept under close control and never reached huge and unsustainable amounts as has been declared.[6]

Debt Efficiency and the Formation of the Roman Financial Market

Despite a poor reputation – utterly undeserved – the papal public debt was a model of technical perfection, as was underlined many years ago by Fernand Braudel.[7] The Apostolic Chamber always managed to keep the debt under control, balancing new loans, repayments and interest payments, and avoiding the bankruptcies which befell Spain and France. Papal certificates were in high demand and from the beginning Rome became an important financial centre, even if it was smaller and less specialized than other European markets such as Antwerp, Lyon, Genoa, Besançon and Piacenza, since it lacked equally sophisticated trading and manufacturing systems.

The Apostolic Chamber carefully managed the issuance and the circulation of bonds, making the supply and demand of saving meet. Even if during the seventeenth and eighteenth centuries we do not find in Rome either a stock exchange building or an official list of securities, demand and supply could easily match both on the primary and on the secondary markets with the intermediation of the numerous banking houses active in Rome. Economic advantages, such as attractive returns, provided the main incentive in purchasing bonds. Interest rates dropped from 10 per cent in the 1530–50s to 3 per cent in the 1680s, but returns offered by investment in bonds remained constantly higher than income from investment in real estate or other returns from traditional financial investments. In the main, the latter offered higher nominal rates, but at a considerably higher level of risk, given the large percentage of debtors who defaulted.

Little by little the administrative procedures guiding the issuance and the trading of papal bonds were simplified by *cameral* offices, which monitored transaction costs. The Apostolic Chamber issued a body of legislation in order to keep the administration efficient, to safeguard the rights of creditors and to establish a degree of market discipline. The legislative process culminated with the publication in 1615 of a compendium of norms providing basic rules to bondholders, administrators and clerical staff.[8]

Transaction costs were quite low. Upon purchasing bonds the buyer had to pay to the administrators a moderate fee, ranging from 0.4 to 0.85 per cent of the nominal price.[9] Taxation on bonds was thus very moderate, in fact no taxes were levied on the possession of certificates, on returns, or on capital gains. Commissions were also low, and this is very important, given the crucial role played by middlemen. Fees did not exceed 0.6 per cent of the nominal price of bonds. Altogether a buyer would have to shoulder an overall cost, including taxes, ranging from 0.7 to 1.2 per cent of the nominal price of each bond traded.[10] Authorities carefully secured the diffusion of reliable information concerning the trading terms and conditions of every issue in regard to managerial efficiency, timely payment of returns, adequacy of pledged revenues and so on. On the Roman market transparency was not assured by public authorities, yet bonds were routinely exchanged above par and transactions revealed little price discrepancies. This convergence in securities valuations indicates that the market possessed an adequate flow of information, mainly coming from the great many relationships among private businessmen and banking houses. The Apostolic Chamber behaved correctly towards investors: during the 1687 conversion of old issues into the new *Monti* of St Peter, the valuation of old bonds was strictly made according to current market prices. Stockholders were given the option either of redeeming their old bonds at market value or of swapping 100 old shares for 130 new ones.[11] In the main it can be said that in Rome the key features which could guarantee adequate market efficiency were in place: i.e. security, long-term profitability, transparency and rates of return proportional to risk.

Investors in Papal Bonds

Papal debt issues met with remarkable favour from investors from the very beginning. Despite the frequent succession of pontiffs – 36 elections in three hundred years – popes always adopted a firm policy of accepting responsibility for financial obligations incurred by their predecessors. After a long period of expansion and of managerial improvements, both the financial size and the pool of investors stabilized in the second half of the seventeenth century. The latter came to display the following features:[12]

1. *Female investors.* On average women made up about a quarter of investors (27 per cent). However women's financial means were less than men's: in fact, taking into account the amount of capital invested, the share of women's holdings drops to 12 per cent. We are not dealing with paltry sums, particularly considering the role women were relegated to in early modern societies. Dowries and inheritances made up most of women's assets.

2. *Distribution between private and corporate investors.* Individuals formed the largest group of investors, however religious and charitable agencies represented about 20 per cent of investors and owned an equal share of the overall investment. In the main these agencies were either based in Rome or in the Papal States (79 per cent). Investments from foreign agencies were rather poor.[13]

3. *Holdings.* A disproportionately large share of bonds was in the hands of a limited number of wealthy investors – mostly aristocrats and international financiers – yet at the same time investors flocked to securities from all walks of life. Since the distribution of wealth in early modern societies tended to be highly skewed it is not surprising to find that a small cohort of well-to-do nobles and professional money-dealers dominated the market. It has to be underlined, however, that papal bonds also attracted the savings of a vast conglomerate of investors of little or of moderate financial means. Investors from the middle and lower rungs of the social ladder displayed a remarkable attitude to saving, which is highlighted by a remarkably high number of tiny purchases of just one share or even fractions of shares.

4. *Bondholders' geographical distribution.* Papal securities offered an attractive investment venue not just to subjects of the Papal States but also to foreigners. As a matter of course investors from Rome and other provinces of the papal domains managed to acquire nearly 55 per cent of papal bonds, yet investors from other Italian cities amassed considerable holdings as well. Most foreign purchases were in the hands of Genoese, who had replaced Florentine money-dealers since the end of the sixteenth century.[14] In the late seventeenth century, significant purchases came also from Lombardy, from Milan and Como above all (it is interesting to note that the reigning

Pope, Innocent XI, was from Como). Adding to Genoese direct investment (about 18 per cent) purchases made from residents of neighbouring dioceses (Albenga, Savona and Ventimiglia), we find that investors from the Liguria region held about 21–2 per cent of papal debt. The significance of the international role played by the Genoese can be gauged against the backdrop of the much more limited purchases of Florentine and Tuscan investors, who claimed just 5–6 per cent of the papal stock.

An accurate organization, an efficient management, a reliable set of guarantees and the Apostolic Chamber's fair dealing with investors contributed to introduce papal bonds to investors well beyond the borders of the Papal States. In turn this development was crucial in transforming Rome into one of the main national and international financial centres of the age.

Revenues to Service the Debt

Since the very beginning papal debt was conceived as funded debt. This means that the service of the debt was based upon fiscal incomes which were both adequate and clearly pledged. Balance sheets, which are regularly available in archives from the mid-seventeenth century,[15] reveal the origin and quantity of revenues which funded debt service in order to guarantee regular dividends and – sometimes – to repay capitals. In small part, revenues came from patrimonial assets; donations and spiritual revenues handled by the Papal *Dataria* also contributed, but this peculiar stream of money began to decrease from the seventeenth century onward. The main source of debt-funding income came from the yield of consumption taxes. The city of Rome itself provided more than 50 per cent of total revenues for the state debt.

In a city with a very high level of consumption, tax revenues from this area were committed to provide adequate and regular funding to a debt system which in turn met with appreciation from investors and enjoyed complete security. The system of Rome's customs – i.e. the collection of consumption taxes – originated in the fourteenth century and had been perfected over time. Collection was routinely farmed out for a period of nine years to the main banking firms active in Rome. In this way a thick and efficient web of intertwined interests coalesced around Rome's taxes, which included the collection of revenues, the issuance of bonds and the relationships between banking firms, which were also *Monti* depositary banks and ran most of state financial business inside the Apostolic Camera. This system came partially to an end only at the beginning of the eighteenth century, when *cameral* bureaucracy claimed the direct management of Roman taxes.

As we can see in Chart 8.3, taxes levied on Rome's consumption for the debt (upper curve, values expressed in silver *giulii* per capita) remained at a very high level for two hundred years, whilst the contribution per capita from the periphery was always very low.[16]

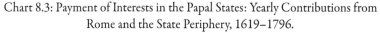

Chart 8.3: Payment of Interests in the Papal States: Yearly Contributions from Rome and the State Periphery, 1619–1796.

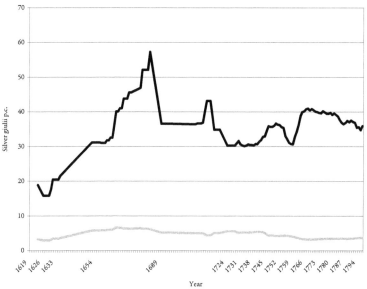

The fiscal income of Rome's taxes (from 1630 to 1790) expanded throughout the seventeenth century and peaked in 1679 (collected revenues equalled 145 grams of silver per capita). It remained high throughout the first half of the eighteenth century (100 grams of silver per capita) but contracted afterwards, slowly at first (80 grams of silver per capita), then dramatically in the last twenty years of the eighteenth century, in coincidence with the introduction of a new custom system at the borders. It thus seems that a true economic crisis hit Rome very late and in a limited way. The consumption of meat, wine and flour provided the solid bulk of the tax yield.

Taking a harder look at archival materials, the hotly debated issues of privilege and fiscal exemptions – often imagined as twin evils bearing the responsibility for a financial bankruptcy which actually the papacy never came close to – have to be reassessed: until 1678 fiscal exemptions increased, reaching 15 per cent of the overall yield of Roman customs. However exemptions were drastically curtailed afterwards and their incidence was reduced to 3–4 per cent of collected revenues.[17]

As a whole the data show the solidity of papal public finance, although in the context of an Ancien Régime system headed for a slow economic decline. We can see a turning point between recourse to the debt lever – which was no longer increased but actually reduced – and recourse to the fiscal lever – per capita fiscal pressure increased to reach nearly 10 per cent. This trend was particularly evident in the period 1630–70, when papal control of state machinery was already well established. Consumption in Rome remained buoyant throughout an age supposedly marked by economic crisis at the national level, and played a crucial role in sustaining government financial strategies.

Looking at the Periphery: The *Legazione* Bolognese

In addition to the development of a vast and complex state debt, the Papal States presided over the peculiar formation of several equally large and composite debt systems at the municipal level – in Rome, in Bologna and in Ferrara – around which the relationships between centre and periphery came to gravitate.

The institution of the *Monti* in Bologna allowed popes to use the city as a sort of coffer from which to draw resources whenever they needed to. From the early sixteenth century onwards the system of Bolognese *Monti* saw a relentless expansion, yet the central decades of the seventeenth century marked a watershed between two distinct periods, dominated by a very different set of priorities. Between 1506 and 1656 Bolognese debt boomed at an almost exponential rate: growth was fuelled by a proliferation of mostly unredeemable (*perpetui*) issues, paying high returns. The number of debt issues increased from 3 to 27, and the total capital borrowed moved rapidly upward from 350,000 lire in 1516 to over 9 million in 1656. In the second half of the seventeenth century the debt system was restructured and issues were concentrated: the number of debt issues decreased to 8 in 1705 and was further reduced to just 5 in 1765. Restructuring did not mean reduced indebtedness though. In fact the public debt of the *Legazione* kept expanding: from 9 million lire in 1656 it grew to 11.8 million in 1705, and reached 22.5 million lire in 1765.[18]

With an overall population of about 200,000 inhabitants in the middle of the sixteenth century the debt/population ratio stood around 5 lire per capita. Given a resident population that remained largely stable (ranging between 200,000 and 260,000 people), the continued growth of the debt translated into a 16-times higher per capita burden, which increased to 28 lire in 1595, 42 lire in 1656, 53 lire in 1705, and 84 lire in 1765.

Plotting the index of Bolognese indebtedness (1550 = 100), we find that the cumulated debt stood at a value of 490 in 1596, grew to 824 in 1660, reached 1,037 in 1700, and climbed to 2,029 in 1765. Looking at the expansion of tax revenues we find that fiscal income expanded at roughly the same pace only during the second half of the sixteenth century: between 1550 and 1596 the index of tax receipts climbed from a value of 100 to 322. It slowed down in the first half of the seventeenth century (the index stood at 410 in 1660), but then contracted to a value of 346 in 1700 (Chart 8.4). The fiscal income/debt ratio moved dangerously upward from ¼ in the middle of the sixteenth century to ¹⁄₁₀ in 1660, to ¹⁄₁₇ in 1765.

Chart 8.4: Debt and Taxes in Bologna, 1550–1765.

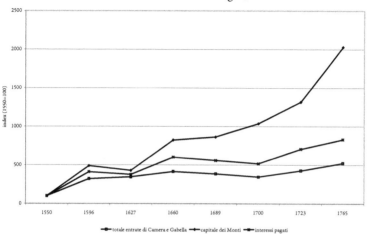

Bolognese *Monti* presented throughout the sixteenth century a twin feature: a multitude of emissions and high returns. Investors flocked to purchase Bolognese bonds lured by attractive interest rates ranging mainly from 6.5 to 8 per cent (but with lows of 5 per cent and highs of 10 per cent). Seventeenth-century debt restructuring was not limited to simplifying the structure and making management more efficient; it worked to stabilize the financial situation, to reduce the cost of servicing the debt and to provide at no additional cost the financial means local authorities desperately needed.

To achieve long-term debt sustainability Bolognese authorities chose to implement a policy of aggressive interest rate reduction that allowed them to contain the amount of revenues tied to debt servicing. Government efforts continued in the eighteenth century with the issuance of the *Monti Clemente primo*, *Clemente Secondo* and *Benedettino*, all at 3 per cent (Chart 8.5).[19]

The restructuring of Bologna's debt system went together with two important changes in the destination of resources and in the social make-up of investors. From the mid-sixteenth to the mid-seventeenth century Rome claimed nearly 60 per cent of capital borrowed in Bologna, whereas from the late seventeenth to the mid-eighteenth century the outflow of Bolognese capital shrank to about 10 per cent.

At the same time deep changes within the body of investors emerged. By and large bonds remained in the hands of Bolognese citizens and agencies, and the overall number of shareholders remained fairly stable – roughly just over 1,000 proprietors – between the late decades of the sixteenth century and the second half of the eighteenth century.[20] This stability conceals an interesting variation within the body of Bolognese investors, most notably a trend away from individual ownership and towards corporate ownership. The steady reduction of interest rates probably contributed to the overall trend. Although Bolognese individuals remained a very large group of bond-holders their relative weight declined stead-

Chart 8.5: Rates of Interest on Bolognese *Monti*, 1550–1765.

Chart 8.6: Holders of Bolognese Bonds, 1555–1765.

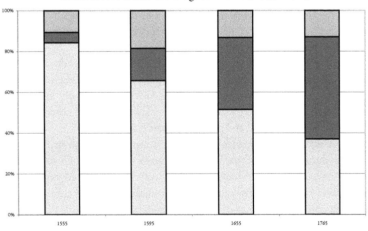

◼ Bol. Citizens ◼ Bol. Agencies ◼ Foreigners

ily: from 84.3 per cent in the mid-sixteenth century, to 65.7 per cent in 1595, to 51.5 per cent in the mid-seventeenth century, to less than 40 per cent in 1765. The drying up of investment from individuals and families was made up by an ever larger flow of financial resources from the city's religious and charitable agencies. Around the mid-sixteenth century corporate investment was modest: agencies were few in number (7.4 per cent) and had small holdings (5.1 per cent). By the end of the sixteenth century, however, corporate investment had progressed markedly: agencies made up 13.3 per cent of investors and owned 15.7 per cent of bonds. At the middle of the seventeenth century they represented 29.5 per cent of proprietors and their investment leaped to 35.2 per cent. In 1765 agencies dominated the market: they made up 47 per cent of investors and owned about 50 per cent of bonds (Chart 8.6).[21]

Investments in the Papal Debt in Nineteenth-Century Rome

The first thirty years of the nineteenth century were years of deep change for the administration of the papal debt, driven by the twin attempts of the French government to centralize and downsize the debt. The traditional trust in papal bonds had already been badly shaken by the suspension of interest payment during the first Roman Republic in 1798 and 1799. In 1801 payments were resumed, at rates reduced from 3 per cent to 1.2 per cent, but they were suspended again in 1806.[22] The collapse of the market value of bonds inevitably followed and market quotations remained very low, at an average value of 10–12 *scudi*, against a nominal value of bonds of 100 *scudi*, for the entire first decade of the nineteenth century.[23] Later on, a papal *Motu proprio* (decree) of 1816 on the one hand recognized French liquidation, and on the other hand tried to limit investors' losses, allotting a nominal value of each bond to be reimbursed from 24 to 25 *scudi* and resuming interest payments. The debt was then consolidated and interest expenses were reduced.[24]

This was the position taken by those who bore the responsibility of managing public finances. But how did investors react to the losses suffered, first at the hands of the French administration, then at the hands of the restored papal government? And who were the financial operators who helped maintain the dynamism of Rome's financial market in the 1820s? From archival sources for the period 1822–31, we can document on average 175 transactions brought to an end in one year, with the notable exceptions of 1822 (22 transactions), 1824 (71 transactions) and 1831 (78 transactions).[25] Vincenzo Cleter and Francesco Cressedi, official Chamber stockbrokers, handled most securities transactions throughout the decade. The former routinely acted as mandate-holder of the firm Torlonia and Company, the trading name of the Banco Torlonia. In addition to them, Pietro Zappati and Ambrogio Valle operated as brokers at the Central Office of the Public Debt.

Chart 8.7: Capitals Traded in Papal Bonds, 1822–31.

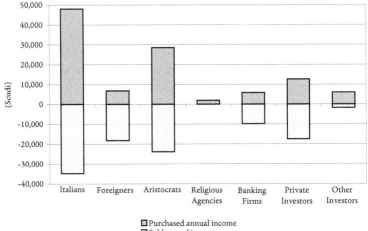

□ Purchased annual income
□ Sold annual income

From Chart 8.7 the tendency of foreign investors to sell bonds rather than to buy is clear. Other categories in the chart make reference to Italian investors only. Italian aristocrats were the most important group of private investors both in terms of transactions and in terms of capital traded. They were closely followed by lay agencies, such as banking firms. Giovanni Torlonia, a man with a deep knowledge of the Roman market, traded during the 1820s the largest batch of consolidated papal bonds. On the one hand he purchased bonds for a nominal value of 300,000 *scudi* and annual income of 15,000 *scudi*, on the other hand he sold stock for an annual income close to 10,000 *scudi*. The dealings of foreign aristocrats could not come even close to the size of Torlonia's activities. In addition they were far busier selling than buying consolidated bonds. Purchases hardly reached an annual income of 1,000 *scudi*, and the Russian aristocrat Nicola de Demidoff alone shed bonds for an annual income of 3,000 *scudi* (and a face value of 56,000 *scudi*).

Somewhat different, and certainly more balanced, was the approach of banking firms, both Italian and foreign, operating in Rome. The banking firms Torlonia and Company and the Dutch Claudio Cromlin, Van Heukelom Frantz and Brantz posted very similar trends for acquisitions and sales. In addition to Giovanni Torlonia, the leading Italian aristocratic dealers were Prince Luigi Boncompagni and Count Giuseppe Antonio Celani, who acquired bonds for annual returns of 2,000 and 1,300 *scudi* respectively. Among non-noble dealers Felice Trocchi stands out, with purchases for 92,000 *scudi* and sales for 80,000 *scudi*. Among non-banking enterprises, the firm of Saverio Scultheis – an importer of colonial products – was quite active between 1822 and 1831. The firm accumulated consolidated bonds for annual returns in excess of 5,000 *scudi*. The firm's financial dealings certainly benefited from the close association of the Scultheis family to Giovanni Torlonia: the banker had married a Scultheis woman and had developed business ties with the family.

In those same years also a number of religious agencies were active financial dealers on the Roman market: the Bambin Gesù monastic house and the Prelatura Chiaromonti stand out, with 13 and 27 transactions respectively. Among charitable agencies Rome's Ospedali Riuniti was the most active, with 20 transactions leading to the acquisition of bonds for a nominal value of 20,000 *scudi*.

The Making of Rome's Stock Exchange

Initially, there was not a building or even an office exclusively appointed for bonds transactions in Rome. Only on 21 December 1821 did a decree claim that the Secretariat of State ordered brokers to establish a public stock exchange open to all traders, 'where dealers could meet according to guidelines set out in the Code of Commerce and where exchange and security rates would be set.'[26] The economic congregation stressed that privilege and predominance of special interest groups had to be stamped out in order to keep Rome's stock exchange on an equal footing with European capital cities, from Naples, 'where the stock exchange is public and bankers and traders meet freely at the ring of the bell', to Livorno, Genoa, Marseille and Ancona, not to mention to London and Paris, where the stock exchanges were open to 'brokers of every nationality' without any form of subjection to local bankers and brokers.[27] The stock exchange in Rome was only virtual and lacked statutes until the French invasion. The Code of Commerce adopted by the restored Papal States retained most of the provisions which had been introduced during the French domination. Article 66 of the new Code of Commerce called the stock exchange the assembly, under the authority of the government, of traders, ship captains, brokers and middlemen.

In the early stages transactions were settled in the Apostolic Chamber main offices or within the offices of each banker. Later on, 'local and foreign bankers were required to seek permission to intervene on the trading floor and to deposit a sum to the Monte di pietà. The latter however was a mere formality and the deposited sum could be withdrawn at will. And the practice was discontinued well before the introduction of the Code of Commerce'. In addition, it was the bankers themselves who screened and authorized new admissions. It was a privilege to be listed among the 'main banking families' and every year the list was published in the *Cracas* (Rome's journal). Torlonia himself stated that inclusion in the list made him well known within and without Rome and allowed him 'to contribute to the wellbeing of the country, since the government protected and trusted the banking profession and to it turned whenever in need'. Torlonia became a banker and purveyor to the court in 1796 thanks to a special *chirografo* issued by Pope Pious VI. After 1790, new nominees were required to make a cautionary deposit of 25,000 *scudi* to the Monte di Pietà or the Banco di Santo Spirito. Bankers formed a closed caste: there were no more than 7 or 8 official bankers in Rome and they met once a week – routinely on Friday – in a room of the Archiginnasio at the Sapienza (the Roman university building) with the assistance of just two *mezzani* (brokers) to set rates of exchange. Transactions determined actual exchange rates between different markets, but rates also fluctuated according to demand and offers of bills of exchange and were influenced by prevailing rates on the main foreign markets. 'The rate of exchange indicates where buyer and seller meets. Therefore the list does not establish the rate but indicates the meeting point between bid and asked level, exactly as the stone measures the water level.'[28]

Legislative provisions recognized the full negotiability of new bonds. Transactions were recorded on ledgers which were kept in the Office of the Public Debt. Bonds were registered but they could be paid to the bearer as well. During the early decades of the nineteenth century consolidated stock continued to be, as in the past, the blue chip of the Roman market. In addition to Roman bonds at 5 per cent, public debt stock included the quotation of bonds of Milan's *Monte* and non interest-bearing certificates (redeemable in cash or against the purchase of public property).

Bonds displayed a high degree of volatility. The erratic trend of bonds' market prices from 1822 to 1848, as shown by Chart 8.8, can be in part explained by economic policy choices and recurrent financial emergencies in the age of restoration.[29] The average quarterly prices of traded bonds in Rome recorded expansive and recessionary trends which exactly matched political, economic and financial events. On average expansive periods lasted 2–3 years while recessionary periods were shorter, just 1–2 years. In accordance to the provisions of the Vienna agreement, from 1821 to 1833 bonds of Milan's *Monte* were also listed. Shares of Rome's Discount Bank were listed from 1826 to 1829 and the 25 ducat certificates of Naples were also listed from 8 August 1823 to 9 July 1824. From 1838 we find listed shares of the Società Pontificia di assicurazioni (insurance company). Towards the end of the 1850s the stock exchange witnessed an upward trend of transactions involving shares of societies operating in the service sector, railways, insurance and banking (the only shares were issued by the bank of the Papal States). As a matter of fact, the trend of the Roman stock exchange was a faithful mirror of the feeble economic system, and at the beginning of Italian unity public debt still played the leading role on the scenery of the Roman financial market.

Chart 8.8: Market Prices for Bonds at 5 Per Cent, 1822–48.

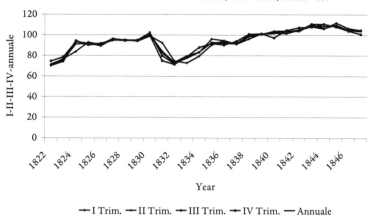

9 TOWARDS A NEW PUBLIC CREDIT POLICY IN EIGHTEENTH-CENTURY SPAIN: THE INTRODUCTION OF THE TESORERÍA MAYOR DE GUERRA (1703–6)

Anne Dubet[1]

The creation of the Tesorería Mayor de Guerra in October 1703 was one of the most fundamental financial and administrative reforms implemented in Spain during the reign of the first Bourbon king, Philip V. The new department, whose head was Juan de Orcasitas y Avellaneda, second Count of Moriana, was charged with the task of monitoring the military spending of the monarchy, and it was directly subordinated to another new department created in September 1703, the Secretaría del Despacho de Guerra, under the control of Manuel de Coloma Escolano, second Marquis of Canales.

The convenience of creating a central treasury had often been debated in Castile in previous centuries and since the sixteenth century there had existed a Tesorería General in Madrid. Yet, as its ambitious title suggests, the new Tesorería was far from being a truly single treasury.[2] The fiscal incomes collected in the Castilian provinces were gathered in a net of provincial treasuries dispersed over the kingdom. Once there, the provincial treasurers paid the current expenses allocated to them, mainly public debt titles (*juros*) and payment orders (*libranzas*). Thus the funds which finally arrived to the Tesorería in Madrid were little more than the remnants of the provincial treasuries. Unlike the Tesorería General, the new Tesorería Mayor de Guerra was devised to fund all war-related expenses of the monarchy, both in the geographical and administrative sense. The military paymasters were transformed into mere subordinates of the Tesorería Mayor de Guerra, so from October 1703 a single royal minister concentrated both funds to pay the military activities of the Crown and its allocation.

Although the War of the Spanish Succession prompted the creation of the Tesorería Mayor de Guerra, it would be wrong to see the new department as a transitional expedient. In reality, it left an unforgettable mark on the later development of Spanish politics and administration. The new institution had to face many problems, proof of which can be found in the fact that the new Tesorería was temporarily suspended twice: between October 1704 and May 1705, and between July 1709 and June 1713. This should not be considered very extraordinary. Another basic piece of the reformist programme promoted during the first years of the new dynasty, the Secretaría del Despacho de Guerra, faced similar difficulties and was also suspended between August 1704 and June 1705, being reintroduced in July 1705 under the control of José Grimaldo, this time with powers extended to the financial and fiscal fields. It should be emphasized here that in 1714 the Secretaría del Despacho de Guerra was split into four different departments: the Secretarías del despacho de Guerra, de Marina e Indias, de Justicia and de Estado. This marked a milestone in the administrative and political history of the country because the new departments had a relevant place in the political process of the monarchy and survived, together with the Tesorerías, until the last phase of the Ancien Régime in Spain.

As for the Tesorería Mayor de Guerra, in July 1718 it was amalgamated with the old Tesorería General. From 1718 on, the head of the new Tesorería, the Tesorero General, controlled a net of paymasters in the armies and, especially, in the provinces, and the range of the single treasury which since 1703 had been confined to military spending was extended to the civilian realm. The spending of the funds allocated to each one of the four departments was in the hands of the Secretarios del Despacho de Estado, de Guerra y Marina y de Justicia, Gobierno Político y Hacienda, and this illustrates better than anything else the decadence of the old council, the cornerstone of the Castilian government until the last decades of the previous century.[3] As in 1704–5 and in 1709–13, there were moments when the Tesorería General was replaced by a combination of the Tesorería Mayor de Guerra and the old Tesorería General. Yet nobody in the political and administrative circles of the Spanish government considered the possibility of returning to the pre-1703 situation.[4]

The relationship between the new Tesorería Mayor de Guerra, introduced in 1703, and the birth of the Tesorería General in 1718, together with the changes in the decision-making process brought by the erection of the new Secretarías del Despacho has attracted the interest of historians over the last decades.[5] The links between the Secretarías and the new Tesorerías have been commonly emphasized, but it seems that the Tesorerías have not aroused as much interest on their own account.[6] At the present date, for example, basic aspects of the structure and daily functioning of the Tesorerías are unknown and we do not have a clear explanation of the reasons for the alternation between the Tesorería General and the Tesorería Mayor/Tesorería General after 1718.[7] Thanks to the work of a group of researchers there have been remarkable advances in our understanding of the financial policy followed by the Spanish Crown in the first decades of the century.[8] Unfortunately, it seems that the Tesorerías have been forgotten and relegated to the field of political and institutional history, yet there are good reasons to question this separation. After all, the 1703 reform was promoted by a famous French financier Jean Orry, who devised it at a time when there was a great need to fund expensive military campaigns in Extremadura, Castilla and Andalucía. The nomination of financiers as treasurers from 1703 onwards is another argument in support of the utility of studying the institutional and political reforms of the period, together with the financial policy followed by the monarchy.[9] Taking these factors into account, then, this paper is focused on the study of the creation of the Tesorería Mayor de Guerra and on the way this department introduced new rules to regulate the relationships between the Crown and its financiers.

Towards a Single War Treasury

It would be impossible to explain the introduction of the Tesorería Mayor de Guerra in October 1703 without taking into account a number of projects surrounding its implementation. In the view of its creator, Jean Orry – sent by Louis XIV to help his grandson, Philip V, put the Spanish finances on a sound footing[10] – the main objective of the new Tesorería was to solve the problems caused by the existence of a net of dispersed provincial and local treasuries and by the diversity of decision-making centres at the higher levels of the financial administration of the country. This had been emphasized by Orry himself in February 1703, after discovering that the funding for military expenses came at least from six different sources: the War Council, the famous Cardinal Portocarrero, the Secretarío del Despacho Universal (the Marquis of Rivas) and three other private individuals ('particulares').[11] As a result of such dispersal, it was nearly impossible to monitor the military spending of the monarchy and even to enforce royal decisions. As Orry put it: 'things went so badly that royal orders were disobeyed; we had enough funds, but we did not spend them; we raised armies, but we did not pay them'.[12]

From October 1703 only one royal minister, the Tesorero General de los gastos para las Guerras (commonly known as Tesorero Mayor de Guerra), controlled the military spending of the Spanish Crown. Every payment needed royal approval and the new Tesorero had to send monthly accounts of the state of his department to the king.[13] At the provincial level, the Tesorería controlled a group of paymasters who, in turn, controlled a network of delegates.[14] When the Tesorería was reintroduced in the summer of 1705, the paymasters were demoted to treasurers and their delegates to paymasters.[15] The Tesorero Mayor selected the treasurers, who had to send him regular accounts.[16] The payment orders were sent to the Tesorero by the Secretario de Despacho de la Guerra,[17] while the paymasters who were sent to the battlefields had to make those payments ordered by the Capitán General and licensed by the Royal Armies controller, the Veedor General del Ejército, or the recently created war commisioners (*comisarios de guerra*).[18] The new paymasters did not replace the old traditional treasurers of royal taxes; they survived. Yet from 1703 it was strictly forbidden for them to pay any military expenses and their role was limited to the remittances of those funds to the new *pagadores*.[19]

Concentrating the funding of the military spending of the monarchy into a single treasury under a new and powerful minister, it is not difficult to see that Orry wanted to sideline the traditional war council, the Secretario del Despacho Universal and Cardinal Portocarrero, as may be gauged from the complaints of the latter.[20] In fact, the creation of the Tesorería Mayor de Guerra was the financial translation of the famous *via reservada*,[21] introduced in the Spanish government during the same years. It seems clear that a stricter control of the financial powers of high-ranking military officers, who were reduced to paying only the extraordinary expenses, was another objective of Orry's plan.[22]

Another Method of Financial Control

The 1703 reform was completed with the introduction of a new method to audit the accounts of the new treasury. The old and traditional audit department of the Crown's finance council, the Contaduría Mayor de Cuentas, was preserved, but there were also innovations.[23] A close surveillance of his subordinates, both treasurers and paymasters, was expected as a matter of course from the Tesorero Mayor de Guerra, something that may be gauged from the testimony of the first Tesorero. Of course, in a world dominated by the importance of personal links, provincial treasurers and paymasters knew too well that they owed nothing less than their complete allegiance to their powerful master, but this did not prevent Orry from introducing other control methods. The funds of the provincial treasuries and the paymasters came from remittances sent to them by the farmers and treasurers of royal taxes. To guarantee that the Tesorero Mayor de Guerra in Madrid knew that such remittances had been effectively made, the farmers and treasurers of royal taxes had to inform him directly and, once this had been done, the Tesorero Mayor, and not his subordinate provincial treasurers and paymasters, sent the tax farmers and local treasurers a receipt recognizing the whole operation. Thanks to this, the Tesorero Mayor was perfectly aware of the amount of funds which arrived to his treasury.[24] As for the spending of such funds, the treasurers and paymasters were strictly and progressively more controlled. Treasurers and paymasters had to pay regularly the wages of the army, yet all extraordinary expenses needed an authorization. In order to avoid fraud, it was strictly forbidden to give cash to the army officers to purchase supplies and it was decided that all supplies needed by the royal armies should be provided directly by the financiers (*asentistas*) instead.[25] As result of such measures, during 1703–5 both the treasurers and the paymasters were tightly controlled from the centre, so, as Orry remarked in 1705, no funds were distributed to them without previously allocating what expenses they were going to satisfy.[26] The complaints of two members of Orry's team, Francisco Ronquillo and Melchor de Flores, are good proof that the new Tesorería Mayor set levels of internal control which had been virtually unknown in the Castilian administration until then.[27]

In return for a tighter internal control, and thanks to Orry's efforts, the control exerted by the Contaduría Mayor de Cuentas on the Tesorero Mayor was simplified and reduced. In 1703 it was decided that the Tesorero would have to send to the Contaduría the payment orders received and the receipts given to him by the beneficiaries of his payments to justify his work.[28] In practical terms, this had the consequence of replacing the ministers charged until then with the task of auditing the accounts of the royal armies, the traditional *contadores* and *veedores*, with new ones: the *comisarios de guerra*, introduced in November 1703 with the tasks of preparing the *revistas*, the military rolls used as basis for supplying the armies and paying the wages of officials and soldiers.[29] In September 1704, the military ordinances introduced a new post in this organization, creating the inspectorates of infantry and cavalry.[30] The *comisarios* were dismissed at the same time as the Tesorero Mayor in 1704, but they were reintroduced in June 1705. The traditional *contadores* and *veedores* preserved their posts, although losing all their power, as may be deduced from the fact that from 1703 the government only admitted those *revistas* compiled by the new *comisarios*. There is no doubt that this was consciously enforced by Orry, who, in fact, wanted to force the resignation of the *contadores* and *veedores* through this method and through the delays in the payment of their wages, as they remarked in 1705.[31]

A More Autonomous Treasurer

The reforms of the years 1703–5 introduced a war treasury to the centre of the Castilian administration. The war treasury was tightly controlled by the Tesorero and it was placed under the Secretario del despacho de Guerra, created in these years to supervise the Tesorero. I have studied the work of the first two *secretarios*, the Marquis of Canales and José Grimaldo, elsewhere. From the autumn of 1703 the *secretario* was in close correspondence with the military officials deployed in the provinces and with high-ranking military officials (*capitanes generales* and *gobernadores de armas*) to compile the rolls of the army and to provide the funds and supplies needed. Thank to this, the *secretarios* were well aware of the real extent of the needs of the army, and this helped them to supervise the work of the Tesorero Mayor.[32]

Far from dispensing with the services of the financiers, the reforms of 1703–5 meant exactly the opposite: from 1703 the war treasury was handed to one of them, the Count of Moriana, who was also allowed to select his subordinates. The new department escaped from the Contaduría Mayor de Cuentas. Not surprisingly, this raised the suspicions of the more traditional sections of the Castilian government, as may be gauged from the evidence provided by the governor of the finance council (Consejo de Hacienda) in 1705, Miguel Francisco Guerra, who voiced the opinion of the Tesorero Mayor prevailing in many circles of the Castilian government.[33]

According to him, while the old Tesorero General could not make any payment without the approval of the Contadores de la Razón, the Tesorero Mayor was only subordinated to the *contadores* when physically present in Madrid. All the payments made by him outside the capital or by the local treasurers were outside the power of the *contadores*, something unfair in Guerra's view, probably because this had allowed an unusual flexibility to the Tesorero. As for the incomes, only a small part of the funds arriving to the Tesorero were audited by the Contaduría Mayor de Cuentas, as it was nearly impossible to audit the rest.[34]

Complaints like these emphasize the key role played by the Tesorería Mayor de Guerra in the reforms introduced in 1703–5, and they also illustrate the strong opposition it aroused. Surely it is not by chance that, apart from the above-mentioned complaints of Portocarrero and Guerra, a stream of similar memorials arrived to the court during the same years from other councils, such as the powerful finances, Castile and war councils, high rank military officials, such as the Marquis of Villarías, Capitán General de Andalucía, the members of the Contaduría Mayor de Cuentas and the treasurers, *veedores* and *contadores de ejércitos*.[35]

Intentions and Evaluations

The strength of the opposition aroused by Orry's project raises two questions. First, why was it introduced, and second, why was it continued with such determination during the period? It would be impossible to explain the reform ignoring the pivotal role played by Orry and his supporters, yet it would be misleading to consider it as the heritage left by a particularly gifted foreign minister surrounded by a small group of brilliant supporters, because this would not explain what induced Philip V and his ministers to preserve the Tesorería Mayor during the war years and, especially, after the peace. Simultaneously, although it would be tempting to consider the reform as the Spanish copy of a set of measures successfully tested in France and imported thanks to the close relationship between the French and Spanish branches of the Bourbon dynasty, this does not explain why it was preserved after 1709 and 1714, when the relationship between the two crowns began to worsen.[36] Admittedly, the presence of elements imported from the French system in making the reform seem undeniable, yet it is probably more relevant to analyse why some Spanish ministers and politicians decided to support it.[37]

One good way of examining this is to try to find the groups which reaped the benefits of the changes brought by Orry. The problem here is that, given the shortcomings of our documentary sources, it is difficult to present a clear and definitive answer. Of course, the Secretarios del Despacho y Guerra, the Tesorero Mayor de Guerra, the staffs of the new departments and even some military officers and local ministers, such as Francisco de Ronquillo and the Prince of T'Serclaes, brother in law of Canales, supported the reform.[38] Yet, once we leave the narrow world of the court and the new departments created in 1703–5, is more difficult to know who the followers of the French financier were.

A clearer answer may be found through the study of the debate surrounding the activities of Orry, Canales and Moriana in 1704–5.[39] As has been previously remarked, during these nearly two years the reform suffered a temporary setback which caused the departure of Orry to France (in July 1704), the amalgamation of the Secretaría del Despacho de Guerra with the Secretaría del Despacho Universal (in Rivas's hands) and the resignation of the Tesorero Mayor, the Count of Moriana. This temporary halt was caused by problems in the supplies of barley and bread to the royal armies deployed in the Castilian and Extremaduran fronts, which prompted many inquiries carried out by French officials and ministers, such as the French ambassador, Gramont, and the war and foreign affairs ministers (Monsieur Chamillart and the Marquis of Torcy respectively). All these high-ranking ministers wondered about the convenience of reintroducing the Tesorería Mayor and the Secretaría del Despacho de Guerra, with or without Orry, and gave him a welcome chance to justify his work. Thanks to these inquiries it is possible to know the aims of the promoters of the reform and their evaluation of the results achieved during its first phase. The consolidation of the royal power was prominent in the list of objectives, but, from a short-term perspective, both the Tesorero Mayor and the *secretario* were expected to improve efficiency in raising and spending the funds devoted to the payment of the armies.

The real amount of the funds devoted to the army between October 1703 and October 1704 caused some controversy,[40] but the main debate was focused on its employment: to quote an example, Orry had always been ready to delay the payment of debts, while to Rivas this seemed a more urgent task. As for the question of the supplies, even Orry admitted that there had been difficulties, yet he had good reasons to justify them: a few weeks after reaching an agreement with a financier (*asentista*) to provide these supplies, the demand for rations had been unilaterally increased when the *asentista* was compelled to include the rations of the French reinforcements sent to Spain, and the course the military operations had caused unexpected changes in the places earmarked for the deliveries of bread to the armies. Of course, there had been some successes. In general terms, it was widely thought that the army's wages had been regularly paid, without serious delays. As for the reduction of the powers previously enjoyed by high-ranking military officials in the financial field, one of the main objectives of the reform, the outcome was less clear and, apart from Orry, only Puységur was ready to admit that this has been achieved. To finish, it should be emphasized that everybody shared Puységur's tribute to the beauty of the *estados* provided by Orry. Unfortunately, it is impossible to establish whether the word *estado* referred to the quality of the royal armies or to the accuracy of the financial accounts sent by Orry, yet it does not seem too wrong to assume that Puységur's praise reflected a fairly positive opinion of Orry's work.

The reasons invoked to favour the reintroduction of a *secretario* in charge of military affairs in the spring of 1705 confirm that this was one of the key points of the reform. It was supposed that the new *secretario* should be an expert both in military logistics, ranging from the delivery of supplies and funds to the armies to the nomination of the appropriate subordinates, and in financial matters he was empowered to arrange supply contracts with the financiers, replacing the old *consejos*. This helps to understand the importance conferred to the Tesorería Mayor de Guerra, directly subordinated to him, and ready to issue payment orders on his behalf in every part of the country.

A More Solid Public Credit

Although, as we have just outlined, some controversy surrounded the reform, its financial and political advantages were widely recognized. Everybody was convinced that the reintroduction of the Tesorero Mayor de la Guerra was a basic step to improving the funding of the royal armies, encouraging the financiers to lend money to the king. The emphasis on the financial accountability of the *secretario* and on the importance of the new Tesorero points to the possibility that the king's creditors might have occupied a prominent place in the ranks of the promoters of the reforms, together with soldiers and officials.[41]

Unfortunately, only a handful of documents deal with this possibility, but it should be borne in mind here that, in his presentation of the whole project to Philip V, Orry took care to observe that the multiplicity of centres empowered to take decisions in the field of military spending and the lack of coordination between them had lowered the quality of the *consignaciones* offered to the *asentistas*.[42] A more efficient way of paying the king's creditors, reducing delays and the subsequent rise in interest on the debt was, in Orry's view, one of the most promising results of his plan. Far from ending the contacts between the royal treasury and private financiers, then, Orry's real objective was to put the relationship between both groups on a new basis, creating a favourable environment for those *asentistas* ready to have dealings with the government.

A New Relationship with the *Asentistas*

The policy followed by Orry was the continuation of a programme first suggested to Philip V in 1701 and 1702, when he had supported the idea of introducing financiers in the control and management of the royal treasury.[43] According to him, it was convenient to reduce the multiplicity of local and provincial treasuries, using the services of big tax farmers to collect all the taxes levied in every fiscal district. This would simplify the fiscal system, lowering the collection costs of the taxes and reducing the opportunities for fraud. To attract the *asentistas*, Orry proposed changes in the rules according to which the taxes were traditionally farmed out, guaranteeing the tax farmers enough profits, longer contracts and protection from judicial prosecution. All this meant that the Crown could renounce the services of the galaxy of small financiers who had traditionally farmed the taxes and avoid the direct collection of them by the Crown's ministers. It also shows that, in Orry's view, the solution to the problems of the royal treasury rested on a profitable partnership between the government and the best financiers.

The reforms of 1703 were seen by Orry as the first step towards the implementation of the project presented in 1701–2.[44] Orry always considered that, thanks to the Secretario del Despacho de la Guerra, it would be easier to farm the royal taxes, and he decided to use the *asiento* of Manuel López de Castro in October 1703 to show it.[45] His idea was that, in return for supplying foodstuffs to the royal armies, Manuel López de Castro would obtain the collection of some taxes, so when the contract was signed in the last months of the year this *asentista* took over the collection of taxes levied on tobacco, paper, cards and *aguardiente* in the whole kingdom, together with other less important ones, being simultaneously placed under the special protection of the Marquis of Canales.[46]

Another project devised in 1701–2 helps us understand the objectives of the supporters of the reform. With the approval of Philip V and Louis XIV, Orry had devised an ambitious scheme to redeem the consolidated debt (the famous *juros*) through the sales of posts in the royal treasury to the owners of these titles, mainly businessmen and financiers. The idea was that venality could be used to reinforce the fidelity of the *juristas* to the dynasty. When combined with the above-mentioned intention of using the financiers as tax farmers, it seems obvious that Orry's idea was to promote the role of the financial community in the royal treasury, either on a permanent basis through the sales of offices, or on a more provisional one through the farm of taxes.[47] Although these projects were not finally implemented, certain marks of them are clearly visible in the redemption of public debt and in the sales of offices carried out during the War of Succession.[48] In any case, it is interesting to remark how the instigator of the reform always admitted that the services on behalf of the king carried out by those financiers serving in the ranks of the royal treasury had to be seen as something attractive, and that public service and private benefit were considered compatible. The ministers who evaluated his plans admitted the same conception of relations with financiers.[49]

Far-reaching changes were introduced the execution and auditing of military spending. During the spring of 1703 many contracts were negotiated to arrange the supplies of wheat and bread to the royal armies. After a first stage, when many ministers tried to arouse strong competition between the financiers, Manuel López de Castro obtained the *asiento*. A few days later, another minister let Orry know that a new and more advantageous offer had been presented, yet, after considering that the author of the new offer was virtually unknown in the financial community and that the breaking of a legal contract would ruin the confidence of the others financiers in the royal treasury, Orry refused to admit it. It was preferable to accept a lower prize in order to preserve the confidence of the *asentistas* both in Orry himself (who was the main negotiator, on the royal side, with the *asentistas*) and in the king's promises.[50] During the autumn of the same year Orry took a further step, turning to the same financiers as he had the previous spring. In the December 1703 *asiento* of Manuel López de Castro, the company of this powerful financier had farmed the taxes levied in many provinces, and in return López de Castro had committed to supply wheat and barley to the royal armies deployed in Andalucía, Castilla la Vieja, Extremadura and Galicia. In Orry's view, the advantages of this deal were clear. The king would not have to pay *anticipaciones* (funds paid in advance) to the *asentista*, either in cash or in *libranzas* (which usually involved the payment of interest),[51] so the royal treasury would make substantial savings. The possibility of ending the frauds traditionally carried out by royal officials such as *veedores*, *contadores*, *pagadores* and *proveedores* was one of the most important advantages of the contract. As for the *asentista*, his interest in the whole operation laid in the farming of some of the most important royal taxes and in the possibility of raising the value of his collections.[52]

More Flexible Payments and a More Efficient Control

The financial policy followed by Orry from 1703 was ruled by the purpose of restoring the king's credit, reinforcing the confidence of the *asentistas* in his word. To do that, Orry followed a two-fold strategy, first easing the participation of financiers in the financial administration, and second establishing rules securing them substantial profits. The introduction of the Tesorería Mayor de Guerra, placed under the Secretaría del Despacho de la Guerra, was the key. The new Tesorería offered two basic advantages to all those interested in financial dealings with the Crown.

First, as Orry frequently stressed, the Tesorería was ruled by a financier whose jurisdiction covered all the war theatres through a net of *tesoreros* and *pagadores*. The Tesorero had the autonomy needed to made payments everywhere. From the perspective of the king's creditors, the new Tesorería was much more flexible than the traditional departments of the government, and, to a certain extent, this could be considered the result of the importation of management methods from the private sector.[53] As an example, Moriana very often used bills of exchange. Simultaneously, the possibility of having clear intermediaries (treasurers and pay-masters at the local level; the Tesorero at the court) to solve any possible difficulty would have seemed to the *asentistas* a useful way of easing their work.

Second, by gathering together all the previously dispersed funds into a sin-gle treasury, it was possible to know at a glance the funds at the disposal of the Tesorero, as can be seen in some accounts compiled by order of Orry, Rivas and Gramont.[54] Simultaneously, the Secretarios del Despacho de Guerra, Canales y Grimaldo, requested and obtained monthly reports showing all the payments made by the army's paymasters.[55] Apart from improving the auditing capacities of the Tesorería, to those in charge of the funding of the royal armies (the Secretarios del Despacho de la Guerra and Orry), such improvements were an essential tool in their dealings with the *asentistas*. For example, the López de Castro *asiento* included an estimate of the amount of the fiscal incomes he was going to col-lect, together with another estimate of the global amount of the funds of the Tesorería.[56] It seems possible that such estimates were shown to the *asentista* to help him to overcome any reluctance in reaching an agreement with Orry, espe-cially when we remember that López de Castro had requested similar information concerning to the post of royal armies' supplier.[57] As we can see, then, the reforms and improvements in financial audit methods, which in another context may be interpreted as an instrument to repress dishonest financiers, were introduced here in their favour, and even at their request.

After considering all the evidence so far, it seems difficult to deny the role of Orry and his team in a reform whose main objective was to create a new partner-ship between the Crown and the financiers, yet it would be unfair to forget that the need for the changes introduced after 1703 was widely agreed by most of the Spanish ministers around Philip V, as may be gauged from the decisions adopted after the war.[58]

Were the Financiers the Authors of the Reform?

The reform of 1703 poses many other questions. The measures introduced by Orry succeeded because they addressed a set of problems which had been acutely felt during the previous decades by many of the Crown's ministers, yet there still remain many unsolved questions: did the financiers play any role in the proc-ess? If so, what was it? Could the success of the reform be explained by their active support? The documentary sources analysed so far do not allow definitive answers to these questions. In fact, they pose more questions than answers, but this does not prevent us from presenting some remarks which could be verified by further research.

To begin with, in his correspondence with Torcy and Chamillart, ministers of Louis XIV, Orry admitted that many of his Spanish informers were tax farmers.[59] Thanks to them, Orry improved his views on the need to reform tax collection methods and the norms ruling the farming of taxes, and he also discovered who might like to buy new offices and at what price.[60] The information provided to Orry by his Spanish interlocutors also extended to the field of military spending, and it helped him to have a clear view of the traffic developed around the *libranzas*.[61] Although he took good care never to disclose the identities of his sources, most of them seem to have been *asentistas* residing at the court. Manuel López de Castro, presented by one of Orry's enemies as a close friend of the French minister, may have been one of most important.[62] Orry was on good terms with López de Castro,[63] although he never referred to him as a trusted informant or a possible councillor. Moriana was first mentioned in Orry's letters at the end of September 1703, just before his nomination, being described as a sensible man who rejected the post of Tesorero Mayor for fear of the threats of the powerful Cardinal Portocarrero, so it does not seem that Moriana had a place in the group of promoters of the reform.[64] The last financier quoted (in 1702) as Orry's interlocutor was Juan de Sesma Díez Tejada, former member of the finance council, presented by Orry as someone with a deep knowledge of all aspects related to the king's incomes.[65] Although Orry never mentioned it, Sesma was linked through family and business connections with many of the big *asentistas* living at the court, such as the Marquis of Santiago, his father-in-law, and the famous Navarrese, Juan de Goyeneche.[66] Sesma could have provided valuable information to Orry on the funding of the royal armies and on the convenience of many reforms, yet the relationship between them would have been strained after the introduction of the Tesorería Mayor de Guerra because, as Orry was well aware, Sesma was a close ally of one his worst enemies, Portocarrero.

Orry gathered all the information he could from many financiers, some of them members of the financial administration, yet there is no proof that they were involved in the development of the idea of Tesorero Mayor de Guerra (although the possibility that Orry may have overlooked the importance of his sources in order to emphasize his own role should not be discarded). In any case, the fact that Orry mentioned such contacts in his correspondence is significant. On the one hand, it shows the French ministers to whom he sent his letters, and possibly even to Philip V himself, that there was nothing wrong in his contact with the financiers and that they welcomed the idea of being placed in the ranks of the financial administration. On the other hand, it leads to the conclusion that the Spanish financiers were always well informed of the Orry's real intentions and that their reaction led him to suppose that they accepted the reform.[67]

At the present stage, further research is clearly needed. It would be interesting to analyse the source of the credit enjoyed by Moriana and López de Castro, the two financiers on whose shoulders fell the burden of the reform. Did Orry expect that the personal credit of those financiers could reinforce the office of Tesorero Mayor and the function of provider? Or was the possibility of achieving control of the most important royal taxes opened to Moriana thanks to the reform that conferred him this credit, and not to his previous career? I cannot offer a clear answer to any of these questions. It is known that Moriana came from a long line of financiers with deep interests in the farming of royal taxes,[68] as was common in the *asentistas* community, yet he was not a particularly powerful or well-endowed member of the group. This suggests that Orry might have deliberately selected a competent, but not top-ranking, financier to fill the post of Tesorero in order to control him better, or even that Moriana was little more than the frontman of more influential financial groups. If that is the case, then it would be necessary to identify such groups to understand the later trajectory of both Moriana and the Tesorería.

This could clarify some aspects of the financial policy followed by the Spanish Crown during the first years of the eighteenth century. It is well known that a group of Navarrese financiers emerged from 1712 onwards as the most efficient and important group of Crown financiers, being the main beneficiaries of the new tax farming policy inaugurated during the War of the Spanish Succession in 1713–14.[69] It would be interesting to verify whether their active involvement in the financial dealings of the Crown was earlier than traditionally thought. What was their role during the years 1703–4? Were they simple spectators, perhaps not too opposed to the reform?[70] Or did they support the reform with their private credit? The nomination of one member of the group, José de Soraburu, in March 1706, as Tesorero de Guerra de Navarra, lends some credibility to the second possibility.[71] As long as we do not know who the interests behind Moriana were it is difficult to give a clear answer.

10 FRENCH PUBLIC FINANCE BETWEEN 1683 AND 1726

François R. Velde[1]

Introduction

From the Peace of the Pyrenees (1659) to Waterloo (1815), France was the dominant power in Europe. Meanwhile, Britain rose, politically and economically. Public finance is one of the areas where the contest and the contrast between the two powers is the clearest. Following a crucial political transformation in 1688,[2] Britain innovated and acquired the financial institutions and tools that enabled its final supremacy.[3] France, it would seem, let its size advantage fritter away and this stretch of time was just as much time lost.

On closer inspection, the picture is not so simple. I argue that the period of French financial history extending from 1683 to 1726 displays much turmoil, experimentation and innovation. France did not suffer from a lack of financial instruments, indeed some in 1720 probably thought it had far too many. As for institutions, they are all experiments that have succeeded, and thus cannot serve as explanations.

Successive French governments were aware of the contest in which they were engaged. The last wars of Louis XIV required extraordinary efforts to raise the necessary resources. After the king's death in 1715, there followed a period of ten years during which solutions were sought, debated, and tried. The brief French career of John Law, theorist and policymaker,[4] might seem exceptional, but was in fact emblematic. Partly to deflect attention from John Law, I will use the career of four famous but poorly-known financiers, the Paris brothers, as a thread through this narrative.

In the rest of this introduction I give a rapid biographical sketch of the Paris brothers, then describe the broad geopolitical context of the period I study and the fiscal and financial instruments then in use. The narrative itself is roughly chronological and naturally divided in three by the John Law episode. I emphasize the innovations in the periods before, during, and after Law.

The Paris Brothers

Who are these famous but poorly known figures of French financial history? The Paris brothers were the children of Jean Paris (1643–97) and Justine Trenannay La Montagne (d. 1722).[5] Of the seventeen children of this marriage, four rose to prominence, and were distinguished from each other, in the custom of their native Dauphiné, by nicknames: Antoine Paris the elder (1668–1733), Claude Paris La Montagne (1670–1744), Joseph Paris Duverney (1684–1770) and Jean Paris de Monmartel (1690–1766). Given the age differences, the quartet was really formed of two pairs. Antoine and Claude, the older pair, led the family affairs until their fall from grace in 1726, and although they both lived to see the family's return to favour in 1732, their career was effectively ended. Joseph and Jean, the younger pair, embarked on a second career that lasted until the 1760s: this second career, which owed much to the prominence of their protégée, the Marquise de Pompadour,[6] will not occupy us here.[7]

The family came from Moirans, a small town in the Dauphiné. In 1675, Jean Paris took over the inn founded by his wife's grandfather and became a prominent citizen of the town, rising to the position of consul (alderman) and, when the office was created in 1693, he became the first mayor of the town. The family's entry into finances came with the Nine Years War (1688–97). Savoy having allied itself with the Netherlands and England against France, an army was sent to Dauphiné to attack the duchy. In 1690, the father, who was a merchant as well as an innkeeper, successfully took up the task of providing the army with food. At the end of the war, Antoine and Claude went to Paris to collect on some of their debts, and with the help of a cousin and cloth merchant they were introduced to various officials in the finance ministry. When the War of Spanish Succession began in 1701, Antoine and Claude went into business again, providing food for the armies in the Low Countries and Germany, and training their younger brothers Joseph and Jean. They forged close ties with the indispensable banker of the time, Samuel Bernard. By the end of the war, Antoine had become receiver general of direct taxes in Dauphiné (a position in which he first experimented with new accounting methods), Claude was a *secrétaire du Roi* (an honorary but prestigious position), and Jean was general treasurer of the *Ponts et Chaussées*. They had thus become part of the financier establishment.[8]

The rest of their career (up to 1726) falls in two phases, separated by the interlude of John Law's System: 1716–19 and 1721–6. In the first phase, the Paris brothers completely reformed the collection of direct taxes, introducing double-entry bookkeeping and close monitoring of tax collection, oversaw the Visa of 1716 which reduced and consolidated the floating debt inherited from the war, and began the reform of the collection of indirect taxes (the general farms). During the second phase, their influence reached its highest point. The Paris brothers liquidated the enormous debt left over from John Law's System in the Visa of 1721–3, continued their accounting reforms, and implemented the financial policies of the government of the Duke of Bourbon (1723–6). The fall from power of the latter precipitated their exile in 1726.

We are relatively well informed about these important figures because they wrote considerable amounts of material. Much is lost, but some has survived. The most important document is an autobiography composed in 1729 by Claude for his children, known as 'Discours de Paris La Montagne à ses enfants', which I use heavily here.[9]

The Geopolitical Context

Chart 10.1 shows military expenditures (war and navy) in France from 1662 to 1816. The period captures of all of the wars between two defining moments in European history, the Peace of Westphalia in 1648 and the Peace of Vienna in 1815. For comparison purposes, I calculated the HP-filtered trend for peacetime expenditures. The trend indicates a long-term upward movement in the peacetime level, partly due to secular inflation. To better compare military expenditures over such a long period of time, Chart 10.2 shows the percentage deviation from this peacetime trend.

Chart 10.1: Military Spending in France, 1662–1816 (in francs or 1726 *livres*). The smooth line is the HP-filtered trend for spending in peace years.

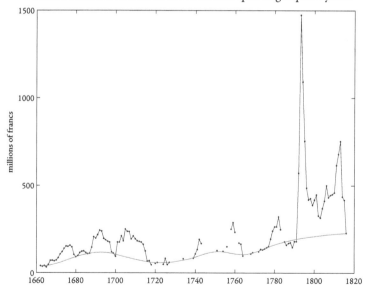

Chart 10.2: Military Spending in France, 1662–1816 (in percentage deviation from the peacetime trend).

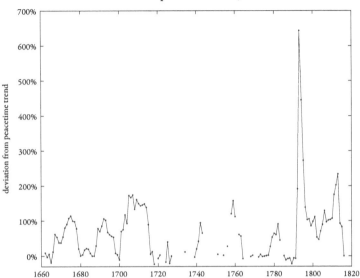

As is well known, the main source of variation in government spending came from wars: non-military spending (excluding debt service) was relatively small and varied much less. Each of the peaks in Chart 10.1 is recognizable as one of the periodic European wars in which France was engaged. In spite of gaps in the sources, especially for the eighteenth century, the graph shows that the last two wars of Louis XIV (from 1689 to 1713) were very long and costly. Not until the wars of the Revolution and Napoleonic period did France exert similar military efforts.

A discussion of the causes and value of wars is outside the scope of this paper. A few points can nevertheless be made. First, aside from 1792–3 and 1814, France did not fight on her territory: the Low Countries, Germany, Italy and Spain were the main theatres in Europe. This is because she did not fight to defend her borders so much as to establish and maintain hegemony over the continent, either by outright conquests or else by imposing her will on others. Second, France usually had allies, but in most of these wars (and in all but one after 1688), Britain was her adversary, bent on countering her attempt at hegemony. For this reason, this century and a half has been called the second Hundred Years War. Third, from a purely geopolitical perspective, the end result of these wars was essentially a draw. From 1648 to 1793 France steadily increased its size and population by a total of 18 per cent, gaining Alsace, Roussillon, Franche-Comté, Lorraine, parts of Flanders and Hainaut, Comtat-Venaissin, Savoie and Nice.[10] In this sense, the wars achieved one of the main goals of French policy since the early seventeenth century, Richelieu's *pré carré* with natural boundaries at the Alps and the Rhine. But the overarching goal of hegemony over Europe was only partially achieved. The Austrian Habsburg monarchy was weakened, but to the benefit of Prussia. Kindred Bourbon dynasties took root in Spain and Italy, but the rise of northern Europe (the Netherlands and Britain) lessened this success in southern Europe. And, in the course of these wars, France was unable to protect her colonial empire, losing all but Haiti and a handful of Caribbean islands in 1763 (although the value of these colonies was highly debatable).

The Tools of Public Finance

Financing these wars, for better or for worse, was the main challenge of public finance. It is clear from the high variance in military expenditures that these conflicts could not be financed in the traditional medieval way, namely by increased taxation in wartime. Raising taxes remained an important tool, and some of the innovations took place on the fiscal side, but tax-smoothing was a necessity. Financing meant borrowing, in some form or other, during the wars, and managing the resulting debt in peacetime.

The Problem as it was Seen

In August 1722, the rRegent of France began to instruct the twelve-year old king on the affairs of state. The main topics to cover were public finance, war and foreign affairs. The regent began his first lesson in public finance by explaining that 'the King can be rich only inasmuch as his subjects are so' and the application of this principle was that

> an exact proportion must be kept between the sums that the King demands of his subjects and their abilities. To reach an exact knowledge of this proportion would require discovering the subjects' resources, but they are unknown, and there is no feasible way to find out what each individual owns. Therefore we must limit ourselves to examining the highest taxes that the peoples bore without seeing their prosperity affected, and compare the circumstances of these taxes with our own.

This in turn leads to a detailed study of each type of tax and the variations of its yield: 'the causes of increases and decreases being well understood will allow us to know what support the peoples can give to the State's expenditures and what precautions must be taken so that the collection of these sums do not ruin them'. In a second step, the expenditures must be set according to the capabilities of the taxpayers.[11] Thus, the government was not oblivious to the impact of taxation on the economy. It saw its main constraint as the maximum sustainable level of taxation compatible with prosperity, and tried to set its level of expenditures (including the service of the debt) to match this ceiling estimated from past data.

The Numbers

To review the main fiscal tools, Table 10.1 presents fiscal revenues in selected peacetime years. The first is the year that Colbert died, the second falls in the brief interlude of peace between the two major wars of Louis XIV, the third at the death of the Sun King, and the last is at the end of the period I study. The table follows the traditional breakdown into indirect and direct taxes, which can be understood in a variety of ways.

Table 10.1: Revenues of the French State, 1683–1715. The *livre* index measures the silver content of the unit of account (1 in 1715).[12]

	1683	1700	1715	1725
Indirect Taxes				
United Farms	62.8	58.6	47.0	77.7
Other Farms	2.2	8.0	12.9	26.3
Direct Taxes				
Taille and Misc.	47.7	41.6	51.8	80.9
Capitation	–	–		25.8
Dixième	–	–		24.0
Royal Demesne				
Woods, Incidental	3.4	4.0	3.9	6.2
Total	116.0	112.1	165.6	191.1
Livre Index	1.05	0.92	1.00	0.67
Total (constant *Livres*)	121.4	103.5	165.6	128.9

Indirect taxes are taxes on consumption, levied at some point along the chain of production of the taxed good. The bulk of indirect taxes comprised five main elements: the salt monopoly on distribution to consumers, with mandatory minimum per capita purchases (*gabelles*), beer and wine taxes (*aides*), duties levied at internal and external boundaries (*traites*), tariffs at the gates of Paris (*entrées*) and various regalian rights (*domaines*). By 1680, these five groups of taxes had been collected into a single farming contract on a standard six-year lease. Tax farming, medieval in origin and widespread in seventeenth-century Europe, was relatively straightforward: private entrepreneurs bid at an open auction and the highest bidder carried the lease. For the duration of the lease (typically six to nine years), the lessee made an annual payment equal to his original bid and collected the specified taxes. The tax rates were set by the king beforehand: any increase or decrease in tax rates were made up at the end of the contract. Disputes between taxpayers and the lessee were handled by specialized tax courts (the *cours des aides*).

Direct taxes were taxes levied on individuals rather than on goods, and were somewhat closer to income or wealth taxes. In 1683, the only one was the *taille*, levied on commoners since the fifteenth century. The king decided every year on the amount he would levy (the *brevet de la taille*), which was then allocated among the various provinces based on information supplied by the king's officials, the *intendants*.[13] Each intendant in turn allocated his province's tax liability between districts, and so on down to the parish level, where residents figured out how to apportion their liability between themselves. The collection was entrusted to local receivers, who in turn sent the monies to the receivers general, who paid off expenses assigned on those revenues and returned the rest to the royal treasury. In some ways this form of tax collection was not dissimilar to tax farming: the receivers were obliged to turn over a fixed sum within fifteen months: how much they actually collected, and what they did with the funds in the meantime was up to them. It was well known, and perfectly acceptable, that they used the funds to provide liquidity and short-term lending.

This method was applicable in the provinces that were French in the mid-fifteenth century. When new provinces were annexed by inheritance or conquest, they were allowed to negotiate with the king the amount they would pay in lieu of the *taille*, and to levy the amount themselves. Thus the *pays d'État* (roughly, provinces acquired from 1450 to 1550) and the *pays conquis* (acquisitions after 1550) collected the equivalent of the taille themselves.[14] As the Paris brothers noted,[15] this tax also had an element of tax farming in it, namely the insurance aspect: the sum negotiated with the local estates (which did not meet every year) was constant for several years like a lease price.

Chart 10.3: Primary Surplus and Debt Service (interest payment) in France, 1662–1715.

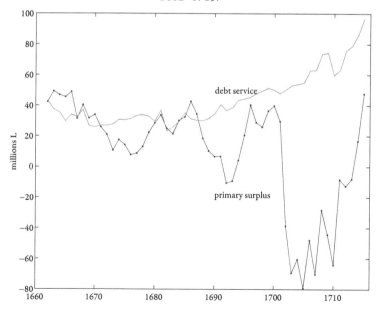

Chart 10.3 shows the evolution of the primary surplus (revenues less non-debt spending).[16] The figure highlights the main features of the time. The medium-

term movements in the primary surplus are driven by wars (each fall in the primary surplus carries the name of a conflict). The first half of the reign (1660–85) looks different from the second half (1685–1715): wars were shorter and better managed financially. By 1715, in spite of a partial default (the fall in debt service in 1713) and serious efforts at cutting spending and increasing tax revenue (the rise in the surplus in 1715 and 1716), a large gap remains in 1716 as the Regency begins.

Emergency as the Mother of Invention (1683–1715)

The 'Great Colbert', who would remain the beacon and exemplar of French public finance and administration until the Revolution,[17] died in 1683. His legacy survived through his nephew Nicolas Desmarets, who was the most senior official under the finance minister, Chamillart, from 1703 and his successor as minister from 1708 to 1715. Colbert's influence continued through Desmarets's protégés and admirers such as Noailles and the Paris brothers. But the great minister, who started his administration with a default in 1661 and spent twenty years establishing the framework within which finances continued to operate until the Revolution, never faced as difficult a task as his successors. How did France marshal the resources that it did during the grim second half of Louis XIV's reign?

Direct Taxation

In Table 10.1, there seems to be little difference between 1683 and 1700, but the war saw one major innovation, the introduction of a new direct tax called the *capitation*. As its name suggests, it was a per capita tax. The *taille* was assessed on a geographical basis first, then broken down at the village level between inhabitants. The resulting inequalities between taxpayers of different villages or provinces were well known. The *capitation* tax, instead, was based on each head of household's social status: 22 classes were defined nationwide, with corresponding taxes ranging from 2,000 francs to 1 franc. No lay person was exempt except the king (the first name in the highest category was the heir apparent); the clergy offered a lump-sum contribution. Moreover, the collection of the tax, and the resolution of disputes related to it, was entrusted to the king's officials, the *intendants*. Its yield in the 1690s was about 24 million francs per year, a sizeable addition to annual revenues. The tax was to cease with the war, and it did, punctually, in March 1698. But it was levied again from March 1701, and one of Louis XIV's last acts was to make it permanent. In its second incarnation the *capitation* was beginning to look like the *taille*, with nominal amounts assessed for each province, and self-assessment for certain groups such as the nobility, judicial officers, Paris residents, etc. In 1708 the king offered to rebate the tax to certain groups in exchange for lump-sum payments, the so-called *abonnements*.[18] The offer was taken up by the clergy as a whole, and by provinces like Languedoc and Provence.

The War of Spanish Succession led to another tax, this one more explicitly on income, the *dixième* (tenth). Levied in October 1710 after the breakdown in peace negotiations, it played a role in convincing the Allies that France was not as destitute as they had imagined. It was again a wartime tax, which ceased in 1717, and was restored from 1733 to 1737 for the War of Polish Succession and again from 1740 to 1748 for the War of the Austrian Succession. It became permanent after the Seven Years War under the different name of *vingtième*. In principle, individual assessments were to be decided centrally in Paris, but quickly, under the pressure of the emergency, the form of tax collection devolved into another simile of the *taille*. Provinces were allowed to buy themselves out, the tax collection on certain groups was in effect farmed out, the clergy once again offered a lump-sum payment, etc.

Both taxes represented major innovations for French finances:[19] they were the first new direct taxes since the fifteenth century, and were based (at least ideally) on nominal lists and assessments of each individual's income or status, even if their practice was far from the income taxes we know. Where both taxes retained a medieval flavour was in their duration. Consistent with the original theory of taxes as an 'aid' to the king, they were to last only for the duration of the emergency. This theory made sense only when the increase of expenditures could be matched by the increase in taxes, obviating the need for debt. Thus, these innovations, as initially implemented, were of little use for supporting debt. As the eighteenth century progressed the taxes were made more permanent, and long-term loans were issued on the basis of their revenues in the 1740s.[20]

Indirect Taxation

Change among indirect taxes came not so much from new taxes as from experimentation with tax farming. The near-complete monopoly set up by Colbert did not survive very long, as the increase in other farm revenues shows. Nor was it really a monopoly, contrary to appearances: the general farmers typically turned around and subleased tax collections (by type of tax and by region) to 'subfarms' (*sous-fermes*). Furthermore, when new indirect taxes were created during the wars, they were farmed out on separate contracts, not to the general farms. The years 1725 and 1726 mark the high point of a process of dismemberment of the monopoly in search of more competition among lessees, sometimes at the risk of inefficiencies, as when a given tax and a 10 per cent surcharge on that tax (the *deux sols pour livre*) were farmed separately (I return to this later).

Here too, looking at peace years masks some wartime changes. The lease contract placed all the risk on the lessee: if tax collection fell short of his annual payment, he was expected to make up the loss from his funds, but conversely the profit was also his. In practice, lessees sometimes defaulted, particularly during wartime when tax collection fell drastically short. This happened in 1709, and the united farms were placed under direct administration (*en régie*): the same person-nel remained in place, but salaried rather than as tax farmers. Only in 1716 was the united farm lease reconstituted. The same process occurred after the end of Law's System: the general farms were run by the farmers for the king's profit (or loss) until 1726. Only after 1726 did the general farms gradually evolve into the familiar centralized, for-profit behemoth.[21]

Long-Term Borrowing

Contrary to the theory behind the wartime levies of the *capitation* and the *dix-ième*, the budget was not balanced during wars. Typically, the government went into deficit and financed expenditures with a mixture of short-term and long-term debt. The short-term debt was converted into long-term debt after the hostilities ended, and (conditions permitting) the long-term debt was converted into lower-interest long-term debt as market interest rates fell. Conversions were possible because the long-term debt traditionally issued was a perpetual annu-ity (*rente perpétuelle*). As with privately-issued annuities, the creditor could not demand payment, but the debtor could redeem the debt at any time. This model worked well for the first half of the reign, until 1685, and Colbert was able to successfully carry out a (voluntary) debt conversion in 1680. Another conversion was carried out partially in 1698 and 1699. Finally, John Law's conversion of the whole debt into equity of the Indies Company in 1719 also used this feature. It is curious that, while Britain's consolidation of its debt into redeemable annuities in the mid-eighteenth century is often seen as a crucial step in its financial develop-ment, France, which had the right tool, relinquished its use. Perpetual annuities were rarely issued after 1720, most borrowing being done either in fixed-term loans or in life annuities.[22]

The other main form of long-term borrowing was through the sale of offices. An officer was someone who held a government position not on commission or at the king's leave, but as of right, and enjoyed various privileges attached to the position (in particular the collection of fees related to his activities). Offices were sold (to qualified purchasers), and the king paid interest on the original sale price, which was called the wages of the office (*gages*). A wage increase was really a forced loan, requiring the officer to put up the additional capital. Officers could not be removed except for misconduct; however, the office itself could be abolished, as long as the king repaid the original sum. Thus, offices as a form of debt also car-ried the same repayment option as annuities. Creation of offices was a feature of wartime, and the War of Spanish Succession gave rise to extraordinary ingenuity in the invention of new offices by the thousands. Offices and annuities could be transferred or sold, but with fairly high transaction costs. Both were considered forms of real estate, and could be mortgaged.

To the extent that the main attraction of an office was the right to collect a fee of some kind, the creation of offices was very similar to another type of operation, which consisted in both creating a new tax (levied for a fixed period of time) and selling the right to collect it in exchange for a lump-sum payment: this combined into a single operation the creation of a tax and the issue of a loan backed by the revenues of the tax, in an efficient manner (subject to the caveat that the government had to properly estimate the future revenues of the new tax).

In some cases we see the government alternating between offices and tax farming for the same tax. For example, in 1705 a hundred offices of inspectors of oils were established in Paris and another hundred in the rest of France: they were given a fee for every pound of oil they 'inspected'. In 1710 the offices were abolished and the fees converted into taxes to repay the finances of the offices; but the right to collect the tax was farmed for eight years in exchange for a total of 3 million *livres*, of which 2.6 million *livres* were immediately paid to the treasury. Likewise the *contrôle des exploits* (a fee on court filings) was collected by officers from 1691 to 1698, then again from 1704 to 1713; the rest of the time by farmers. The creation of offices (in 1691 and in 1704) allowed the raising of a loan backed by the tax: the suppression of offices (in 1698 and in 1713) allowed the refinancing of the loan.[23]

In the late seventeenth century the French government, like others in Europe, had begun experimenting with life annuities (1693) and tontines (1689).[24] In 1700, taking advantage of a craze for private lotteries, the government sold 0.5 million *livres* in life annuities for 10.4 million *livres*, at a rate of 4.8 per cent far lower than the actuarially fair 7–14 per cent it had offered on the same amount of annuities in July 1698. The sum was raised by selling 400,000 tickets at 26 *livres* each, for which 475 prizes ranging from 400 to 20,000 *livres* were awarded.[25] The government explicitly allowed the formation of associations to buy blocks of tickets and made it possible to divide the prizes as long as the resulting annuities were no smaller than 75 *livres* (a quarter of the smallest prize). Use of lotteries to lower the cost of debt continued on and off until the Revolution.

Monetary Manipulations

The peacetime snapshot misses a large number of alternative sources of revenues. Aside from many small indirect taxes levied and auctioned off (often for a single upfront payment), a major source of revenue was seigniorage, which added about 100 million over the course of each war, not far from a year's worth of peacetime revenue.

The monetary system of the time consisted of two distinct elements.[26] One was made up of the monetary objects themselves, coins made of gold and silver bearing the king's effigy but no indication of value. The specifics of the coins (weight, fineness, size, imprint) are set by edicts of the king. The other was the unit of account, the *livre* or *franc*. The use of the *livre* is general and required for all contracts and debts, including bills of foreign exchange. The relation between the two elements is set by the king with an order in council (*arrêt du conseil*) which has immediate effect and is not subject to control or registration in any court. In other words, the king can, literally overnight, change the legal tender value of coins.

The use of monetary manipulations to generate seigniorage had by and large ceased with the Hundred Years War in the fifteenth century. Changes in legal tender values were henceforth used to adjust legal values of coins with their relative values in the market (either bimetallic issues, or small change problems).[27] From 1640 to 1686, the French coinage and its legal tender values had been stable. In 1676, Colbert had even abolished seigniorage altogether, on the English model. From 1690 to 1726, however, France experimented with a new form of currency manipulation inspired by Spanish practices of the early seventeenth century.

A reformation consists in levying a tax on the whole stock of coinage. To do so, the following method is used. The legal tender value of each coin is increased from 1 to 1+x, but only in exchange for a payment by the coin-holder of y with 0<y<x. To verify that the payment has been made, the coin needs to be surrendered to the mint where it will be restamped with a new design ('reformed').[28] The change in values is declared to be permanent; in practice, however, the government after a while decides to return to the old face value of coins, and announces a decreasing path of face values for the coin: $\{1+x(t_i)\}_{i=1,\,...}$ returning the coin to its original value of 1. If the situation requires it, the operation is repeated. This was carried out in 1690, 1693, 1701, 1704 and 1715. More traditional forced recoinages (where all coins are demonetized and everyone is obliged to buy new legal tender at the mint and pay the seigniorage rate) occurred in 1709, 1718, 1720 and 1726. Chart 10.4 shows the mint equivalent (the face value of a fixed weight of coins) and the mint price over time; the distance between the two lines measures the seigniorage rate, and the monetary reforms are plainly visible.

The money stock in 1690 was estimated to be about 500 million (in pre-1690 *livres*) and the first reform was fairly successful, since minting amounted to about 85 per cent of the existing stock. Later ones were less successful. Individuals were less willing over time to submit to the tax as they knew from experience that the operation would soon be reversed and that demonetized old coins would in fact be remonetized at a later date. Also, counterfeiting proved to be an increasing problem, as people shipped their coins abroad to have them restamped by foreign competitors out of the reach of enforcement. In the 1709 reform, the weights and sizes of coins were changed so as to make counterfeiting more difficult. The difficulty of extracting profit from the operation is suggested by the rising seigniorage rates.

The monetary reforms and recoinages of 1690, 1693, 1701, 1704 and 1709 all took place in wartime. The recoinage of 1720 can be excused in part as a recreation of the coinage after the disorders of the Law period. But the reforms of 1715,

Chart 10.4: Mint Equivalent (upper line) and Mint Price (lower line) of Silver in France, 1685–1730.

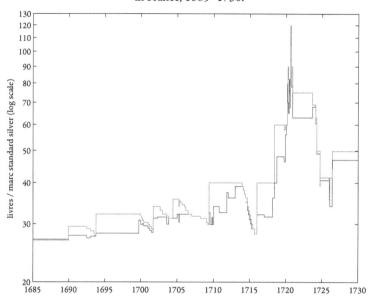

1718 and 1726, although carried out in peacetime, are clearly on the same pattern as the wartime reforms. Although governments were never too proud when resorting to this method (and faced vehement political opposition in the unmuzzled parliament in 1718), it seemed difficult to dispense with it. It is all the more remarkable that 1726 marks the last instance of a seigniorage-driven debasement in French history.

Short-Term Borrowing

The flows of revenues and expenditures were very complex, because of the multiplicity of individuals involved in the collection and disbursement (the Paris brothers speak of eight to nine thousand *comptables*). For direct taxes, the receivers general collected sums from the local receivers; for indirect taxes, the farmers often subcontracted to 'sub-farmers' by tax and by region. Similarly, the royal treasury was but one of a number of treasuries. Various individuals with the authority to spend funds (e.g., the ministers) issued orders to their respective general treasurers to disburse funds (they, in turn, typically had local treasurers in various provinces). The finance minister funded the treasurers by issuing orders to the tax collectors to transfer funds. If the treasurers lacked the funds in cash, they could issue promissory notes payable at a future date. Likewise, the finance minister could specify that the transfer be carried out at some future date. To net out the cash flows from the provinces to Paris and back to the provinces, the minister often ordered a local receiver to transfer his funds directly to a local treasurer rather than to the general receiver of his province.

In practice the treasurers' notes, as well as as the minister's orders, were negotiable instruments, bearing a variety of names such as *billets d'emprunts, billets de subsistance* (issued to military officers to pay their expenses), *assignations, rescriptions, promesses*, etc. These instruments were endorsable and negotiable. It was often said that the king was using the credit of private parties for his purposes, and it is true that some were legally the liabilities of of their issuers, but others were like cheques written by the government on its tax collectors, and nothing prevented the former from going overdrawn. The promissory notes were indeed frequently rolled over until payments were suspended, as happened in October 1710 for the assignations on the revenues of the next three years, which were converted into perpetual annuities at 5 per cent. Similar suspensions occurred in 1759 and in 1770, as a consequence of the Seven Years War. These operations amount to refinancing short-term into long-term debt.

Colbert had created a new institution in October 1674, the *Caisse des emprunts*, a facility where private parties could buy short-term loans from (lend to) the government. Dissolved after his death, it was recreated in March 1702 and backed by the credit of the salt tax collectors; these notes came to be known as the *promesse des gabelles*. They were bearer bonds, carrying 8–10 per cent interest. Their reimbursement was suspended in October 1704, the interest reduced to 5 per cent in October 1710, and reimbursement resumed on a limited basis (6 million per year) in 1713.

Finally, another sort of paper was issued in 1710. A common treasury was created to collect all the payments of the receivers general (the direct taxes), and it issued its own notes in part to redeem some of the existing paper, in part to finance continuing expenditures. These notes were known by the name of the cashier, as the *billets Legendre*.

There existed an active over-the-counter market in these instruments, as witnessed by the numerous quotations in the *Gazette d'Amsterdam* from January 1711 to May 1715.[29] Chart 10.5 displays the implicit interest rate (coupon/price ratio) in the prices for perpetual annuities (*rentes*), *promesse des gabelles* and *billets d'État* which will be discussed shortly. The rates are high, although Sussman and Yafeh have recently argued that British rates remained at a similar level long after the Glorious Revolution.[30]

Chart 10.5: Interest Rate on Various Liabilities of the French Government, 1711–19.[31]

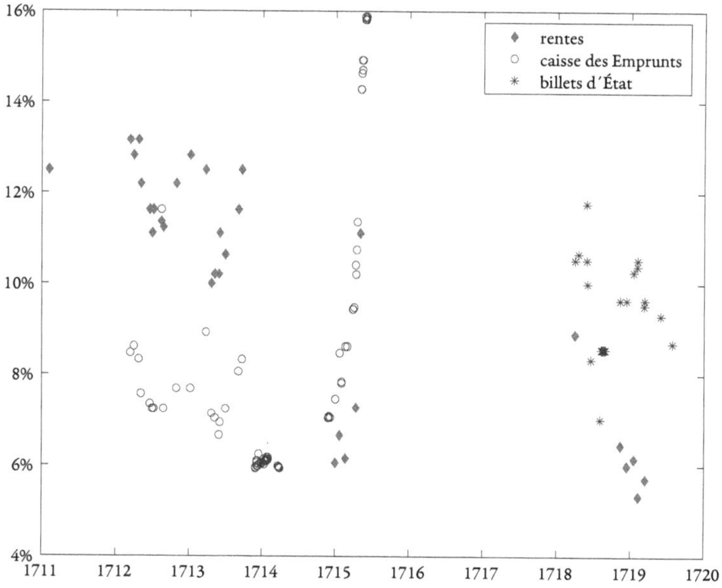

The Billets de Monnaie

The monetary reforms of the War of Spanish Succession occasioned one early experiment in paper money.[32] When the reform of 1701 started, the mints did not have sufficient inventories of bullion on hand to pay for old coins with new coins immediately, and even though restamping (instead of melting) reduced the turnaround time, it was still not possible to return the restamped coins immediately to their owners. The mint directors began to deliver receipts payable to the bearer for the exact amount brought in, to be redeemed a few days or weeks later in restamped coins. These *billets de monnaie* were issued in increasing quantities, and their redemption postponed repeatedly, although they were given an interest. The government started issuing them to make payments rather than for their original purpose. When the reform of 1704 ended in 1706, there was no way to redeem them in restamped coins. They were made legal tender for private debts in Paris (including for bills of exchange) in August 1706, then legal tender for a quarter of all payments in October 1706. They ceased to bear interest, and were reissued on demand in smaller standardized denominations (200 *livres*, then 50 *livres*). In 1707, they ceased to be legal tender, and were converted partly in five-year notes on the tax collectors (54 million *livres*) and partly in circulating notes ultimately redeemable for perpetual annuities (72 million *livres*). From October 1707 to February 1708 they were again made compulsory tender for a fraction of all payments. Most of the remaining billets were retired through the reminting of May 1709. All coins were to be reminted, subject to an 18.75 per cent seigniorage tax, of which 16.67 per cent was payable in *billets de monnaie*. The rest was eventually converted into perpetual or life annuities and they were withdrawn from circulation in October 1711.

The Visa of 1716

The mass of floating debt created during the War of Spanish Succession, a total of 596 million *livres*, was subjected in December 1715 to a liquidation process directed by the Paris brothers. All notes had to be submitted to commissioners who would verify the validity of the claims and liquidate them to a nominal value, for which a new form of instrument would be issued. These bearer bonds were called *billets d'État*, carrying a 4 per cent interest with no specified redemption date. A total of 250 million *livres* were issued, although only 198 million represented conversion of the existing notes; the rest was used by the treasury to finance its deficit.[33]

A reduction from 596 million to 198 million looks like a disguised default, and the Visa of 1716 is often described in these terms. However, it was the occasion for a wholesale examination of the accounts of the war, and it is not clear what proportion represented an audit of the notoriously unscrupulous methods of financiers and accountants. An example illustrates the point. A decree of 2 May 1716 appointed François Brehamel to examine the accounts of the treasurers of war expenditures (*trésoriers de l'extraordinaire des guerres*).[34] At his suggestion, Brehamel was promised a 10 per cent bonus on all the notes of the treasurers he could identify as having been lost, and therefore for which the treasurers could be held accountable in discharge to the king's obligations. From his after-death inventory[35] it is possible to determine that he earned a total of 206,544 *livres* as a result: in other words, he alone managed to cancel over 2 million *livres* of the king's obligations.[36] In the end, 110 million of the reduction operated by the Visa represented double accounting, and 100 million represented expenditures that were appropriated but never made by the treasurers; thus the actual reduction operated by the Visa was only 49 per cent.[37] The Visa had other advantages: the Paris brothers were able to start from the clean slate created by this audit to initiate their accounting reforms among the receivers general (see below).

What became of the *billets d'État*? The interest payments (a total of 10 million) were assigned on several farms whose income was already pledged, and the payment of the interest remained uncertain. Ultimately, they were eliminated through a variety of channels, the most important being the seigniorage tax levied by the reformation of May 1718, which was partially payable in *billets d'État*, and the creation of John Law's companies (the Banque and more importantly the Company of the West).

The John Law Episode (1716–20)

I will not retrace here the long and complex episode known as John Law's System,[38] but rather describe its most innovative aspects. Suffice it to say that John Law, who arrived in France in 1712 or 1713 with proposals to improve the government's credit, was finally allowed in May 1716 to establish a privately-owned bank issuing notes payable to the bearer on demand into specie of a particular type. Soon after, he launched a venture to develop the hitherto profitless colony of Louisiana, under the name of the Company of the West. Both companies began with initial public offerings of shares payable in the form of *billets d'État*, which became the Company's assets and provided working capital through the earned interest. To better ensure the payment of the interest, Law proposed to take over the tobacco monopoly farm on which they were assigned, and cancel out the interest payment with the lease price. This started the Company on a series of mergers and acquisitions that led to its merger with the existing French Indies Company, whose name it took. By December 1718, the bank, which took credit for the coincident economic recovery, was nationalized and became accountable only to the king, and, in practice, wholly managed at the discretion of Law.

The summer of 1719 brought far-reaching changes in Law's operations. Having bought out virtually all the trading companies then in existence, the Indies Company branched into tax collection and mint management. In August 1719, it had the existing lease on the general farms rescinded, and was awarded a new lease. At the same time, it proposed refinancing the whole national debt at a lower interest rate. To finance this gigantic operation, the Company proceeded as it had done with its earlier acquisitions, with further share issues, at prices that tracked the bullish market. The operation ended up being a conversion of government debt into equity in a company that, at the same time, collected virtually all the taxes in France. I call this 'government equity'.

The plan might have worked, but a particular feature of the share issues, a form of down-payment and instalment plan, made the operation contingent on the former bondholders being willing to exercise options on the shares of the Company. To induce them to do so, Law felt compelled to sustain a rising share price, through covert and then overprice manipulations and interventions on the stock market. For this purpose, the bank proved very convenient, as further note issues went essentially unchecked. By January 1720, when Law became finance minister and seemingly omnipotent, the system's apparent success pushed the British authorities into their own version of the scheme with the South Sea Company.

Law's peak was short: the price support for the shares had the effect of monetizing the debt and unleashing foreign exchange depreciation and incipient inflation. Law tried to contain this side effect by demonetizing gold and silver coinage to shore up the demand for his currency; then, he tried to reduce the nominal money supply in the way governments before him had done, by cutting the nominal value of notes and shares in May 1720. This led to a run on the bank and a major crisis of confidence. Law briefly lost his position as finance minister, but was partially reinstated. He spent another six months searching for ways to save the Company and his bank, reducing the money supply by other means (purchasing notes on the open market where they were sold at a heavy discount, issuing more shares, creating bank accounts modelled on the Bank of Amsterdam). Finally, in the autumn of 1720, he demonetized the notes. The Company, meanwhile, had exhausted its funds and was nearing bankruptcy, which meant the government itself was broke as well. In December 1720, he fled France; cleaning up the wreck would be left to others.

Centralization of the Fiscal System

Although Law had made plans to radically change France's taxation system, as others such as Vauban had proposed before him, he never came near to implementing such changes. Nevertheless, the brief period in 1719–20 was as close to a rational and centralized fiscal system as France ever got before the Revolution. Not only was his Company awarded the lease for the general farms, it also bought out the offices of the receivers general in October 1719, transforming them into mere employees. Almost all taxes were now being collected by a single entity. Furthermore, the existence of the bank (whose notes had been made redeemable by the tax collectors as early as 1717, and had been made the mandatory instrument for all financial flows in 1719), meant that a single system was also available for the transfer and management of funds.

The Company was a privately-owned, for-profit concern: in that sense it stood in the tradition of French finances. The novelty, however, was the structure of ownership. Whereas public finance had been the preserve of the financiers, *gens intéressés aux deniers du Roi*, the owners of the new system were a vastly larger class: not only the six or eight hundred shareholders the Company had in the summer of 1719, but by the autumn of the same years thousands more, all the former office-holders and debtors of the Crown. Whereas the farmers had to finance their ventures with their own funds or by appealing to friends and associate investors, Law's System was financed by a broad class, whose membership was completely open since the shares were not registered and were freely traded on the open market. In his later writings, Law would remark on the element of 'shareholder democracy', as we might call it, that his system imparted to the old absolute monarchy. It aligned the interests of the taxpayers with those of the king.

It also made it possible to think of debt financing in a whole new way. Instead of issuing bonds with a fixed, nominal rate of return whose constancy was far from assured, as any rentier who had lived through the painful reductions of 1710 and 1713 knew well, the government made explicit the fact that the stream of revenues backing its commitments was inherently stochastic. In times of war, dividends could be expected to be lower; there was no need to readjust the value of the debt, either by default or through monetary manipulations, to satisfy the government's budget constraint. In particular, by freeing the price level from any demand that the budget constraint placed on it to maintain balance (as the fiscal theory of the price level asserts it does),[39] Law opened the way for monetary stability. It had been one of his long-standing theoretical arguments for the superiority of paper money that it could deliver better price stability than the metallic currencies in use at the time.

The Ascendancy of the Paris Brothers (1721–6)

When Law left France in December 1720, he left a mess behind him. The first act of the new finance minister was to recall the Paris brothers from the exile into which Law had sent them six months earlier. They arrived in Paris in early January and presented submitted a plan of action to the regent, who approved. While preferring to stay out of the limelight, the brothers became influential advisers to the regent and his successor as prime minister, the Duke of Bourbon.

An Accounting Revolution

The Visa of 1716 had allowed the Paris brothers to carry out their first attempt at introducing monitoring and accountability in the tax collection mechanism.[40] One of the elements of the Visa was to close all the accounts of the general receivers of the direct taxes. Beginning in July 1716, they were subjected to a new accounting regime designed by the Paris brothers. Although the receivers were not obliged to adopt double-entry bookkeeping, they were obliged to keep a daybook with an exact record of all their receipts and expenditures, and to forward a copy every two weeks to the ministry of finance. The Paris brothers gathered this information into double-entry registers, allowing them to monitor in real time the process of tax collection and the cash flows to the a central account, and thence to the treasury. Some material has survived[41] and shows how they calculated on a monthly basis the recovery rate for each general receiver.

In August 1718, the Paris brothers had won the lease for the general farms, submitting a bid that took the incumbents completely by surprise. Their syndicate had one original feature: taking a leaf from John Law's book, they issued shares to the public in their enterprise, payable in government bonds. This operation came to be known as the 'Anti-System', and is thought to have been set up as a rival to John Law's System, although it is far from clear that Law opposed it, at least initially. Later, Law approached the Paris brothers and proposed a merger, which they turned down: he then had their lease cancelled and took over the farms in August 1719, as described above. Thus their attempt at introducing the same reforms in the farms initially failed.

When they returned to power in 1721, they predictably tried to pursue their earlier attempts. They easily extended the requirement of keeping day-books to the farms in January 1721, since they were placed under direct management rather than farmed out, as I describe below. When Dubois became prime minister in August 1722, his first goal was to extend the accounting system to all accountants.[42]

By 1725 the Paris brothers had introduced the same reforms among most treasuries, both on the receipts and the expenditures sides, but the Duke of Bourbon did not allow them to push to completion because of increasing political resistance. They were nevertheless able to compose a *livre du Roy* in two copies, one which they kept and updated daily, the other kept by the minister of finance and updated weekly. The government was thus in a position to ascertain its fiscal position on a continuous basis, and make the necessary adjustments.

A Bureaucratic Revolution: The Visa of 1721
The wreck of Law's System consisted of a number of liabilities or instruments that differed both in their nature and terms (notes, bonds, deposits, shares) and in terms of their issuer or originator: the Crown, the Company, the bank. It was debatable to what extent there was any real distinction between these entities. Initially, the government made the Company responsible for the bank, but later realized that this was incompatible with one crucial premise of the Paris plan, namely the survival of the Company. Furthermore, it was difficult to make a distinction between the Crown's bonds, issued in June 1720 to reverse Law's debt conversion scheme, and the shares and notes of the Company held by former bondholders. In the end, all liabilities and instruments went through the same process.

The procedure adopted was the following. The shares of the Company remained as shares, to form the basis for its legal ownership. All other liabilities and instruments were submitted to the government, to be exchanged for government bonds. The Company redeemed its liabilities from the government, as much as it could, using evidence of indebtedness it received from the government in 1719 and 1720. As these were insufficient, the Company remained a debtor to the crown for 580 million *livres*. The shortfall was simply written off by the government in 1725, thus securing the Company's legal discharge, and leaving it free to continue its commercial activities.

How were the liabilities converted into government bonds? The Paris plan relied on two principles. One was to commit the government to the level of debt service that prevailed in 1718; to this effect, the government announced that it would reconstitute the debt to the level of 40 million *livres* in annual interest. The second was to treat the claimants as fairly as possible. The main distinction that the Paris plan saw between claimants was the manner in which they had acquired the claims they owned. A bondholder who had been led into the debt conversion scheme, or an individual who had been forced to accept Law's paper money as legal tender in repayment of a private debt, should be treated differently from a speculator who had bought the securities on the cheap on the open market, or sold goods of his own free will. Making such distinctions required precise knowledge of each individual's claims and their origins.

To acquire this information, the Paris brothers set into motion what can only be called a masterpiece of the bureaucratic art. All claimants were required to present their securities for inspection, along with identifying information about themselves, and statements detailing the manner in which they had come to acquire their securities. About 510,000 individuals (out of a total population of 20 million) filed claims. The claims were catalogued and tabulated by type and by origin. An alphabetical register of all claimants was created. The information being volunteered was obviously suspicious; to verify the claims, the government later required all notaries in France to submit copies of all financial transactions they had registered during the eighteen-month duration of Law's System. A total of 1,393,000 transactions were thus reported to the government.

Once in possession of this information, a total of the claims by type and origin could be tabulated. Given the total amount of debt the government was willing to take on, a matrix was created, with the rows corresponding to the type and size of claims, and the columns to the origin of the debt. The entries were the coefficient to be applied to the size of the claim, ranging from 100 per cent for the best claims to 5 per cent for the totally undocumented claims. Each claimant then received a liquidation certificate, whose nominal amount was the size of the claim multiplied by the relevant coefficient; the certificates could then be converted into government bonds. It is particularly remarkable that no account was officially taken of the status of the claimants: the decisions were made purely on the published criteria. (A few privileged individuals with special access to the regent, and also diplomats based in Paris, were given separate treatment; but all reclamations filed after the deadline were turned down.)[43]

This colossal enterprise lasted from January 1721 to September 1722, mobilized thousands of clerks and cost 9 million *livres*. The Paris brothers were clearly proud of their achievement, because they commissioned an author to write a history of the entire operation, in five volumes (three volumes of text and two volumes of appendices containing all the decrees, regulations and instructions). The writer continued to be paid by them to finish the work after their dismissal in 1726. The work itself is lost, but an abridged version still exists, in an unpublished document.[44] This manuscript contains the detail of the operation, in particular the manner in which a 'dictionary' of all claimants was compiled to cross-check all the information that was submitted, and also the various mechanisms by which fraud could be detected. One instance of fraud did take place: two of the twenty-four commissioners appointed to carry out the liquidations fabricated false certificates to sell them on the secondary market. The fraud was detected, a much-publicized trial took place and the guilty individuals were sentenced to life in prison.[45] At the end of the process, all the information gathered by the government was solemnly burned in public, to preserve *le secret des familles*.

A total of 2,222.6 million *livres* in instruments were presented to the Visa from January to August 1721. They were liquidated at a face value of 1700.7 million *livres*, a 23.5 per cent average reduction, but with much variation across individuals. The authors of the Visa[46] insisted that their goal was to bring back the debt to a sustainable level while maintaining fairness, by which they meant a bias for small holders. No claim of 500 *livres* or less was reduced: these small claims represent half of the individuals and 40 per cent of the sums involved. This means that the remaining 60 per cent of the sums were reduced by 39 per cent on average.

Starting in February 1722, claimants were required to turn in the instruments they had presented in exchange for certificates bearing a liquidation face value. Only 2,211.2 million *livres* of instruments were turned in from February to November 1722; they were exchanged for 1,661.6 million *livres* of certificates of liquidation, of which 62.6 million *livres* were never used. A supplementary tax on excessive profits from trading in Law's System was levied on about two hundred individuals (the most notorious 'Mississippians'), which further reduced the debt by 190 million *livres*.

The certificates were convertible into life annuities at 4 per cent and perpetual annuities at 2.5 and 2 per cent created from 1720 to January 1724, of which a total of 1,700 million *livres* in capital, 47 million *livres* in perpetual annuities, was available. These annuities became the core of the national debt; the bulk of the perpetual annuities were still in existence in 1789.[47]

The cash value of the liquidation certificates on the open market averaged 22 per cent of face value from February 1722 to February 1724. This means that the average holder of a bank note ultimately got about 17 per cent. Chart 10.6 plots the interest rate on French debt, assuming that a liquidation certificate was used to buy a 2 per cent perpetual annuity.

There was much complaining about the Visa, but this unprecedented effort on the part of the government remains a powerful testimonial to its desire to treat the debtors of Law's System as best it could. It is hard to imagine a government intent on defaulting on its debt settling on such a costly and time-consuming way to go about it. The main concern was clearly fairness, and undoing as much as possible the redistributive impact of the inflation generated by Law's System.

The event that dominates France's eighteenth century is the one that closes it, the Revolution. The standard question is: what were its causes? A related, more difficult question is: why did it not happen sooner? In recent years, the historiography has focused on the emergence of a public consciousness or discourse (shaped largely by the Enlightenment) within which the radical questioning of the existing institutions could be conceived. It remains acknowledged that a major fiscal crisis precipitated the events of 1789; the Revolution started out as a

Chart 10.6: Interest Rate on French Debt Derived from the Market Price of Liquidation Certificates, 1722–4.[48]

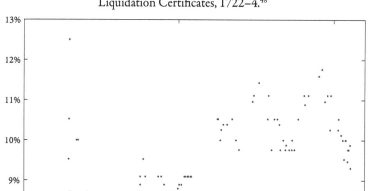

movement of stakeholders reclaiming the conduct of policy from a government perceived as incompetent. The monarchy's position was at least as financially precarious in 1715 or in 1721 as it was in 1788. I submit that the Paris brothers' extraordinary action may have defused the kind of discontent and sense of injustice that could have fuelled radical changes much earlier.

A Financial Encyclopedia

The Paris brothers, in their narrow way, were in the same mould as the encyclopedists of the later half of the century. Their belief that information was key to good management of finances did not limit itself to the monitoring of fiscal flows. They knew well that the French fiscal system was an incredibly complicated accumulation of taxes created at different times and in different regions of France with little regard for coherence. It was universally believed that the 'science' of fiscal administration was extremely complicated and in the grasp of very few: they wanted to collect all this knowledge as completely as possible, and their privileged position inside the Bourbon administration gave them full access to it. In La Montagne's autobiography there is a description of a *plan général des finances*, as well as a list of the treatises they had completed and those they did not have time to finish, a total of thirteen in all, each in several volumes.[49]

Some are historical in nature, like the history of all perpetual and life annuities created in France since the sixteenth century. Others are compilations, such as the listing of all import and export duties from 1664 to 1726, while others also include plans for improving the management and collection of taxes (such as the salt monopoly or the gunpowder monopoly). The treatise on salt includes detailed maps of the location of every warehouse, as well as a listing of all villages and the number of households in each subject to compulsory salt purchases. A treatise on the navy and another on military spending are in the form of plans for expenditures, depending on the desired level of strength to be reached in wartime and peacetime. Another is a plan to improve the collection of taxes and the flow of funds to the armies for their supplies. Just as Desmarets had started a rational archiving system for the ministry of finance,[50] the Paris brothers wanted to establish a permanent library in the ministry to store this information for the use of future ministers.

One should not overstate the radical nature of the Paris brothers' project. They did not seem to be animated by a desire for wholesale reforms, as Vauban had been in his *Dime royale* project of 1707, and as became increasingly common towards the end of the monarchy. In this sense, they belong to an earlier generation than that of the Enlightenment. They were still working within an existing system of taxes, but wanted to be as efficient as possible in using the available fiscal tools of the monarchy, and be in a position to propose new ways to sustain the budget under future emergencies.[51]

One of the Paris brothers' great obsessions was information. The adoption of their accounting reforms in the direct taxes in 1716, and their extension to the indirect taxes included in the general farms in 1721, had provided them with the means to monitor all the financial flows of the French monarchy (they had plans to extend the accounting rules to the gunpowder and post farms, but these were not carried out).

The Debate over Tax Farming

In January 1721, the Indies Company was stripped of almost all its non-commercial activities. The receivers general were restored to their former offices, although they remained under the accounting regime established by the Paris brothers in 1716. As for the general farms, the former farmers made a bid of 45 million *livres* (less than the lease of 1718, when the *livre* contained 25 per cent more silver), which the government turned down. Instead, the taxes that formed the contract of the general farms were placed under direct management (*régie*), with the former farmers as employees (earning 18,000 *livres* each). The receipts in the first year were 59 million *livres*, and increased even further thereafter. The farms (as well as several other taxes that had been farmed separately) remained under the *régie* system until 1726.

Which system was preferable, farm or *régie*? The debate had been going on within the administration for a while, especially after the experience with *régie* from 1703 to 1715 (during which time the farmers had been unwilling to commit to a lease contract). An undated memo comparing the *régie* and the farm (and clearly leaning towards the former) sheds some light on this debate.[52] Under the *régie* system the king is self-insured: 'if he loses one year the surplus of another year compensates him'. Under the farm system, the farmer insured the king: this was touted as an advantage by the supporters of the farm, since it made fiscal planning easier. In effect, the farm system can be seen as the combination of a simple tax system with an insurance arrangement with the farmer (the same was true, as noted above, with direct taxes collected by the receivers general). This insurance was deemed very valuable by finance ministers who wanted to rely on solid estimates of revenues to meet fixed obligations such as debt payments and the wages of officers. The memo disputed that much insurance was provided in practice, pointing out the difficulty of enforcing the contract in the times when it was needed most. Past experience showed that farmers could and did renegotiate ex post their obligations. This took the form of an *indemnité* granted by the king after the farmers had convinced him that they could not meet their obligations. In 1701, the farmers' lease price for the *aides* for the previous four years was cut by a third; in 1712, the lease price of the previous five years was cut by 18 per cent.

The incentives for the farmer were one of the main advantages put forward by supporters of the farming system. Under a *régie*, salaried tax collectors had no incentive to be efficient: 'they don't care to deserve their wages as long as they receive them'.[53] The memo argued that, in fact, the *indemnité* system created a perverse incentive under certain circumstances: if the farmer expected to miss the revenue target, he had every incentive to make his losses worse so as to secure as large an *indemnité* as possible. Furthermore, incentives could be provided to the *régisseurs*, by giving them bonuses for meeting predetermined revenue targets.[54] The threat of being fired (an extreme penalty) was also present. The government separated some of the taxes from the general farms and assigned them to a competing *régie*, and year by year shifted taxes from one to the other, possibly as a result of competition between the two sets of *régisseurs*.

The memo discusses other pros and cons of the two systems. It was also argued that farms offered the advantage of being a source of short-term finance for the government. The farmers were frequently called upon to make formal advances to the treasury. But the loans only came at a cost in terms of foregone revenues and high interest. Farmers were subject to legal difficulties: to prevent them from abusing their power, they were subject to elaborate procedures in cases of disputes with taxpayers. Such safeguards did not apply in the case of the *régie*. Farmers not having generally the resources to take on the collection of any given tax at the national level had to share its collection by region, through the mechanism of subleases (*sous-fermes*): this, according to the memo, did provide extra sources of credit for the government, but only at the cost of inefficiencies, incoherences and redundancies.

An attraction of the farming system was the minimal accounting cost, or more generally of any monitoring. The accounting cost was the motivation for a curious procedure that was used in 1714, namely, converting a *régie* into a farm ex post. It was decided that the employees (farmers) would not have to account for their management of the revenues from October 1709, as long as they could document that they had turned over to the royal treasury an amount which was declared to be the lease price for each year.

Finally, an important element in the debate over the merits of the two systems was the question of information. Malézieu argues that the finance minister's desire to acquire information about the real product of the farms was a motivation for the choice of the *régie* system in 1721.[55] Interestingly, when the taxes of the general farms were increased by 10 per cent in 1705, the collection of the increase itself (the so-called *deux sols pour livre*) was handled by a separate *régie* than the rest of the taxes; and, in 1715, after the return to the farming system, the farmers general manoeuvred to have the *deux sols pour livre* taken out of the *régie* system, because they knew it gave the government information on the true amount of taxes collected. Of course, such an advantage of the *régie* system matters only if the government were to alternate between the two systems, regularly updating its knowledge of the tax income at the (potential) cost of inefficiencies during the *régie* period.

Creation of a Stockmarket

The Paris brothers, as part of their plan, had salvaged the Indies Company from bankruptcy. It continued as a chartered corporation with shareholders. The Company was substantial in size: with 55,000 shares valued somewhere between 700 and 1,800 *livres*, its capitalization was of the same order as that of its British rival. The shares were traded, and prices were regularly reported in newspapers such as the *Gazette d'Amsterdam* as well as handwritten newsletters (*nouvelles à la main*). Other securities were doubtless traded, but I have not seen other prices reported except for liquidation certificates of the Visa until March 1724. The Company stock price varied wildly from 1722 to 1724 (see Chart 10.7), and options or futures were traded anew. The government grew alarmed at the apparent disorder in the market and incidences of forged securities, and decided it was better to regulate the market than to ignore it. Law had briefly established a market in the summer of 1720 but shut it down after a few months. In September 1724, a new body of sixty brokers in securities was established, and they were given a space near the Indies Company's offices, the Galerie Mazarine. The market's regulations were drafted by Paris Duverney, and the lieutenant of police of Paris officially inaugurated the new location on 17 October 1724. Initially a permission slip was required for anyone to enter the place, but in March 1726 this requirement was removed. The Paris bourse remained essentially unchanged until it was shut down during the Revolution in 1793.

Chart 10.7: Price of the Compagnie des Indes Stock, 1722–6.[56]

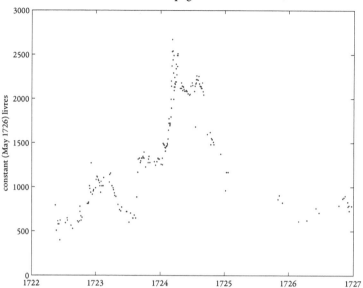

Price Stability

The period from 1723 to 1726 witnessed a remarkable and somewhat unprecedented period of monetary deflation. It had been customary, since the Middle Ages, for the government to undo currency depreciation after debasements. The multiple reformations of Louis XIV were likewise each followed by a programmed and pre-announced return to the old parity of the unit of account with silver, although the onset of the next reformation often occurred before a complete return was achieved.

In the autumn of 1720, when France returned to a metallic standard after the collapse of John Law's paper currency, the explicit intention was to return from the current parity of 90 *livres* per mark of silver to the 1718 parity of 60 *livres*, or perhaps even that of 1716, 40 *livres*. More urgent tasks took priority, however, and the appreciation stopped at 75 *livres*. It resumed in 1723, and then took place in a series of four unannounced decrees, in August 1723, February, April and September 1724, by which time it was 41.5 *livres*. This last step was announced to be the last, and the stated policy was thereafter price stability, once the general price level had returned to its level of 1716–17.

The motivation for such a drastic policy was that prices were deemed too high, and the government wanted to revalue the national debt, as it had been refounded in 1721–2. Of course, since many taxes were levied in nominal terms, this also implied to some degree an increase in tax revenues; the policy is nonetheless remarkable. France under the absolute monarchy is mainly remembered as an incorrigible defaulter; this episode is rarely noticed for what it is, a costly and seemingly unnecessary transfer to debtholders.

How costly it proved to be was not forecast by the government. The economy simultaneously experienced a severe depression, in which the textile industry contracted by a third from a peak in mid-1723 to a trough in mid-1726.[57] Whether or not there is a causal relation remains to be determined. Prices did not adjust to the revaluation of the currency, with the single exception of the foreign exchange markets, where prices adjusted instantaneously and fully. All other markets that I have been able to document, whether it be foodstuffs at the Paris Halles, producer prices at the places of production, wholesale markets at the fair or retail prices, adjusted slowly, and never by the full extent of the revaluation. On top of this, the year 1725 was marked by a very poor harvest in the north of France, resulting in serious disturbances in Paris. The government's attempts at improving supplies by purchases of wheat from more distant provinces and from abroad served to fuel the first apparition of the 'famine plot' legend.[58]

The policy proved costly in another dimension. In spite of the promise to maintain fixed parities, the government found itself forced to manipulate the currency once more, in February 1726. The international political situation deteriorated sharply in the spring of 1725, for dynastic reasons. The young king, whose health was still uncertain, had been engaged to a Spanish princess much younger than him, and the government felt the need to secure the succession and avoid the risk of a war with Spain by breaking the engagement and marrying Louis XV with the daughter of the deposed king of Poland.[59] The move outraged the Spanish court which, in retaliation, concluded a surprise alliance with its erstwhile enemy, the German emperor. The possibility of a renewed European conflict was very serious, and the French government felt the need to raise taxes to prepare for war. At the same time, however, it had decided to start a sinking fund for the debt with the revenues of a new income tax, the *cinquantième*. The quickest way to secure more funds was to launch yet another reminting; the value of coins were lowered by 12 per cent in January 1726, then a reminting was ordered in Febuary 1726 back to the earlier level. Although the parity remained the same in the end, the monetary manipulation still violated the spirit of the government's earlier commitment.

Finally, in an abrupt reversal of the deflationary policy, the government increased the value of the mark of silver from 41.5 *livres* to 49.8 *livres* in May 1726. Again, coincidentally or not, textile output picked up immediately (and prices adjusted much more quickly), and the economy revived. The government's credibility, however, was shattered, and discontent had grown large enough that the Duke of Bourbon was fired on 11 June 1726 and the whole cabinet replaced. Its successor government, led by the Cardinal of Fleury, would reap the benefit of the turnaround.

The role played by the Paris brothers in the formulation of this monetary policy remains uncertain, since it remained tainted by the concurrent depression, and in their later writings the Paris brothers were a bit cagey about claiming credit for it.[60] What is nevertheless apparent from their contemporary writings is their attachment to the revaluation of the debt, both through the deflationary policy and through the establishment of the sinking fund, and to price stability. As Paris-Duverney wrote in a text published in the Gazette d'Amsterdam in August 1725, 'the more one has acted hitherto in a way contrary to trust, the more the government must exercise care and punctuality with its promises in order to regain this precious trust and use it with moderation for the benefit of the State when its preservation is at stake'.

The Revolution of 1726

The abrupt dismissal and exile of the Duke of Bourbon was carried out on Louis XV's direct orders. This first personal act of the sovereign impressed his contemporaries by the speed and duplicity with which it was executed. At the first council he headed, the king abolished the position of prime minister, appointed new ministers and announced that the Cardinal of Fleury would henceforth always attend the meetings.

The fall of the Duke of Bourbon had a number of other consequences for French finances. His administration, and the Paris brothers, had fallen into such discredit that the Fleury administration acted in precisely the opposite way. As Fleury wrote on 13 June to the Duke of Bourbon to explain his role in his downfall, 'a change was needed to change minds, and this has always seemed necessary when the affairs of State were in disarray. It was even less unavoidable given the unfortunate, albeit unfair public prejudice against Your Highness, because it was feared that anything coming from you would have been ill-received.'[61]

The official programme was a return to the glory days of Colbert: 'No sooner had M. Le Pelletier des Forts become comptroller general that he declared his intention to administer finances the way they were under M. Colbert, whose precepts had not been followed since the ascent of the king [in 1715]'.[62] The programme is made more explicit in a remarkable memorandum on internal affairs drawn up at the request of Le Pelletier des Forts for himself and Fleury alone:[63] 'During the continous wars of the last reign many abuses were committed and a number of disorders followed. During the king's minority two systems were formed ... one confused true finance with the greedy *traitans*, the other accepted only paper and found specie useless for trade.' It is easy to recognize Law's System in the second, and the first represents the Paris brothers' *régies* and 'impractical accounts'. The memo's anonymous author, with unbridled cynicism, vaunts the traditional system of the *taille* because it keeps the common people in petty debates over its allocation: 'the true policy is to maintain the little people in a perpetual state of discord and jealousy and great mediocrity so that it busies itself only with living without ease and paying taxes'. The nobility must be kept dependent on the king, perpetually in debt: one of the ill effects of Law's System was that it allowed debtors to free themselves. Financiers enrich themselves and intermarry with the nobility, merchants ally themselves with the financiers and the king remains absolute master. Economic principles are incompatible with a monarchical government, which is why Vauban's flat tax was rejected. The *cinquantième* tax must be abolished: similar taxes made the Netherlands independent and weakened the king's authority in Britain. Monetary mutations, when they are too frequent, make the public too knowledgeable about the intrinsic content of coins and makes future use of seigniorage difficult. The memo argues for the return to the farms and the receivers general, whose freedom to use tax funds for their own lending enhances their credit and offers resources in times of need. The *régie* system must only be used for new taxes to ascertain their revenue, after which they must be farmed. It also recommends defaulting on the debt, by at least 10 per cent.

The plan was faithfully executed. Among the first measures taken in July 1726 was a return to the old system for both direct taxes and indirect taxes. The *caisse commune* of the receivers general was abolished, the inspectors were suppressed, and the accounting system established by the Paris brothers was essentially dismantled as too costly (it was claimed to cost over 2 million *livres*) and too burdensome.[64] For indirect taxes, the Fleury administration promptly returned to the farming system, awarding a lease without any bidding. A serious competing bid was put together by the former farmers in 1728, complete with a detailed comparison with the current lease showing how undervalued it was. This counterbid forced the incumbents to raise their lease price to some extent, but it ultimately failed.[65]

Any plans to repay the debt were abandoned,[66] and the *cinquantième* tax, designed to fund reimbursements but which had not been managed well, was abolished. Quite the reverse happened now: in November 1726, the new government simply eliminated the small perpetual and life annuities of less than 20 *livres* per year, annuities held by the small holders whom the Paris brothers had taken care to protect during the Visa. More seriously, the life annuities created since 1720 were reduced by a factor ranging from one-sixth to two-thirds, reducing the total charge of the annuities by nearly 30 per cent (although in the end the cut was about 10 per cent).[67]

In monetary policy the new government changed nothing, and neither did any successor until the Revolution (save for an adjustment of the gold/silver ratio in 1785); the *livre* (and later the franc) retained the same silver content until 1914.[68] Just before his dismissal, Dodun had decided to temporarily reduce the seigniorage rate on the ongoing recoinage from 11.7 to 5.8 per cent until January 1727. The incoming administration published the decree, and regularly postponed the date at which the higher seigniorage rate was to resume, until it was made permanent in 1738.

It is common to oppose John Law to the 'financiers', but the foregoing shows that things were more complicated. In reality, the period from 1715 to 1726 is one of persistent attempts at reform. The triumph of the old guard did not occur in 1720, but in 1726.

Conclusion

A discussion of French finance in the eighteenth century inevitably raises the comparison with France's arch-rival, Britain. Chart 10.8 makes the comparison of per capita military spending in the two countries.[69] The contrast between the early and the late parts of the period is stark. The Revolutionary and Napoleonic wars represented a quantum leap in terms of intensity and duration (France fielded 300,000 to 400,000 soldiers under Louis XIV, and 1.2 million in 1794), just as World War I did a century later. While France's efforts were comparable to Britain's in the early period, they were clearly outpaced in the later period.

Chart 10.8: Ratio of British to French Per Capita Military Spending, 1689–1816. The shaded areas indicate periods when Britain and France were at war.

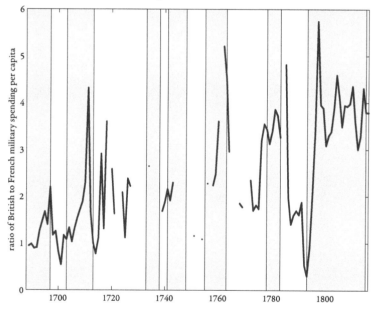

What accounts for this difference? The differential in per capita output alone is not enough to explain a ratio of four to one in the late eighteenth century. Is it a matter of financial technique? This paper argues that financial innovation was possible, indeed was tried frequently, in France. But the emphasis on tools and instruments is misplaced. French governments proved either incapable of successfully implementing these innovations, or else simply abandoned them. The means were there; was the will?

11 LONG-TERM WAR LOANS AND MARKET EXPECTATIONS IN ENGLAND, 1743–50

Christophe Chamley[1]

In the eighteenth century, debt financing enabled England successfully to muster war resources against an enemy of larger size and set the path towards its empire. Previous studies do not focus on the composition of this debt.[2] This paper focuses on the debt financing of the War of the Austrian Succession (1743–8) that set the stage for the financing of subsequent wars in the eighteenth century. It is shown that deficits were financed by long-term debt in each year of the war when the interest rate was high. A critical feature of the debt policy was the issuance of callable bonds. At the end of the War of the Austrian Succession, the rapid decrease of the interest rate allowed the government to exercise the callable option and to lower the debt service. The callable feature was thus an important contribution to the low debt service that enabled England to issue more debt than France for an interest service that was about the same.

In November 1749, Prime Minister Henry Pelham presented his plan to reduce the interest rate on the debt from 4 to 3 per cent. Dickson gives him much credit in carrying this difficult project without market disruption. By contrast in France, when the abbé Terray reduced the interest rate on some government liabilities in 1770, the price of the marketed debt fell by half. An interest reduction was considered a default in France but it was accepted in England because of the type of debt contract: all long-term debt in England was in callable bonds.

There is a view that war deficits were financed by short-term and refinanced by long-term instruments after the war, when the interest rate was lower.[3] This view does not hold for the War of the Austrian Succession or the Seven Years War (1756–63). Even in the War of American Independence (1777–83) short-term debt was a minor part of financing.

The first part of this paper therefore describes the market instruments that were issued during the War of the Austrian Succession, which came at the end of the period in which both the capital market and the credibility of the government were strengthened.[4] The financing of this war set the pattern for the Seven Years War, and the War of American Independence, which deserve separate studies.

From the description of the characteristics of the loan issues, we will determine a correct value of the cost of borrowing *ex ante*.[5]

The dominant financial instruments were long-term bonds with coupons of 3 and 4 per cent. Both were callable bonds: they were legally redeemable at par. In eighteenth-century England, the optimal rule of calling the bond as soon as it reaches par could not be applied because of the fixed costs in floating a large amount of new debt, and also because of issues of moral hazard and fairness. The recall of the high coupon debt could not and was not expected to take place at par.

Market participants viewed the 4 per cent debt as a contingent asset that paid a coupon of 4 per cent as long as the price of the 3 per cent debt was below a specific value, which can be taken as the par level. When the 3 per cent debt reached par and was stable, the 4 per cent debt could be redeemed. In order to save on the transaction cost of refinancing with new 3 per cent bonds purchased by the same individuals as held the 4 per cent debt, the government announced an 'interest reduction': the coupon of the 4 per cent debt was reduced gradually to 3 per cent during a relatively short transition period. That reduction was equivalent to a conversion of the 4 per cent into a 3 per cent, one for one, with an additional payment equal to the present value of the coupons over 3 per cent during the transition (an amount equal to about 4 in 1749). A 4 per cent bond was therefore a derivative financial asset of the 3 per cent bond: all its payments depended solely on the price of the 3 per cent: it would pay £4 per face value of 100 per year until the price of the 3 per cent reached par. Around that date, it was converted into a 3 per cent bond with a additional payment that was not specified at the time of issue but could be anticipated by the market.

The representation of the prices of the 3 per cent and the 4 per cent annuities (traded almost daily) will show that, for the debt that was issued during the war, the terms of the Pelham interest reduction on the 4 per cent annuities were expected long before they were announced. The redeemable feature of the debt enabled the government to benefit from market pessimism that turned out to be excessive. A 4 per cent annuity was the sum of a 3 per cent annuity and an annuity paying £1 per year until the long-term interest returned to about 3 per cent. As the market believed this date to be distant in the future, more than 10 years, it bought the contingent annuity from the government at a price that grossly exceeded the ex post payments by the government.

The Financial Instruments

During the period of peace that followed the wars with Louis XIV, the long-term interest rate decreased regularly from 8 per cent in 1710 to 3 per cent in the mid-1730s, in this period of 'financial revolution'.[6] When war resumed in 1743, the

Chart 11.1: Loans and the Long-Term Interest Rate in England, 1741–51.

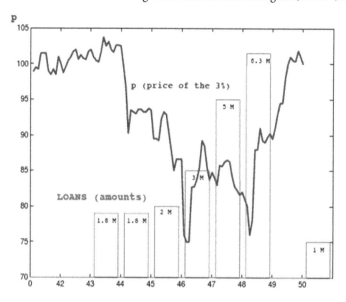

long-term interest rate had been around 3 per cent for ten years and the stage was set for the financing of the next three wars until 1783.

Debt financing in the War of the Austrian Succession is summarized in Chart 11.1. The price of the 3 per cent annuity (whose features will be discussed below) fell during the war years, with record lows around 75, and recovered rapidly to the par at the end of the war. The amounts of the loans (M stands for millions of pounds) rise gradually. Government borrowing occurs only during the war years and the bulk of borrowing takes place when the long-term interest rate is high.

The evidence does not support the view that war deficits were financed short-term and refinanced in long-term instruments after the war, when the interest rate was lower. War borrowing relied on a limited set of financial instruments, which were long term. Short-term credit played its standard role over the yearly cycle to match expenditures and resources, but it did not accumulate to be refinanced at smaller rates after the war. The best-known short-term instruments were navy bills at rates of 5 per cent and higher. Some accumulation of these bills took place, but their refinancing of £3 million in 1749 was charged on a loan issued under war conditions with an interest rate higher than in the previous year.[7] The accounts do not show refinancing of short-term debt after the end of the war, except a small conversion of the navy victualling bills in 1750 (£1 million compared to £20 million for the war).[8]

An Overview of War Loans

A war loan issue was an important affair, as it would be today with the privatization of large state companies or 'Initial Public Offerings', and it entailed significant fixed costs. Moreover, the large market that we see today in short-term treasury bills did not exist at the time. Contemporary accounts emphasize that for the government it was essential that each single issue should be 'successful', which meant at the time significantly oversubscribed, as it would be today with investment banks and 'Initial Public Offerings'.

Table 11.1: New Loans in England, 1743–50.[9]

Date	Amount (£million)	Instruments	Rate (%)	Ex Ante Rate (%)	Ex Post Rate (%)	Prices
1743	1.8	100 (3%)	3.42	3.42	3.32	3%: £100
1744	1.8	100 (3%)	3.33	3.33	3.33	3%: £93
1745	2.0	100 (3%)	4.02	4.02	4.02	3%: £89
		L (1.125)				
1746	3.0	100 (4%)	5.4	4.81	4.72	3%: £75–83
		L (1.5)				4%: £91–4
1747	4.0	110 (4%)	4.4	3.73	3.54	3%: £85
						4%: $96
1747	1.0	100 (4%)				
1748	6.3	110 (4%)	4.4	3.71	3.51	3%: £80
						4%: £90
1750	1.0	100 (3%)				3%: £100
SUM	20.7					

The process for a new issue began in the late autumn of each war year with the parliamentary session which assessed the amount and the broad terms of the loan. Preparation continued during the winter in discussions with the 'moneyed men' and the fine-tuning of the terms of the loans to contemporary market conditions. The subscription was paid in monthly installments of 10–20 per cent beginning at various times from December to May. Investors seem to have appreciated gambles and often a significant fraction of the loan was raised by lottery tickets with government bonds as prizes. The total value of the prizes was equal to the value of the tickets and could exceed it when special prizes were added in the fine-tuning to secure success of the issue.

The amounts and types of loans are presented in the second and third columns of Table 11.1.[10] In 1743 and 1744, a payment of £100 would get a 3 per cent annuity with a face value of 100. In 1745, as interest rates increased (Chart 11.1), for the same payment of £100, a lifetime annuity of £1.125 per year (to be written on any chosen person regardless of age) was added to the 3 per cent annuity. Lotteries were popular in the eighteenth century. Almost all the loans was partially issued through a lottery: in the case of the 1745 loan, for each £400, the investor would receive a 300 face value of 3 per cent bonds and 10 lottery tickets (at £10 each). These tickets would entitle the investor to a lifetime annuity of £4.10 shillings in addition to the prize of the lottery. The prizes were in 3 per cent bonds with fair odds. A similar scheme was used in 1746.

Lifetime annuities represented less than 5 per cent of the borrowings during the war, which essentially relied on 3 and 4 per cent annuities. In eighteenth-century England, all annuities were perpetually redeemable at par, unless specified otherwise. This feature is essential in the financial policy of England and contrasts sharply with the loans issued by France at the same time, which were mainly in lifetime annuities, or with terms of 9–32 years.[11]

The 3 Per Cent Annuity

The 3 per cent annuity was the workhorse of debt financing in eighteenth-century England. It was redeemable at par, like any other annuities, but market conditions and policy constraints were such that their probability of redemption was negligible. (Their rate was reduced to 2.5 per cent only at the end of the nineteenth century after a long period of low rates.) The 3 per cent bond had been above par only temporarily. We will see that redemption meant in fact a conversion into a debt instrument with a lower coupon when that financial instrument was around par. No debt was ever issued at less than 3 per cent in eighteenth-century England. We will focus on the conversion of the 4 per cent annuities into 3 per cent annuities.

The 4 Per Cent Annuity

These annuities supported two-thirds of the war loans between 1743 and 1748. At the onset of the war, more than 85 per cent of the public debt was at 4 per cent.[12] A redemption of the annuities with a rate of 5 per cent or more had taken place after the wars with Louis XIV, and an attempt had been made in 1737 for the 4 per cent debt, but it failed. We will see that during the War of the Austrian Succession, the possibility of redemption was very much taken into account by the market. We will also examine some particular features of the redeemability of an eighteenth-century British government bond which were somewhat different from those of a standard callable government bond in the twentieth century.[13]

The Ex Ante Cost of Loans

Two measures of the cost of loans are reported in the fourth and fifth columns of Table 11.1. In the fourth column, 'Rate' stands for the internal rate of return computed by Grellier, who used an accounting method.[14] His numbers are useful because he probably had information on additional prizes and on lifetime annuities. The accounting method overstates the borrowing cost because it cannot take into account the redemption features of the assets and it must assume that coupons are paid forever, contrary to market expectations. For example, in 1747, it generates a rate of 4.4 per cent on an initial investment of £100, which gets a face value of £110 in 4 per cent annuities.

The fifth column reports the true borrowing cost at the time when the loan was issued, that is the internal rate of return or yield using the market data at the time of issuance of the loan. This yield is computed with the equivalent financing though a 3 per cent annuity. For example in the 1747 issue, the public should expect to receive for £100 an amount equal to the product of 110 and 96/85 in 3 per cent annuities, where 96 and 85 are the prices of the 4 per cent and the 3 per cent annuities (see the seventh column). This generates a coupon of 3.73. Assuming this coupon to be perpetual (if not, we have an upper limit of the rate), this value is equal to the rate reported in the fifth column.

The 1745 loan bundled for each £100 a package of one 3 per cent annuity at face value 100 and a lifetime annuity of £1.125 per year. These were not rated by age and we have no information on the age distribution of the subscribers. Grellier reports a rate of 4.02 per cent. There is no need to refine that number, which is the true long-term interest cost of the loan, but we can extract from that number the implicit maturity of the life annuity. The maturity that best reproduces Grellier's result is exactly sixty years, which is the number given for the computation of the 1745 yield. Note that this rate of 4.02 per cent is much higher than the market yield of 3 per cent annuities, which was around 3.37 per cent (with a price of 89 in the sixth column).

In 1746, we have a mix of a 4 per cent annuity and a lifetime annuity. We can assume that the 4 per cent component is equivalent to a perpetual payment of $3 \times 94/83 = 3.3976 = c$, where 94 and 83 are the prices of the 4 per cent and the 3 per cent annuities in the spring of 1746 (which are more relevant than the prices at the beginning of the year because the payments for the subscription were made in the spring and the summer).

The life annuity is taken as a payment of 1.5 for 60 years. The yield R is such that $100 = \sum_{1 \le i \le 60} (1.5+c)/(1+R)^i + (c/R)/(1+R)^{61}$, which gives a value R=4.81 per cent.

The yields in the fifth column illustrate the high cost of life annuities: in 1747 and 1748, when the level of borrowing was at its highest (at £5 and £6 million), and the long-term rate was as high as at any other time in the war, the yield was significantly lower than in 1745–6, when the amount of the loans was only half. Raising loans through financial instruments actively traded in the market and with a contingent redemption date was much more effective than life annuities.[15] We will see that, because of the redemption feature, the government was also able to benefit from good surprises on the market, a possibility that could not be exploited in the lifetime annuities.

Redeemable Annuities as Derivatives

In a setting without frictions, the optimal policy is to redeem a callable bond as soon as its price reaches par, according to a standard result in finance. It is well known, however, that both governments and private firms have delayed the redemption of callable bonds. In eighteenth-century England, neither the market nor the government expected that bonds would be redeemed at par. We will first describe what was actually done in 1749, and then discuss the constraints on the redemption of callable bonds that the government faced.

The Interest Reduction of 1749
In the autumn of 1749, the 3 per cent annuity had been around par for a few months. The long-term rate was therefore back to 3 per cent, and was not expected to increase in the near future. The price of the 4 per cent had reached 105. The king, in his opening speech to the session of the parliament, made it official that interest payments should be lowered on the entire 4 per cent debt, which greatly exceeded the debt incurred in the last war. The government of Pelham ruled out an immediate reduction of the rate to 3 per cent and fixed the terms at the end of November:[16] the 4 per cent bonds would receive a coupon of 4 per cent for the year of 1750, and then 3.5 per cent for the following six years during which they were not redeemable. After seven years, there would be no distinction between these bonds and the 3 per cent bonds. For a holder of a 4 per cent annuity, the interest reduction was equivalent to conversion into a 3 per cent annuity with a payment of about 4 pounds per annuity, paid in instalments.

That plan was implemented with minor variations for the total debt of £57.7 million at 4 per cent. By May 1750, only £7 million from the £57.7 million was not converted. The holders of these bonds were paid off by a new loan. According to Dickson the plan was resisted, in particular by the large institutional investors, and was apparently in jeopardy during the winter.[17] His account cannot be repeated here but its reading may be useful for the discussion of the calling rules and the contradictory evidence by the market which will be examined later.

Why Not Redeem at Par?
For United States callable treasury bonds (available up to 1995), the call had to be announced 120 days in advance. Since the interest rate fluctuates randomly during this period, the optimal price at which the bond should be called is strictly above par, and depends on the volatility of the interest rate. There was no formal delay for implementation in eighteenth-century England, but a delay and a special compensation at the time of redemption had to take place because the of following constraints.

The redemption of the 4 per cent debt could be done only by issuing new debt at 3 per cent. However, issuing costs were large. Since the new annuity holders would be the same people holding the old annuities, transaction costs would be saved by reducing the interest of the debt. However, the reduction of the interest rate was not in the debt contract. Hence the government and the debt holders were competing to capture the rent of the fixed costs. Not surprisingly, the three large companies that represented a dominant fraction of the debt holders and had more bargaining power, the South Sea Company, the East India Company and the Bank of England, opposed the plan at the beginning. These companies eventually agreed, but the discussions imposed a delay between announcement and implementation.

Annuity holders could always reject the conversion at a lower rate and, despite the good terms offered by Pelham, some did. Because the government had to provide an interval of time to convert their holding, it had to provide a premium that would dominate possible price losses of the 3 per cent annuity in the short term. The payment of 4 per cent face value of 100 provided some guarantee in this respect.

In eighteenth-century England, the interest rate depended mainly on the government fiscal policy, which itself depended on the military policy. Reputation was essential during this period of growth of the public debt. The redemption of an annuity raised issues of asymmetric information, moral hazard and fairness. An increase of interest rates and a fall of the annuity price soon after the conversion would have raised the suspicion of 'inside trading' and a government taking advantage of private information about the future evolution of interest rates. Hence, there was additional incentive for the government to give some compensation against a possible capital loss on the newly converted debt, at least for the near future after the time of the conversion.

Contemporary discussions of the policy emphasize that the 3 per cent annuity had been around par for a few months and was likely to stay at that level in the future. The issue of moral hazard is similar: the government had to avoid any suspicion that it would take advantage of the interest reduction and the lighter burden of the debt to start on new ventures.

Redemption, Swap or Interest Reduction?

Instead of a swap where each 4 per cent annuity was converted into a multiple of 3 per cent annuity, Pelham implemented a schedule of gradual interest reductions to the level of 3 per cent. Both methods may have the same present value, but two differences should be mentioned. First, in the interest reduction, the face value of the loan is not changed, while it increases in the swap. Hence, once the interest reduction has been phased in (seven years in this case), the service of the debt is smaller after the interest reduction than after the swap. The interest reduction is thus a method to repay some of the debt and it saves on the fixed costs of any operation of debt reduction in the future.

Second, agents may have different perceptions of the two policies. The interest reduction may have looked more 'natural' than the conversion in a multiple of 3 per cent annuities: in November 1749, the long-term rate was stable at 3 per cent. It the context of unspecified contingent agreements, perceptions of ex post fairness matter and may rest on idiosyncratic and subtle details. Holders of 4 per cent annuities seemed to have had a special advantage, with some justification, but, given the conditions of the time, they 'should have been satisfied' to enjoy this advantage for a limited time. Under a swap that provides an amount of 3 per cent bonds with a face value higher than 100, the rate of the swap may end as a benchmark that could put an additional constraint on similar redemptions in the future.

The 4 Per Cent Annuity as a Derivative of the 3 Per Cent Annuity

The previous discussion of the historical context and events shows that the payoff of the 4 per cent annuity was contingent on the price of the 3 per cent annuity, paying a coupon of £4 per year before its redemption and converted into a 3 per cent annuity with the addition of a premium when the 3 per cent annuity price had regained 'stability' at par. Therefore, the 4 per cent annuity can be viewed as a derivative on the 3 per cent annuity. The prices p and q of the 3 per cent and 4 per cent annuities are presented in Chart 11.2. We can make the following remarks.

1. For all trading days, the points of coordinates (p, q) are between the two lines $q=p$ and $q=(4/3)p$, hence $p<q<(4/3)p$. The price of the 4 per cent annuity is higher than the 3 per cent price since it pays a higher coupon and is eventually redeemed into a 3 per cent with a conversion ratio greater than 1. The price q was much lower than $(4/3)p$, which would be its price if the market expected no conversion into 3 per cent. A glance at the figure shows that expectations about a conversion played a major role in the determination of the price of the 4 per cent annuity.

2. The observations after 2 October 1749 are represented by stars. There is no apparent discontinuity of the *level* of q in relation to p at the time of the redemption, but there is a discontinuity in the two *schedules* before and after the event. The new schedule is a line $q=p+h$, with h equal to about 4. After 1 October, two months before the official announcement of the interest reduction plan, the market treated that plan as a *fait accompli* for the debt issued during the war; from that date on,[18] the premium of the 4 per cent over the 3 per cent annuity is constant and equal to the value that will hold through the year 1750.

3. The difference q-p is the value of an annuity paying £1 per year until the consol reaches its par value (the time of the interest reduction), with a final payment of £4. The difference evolves randomly over a decreasing trend following the events of the war and the gradual nearing of its end. However, the levels of this difference are high throughout the war, more than 10 usually:

people expected the interest rate to stay above 3 per cent much longer than it actually did.

4. On Sunday, 24 April 1748, the peace conference began at Aix-la-Chapelle. Between the previous Friday and the following Tuesday, in the largest jump of the war (except for the days around Culloden, 27 April 1746), the price of the 3 per cent rose from 80 to 85, with further gains immediately after. April 1748 marks a sharp difference in Chart 11.2 between two regimes of asset pricing.

5. The beginning of the peace negotiations did not mean the end of uncertainty. The guns of Maurice de Saxe conducting the siege of Maastricht could be heard a dozen miles away. Long lists of ships captured at sea were geven each month in the *Gentleman's Magazine* until the signing of the peace treaty on 18 October 1748. Nevertheless, April 1748 had simplified the issues that had to be addressed for the computation of expected future prices: the trend for interest rates was definitely downward and the main question was how fast they would come down. This new context is reflected in the relation that appears between the prices of the two annuities in Chart 11.2. This relation can be explained by the random evolution of one factor, the interest rate, in a model,[19] which quantifies the expectations of contemporaries about future interest rates and the time and the terms of an eventual redemption.

6. Before 1748, no simple relation appears in Chart 11.2 between the prices p and q of the two annuities. In this very complex war[20] between England, France, Holland, Austria, Prussia, Spain and Russia, alliances shifted a number of times and news could arrive about future developments with no immediate impact on the short-term interest rate. The term structure of interest rate was probability not decreasing over the foreseeable future and, for a given long-term rate as measured by the price of the 3 per cent, there could be different structures of the future interest rate and therefore different prices of the 4 per cent annuity. For a given price of the 3 per cent at 85, there are in Chart 11.2 at least three different levels of the 4 per cent annuity price, each with a specific local schedule. Before April 1748, the asset prices do not move in a space of dimension one, thus reflecting the uncertainties of the multi-faceted war.

The Impact of a Possible Default

When a government implements a partial default, the higher interest rate is reduced first, as in 1770 France. In this case, the 4 per cent annuity could be singled out because of its higher coupons and its junior status. The selective default would be a default on the £1 per year premium paid by the 4 per cent over the 3 per cent annuity. Hence, such a probability would decrease the observed price of this premium, which is q-p. Since the observed market price shows that the market overpriced the 4 per cent annuity over the 3 per cent in view of the actual redemption date, a probability of default would strengthen that property.

Chart 11.2: Prices of the 3 Per Cent and the 4 Per Cent Annuity in England, 1746–50.[21]

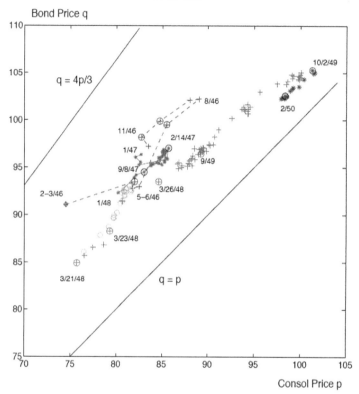

Conclusion

It has sometimes been argued that bond prices overreact in times of bad news and war. The observation of annuity prices during the War of the Austrian Succession provides some information about such an excess fluctuation. The main issue at the end of war, as attested by the policy of issuing redeemable bonds, was the speed of convergence of the bond to its par value. If people expected a slow convergence, then the price of the 3 per cent annuity did not overreact.

First, the market was remarkably rational in pricing financial assets consistently, as shown by the evolution of prices after April 1748 in Chart 11.2, and confirmed by the quantitative study in Chamley.[22] Moreover, the absence of discontinuity in the level of the 4 per cent price with respect to the 3 per cent price shows that the terms of the payoff at the time of the interest reduction at the end of 1749 were accurately predicted and taken into account long before that time. Second, the market showed an excess pessimism about the recovery of bond prices after the war. The large premium of the 4 per cent over the 3 per cent annuity shows that the expected time for the bond reaching its par value was strongly overestimated.

In this context, the debt policy during the War of the Austrian Succession offers a spectacular illustration of the power of marketed contingent financial instruments. The loans of 1745 and 1746 included non marketed lifetime annuities and were more expensive *ex ante* than later loans, although the long-term rate was not smaller in 1747–8 and the amount of the loans more than twice as high.

The contingent feature of the callable bonds enabled the government to take advantage of the excess pessimism. Simply put, in April 1746, during the subscription of the 4 per cent bond, the market paid a price of £12 for the contingent annuity of £1 per year until the call of the bond. It was willing to pay that price because it was pessimistic about future interest rate. Its expectation was that the annuity would pay for about ten years with a final payment of £4. In fact, the annuity lasted only for three years. That price of £12 was much more than the total amount collected on the annuity, ignoring discounting, since the government paid a total of £7 (£1 per year from 1746 to 1748, and a total of £4 after). On the main loans, which were floated after 1746, the government paid a rate ex post that was equivalent to less than £3.5 perpetual. The government was therefore able to bet with great success against the pessimism of the market.

The success of the contingent policy is measured by the ex post rate of return that the government paid on its loans. This rate (the long-term internal rate of return) is presented in the sixth column of Table 11.1. Once the government abandoned the inefficient life annuities for the redeemable 4 per cent, it was able to finance the war a long-term rate that, even during the worst years, turned out to be only 3.5 per cent.

Finally, the successful betting by the government against pessimistic investors was repeated recently and in a similar context. In the early 1980s, the British government faced adverse expectations of private investors who were pessimistic about the government's conduct and the evolution of interest rates. This time, the enemy was not France, but inflation. Prime Minister Margaret Thatcher was more confident than the market that she would prevail and her government issued inflation indexed bonds, with coupons linked to the inflation rate. Expecting high coupons for a long time, investors paid high prices to the government, like the buyers of 4 per cent annuities in 1747. Inflation came down much sooner than expected (with some help from Paul Volcker, Chairman of the United States Federal Reserve). In the 1980s as in the 1740s, the government won against excessive market pessimism.[23]

12 MERCANTILIST INSTITUTIONS FOR THE PURSUIT OF POWER WITH PROFIT: THE MANAGEMENT OF BRITAIN'S NATIONAL DEBT, 1756–1815

Patrick Karl O'Brien

The Rise of Britain's Fiscal Naval State

In outline (if not in the chronological detail required for a complete and satisfactory historical narrative) the reasons why the United Kingdom evolved, between the Glorious Revolution of 1688 and the Congress of Vienna of 1815, into the most powerful fiscal military state in Europe have become clearer since Peter Dickson inaugurated the modern debate with the publication of *The Financial Revolution in England* some four decades ago.[1] That seminal book (subtitled 'A Study in the Development of Public Credit 1688–1756') directed attention to the economic and geopolitical significance of a political consensus and network of institutions for the accumulation of a national debt required for the rise of British power.[2]

Over the long eighteenth century public debt increased from a nominal capital of under £2 million in the reign of James II to reach an astronomical level of £854 million or 2.7 times the national income when Lord Liverpool's administration returned the monetary and financial system to the gold standard in the aftermath of the Napoleonic War.[3] Up to 85 per cent of the money borrowed as long-term loans or raised as short-term credit between 1688 and 1815 was allocated to fund a sequence of costly armed conflicts against enemies who threatened the security and stability of the realm, as well as the kingdom's rivals who challenged its mission to command the oceans, engaged in mercantilistic competition with British businessmen for the profits of global commerce, or obstructed the nation's ambitions for colonization overseas.[4]

The institutionalization of public debt was but one symptom and sinew of a combined financial, fiscal and naval strategy for the projection of British power overseas.[5] State debts could only be accumulated, sustained and serviced by reve-

179

nues from taxation assessed and collected with difficulty from the realm's evolving but narrow fiscal base and recalcitrant bodies of taxpayers. That is why a 'fiscal revolution', the outcome of a political consensus that succeeded an interregnum of destructive civil war, the innovations of a republican regime and the construction of relatively efficient institutions for the assessment and collection of taxes (particularly excise and customs duties) under the restored Stuart monarchs, together with sustained support for a standing navy – have all been analysed by a recent wave of historiography as 'preconditions' for the rapid (and, in European terms, extraordinary) accumulation of public debt that succeeded the change of monarchical regimes in England in 1688.[6]

Whatever might be claimed for the origins and representations of the Glorious Revolution as the final victory of parliament over despotism, 1688 certainly marks three interrelated upswings in revenues collected for and expenditures made by the English state.[7] Between King William's War and final victory at Waterloo taxes, loans and allocations for the navy and the army all rose and continued to increase war after war to peak at the close of the Second Hundred Years War with France, 1803–15.[8] Revenues from taxation increased far more rapidly than national income – a fact which relocates economic explanations for the rise of the state to a subsidiary place.[9]

Chart 12.1: Allocations for Debt Servicing as a Proportion of Total Net Income from Taxation in Britain, 1688–1814.[10]

Most of the extra money appropriated by the state from the kingdom's relatively compliant body of taxpayers serviced its national debt. Apart from the tiny residual allocation to support the court and organs of central governance, the remainder of tax revenues available to the state (after hypothecated debt servicing changes had been met) funded the realm's fluctuating but increasing expenditures upon the military and naval forces of the Crown.[11]

Despite some rather minor episodes of resistance at home and a serious tax revolt by subjects of the Crown residing in thirteen colonies in New England, the degree of compliance secured by an 'ancien regime' from parliaments and tax-payers for an extraordinary and sustained uplift in demands for taxes has been retrospectively constructed as a narrative of political, legal and administrative success.[12] Britain's achievements as a fiscal state embodied a consensus among the elite concerning expenditures upon external security, internal order and aggressive mercantilism vis a vis European rivals for gains from commerce and colonization overseas.[13] As Peter Dickson appreciated, it also included recognition of their stake in the national debt by the nation's wealthy elites – represented in parliament.[14] They groaned but paid a due share of taxes, and took the opportunities provided by well-managed issues and market for public securities to diversify their portfolios of assets in order to provide pensions and insurance for their dependants.[15] Many also recognized the role played by governments' credit in widening the capital market, in attracting foreign investment to London and promoting the development of banks and other institutions for financial intermediation.[16]

Despite the rapid accumulation of debt, the high shares of total tax revenues allocated as transfers to government creditors, the antipathies of radicals to moneyed and aristocratic interests as well as episodes of political anxiety and controversy over the scale of debt, the realm never experienced fiscal crises of the kind that afflicted other powers on the mainland.[17] Once a system and institutions for regularized borrowing were up and running, the debt matured along the lines depicted by Peter Dickson into another sinew of power – as envied and feared by other states on the mainland as the kingdom's fiscal prowess and its royal navy.[18] That achievement took several decades of experimentation and innovation to mature. With lapses, the system survived the strains placed upon it by the Seven Years War (1756–63), the War of American Independence (1776–83), and above all by costly wars against Revolutionary France and Napoleon (1793–1815), because the operations involved in providing the royal navy and armies with the real resources required for the prosecution of warfare and defence of the realm were managed with relative, if not with remarkable, efficiency by those in charge of the nation's finances during its long transition to geopolitical hegemony.[19]

This essay follows the historical themes explored by Peter Dickson in *The Financial Revolution* and analyses the principles and practice of debt management from where he left off in 1756 through to the apogees of Trafalgar and Waterloo. Thereafter, and for roughly a century, the United Kingdom's fiscal and financial system supported an altogether cheaper imperial state – mortgaged to its creditors, unavoidably in thrall to laissez faire and free trade, but fortuitously in no danger from its rivals before the rise of Germany.[20]

Principles of Eighteenth-Century Debt Management

The Accountancy of Bond and Bill Finance

Government borrowing was achieved through the sale of paper securities to private capital markets. This task involved British chancellors of the Exchequer and their advisers in the business of managing a national debt. The complexity of that task can only be appreciated by close investigation into the range of decisions behind the marketing of public securities.

Given the level of expenditure, the higher the level of taxes levied on the population the lower was the amount borrowed by the state. In Britain (at or preparing for war for about half the years between the Glorious Revolution of 1688 and the final victory over its European rivals in 1815) borrowing took one of two forms: funded or unfunded. Contemporary discussions of public finance hardly mentioned the latter and regarded a balanced budget as one where revenues from taxes covered expenditure and the government had no recourse to funded borrowing.[21] It is easy to see how unfunded borrowing could be ignored. In peacetime most bills issued by departments of state to obtain goods and services on credit provided funds to anticipate revenue accruing during the current year and were automatically paid off (redeemed) when taxes, or receipts from loans, arrived at the Exchequer. 'Contingent' unfunded borrowing of this kind made no contribution towards the finance of annual expenditure; it simply met the needs of the Exchequer, the navy, the army, the ordnance and other departments for ready cash. Whenever governments borrowed short term on the security of revenues which subsequently failed to arrive at the Exchequer or departments of state, or issued bills to secure credit for unforeseen increases in levels of expenditure, clearly the state had employed unfunded borrowing to finance its current expenditures. The case is even more obvious when departments issued bills redeemable from tax revenues accruing in future financial years.[22]

Since the state both borrowed money and repaid debt during most financial years (1688–1815), only the net amount of money borrowed could be used for the purchase of commodities and services by public departments and to meet interest payments on the national debt. Clearly, the wider the gap between total receipts from the sales of bonds and bills and expenditures upon their redemption, the higher the proportion of borrowed money available for the finance of 'real' expenditure would become. At the same time the national debt would accumulate more rapidly. As the volume of debt redeemed grew the amount of current loans available for other forms of expenditure became comparably smaller. When the repayments of debt exceeded funds borrowed over the year, the government in effect allocated taxes to meet obligations to its creditors, and the amount of debt outstanding and the interest bill then declined. As discussions on the Sinking fund under Robert Walpole and William Pitt revealed, only if the government possessed a surplus of tax income over expenditure on resources could effective reductions be made in the size of the national debt.[23]

The net amount borrowed by the government for the finance of 'real' expenditures consisted then of receipts from bonds sold minus payments for bonds redeemed in the market by the Treasury, plus revenue from bills marketed minus revenue used to redeem matured bills. These four operations encompassed the business of debt management. Receipts from bonds sold usually exceeded the amount of revenue employed to buy bonds and funded borrowing almost invariably made a large contribution (up to 80–90 per cent) towards the finance of expenditures on warfare. But the contribution from unfunded borrowing could be either positive or negative. When bills repaid exceeded bills issued part of the revenue from funded borrowing had in fact been diverted to redemption of the floating debt. Furthermore, the net volume of bonds sold over the year bore an inverse relationship to the net volume of bills issued. Unfunded and funded borrowing provided chancellors with alternative ways of raising money and the higher the level of one the lower the level of the other.

This basic accountancy must be kept in mind for the purposes of discussing all policies and operations concerned with public borrowing. Management of the funded debt involved the sale of new bonds, an operation called floating or negotiating a loan, and the redemption of debt through the purchases of bonds from the money market by the Commissioners for the Sinking Fund. Although eighteenth-century governments could opt to purchase bonds and redeem them at par values, bonds were not legally promises for the repayment of debt. Nevertheless, after the American War of Independence, public opinion and statesmen became deeply concerned about the size of the country's debt, which had doubled in size (1775–83). Sir Robert Peel wrote a pamphlet to show 'the apprehensions which have surrounded the debt are unjustified', and William Playfair wrote another to disprove the prevalent notion of the debt 'as the great disease of the constitution'.[24] William Pitt the Younger shared fears about the size of the post-war debt and resolved to place it under a regular course of redemption.[25] His plans leaned heavily on the ideas of Richard Price.[26] Briefly, Price recommended the establishment of a sinking fund fed by taxes formerly paid as interest on bonds redeemed by the government. Thus the annuity payments formerly transferred to bondholders would provide the government with an accumulating fund for the redemption of more and more national debt. As Price himself put it, 'A Sinking Fund fed by interest is a fund constantly increasing'.[27] His ideas had much to commend them. Of course taxes had to be imposed to provide funds to buy an initial amount of bonds from the capital market, but as time went on the sinking fund depended less on the imposition of new taxes and more upon receipts from taxes formerly levied to pay annual interest to the government's creditors. Further taxes would not be imposed and the governments would simply maintain the existing burden of taxation in order to support a strategy for debt redemption. To statesmen faced by a society which exhibited such a marked reluctance to comply with demands for higher taxes, the attractions of Price's scheme were obvious.

In 1786 Pitt established his famous sinking fund when he allocated £1 million every year from surplus revenue for the purposes of debt redemption. He also used the interest formerly paid to the owners of the redeemed stock for the redemption of even more bonds. When the annual income of the sinking fund reached £4 million Pitt proposed that the interest on the bonds redeemed thereafter could be cancelled and taxes reduced accordingly.[28] Calculations among his papers show that if the price of consols had remained at 75, and no further borrowing occurred then through the operation of this plan, the national debt might have been paid off over thirty-five years.[29] Pitt was most anxious that his scheme should avoid the fate of previous sinking funds whose income had been diverted away from their original purposes towards the finance of other pressing items of public expenditure. In order, as he put it, 'to convince the kingdom something effectual is meant and public debts are indeed on the way to be extinguished', he attempted to design the legal and administrative framework of his sinking fund in such a way that it would become mandatory for all future chancellors of the Exchequer.[30]

For the five years prior to the wars of 1793–1815, the sinking fund operated as Pitt intended. The fund purchased bonds with surplus revenue from taxes and received interest on redeemed stock.[31] When the war against Revolutionary France began in 1793 the government once again commenced borrowing on a large scale, and with the disappearance of the budget surplus the whole purpose of the sinking fund obviously required reconsideration. For reasons discussed below, the government persisted with the sinking fund and between 1793 and 1815 allocated revenue for the redemption of debt at the same time as it sold bonds to the market.

Management of the unfunded debt involved decisions about the issue, renewal and redemption of bills. Every year the Treasury, confronted with blocks of matured bills due for redemption, could meet the government's obligations to its creditors in one of four ways. First, the bills could be repaid from the cash received from tax revenues and the unfunded debt would then decline. Second, the chancellor could allocate cash received from loans towards the repayment of bills. In this case the funded debt would rise but the unfunded debt would decline by a comparable amount. Whenever the government borrowed on bonds and at the same time reduced the unfunded debt, the Treasury had in effect allocated part of the loan towards the redemption of bills. Third, the chancellor could opt to renew matured bills for a further year. This occurred whenever the amount of bills issued over the year exceeded the amount repaid and the unfunded debt increased. The renewal of floating debt involved no transfer of cash from the public to the government and implied that the chancellor had deferred making proper provision for the redemption of bills until some future date. Finally, the Treasury could convert bills directly into bonds by means of an operation called funding, which simply involved the exchange of bills for bonds of comparable market values. Again no cash passed between citizens and the state. The Treasury reduced floating debt but added a comparable amount to the funded debt. Funding operations increased the supply of bonds offered to the money market over the financial year, which meant that past expenditure, met in the first instance through the sale of bills, was ultimately financed in a subsequent year through the sale of bonds.[32]

To sum up: eighteenth-century debt management was concerned with the sale and redemption of bonds and bills. It aimed to facilitate the flow of revenue into the Exchequer at the lowest possible cost to the public. To implement financial policy, the Treasury operated within the laws, conventions and institutions – analysed in Peter Dickson's classic text and other secondary sources. Nevertheless, economic constraints seriously limited the government's freedom to change conditions in the capital market for its bills and bonds. At any one time the distribution system in place for the sale of public assets had to be taken as given. For example the Treasury had to bargain with loan contractors and market bills through London bankers. Ministers continued to depend heavily on the Bank of England not merely to act as a private intermediary with the money market but to support both the government and the private institutions involved in supplying the state with whatever credit was deemed to be necessary. Furthermore, chancellors of the Exchequer also operated within the legal framework and constitutional conventions of a long established fiscal and financial system. They required approval from parliament for all their actions, and money had to be borrowed and spent within a single financial year.

Chancellors of the Exchequer could certainly, however, exercise some degree of influence on the terms upon which they borrowed money. First they could regulate flows of assets onto the London capital market in order to take advantage of changes in demand. They could also offer the kind of assets popular with the market and profitable to the government. Finally, they could seek to promote competition among those who purchased public securities.

Timing and Arrangements for the Issue and Redemption of State Securities
Chancellors of the Exchequer attempted to regulate the flow and composition of assets offered to the London capital market in order to take every possible advantage of variations in demand. Thus, when the market's preference for liquidity seemed high, interest charges could be contained by borrowing through the medium of bills. If bonds seemed to be in favour then it obviously benefited the Treasury to fund part of the floating debt. Strategy consisted essentially of reacting to changes in the disposition of the capital market towards different types of public securities. It was, above all, a matter of making the right arrangements at the right time. To appreciate the opportunities open to any chancellor it is

illuminating to outline the factors affecting market demand for securities and the methods available to him for taking advantage of such changes in demand.

In seeking funds the government always competed with demands for savings for profitable investment elsewhere in the economy. But while the market for the government's assets overlapped with the national market for capital, that market was neither homogeneous nor perfectly integrated. Bondholders lived on the whole in and around London. For most, their investment horizons probably did not extend to the possibility of owning industrial property in the north or the Midlands, and the ways in which industry was financed did not accommodate or normally appeal to them. The range of feasible alternatives open to investors in government paper may well have been confined to mortgages on real estate and the limited range of securities negotiated on the London capital market, which included stocks of the Bank of England, the East India Company, the shares of several insurance companies, public utilities and the more numerous canal companies. Moreover, since government borrowing resulted in the sale of assets legally exempt from the operations of the Usury Laws, it became difficult for the private sector to compete whenever interest rates moved above the legal maximum of 5 per cent.[33] The low risk, higher yield and marketability of public securities rendered them a favoured outlet for whatever funds happened to be available in London. While merchants, landowners, canal companies, builders and industrialists found it difficult to obtain loans or credit in wartime because of the diversion of investible funds into government securities.[34]

First-time buyers for new bonds included loan contractors, banks, insurance companies, bill brokers, gentlemen of the stock exchange, wholesalers, retailers and merchants of every kind, who together made up the London capital market. Although it might be difficult at the margin to distinguish dealers from investors, most of the immediate and possibly the second line of demand for bonds came from 'speculators'; that is from people more interested in realizing a capital gain on their transactions than in a steady income from interest. Government bills, on the other hand, provided the market with an asset less likely to fluctuate in value, more easily exchanged for cash at a London bank, of short maturity but which in general earned lower rates of interest than bonds. Investors in bills hardly expected to make serious capital gains, but bills did provide them with a fairly profitable and highly liquid outlet for surplus cash.

At any point of time the market distributed the funds available for investment in public securities between cash, bills and bonds. Cash balances offered little or no interest and maximum security. Bills paid interest and were easily realized for cash, while bonds paid higher rates of interest and offered prospects for capital gains. Movements of funds between different types of asset in response to pressures for liquidity was already evident during the eighteenth century, and reasons for changes in the disposition of the market are not difficult to trace.[35]

First of all, the propensity to purchase bonds grew stronger when investors' wishes for cash and bills had been satisfied. That depended rather heavily on the Bank of England. If the Bank imposed any restraint either upon purchases of bills from the government or upon the value of loans to the private sector, its action immediately reduced the overall demand for bonds. Apparently even rumours of stringency in overall monetary conditions produced the same result.[36] But apart from the absolutely crucial position of the Bank vis à vis the London money market, the government itself could also influence general liquidity. For example, if the Treasury issued more bills than it repaid over the financial year the volume of unfunded debt held by the market increased, while any contraction of the floating debt reduced both the market's liquidity position and its propensity to buy bonds.[37]

Similar effects could be occasioned by large-scale transfers of cash to or from the private sector to or from the government. For example, Abraham Newland, the Bank's cashier, explained to a House of Lords committee in 1797 how cash accumulated at the Exchequer for several weeks before quarterly dividends payments on the national debt, which made a considerable difference to the volume of money in circulation. Twenty-two years later another Lords committee put the variation in the note issue during the period preceding and following the payment of dividends at between £3 and £5 million.[38] Any fluctuation in the flow of government expenditure over the year also produced comparable variations in the volume of cash on deposit with London bankers and, through variations, expansions or contractions in the overall supply of credit afforded to its clients by the banking system.

The propensity of the market to buy bonds was also strongly influenced by expectations of future movements in their values. If prices moved upward and investors expected the trend to continue, their disposition to buy bonds became stronger, but if they anticipated a fall in prices their antipathy grew. They preferred to hold bills or cash. In an organized and interlocked market, speculators' dispositions to optimism or pessimism tended to become generalized quickly and in wartime their swings in mood could become highly volatile.[39]

This is not to say that the factors normally taken into account by speculators in their predictions were irrational. They knew, for example, that their customers could invest only a certain amount at any one time and that large and rapid increases in the supply of bonds could only be disposed of at lower prices. Thus, when purchasing bonds from the government or from their fellow dealers in the capital market, they had to make some estimate of the effects on prices of potential future flows of bonds onto the market and of the willingness of investors to absorb all the bonds offered for sale over finite periods of time.[40] In aggregate the relevant flow consisted of the annual loan, bills funded by the Treasury and old stock marketed by the public. Usually the chancellor informed the market about the amount of the loan early in the financial year, but funding operations occurred as and when his advisers considered it expedient to reduce floating debt. Dealers had no way of ascertaining the amount of bills scheduled for funding during the year, but they could reasonably anticipate such operations whenever the volume of floating debt outstanding had risen rapidly and when the discount on bills was falling.[41]

Additions to the amount of old stock normally sold by investors remained more unpredictable and depended upon their anxiety about the capital value of their holdings in the funds. Political events had been recognized throughout the century as perhaps the most significant influence on the disposition of both dealers and investors to buy and sell bonds. In peacetime the illness of the king, a change of administration, or, as Thomas Mortimer amusingly writes: 'the advancement to the highest offices in the state of men of weak minds, corrupt hearts and debauched manners' had tended to lower the demand and the prices of public securities.[42] By the end of the century investors concerned themselves very little with the risk of default by the government on its interest payments, but they knew that war would radically increase and peace seriously diminish the amount of money borrowed by the state. War, or the expectation of war, presaged an increase in the supply of bonds and bills and some predictably sharp reduction in their prices. Peace portended the opposite. Investors who had purchased assets cheaply while the war continued could expect to make capital gains when hostilities ceased, and people who had purchased bonds before war broke out could expect to make a loss if they realized their assets during the conflict. Thus speculators and investors concerned to preserve the capital value of their investments usually hurried to sell out at the onset of war and to buy when peace seemed imminent.[43] The influence of this body of 'floating assets' on prices could be considerable. Consol prices, for example, fell sharply at the onset of war in 1756, 1776 and 1792 and appreciated again when peace terms were agreed to in 1762, 1782, 1802 and 1814.[44]

During wars any political or military event which suggested either the prolongation of armed conflict or an early peace affected bond prices and the bids submitted for loans by contractors. For example, the contractor James Morgan observed that his bid 'would be governed by reference to the market price in the first instance, next the disposition of the public towards peace'.[45] Thus alliances formed against the kingdom; the loss of naval engagements or land battles and the termination of peace negotiations all served to depress bond prices, while victories, diplomatic success or the opening of talks with enemy powers invariably led to an appreciation of prices.[46]

Not all speculation about possible movements in the value of securities can be described as rationally based. For example on several occasions during the wars the stock exchange and other parts of the market apparently bought and sold on the basis of wild rumours and at least once the market succumbed to a deliberate fraud designed to persuade it that peace was in the offing and prices would rise.[47]

Many pamphleteers accused stockbrokers and other groups of dealers of rigging the market in order to further their own interests. Those about to buy bonds certainly possessed an interest in affecting reductions in their prices, while 'bears' about to sell obviously appreciated rising prices. But whether either group could effectively bring about changes in prices sufficient to affect the overall demand for bonds and the cost of borrowing by the state seems doubtful, whatever Mortimer and other opponents of the stock exchange might say to the contrary.[48]

Major decisions about debt management had usually to be made before the chancellor presented ways and means estimates to parliament and at that stage he decided upon the proportions of total revenue to be raised from taxes, from loans and through the medium of bills. Theoretically the chancellor should have favoured bills over bonds whenever the prices of the latter were falling and whenever the market displayed a propensity to remain liquid. The loan could be delayed and subsequently allocated towards the repayment of bills issued to anticipate its revenue. Unfortunately the chancellor could rarely calculate the relative advantages of funded against unfunded borrowing simply because he could not predict with any accuracy the likely flow of bills onto the market over the year. While he certainly knew the amount of bills due for repayment and could estimate the possible increase in the issue of bills for the finance of foreseen expenditure, the volume of bills circulated to cover either inaccuracies in the estimates of departmental (especially naval) expenditure or to anticipate receipts from taxes and loans over the current year could not be brought within a framework of calculation necessary for any rational policy of debt management. In particular, contingent short-term borrowing by the armed services frequently accounted for the greater part of additions to the flow of bills onto the capital market over the year. When sudden and rapid increases in the supply of bills could alter the whole basis of the chancellor's estimates about the relative movements in the prices of bonds and bills, the Treasury could do little more than attempt to contain contingent short-term borrowing within narrower limits. Fine calculations as to the relative advantages of borrowing on bills or bonds never really became feasible. The Treasury could not be expected to operate a 'rational policy' of debt management but usually reacted to the accumulation of floating debt by funding bills whenever profitable opportunities for conversion arose.[49]

Floating debt might also have been contained if the government repaid matured bills from the proceeds of loans. Such funding operations possessed certain advantages. First, the Treasury sometimes managed to convert bills into bonds of 4 and 5 per cent denomination, bonds which loan contractors usually refused to accept, but which had the merit of being convertible after the war into 3 per cent consols, thereby reducing the government's interest bill.[50] Some authors considered funding had an added advantage because it permitted the Treasury to bypass loan contractors and to deal directly with a larger number of bill proprietors, but whether cutting out one group of middlemen seriously reduced the overall interest bill is impossible to say.[51] It probably did not, because negotiations for funding were usually conducted with a fairly small group of London bankers who represented the market and reached prior agreement on the terms generally acceptable for the conversion of bills into bonds.[52]

Perhaps the most important advantage of funding was that it presented the Treasury with opportunities to regulate flows of bonds offered to the market. For example, the loan could be used to pay off bills or, if it seemed more efficient, the Treasury could float a smaller loan and follow with a funding operation. Calculations of this sort must have been difficult to make since they involved comparing the known prices of bonds on the date chosen for negotiating the loan with their expected prices on the date proposed for funding bills sometime later in the year. Additions to the loan would, moreover, depress bond prices while deductions from the volume of bills funded usually gave better terms on the conversion. Theoretically the Treasury should have funded an amount of bills or borrowed an amount of money so that the interest payable after both operations was minimized, at the point where the annual cost of the last pound borrowed equalled that on the marginal bill funded.[53]

Funding could also be timed to take advantage of changes in the disposition of the capital market. Negotiations to convert bills into bonds should theoretically have taken place when bond prices were rising. In wartime daily and unpredictable fluctuations in bond prices also rendered the selection of optimal dates extremely difficult and in any case the time for funding operations had to be negotiated with bill holders who had different views from the Treasury. Both they and the Treasury had, however, a common interest in selecting a time which did not overlap with the release of bonds on the current loan. Both parties attempted to avoid occasions when contractors were disposing of new stock, that is when additional supplies of bonds could depress their value.[54]

Dates for the negotiation of loan contracts were selected by the chancellor and presented him with opportunities for choosing times when demand seemed buoyant. He could avoid opening discussions about a loan when the market expected bond values to fall and displayed a strong tendency to remain liquid. For example, whenever adverse political or military conditions coincided with negotiations for a loan the government could expect the cost of borrowing to rise. Diplomatic and military intelligence could provide the Treasury with advance information about current events and the chancellor could then decide whether to float a loan late or early in the year in order to take advantage of possible fluctuations in bond prices. The government could also create more favourable conditions for the negotiation of a loan either by issuing Exchequer bills or by timing the contract to follow the payment of dividends on the national debt and the purchases of stock by the Commissioners for the Sinking Fund. Accessions of cash or issues of bills helped to satisfy the market's demand or liquidity and disposed it towards bonds.

Other things being equal the Treasury obtained better terms for loans if it gave contractors some degree of control over the supply of new bonds offered to the market. This could be achieved by timing contracts for loans and funding operations in such a way that the supply of bonds remained in the hands of a single group of middlemen. If loans overlapped or coincided with funding operations, the distribution of bonds to a wider market passed into the hands of several rival groups of bankers and contractors all competing for a finite demand. In this situation contractors could adjust their bids for the loan upwards and the cost of borrowing would rise. If, on the other hand, the Treasury made arrangements to allow a single consortium to monopolize the supply of bonds, at least for short periods, contractors were more likely to take an optimistic view of their prospects for capital gains and would raise their bids on the loan accordingly.[55]

It was difficult, however, for the Treasury to widen the gap between loan negotiations without shortening the total time allowed to contractors for the payment of instalments into the Exchequer. Unless subscribers had large personal resources or credit available, they frequently sold the scrip of one instalment to make the next payment. Thus, it became the interest of a consortium to have its liability spread out over the financial year. If the Treasury required payment within a shorter period the rate at which new bonds came onto the market accelerated; profits fell, and bids for the loan would inevitably go down. To help contractors, the Treasury tried to arrange its borrowing operations in order to avoid overlaps and gave them the maximum possible time in which to pay the instalments on a loan.[56]

Denomination of Bonds

By the late eighteenth century the government had marketed bonds of 3, 4 and 5 per cent denominations and could presumably experiment with stocks of higher or lower face values if it so desired.[57] Borrowing money or funding bills into stocks of higher denomination gave the chancellor opportunities for reducing the long-term interest charge on the national debt through conversion operations. Conversion consisted of borrowing money at lower rates of interest in order to reduce old debts contracted at higher rates. Since the government retained the right to redeem bonds whenever their value reached par, when prices rose to that level the Treasury could readily reduce the state's interest bill by converting debt.[58] Perhaps an example will reveal more clearly how these operations could be advantageous to the state. Suppose during the war the government could borrow in 5 per cent bonds issued at par or in 3 per cent bonds valued by the market at 60. In the short term the interest bill on either option is identical because the rate of interest is 5 per cent. Assume further that after the war bond prices rise by 50 per cent and the rate of interest thus falls to 3.33 per cent, bonds of 3 per cent denomination would then sell for £90, that is £10 below par, and 5 per cent bonds for £150 or £50 above par. If the Treasury had borrowed in 3 per cent bonds it would not be presented with an opportunity for reducing the government's interest bill. But if borrowing had occurred in 5 per cent stock (repayable at par), interest could be reduced by 1.66 per cent. 'Borrowing at par enables the state to redeem whenever the stock rises above par ... the other fixes the rate of interest for ever.'[59] Not only was Rickard's argument theoretically tenable, but a long list of conversion operations dating from the early years of the eighteenth century testified to its efficacy. For example, interest on loans from the Bank of England and the South Sea Company had been reduced from 6 to 5 per cent in 1717, to 4 per cent in 1727, to 3.5 per cent in 1750 and to 3 per cent in 1757 by well-timed conversion operations. Between the close of the War of Succession and the opening of the Seven Years War the Treasury reduced by stages the interest on nearly £58 million of stock from 4 to 3 per cent and all of the stocks bearing interest at 4 and 3.5 per cent in 1761 were subsequently reduced to 3 per cent. But from 1763 opportunities for conversions became more limited because nearly two-thirds of the bonds issued after that date consisted of consols and the remainder were nearly all 4 per cent stock. Furthermore, from 1786 the government preferred to rely on the sinking fund to bring about reductions in the charges paid on the national debt. Nevertheless, the country's 'long term interest' demanded that the chancellor market bonds of the highest denomination acceptable to the market.[60]

Competitive Tenders

Firm adherence to the system of competitive tender represented another means open to the Treasury to influence the price it obtained for bonds. At the outbreak of the long wars with France, this system was still of recent origin.[61] Negotiations for loans in the early part of the eighteenth century had frequently been conducted with the East India Company, the Bank of England or the South Sea Company.[62] Only public companies with their resources and status could guarantee the success of a government loan. Later private bankers and prominent mercantile houses took over the function of selling bonds for the government, but up to the War of American Independence the numbers of firms who could guarantee to market an issue of government bonds remained small. Already during that war sufficient groups of speculators had expressed interest in the transaction for two rival consortiums to be formed for the loans of 1782 and 1783, but the Treasury preferred to retain the power to allocate and incurred the charge of partiality. Pitt insisted, however, upon sealed tenders for the loan of 1784 and thereby set the precedent for the system of competitive tender.[63]

However, negotiations with select groups of City financiers even in competition with one another, was not without its opponents who favoured 'open subscriptions'.[64] Critics often failed to realize that open subscriptions placed the onus on the chancellor to fix the price at which he proposed to issue new bonds and attract subscribers and it would have been difficult for him to discharge such a responsibility with competence. His proposed price had to be sufficiently high to obtain all the cash required and the Treasury needed to assess the reliability of all potential subscribers to honour their engagements. If bond prices moved downward after the contract the risk of default increased and if they moved upward the chancellor stood exposed to the charge of extravagance with public money.[65] An open subscription implies a developed stock market ready to subscribe to any reasonable offer from the Treasury. Such a market had not developed by the late eighteenth century for anything but closed and competitive tenders to be the appropriate method to deploy.

Among those not impressed with the system of competitive tender was the economist Sir John Sinclair. He thought that competition encouraged speculators who took up new loans in order to sell out quickly which lowered the price of bonds and thereby increased the cost at which subsequent loans could be floated. Competition, Sinclair considered, had raised the rate of interest, because it augmented the risk and diminished the profits of lending to the government. Sinclair preferred the old system whereby established banking houses received their allocation of scrip which they sold gradually at a reasonable profit to themselves and for the benefit of the government.[66]

There is no substance to his first argument. Certainly it would be impossible to prove that the list of subscribers to loans offered to competitive tender contained more 'speculators' (so often a term of disapprobation during the eighteenth century) who sold scrip more rapidly than old established houses. Upon inspection many speculators, with or without competition, turn out to be the old established houses anyway. Furthermore, how a competitive system of tender per se influenced decisions about selling or holding bonds is difficult to comprehend. Such decisions depended primarily upon movements in bond prices. If speculators expected prices to rise they held bonds, and sold if they anticipated a downward trend. Of course, proponents of Sinclair's view might argue that the existence of competition itself leads to pessimistic expectations about bond prices. Competition represented, however, a continuing factor in the capital market and only one among the multifarious influences on price changes, actual or anticipated. Even in theory it cannot be held responsible for a tendency towards more rapid turnover than might have occurred if loans continued to be allocated among contractors.

There is more to Sinclair's second criticism. In so far as competition raised the bid made by a loan contractor for bonds it reduced the margin within which he could profit from their subsequent sale, and also increased the risk of loss if bond prices declined while the loan remained under payment. Bond prices fluctuated unpredictably in wartime and when a consortium suffered losses the capital market in general revised its assessment of the risks involved in loan contracting. Bids for the subsequent loan might be revised upward.

Chancellors of the Exchequer seemed to be aware of this factor and in expressing satisfaction with the terms of a loan usually added that they hoped the terms would prove profitable for the contractors. Pitt, for example, told parliament the terms of the loan for 1794 'were highly favourable to the public and what was desirable he hoped safe to the lender'.[67] His attempt to compensate the capital market for its losses on the loyalty loan of 1796 displayed an appreciation that over time the government would not be in the public interest, which characterized Treasury negotiations with the capital market.

To point out that certain of the loans negotiated in closed contract between 1793 and 1815 cost less than others offered to competition is an invalid criticism. Adherence to the system of competitive tender remained the only real guarantee that money had been borrowed as cheaply as possible. Competition prevented corruption and did away with patronage. Under the alternative system of allocation, the market price of bonds on the day of the loan contract invariably formed the basis for settling the price at which contractors purchased bonds. Thus, they had a joint interest and sometimes took steps to artificially depress bond prices before negotiating for loans. As a group they gained and the public lost from subsequent appreciation in prices. Under a system of competitive tender, their interests did not coincide. Efforts to depress the current price of bonds for a loan contract certainly continued during the war years, but the presence of rival consortia at negotiations implied an interest by some groups, to bid close to, sometimes below, a market price which they knew to be artificially depressed. Furthermore, had loans continued to be allocated to old established houses the boundaries of the capital market and the development of specialization within it would probably not have been extended to anything like the extent witnessed between 1793 and 1815. Departures from competitive tender could only be defended by the circumstances of a particular case.

The Management of the Debt, 1793–1815

Historical Contexts for an Appraisal of Debt Management

Before, during and after the French wars, the management of the national debt aroused controversy and criticism. Much of the criticism consisted of ill-informed assertions which often degenerated into political vituperation. This can be ignored and so can almost all arguments by comparison or analogy. For example, Pitt and his successors at the Treasury were often condemned or praised for borrowing money at higher or lower rates of interest than their predecessors in charge of Britain's finances in earlier wars. Since even the most capable of chancellors could exercise only a marginal influence on the price obtained for bonds, (the rate of interest being determined by a range of factors outside the control of the Treasury), comparisons between the cost of borrowing in one war and another indicate very little about the efficiency of debt management.

The most persistent focus for controversy during the wars with France was the size of the debt itself. On one side can be found prophets of woe, like Thomas Paine and William Cobbett opposed to the wars altogether. Along with most radicals they disliked the whole system of funded borrowing because it increased the power of the state, and the affluence of the Bank of England, the stock exchange and loan contractors. Their antipathy is really to an unreformed aristocratic constitution backed by the City of London. Appalled by the rapid accumulation of debt, the size of the loans and mounting burdens of interest payments radicals predicted ruin, national bankruptcy, the collapse of the whole financial system and other dire consequences unless the government ceased to borrow money. Less politicized critics combined gloomy forecasts with recommendations, not as one might expect to finance wars with taxes, but with implausible schemes for the immediate redemption of large portions of the debt.[68]

On the other side of the controversy supporters of the government (many no doubt paid by the Treasury for their efforts) attempted in print and in the House of Commons to counteract all dangerous talk of financial chaos. They pointed out that the nominal capital of the debt really indicated very little at all. For proof of the country's ability to meet government demands for loans, public opinion needed to be well informed about the nation's resources and production. Usually they coupled this injunction with as many statistics as they could muster to demonstrate that trade, industry and agriculture all flourished and that incomes had risen since the onset of war.[69] As supporters of the government they properly observed that the British system, which rested upon consent, could not collapse as long as the government continued to abide by the established constitutional rules and conventions for borrowing money.

Certainly, the size of the debt is largely irrelevant to an investigation of its management, and the voluminous controversy on this subject in the press, in pamphlets and in parliament diverted critical attention away from a proper and potentially efficient scrutiny of day-to-day Treasury policies. As Peter Dickson correctly anticipated the only way to understand the management of the debt at any time between 1689 and 1815 is to place financial policy and administration firmly in historical context. He recognized it is essential to bear in mind the constraints of the financial system, the difficulties of borrowing in war time and the war aims of the state.[70] Peter Dickson's example (pioneered by Grellier and Newmarch) to reconstruct historical contexts on the London capital market for the entire gamut for funded, unfunded and redemption operations conducted by the Treasury for 1793–1815 were followed *à la lettre* in my doctoral thesis submitted to the University of Oxford in 1967. Alas there is no space (and it would be tedious) to repeat the detail gleaned here.[71] For present purposes I propose to summarize my general inferences and conjectures from a day-to-day investigation of debt management; leaving readers to consult my thesis for further details and full references.[72]

During the war years, governments of the day modified their managerial practices and passed laws designed to alter the established framework for the London money market in their favour – including that most innovatory and important measure of all, the suspension of specie payments by the Bank of England in 1797. This famous departure from traditional financial policies, previously pursued by the Hanoverian state has been analysed in several works.[73]

Apart from the major discontinuity in monetary policy some rather less than successful attempts were made to reform procedures used by the navy, army and ordnance to estimate their annual expenditures and thereby reduce their unpredictable demands for credit as well as some administrative endeavours to speed up the collection of taxes and their despatch to the Exchequer in London.[74] The assumption behind historical analysis conducted here is that ministers and their advisers could do little more than to manage the debt in ways designed to take a rather limited range of options open to governments at the time to borrow as efficiently as possible. As elaborated above, the Treasury could bring about reductions in the cost of borrowing in four ways. First, it could control the flow and composition of securities offered to the market in order to take advantage of variations in demands. Second, it could foster competition. Third, by pressing stocks of higher denomination on a reluctant market to purchase bonds of denominations higher than 3 per cent the chancellor left the way open for conversion operations which diminished the cost of borrowing over the long run. Finally the government deliberately eschewed the option of abandoning the sinking fund at the outbreak of the war, which if taken could have seriously reduced the total supply of bonds offered to the market between 1793 and 1815.

Flows of Bonds and Bills

Before 1797 the Treasury could not, however, take advantage of the possibilities for alternating between funded and unfunded borrowing, by selling bills whenever bond prices seemed depressed and funding bills whenever bond prices appreciated again. Under pressure from the Bank of England and anxious about the large and unpredictable issues of naval and military bills onto the market, Pitt became more concerned to contain the floating debt.[75] His funding operations over the years 1794–7 seem to be more of a response to credit restrictions imposed by the Bank and unpredicted accumulation of debt for the Crown, than a considered technique of debt management.[76]

After the suspension of cash payments in 1797, followed by reforms to the format of the navy bills and some improvements to military and naval estimates, the employment of unfunded borrowing became a real possibility.[77] Yet between 1798 and 1807, anxious about the stability of the kingdom's inconvertible currency, the Treasury exercised caution in marketing bills followed by funding operations as a way of forcing 4 and 5 per cent stocks onto the market, even though funding possessed the merit of reducing the loan and a smaller loan generally stimulated competition in the capital market. Later in the war from 1807–15 the technique of mortgaging future revenue in order to finance current expenditure became an important part of policy which included a loan and one or more funding operations.[78]

Yet critics, observing the rapid accumulation of floating debt during the early and closing years of the war, argued that at times the Treasury pushed unfunded borrowing to excessive lengths.[79] They failed to recognize that the accumulation of unfunded debt can be attributed in large measure to issues of bills by the army and navy. Despite some reforms to forecasting techniques, naval and military expenditure (over and above the budgetary provisions sanctioned by parliament) continued to complicate the task of debt management. Only after 1808 did the Treasury deliberately resort to bill finance on any significant scale. Even then it would be difficult to prove that the employment of unfunded borrowing over the latter years of the war occasioned any rise in the overall and long-term cost of borrowing.[80] In fact the opposite seems more likely. The only valid case that can be made against unfunded borrowing is that it exacerbated wartime inflation.[81] The government might, however, be criticized for its failure to really reform the methods employed by the armed forces to predict expenditure. Their forecasts not only complicated the Treasury's financial operations but led directly to wasteful expenditures by the armed forces.[82]

To discern just how well the Treasury timed the release of securities onto the capital market seems almost impossible, largely because the question is concerned not simply with historical facts but involves an understanding and appraisal of numerous predictions made by the chancellor and his advisers between 1793 and 1815.[83] In these highly unstable years the apparent failure of a particular loan or funding operation cannot in all fairness be condemned if it can be attributed to factors the Treasury could neither control nor reasonably anticipate. Looked at in historical context the evidence marshalled to comprehend conditions in the capital market at the time when decisions were made suggests that historians might be able, ex post, to sustain a rather limited number of criticisms of the ways that chancellors timed their borrowing operations between 1793 and 1815. For example, Pitt might be awarded black marks for not delaying the loan of 1793 until after the commercial crisis that accompanied the outbreak of war had run its course, and reprimanded for minor mistakes in 1796 and 1805.[84] Henry Petty failed to time the loan of 1806 to coincide with the payment of dividends in April of that year.[85] Nicholas Vansittart appears to have been guilty of three serious errors of judgement between 1813 and 1815, errors which transferred a great deal of money from taxpayers into the pockets of loan contractors and bondholders.[86] This is not, however, a lengthy catalogue of managerial mistakes for twenty-two years of operations on a highly volatile capital market.[87]

Competition

When they observe that no less than eleven out of the twenty-six loans floated between 1793 and 1815 were not subject to competitive tender, historians may well agree with economists who dismissed the whole process as 'a mere façade'.[88] They may not realize, however, that competition constituted only one among several conflicting ways open to the Treasury for affecting reductions in the cost of borrowing. For example, if the chancellor opted to time the sale of bonds so that loans overlapped with each other or with funding operations, competition often ceased to be possible, but the public might well have gained more from successful timing than it lost from the absence of competition. Similarly, decisions that sacrificed competition for the advantages of selling bonds of 4 and 5 per cent denomination eventually paid off.[89]

Furthermore, the government could not insist upon competitive tenders when faced with determined collusion among loan contractors and it did not pay to push competition to the point where contractors made losses and the capital market revised upwards its estimate of the risks involved in speculating in public securities.[90] Nevertheless chancellors in charge of debt management over this period (with the possible exception of Spencer Perceval – advised by William Huskisson) appear unduly conservative in experimenting with ways of stimulating competition, by such devices as dividing the loan, by strategic funding operations and by diverting revenues from the sinking fund in order to reduce the net supply of bonds marketed over the year.[91] Nevertheless, detailed surveys of conditions in the London capital market year by year from 1793 to 1815 led me to the post hoc conclusion that no more than two of the eleven departures from competition during the French wars can be termed indefensible. Both occurred with Vansittart in charge of negotiations in 1813 and 1814.[92]

Consols and Bonds of Higher Denomination

During the long wars with France only a small proportion of the money borrowed by the government came from the sale of bonds other than consols.[93] At the time several writers rebuked the Treasury for marketing too many consols compared with other stocks.[94] After the war when bond values appreciated and when falling prices made interest payments on the national debt a greater and regressive burden on taxpayers, this line of criticism became more vehement.[95] But before support is given to such views (typified by McCulloch) it is essential to make two basic qualifications. First, the range of possibilities open to the Treasury should be elucidated, and second, the precise advantages, both in the short and the long run, of marketing 4 and 5 per cent bonds must be clearly defined.

All the evidence suggests that possibilities for selling stocks other than consols were considerably more limited than critics allowed. As Parker correctly observed, 'contractors have uniformly opposed the funding of debt in stocks bearing a high rate of interest'.[96] They frequently resisted the chancellor's attempts to float the loan in stocks of 4 or 5 per cent denominations, and at negotiations for the loan of 1806 the contractors pressured the chancellor to change his offer between 3 per cent stocks because they claimed 3 per cent reduced stocks were less marketable than consols.[97] They displayed extreme reluctance to experiment with any new forms of public securities such as debentures which first Huskisson and later Vansittart attempted to sell.[98] Their refusal was not a matter of conservatism. Throughout the war years between 60 and 70 per cent of the national debt consisted of consols, which gave that stock a much wider potential market than any other asset. Lower prices for consols widened the market still further and improved prospects for capital gains.[99] Certainly the stock exchange favoured consols and conducted forward dealings in no other assets.[100] Whenever the Treasury gave the market the option of subscribing to different kinds of bonds it invariably opted for 3 per cent stocks. No doubt investors over the eighteenth century had been well schooled in the risk of conversion attendant upon the purchase of 4 and 5 per cent bonds and knew that consols seldom rose above par.[101]

In the face of marked antipathy Pitt certainly made determined efforts to push unpopular stocks onto the contractors, with only a limited amount of success. For a decade from 1797 to 1807 and for the closing years of the war (1812–15) the minutes of loan negotiations give no indication that chancellors attempted to force 4 and 5 per cent stocks onto the contractors.[102] Perhaps the relatively large loans of those years made such initiatives possible only at the expense of frustrating the system of competitive tender.

Throughout the war the Treasury achieved far greater success in marketing unpopular paper assets through the medium of funding operations. Unlike a loan contract, when converting bills into bonds the government dealt directly with the wider and more atomized market, in which few opportunities existed for collusive refusal to accept particular types of public securities. Bill holders seem less reluctant than contractors to purchase such bonds. They took only a small portion from the amount of each individual issue and could take more time than contractors in disposing of it to a wider circle of clients.[103]

Between 1822 and 1854 conversion operations affected a saving of £3.6 million on an interest bill which then averaged about £28.6 million a year.[104] McCulloch calculated that if the Treasury had persisted with stocks other than consols between 1793 and 1815 the annual saving might have been pushed up to the £10 million mark.[105] Perhaps the Treasury could have marketed 4 and 5 per cent bonds, but only at the cost of additions to the annual interest bill until their conversion at some unknowable time in the future. As Ricardo pointed out, 'the ultimate gain to taxpayers from borrowing in stock of high denomination depended on their relative prices compared with consols at the point of sale'.[106] For example, in February 1796, when 5 per cent consols were at par, money could be borrowed in the market at £4.7 shillings in 4 per cent bonds and at £4.3 in consols. Of course this differential between stocks varied over time, but if prices of 3 and 5 per cent bonds are compared for dates just prior to loan negotiations conducted at that time it can be shown that the government would have paid 0.57 per cent more for the privilege of raising money in unpopular assets.[107] To have persisted with 4 or 5 per cent bonds would undoubtedly have depressed their value still further. Such a policy might also have frustrated the system of competitive tender and raised the rate of interest on loans by as much as 1 per cent. This involved the imposition of more taxes at a time when chancellors found it extremely difficult to discover productive sources of tax revenue.

McCulloch and his fellow critics should in all fairness have tried to appreciate the time horizons of Pitt and his fellow chancellors, who regarded bonds sold during the war years as assets with defined maturities. They anticipated that each and every issue of government stocks would eventually be redeemed through the operation of Pitt's established sinking fund. They had no clear notion of when wars would end, or when 5 per cents would rise sufficiently above par to present governments in the future with opportunities for converting public debt to lower rates of interest. Their strategic problem was to weigh possible gains from reductions in the interest bill through conversion operations sometime later in times of peace against the disadvantage of paying more interest at least while warfare continued and possibly longer.

To illustrate the point, let us take the loan of 1804. Henry Addington then had a choice of borrowing in consols or a 5 per cent stock. From his perspective the duration of the war must have seemed indefinite. Yet he expected bonds issued in 1804 to be redeemed after forty years through the operation of the sinking fund. If he opted for consols the state could expect to pay £227 in interest over the life of a single bond, but by choosing 5 per cent stock, the chancellor would have increased the total interest paid per bond to £243. At that point in time he could not be certain that any possible conversion operation after the war would affect a sufficient reduction in the total interest bill to compensate for the difficulties of and additions to taxes in wartime. Of course from the vantage of the mid-nineteenth century with external security taken for granted, and when the sinking fund had been dismissed as a 'delusion', it was all too easy to assert that 'the grand error of our Finance Ministers ... consisted in their attempting to secure an inconsiderable advantage at great ultimate cost'.[108] During the war the problem appeared considerably more complex and the possibilities for marketing stocks other than consols much more limited than economists with hindsight are wont to admit.[109] Perhaps, however, they might argue that the sinking fund deluded chancellors into not attending assiduously enough to the options open to them to reduce the burdens of servicing debt carried by future generations of the kingdom's taxpayers.

Pitt's Infamous Sinking Fund

Between 1793 and 1815 the Treasury sold bonds worth £447 million and over the same period another public body, the Commissioners for the Sinking Fund, purchased £176 million of bonds.[110] Since these securities continued to be issued as perpetual annuities, legally redeemable at the option of the state, the government's clear policy to borrow and pay back money at the same time appears prima facie curious. Repayment of debt in wartime represented, moreover, a complete departure from traditional policies for debt management.[111] Yet the policy received unanimous approbation from contemporaries and condemnation from almost all economists and historians who subsequently examined the financing of the French wars. McCulloch referred to it as a 'miserable juggle', and Doubleday as a 'contemptible hocus pocus'. Lord Grenville, who supported the policy during the war, later called it 'the greatest of all misconceptions', and Newmarch called it 'a hallucination'.[112] Recent and more historical studies by authors like Hargreaves, Acworth and Reese have lent their support to this tradition of castigation.[113]

Almost all criticism of the operation of the sinking fund between 1793 and 1815 leans heavily upon Hamilton's famous essay, *An Inquiry Concerning the Rise and Progress, the Redemption and Present State of Management of that National Debt*, written in 1812. The most important section of this essay is concerned to demolish the ideas of Richard Price.[114] Price had published views categorically opposed to any suspension of the sinking fund in wartime. He considered that war increased efficacy of the sinking fund because in wartime money was borrowed at higher rates of interest and bonds bearing elevated rates of interest could be redeemed in less time than debt contracted with the same initial sinking fund but at lower rates of interest.[115] An example will clarify his argument: a loan of £10 million at interest of 6 per cent would be redeemed by a sinking fund equal to 1 per cent of the loan, or £100,000 in thirty-three years. If the rate of interest was only 3 per cent, with the same initial 1 per cent sinking fund, redemption would take forty-seven years. Under Price's plan when the cost of borrowing went up the absolute sum transferred annually by the Treasury to the sinking fund also rose and obviously accelerated debt repayment. Price virtually ignored the annual charges involved. If the rate of interest rose to 6 per cent the government would every year have to meet interest and sinking fund payments of £700,000 compared with £400,000 if the rate of interest had remained at 3 per cent and the overall cost of amortizing a loan of £10 million at an interest rate of 6 per cent would be nearly a third higher.[116] War made the sinking fund efficacious simply because more taxes would be transferred to it annually for debt redemption. Yet the additional revenue required to operate the fund could only be obtained either by the imposition of new taxes or borrowing. With the disappearance of surplus revenue from taxation after 1792 all allocations to the sinking fund could only be financed with borrowed money. If the annual income for the sinking fund is borrowed at the same rate of interest as the original loan the government will simply be adding to the national debt an amount identical to that redeemed in any given year. If money is borrowed at a rate of interest higher than that formerly paid on redeemed bonds, the national debt and the interest bill will increase.

Even before the war the flaws embodied in some of these arguments had been exposed.[117] Later Hamilton and his followers showed how Price had become confused by compound interest to the point of arguing as if it alone provided the government with funds to redeem debt. But if the historians' concern is not Richard Price but government policy, one crucial question about the sinking fund and debt management during the French wars has never been answered. They must surely enquire as to how far Pitt and his fellow chancellors shared the opinions of Price. Was the sinking fund maintained in operation in wartime for the reasons Price proposed, or were there other and perhaps more sensible political arguments for its retention? The question needs emphasis because Hamilton and his followers tacitly assumed that because Price's plan looks illogical governments of the day also suffered from his delusions. Upon examination, their condemnation of the sinking fund is often based upon little more than a refutation of the worst errors of Richard Price.[118]

Yet evidence that the men in charge of finances during the French wars shared Price's more irrational views on the sinking fund is thin. On the contrary, their budget speeches demonstrate an awareness that income for the sinking fund came from taxation or had to be borrowed.[119] To credit statesmen of the calibre of Pitt, Perceval and Huskisson with an incapacity to perceive that the sinking fund had failed to reduce the national debt is to malign their intelligence. Had Pitt not established his original sinking fund with surplus revenue?

But if the sinking fund did not in fact decrease accumulation of public debt, what then was its function in wartime? On several occasions Pitt publicly answered this question. 'All other wars left a burden to posterity the successful institution of the sinking fund has made a most material alteration to that system.' 'We ought to consider', he said in 1797, 'how far the effort we shall exert ... will enable us to transmit the inheritance of posterity unencumbered with those burdens which would cripple their vigour'.[120] To this end Pitt, as early as May 1790, decided that 'We ought to aim at providing new funds not just for the interest but also sufficient so that *the period of the discharge of the debt* may not be altered'. 'Our debt may be considered', he told parliament, '*as an annuity for a limited number of years*'.[121]

Pitt made provisions in 1786 to pay off the existing capital of the national debt over a finite number of years.[122] Six years later, at the very beginning of the war, he introduced legislation designed to transform all future debt contracted by the state into terminable annuities. Pitt's scheme committed the government to the imposition of taxes sufficient to pay interest and amortization charges over a period of forty-five years on all loans negotiated after 1792. The money was to come from additional taxes equal to 1 per cent of the nominal capital of any loan, together with continued payment of annual interest on bonds redeemed.[123] Although Pitt persisted with the complex administrative device of allocating interest on redeemed bonds into a fund to redeem more bonds, the essential idea behind his legislation was to impose taxes sufficient to place all future loans into a regular course of redemption.[124] As George Rose, Pitt's minister at the Treasury, wrote in 1806, 'every debt is now reduced to an annuity and a large proportion of the persons in existence at the time of debt being created must, in the ordinary course of nature, live to see the end of it'.[125]

Pitt aimed to relieve posterity from the burden of interest payments on the national debt, a goal which received universal praise from his contemporaries, and his legislation provided a model for all subsequent policy regarding the sinking fund.[126] Those who lectured the governments of the day for failing to see 'the only means of redeeming the National Debt is to reduce expenditure and increase taxes' or to perceive 'a Sinking Fund can only operate in peace time' were mistaken if they supposed chancellors of the day could not understand such an elementary point.[127] Their criticism is irrelevant because Pitt, Addington, Perceval and Vansittart regarded the sinking fund as a political device for making provision in taxation (even in the midst of the most expensive war in the kingdom's history) for the ultimate redemption of the entire national debt.[128]

No other interpretation can make sense of their speeches and legislation after 1792. For example, in 1802, when Addington repealed provisions of the original Sinking Fund Act of 1786 (which promised relief from taxation when £4 million of bonds were being redeemed annually), he explained to the House of Commons they had a choice of providing for the repayment of more debt or affording the country relief from immediate rising taxation. With a few dissenting voices the chancellor secured parliamentary approval for continuing taxes previously used to pay dividends on redeemed debt to buy up still more bonds.[129]

When Grenville's government assumed office in 1806 they sought to avoid the imposition of more taxes, and the chancellor of the Exchequer produced a 'New Plan of Finance' which expressly involved borrowing money to pay both interest and the amortization charges on all future loans. Petty's scheme modified existing policy under which the government imposed sufficient taxes to redeem every loan over a set period of time, but he met the objection that he had departed from Pitt's sinking fund by a proposal to continue to employ 'war taxes' to redeem bonds after the end of the war. Thus, under the 'New Plan' (which did not sur-

vive the fall of the Ministry of All Talents), bonds sold during the war would
be redeemed in peacetime with taxes that parliament and the public classified as
temporary or war taxes. The national debt remained an aggregation of annuities
but the time taken for their redemption grew longer.[130]

Perhaps nothing illustrates the essence of wartime policy with regard to debt
redemption better than Perceval's scheme of 1808 which gave creditors the option
of exchanging their bonds for life annuities payable out the sinking fund.[131] Yet
another revealing discussion on the sinking fund emerged at the end of the war
when Vansittart proposed to divert income from the sinking fund towards the
payment of interest and redemption charges on loans contracted after 1813.[132]
Both Lord Liverpool and his chancellor pleaded the necessity for respite from
additional taxation, but also argued that the income of the sinking fund could
become excessively large. They thought it undesirable to devote £30 million a year
in peacetime to debt repayment.[133] For political reasons Vansittart presented his
plan as a 'restoration' of Pitt's original intentions to limit the annual sum devoted
to debt redemption but his critics insisted he had departed from the great man's
later ideas.[134]

Sir Francis Baring, Henry Thornton, Huskisson and Petty claimed that
Liverpool's government had broken faith with public creditors who had loaned
it money on the understanding that a progressively increasing sum would be
devoted to the repayment of debt each year.[135] Vansittart, argued, however, that
bond holders had no right to expect that taxes used to meet interest upon a debt
incurred before 1786 would continue to be employed to redeem loans contracted
after that date, and insisted that part of the income of the sinking fund could be
diverted without violating faith.[136]

Huskisson, probably the most reliable guardian of Pitt's intentions, clarified
for the last time the character of the wartime sinking fund. Its operation had,
he argued, 'made loans equivalent to annuities, repayable over 45 years'. It also
induced contractors to offer better terms to the public because redemption was
clearly provided for in each loan contract. He criticized Vansittart for being over-
concerned with temporary respite from taxation; 'Pitt', he said 'would never
shrink from imposing taxes' and concluded by recommending that taxes be continued after the war to redeem the national debt.[137]

Once Pitt had persuaded parliament to regard bonds as debts of a defined
maturity, it became difficult for anyone to see anything illogical in redeeming
them with borrowed money. After all, if governments had traditionally contracted
debts in terminable rather than irredeemable annuities, the Treasury would have
been compelled long before 1786 to repay and borrow money at the same time.
Agreed, as Petty observed, 'the Sinking Fund could be used as the country likes'.[138]
Had the annuity concept been abandoned at the outbreak of the long wars with
France, no revenue would have been raised between 1793 and 1815 to redeem
debt and the total sum borrowed reduced by a corresponding amount. Why then

did ministers persist with the annuity concept during such a long and expensive war?

The only plausible answer is that statesmen of the day regarded the sinking fund as a device to allay fears about the growing size of the national debt. From even a cursory reading of contemporary newspapers and pamphlets, published from 1783 to 1819, it is apparent that people living at the end of the eighteenth century felt much less sanguine about the national debt than we do today. Anxiety became widespread during the War of American Independence when the nominal capital of the debt increased by nearly 100 per cent in little over six years.[139]

Against a background of widespread unease in 1786 Pitt had introduced plans for its ultimate redemption. Previous sinking funds had failed because statesmen diverted their income to other uses.[140] In order to assure the public of the seriousness of his plan, Pitt promised parliament the sinking fund would become inviolable.[141] By quasi-constitutional statutes and administrative arrangements he endeavoured to keep that promise.[142]

When the government began in 1793 to borrow more than ever before anxieties about one known and large fact, namely the absolute size of the nominal capital of the national debt, intensified. Prophets of woe appeared on every side employing false analogies from private debt to argue 'the country stood on the verge of bankruptcy' or 'brought to the brink' by the immense size of the national debt. As William Frend said of these pundits 'they ... confidently asserted and arithmetically proved we are ruined'.[143]

Apprehension about the mounting burden of taxes imposed to pay interest looks more realistic. 'The evils already produced by taxes to pay interest on funds are likely to prove fatal to our national prosperity', exclaimed one writer in 1799. His fears found echoes both inside and outside parliament and gave rise to more than a century of intense debate about the wisdom of accumulating national debt. What is striking about this discussion is that pessimists (who thought the burden of debt would become unbearable) and optimists (who argued that burdens had diminished with the general rise in income) both found solace in contemplating its ultimate redemption, through Pitt's sinking fund. 'The experience of this country has shown', wrote a bishop in 1797, 'that a debt which would at one time have overpowered the resources of the nation, may at another from its increased agriculture, manufactures and commerce be scarcely felt as a burthen'.[144] Three years later he felt 'happy in the conviction ... that the nation's debts are in regular course of repayment'.[145] Statesmen's papers indicate an almost obsessive interest in schemes to reduce the debt.[146] Their speeches eulogized the sinking fund and their annual finance resolutions invariably contained a rhetorical paragraph to the effect that its income was rising as a proportion of the national debt.[147] 'Your Committee', exclaimed a parliamentary report of 1797, 'have great satisfaction in contemplating the large means which are now annually employed for the redemption of public debt'.[148]

Public opinion could not be ignored by a warring state, concerned to maximize yields from taxes. Budgets of the period classified all taxes imposed between 1793 and 1815 into 'war taxes', which ministers claimed would terminate with the war, and 'permanent taxes', imposed to meet the interest on loans. Pitt certainly realized how useful the sinking fund had been in persuading people to expect relief even from permanent taxes within their own lifetimes. As he more than once observed, 'it animated the hopes of commercial men'.[149] When Philip Francis expressed criticism of the sinking fund in 1806, he was challenged by Castlereagh 'to recollect any period in the history of the country when discontent was less apparent and when the nation submitted with more share of manliness and even satisfaction to every sacrifice the exigency has imposed'.[150] One positive function of the sinking fund was to divert the attention of industrialists, farmers and commercial men away from gloomy contemplation of the national debt and to create a climate of opinion which reduced their strong inclinations to evade taxes.

Undoubtedly the basic criticism against the wartime sinking fund was that it wasted public money and in the long run led to higher levels of taxation. Whenever the price at which the government sold bonds fell below the price the Commissioners for the Sinking Fund paid to redeem bonds, the difference represented a loss to taxpayers which could have been avoided by abandoning the promise of debt redemption. Since contractors demanded a premium for the risks and trouble attached to marketing a loan over the year, the Treasury sometimes sold bonds more cheaply than the prices paid by its Commissioners.[151] Losses were, however, neither invariable nor persistent. They depended on day-to-day movements in security prices. If prices fell after contracts for loans had been concluded, the government might still profit, despite premiums paid to contractors.[152]

Treasury opinion maintained that the operations of the sinking fund kept up the price of bonds and enabled loans to be floated on better terms.[153] Against this view, Hamilton argued that 'if payment be made by means of borrowing it can produce no alteration in the price of bonds at all. Demand and supply cancel out.'[154]

Ricardo was more pessimistic and maintained the larger loan, occasioned by expenditure on a sinking fund, encouraged contractors to sell omnium forward before negotiations opened, which depressed bond prices and, since the contractors determined their bid by reference to the price of bonds on the day of the contract, this raised the overall cost of borrowing.[155] Ricardo's view deserves respect because it belongs not only to a famous economist but to a prominent loan contractor. And it could also be argued that smaller loans might have reduced the cost of borrowing by stimulating greater competition among contractors. Grenfell suggested using the revenue of the sinking fund for just this purpose in 1814, but Vansittart retorted that he had made better bargains without resorting to such operations.[156]

Even if demand and supply did cancel out and greater competition was stimulated, the conception of a sinking fund as a device for transforming the debt from perpetual to terminable annuities constituted a completely new element in the capital market after 1786, which may well have led to more optimistic tenders for bonds. City opinion represented other loan contractors like Walter Boyd and Baring as more disposed to the Treasury view than Ricardo. The maintenance of a 'constitutionally' inviolable sinking fund certainly assured the money market that the supply of new bonds would not reach unlimited amounts. The government's creditors knew that its revenues would not be diverted towards tax relief, but employed year after year to buy up ever increasing amounts of bonds, guaranteeing augmented levels of demand whenever they wished to realize their assets. In wartime, when security prices fluctuated violently and unpredictably, the sinking fund provided for an element of stability in a very uncertain situation.[157] When Petty, Perceval and Vansittart diverted the income from the sinking fund, their policy occasioned alarm in the capital market and accusations of bad faith with those who had loaned money to the government.[158]

Criticisms of the day-to-day operation of the sinking fund may be more valid. The Exchequer transferred income to the Commissioners for the Sinking Fund quarterly, but their purchases, contrary to what Sinclair supposed, were spread evenly over each quarter.[159] The Commissioners bought stock whenever the transfer books at the Bank were open and they made no attempt to reduce the cost of borrowing by purchasing those stocks the Treasury offered contractors. More often than not, the Commissioners arranged their purchases to interfere as little as possible with negotiations for loans. If, for example, the chancellor planned for a loan in consols, they purchased 3 per cent reduced stock or South Sea annuities in the weeks before he met with contractors.[160] Only Perceval, when he endeavoured to persuade the market to accept 4 per cent bonds, applied the sinking fund to buy up large amounts of the same stock before and after a loan. Surely sophisticated and continuous use might have been made of the fund to stimulate competition, to persuade contractors to accept bonds of higher denomination and to influence the terms for loans.

When the war ended and the government found itself in receipt of £13 million of taxes set aside for debt redemption, Ricardo and others favoured using the money as Pitt intended, to make substantial reductions in the national debt.[161] But the times did not favour high taxation. Prices had fallen. Agriculture was in a state of depression and unreformed parliaments of landowners, no longer led by men like Pitt, were unwilling to pay taxes for the remote benefits of debt redemption. Once the policy had been abandoned and a rising national income made taxes easier to pay, men forgot the anxieties of their forebears and began to scoff at the steps they had taken to protect them from burdens of a national debt.[162] Aristocratic politicians advised by economists turned to laissez faire as a cheap ideology to protect their power and interests from further accumulations of public debt.[163] Fortunately for them by then the debt had done the job anticipated for the fiscal and financial system reconstructed in the wake of a republican interregnum by restored monarchical governments and the dramatic shift in geopolitical strategy that flowed from the execution of Charles I and William III's coup d'état of 1688.[164]

13 ITALIAN GOVERNMENT DEBT SUSTAINABILITY IN THE LONG RUN, 1861–2000

Giuseppe Conti

In 1914, Luigi Einaudi, one of the most eminent Italian economists, stated that a government supported by social consensus would be able to meet some additional expenses (even for a new war) by capital levy, or other additional taxes, while a politically weak government would prefer to issue debt. This statement joins the Italian fiscal school doctrine and the elitist tradition of the Machiavellians with Mosca, Pareto and Michels. Taxation immediately submits taxpayers to a lump sum to cover all fees, while debt defers their payments. Debt has other advantages too: first, it provides immediate cash; second, it offers a profitable asset to holders; third, it allows the state to amortize its own liabilities with delaying charges on the taxpayers which are charged according to the fiscal rules of the moment. In an indebted state, any change in its fiscal system can allow the transfer of interest payments onto other shoulders. In this way, a break in the Ricardian equivalence between tax and debt occurs. Then, governments can manage their fiscal choices in order to handle social consensus. This device can benefit those social groups which are able to influence the ruling class to avoid all or part of their fiscal burden. Public debt turns into a fiscal device which gradually transfers incomes from those who should bear taxes to other taxpayers who should not have to pay them. In addition, future taxpayers would pay debt service (interest plus principal) to state creditors. If there are few overlaps between those taxpayers and those creditors, then there is a distributive effect. In these cases, the fiscal illusion created by debts is realized: security holders have actually become richer than before and initial taxpayers have transferred the burden of debt (all or at least a part of its amount) onto others. Through debt, governments modify distributive mechanisms; in fact taxpayers and security holders are only slowly aware of some income transfers and they can maintain their own social consensus towards government and political institutions. In this way the state can preserve its own fiscal legitimacy. However, debt, as a delayed taxation, is a political decision that can only be used until public debt is sustainable. Later, a rising fiscal instability may destroy public debt credibility and crumble social consensus.

From 1861 until 2000, the history of high public debts in Italy followed three distinct systems of government finance. Each of these three systems had its own consensual rule. Before 1914, during the liberal era, property owners lent to governments, which were kinds of auto-controlled corporations as security for debt redemption. The interwar period was an age of fiscal transition and of reaction towards the access of the masses to political life. During World War I and the post-war years, the collapse of the liberal democracy was due, first of all, to a great fiscal shock. The war costs exceeded the financial resources that the current fiscal system could ensure and also exceeded the fiscal tolerance of taxpayers in the medium run. The fascists took advantage of the widespread discontent and social strains in order to restore a fiscal stability. To do this the fascist government let inflation run without control until 1925. In this way the real value of the public debt was reduced and so a fiscal equilibrium was restored. All this led to a new social order under fascist totalitarianism. The overthrow of fascism gave rise to the democratic republic. During the two post-war periods, fiscal and consensual mechanisms were reshuffled. In fact the entire fiscal system (characteristics and levels of expenses and revenues, net private savings and contributory burdens, debts and debt management) changed. A new fiscal order was established after 1945, with the liberation and the first republican government. So the fiscal state was based on the acknowledgement of the mass consensus.

According to the sociological approach to public finance,[1] I emphasize that social conflicts guide government choices. In each of the above-mentioned three systems of public finance, governments can pursue their aims within a specific fiscal perimeter. Only a new social pact, with its own fiscal pattern, can shift forward the debt burden, which limits expenses by the credibility conventions, although some institutional arrangements are experimented with in order to enlarge these boundaries. The main route had been the one of developing financial markets and of organizing some institutional investors in government securities. But these boundaries were not always flexible. This forced governments to redress their budgets when public debt turned towards a stronger risk of losing debt sustainability. Governments have three different ways to fulfil the debt service (payment of interests and principal): first, by issuing new debts (perhaps at increased costs); second, by raising new taxes; and, finally, by cutting expenses. In any case, in a very risky situation, prudent ruling classes aim to get or to maintain a sound fiscal state for a stable consensus. In order to regain sustainability, different methods were used during each fiscal system. So the ruling class managed distributive conflicts by exploiting all fiscal opportunities that debts offered (i.e. they eased expenses via fiscal illusion). During the liberal era the fiscal illusion, created by issuing debt, was exploited until it threatened to bring about a loss in credibility, thus threatening an intergenerational pact. This pact did not allow the debt burden to shift from fathers to children. What was a fiscal illusion would become reality if the ruling classes were able to transfer the charges for debt redemption from actual taxpayers to other and future taxpayers. As monetary illusion gained acceptance, social conflicts could be appeased. Moderate inflationary processes were able to lighten debt through letting their distributional effects take their course. In this case two pillars of liberal era were damaged: the strong intergenerational pact and the representative rule relative to this fiscal system. Both these pillars changed after the overthrow of the democratic republic. Multi-party competition and interest mediation established new delegation rules and different ways of running distri-butional conflicts. The liberal ruling classes referred to relatively small taxpayers' fractions, quite precisely defining in this way the limits to fiscal policy. In a mass democracy in an industrialized country, the dominant class could mediate among various interest groups and social sectors. All this pushed governments into out-lining new frontiers for their political and fiscal action: of course using income transfers, promoting growth and, sometimes, forgetting inflationary tendencies to settle the burdens of high debt stocks. In most empirical work it is supposed that democracy is the main cause of high and unsustainable public debts. In this paper I try to analyse another interpretation of these facts. In modern fiscal states, the problem of government debt is how to redeem it, but I think each regime has had its own way to make it. In any case, raising tax is not a priority, especially in recession periods or when there is a growing fiscal intolerance. In a democracy, the ruling classes have many more signals of fiscal discontent, but they maintain the same fiscal instruments for pursuing greater stability. Thus they are more pru-dent and more inclined to use every available means of fiscal illusion.

Nation-Building and State Credibility

The Italian kingdom rose on debt because its political elite was too weak to extract more funds from taxation in order to cover the high expenses of Risorgimento wars. The new state did not have at its disposal a fiscal bureaucratic body able to raise taxes. Its political cohesion depended on a combination of regional elites accustomed to very different degrees of tax tolerance. In return, those elites expected to reach economic and social integration both at regional and European levels. That integration demanded some large-scale public utilities (such as rail-ways and ports) and more modern services (such as order, army and schools) as other great European powers had. The emergence of the new state on the basis of this social contract led to great fragility, considering the narrowness and fragmen-tation of its consensual bases. A new tax increase would not have been tolerated, above all because of low per capita incomes.

However, the liberal 'historical Right' governments bravely imposed taxes on land property, trading and incomes. This action was insufficient to balance all extraordinary expenses. In order to cover budgetary deficits the Italian state incurred debts mainly by issuing securities and fiat money. In the first decade after unification some large annual deficits were accumulated into higher debts (see Chart 13.1).

Chart 13.1: The Italian Public Debt, Expenditures and Revenues to Output, 1862–2000 (in percentages).[2]

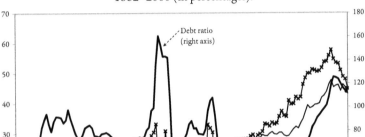

Gaining confidence among landowners and demonstrating that the national unification was not simply a colonization of the Sardinian kingdom but a total victory demanded, in 1862, that the government should set up the 'Gran Libro' of the public debt in which all debts of ancient states were admitted. In 1866 a new war against Austria increased the public debt and compelled the state to suspend money convertibility. Until the end of the nineteenth century high debts limited fiscal policies. These policies were used to keep the equilibrium of financial conditions in the state. In fact, the state was always at risk of being weakened by the heavy debts, causing the failure of the national unification process.[3]

The severity of the fiscal situation is showed by the sustainability index (see Chart 13.2). A combination of rising real interest rates and of primary deficits (defined as an excess of expenditures, excluding debt interests, over revenues) caused a lot of troubles. The creation of an inflationary fiat money was neither able to bring a decline in interest fees nor to discharge the debt burden. Nevertheless primary deficit was eliminated and a substantial primary surplus was produced, the ratio of debt to nominal Gross Domestic Product (GDP) rose and it became increasingly difficult to keep the situation under control.

Chart 13.2: Indexes of Sustainability, Convergence and Annual Change of Prices, 1862–2000.[4]

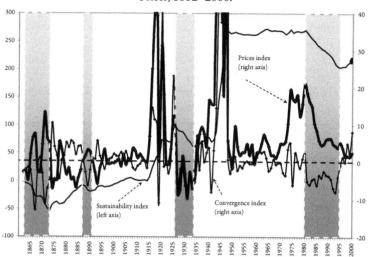

All these results can be clarified by means of an algebraic relation which is able to illustrate the dynamics underlying the debt problem.[5] By making D/Y equal to the debt to national output ratio, and Sp/Y equal to the primary deficit (or surplus) to output ratio, then a level of debt is sustainable if the following equation is true: Sp/Y≥(i-g) D/Y, where i is the average of the nominal interest on debt and g is the annual growth rate of nominal national output. Some simple debt dynamics can be drawn from this equation. If i>g, that is, if the interest rate exceeds the nominal growth rate of the economy, only a sufficiently large primary surplus can make the current state debt sustainable. In the case of an economic growth exceeding the interest rate, then a high debt to output ratio can be sustainable even if there is a budget deficit. The sustainability index is given by a cumulating sum of the first term minus the second term in the above equation. The shaded stripes in Charts 13.2 and 13.3 indicate periods of debt unsustainability, i.e. when the slope of curve tends downward.

Until 1873 a tendency towards the unsustainability of debt persisted. The rising debt ratios could threaten the repudiation of the debt or the gradual payoff of it by means of its monetization. None of the above-mentioned solutions was practised. The government preferred to pursue a balanced budget. This resolution required some severe measures for ordering the fiscal balance sheet. In 1864 a fiscal reform introduced an income tax, and other indirect taxation schemes increased with very unpopular consequences which led to a widespread discontent and strengthened outbursts of revolt. Although unpopular, the government was trying to improve debt management. The *Cassa depositi e prestiti* and a system of post office savings banks (*Casse di risparmio postali*) were instituted in order to invest in state securities and to finance the budget deficit without monetizing it. In 1876, when a budgetary equilibrium was almost achieved, the Right party was swept away by a so-called parliamentary revolution which saw the climbing of the liberal Left opposition to the government.

This event did not change the bases of the fiscal policy. Almost during the whole liberal era, especially before 1914, the ruling classes aimed to strengthen the financial credibility of the state. After 1867, all governments kept a primary surplus (see Chart 13.3). Monetary illusion (also as a moderate inflation) was not practised by those governments in order to gradually redeem debt and to relieve taxes. In fact, monetary funding came to almost 10 per cent of the total debt in 1876.[6] If we examine the path of the consumer price index before 1914 (in Chart 13.2) in comparison with the one of the convergence index – which measures the movement towards and away from the theoretical frontier of debt sustainability – we can observe a strong inverse correlation. This phenomenon will not take place again in the next ages. It can be explained in the following way: during inflationary waves government budgets tended to move away from their sustainability frontier, while during deflationary waves they moved towards or went beyond their sustainability frontier. During this long period the rising or falling prices carried out an opposite effect in terms of sustainability, instead of performing a corrective (or uncorrective) effect on public finances. This phenomenon can be better explained by the Gibson paradox, according to which nominal interest rates adjust themselves in relation to price expectations.[7]

We will return to this aspect. It is important to consider that after national unification the output growth was too weak to allow automatic debt redemption. Thus recovering sustainability depended principally on a series of primary surpluses. These surpluses were not high enough to make the debt ratio go down until the interest burden decreased, after the beginning of twentieth century (Charts 13.1 and 13.3). If we observe the difference i–g (the decisive factor in deciding the sign in the second term of the equation discussed above) before 1914 in Chart 13.3, we can observe that it is positive except for a few years over a short period, between 1880 and 1886, in relation to the expectation and resumption of money convertibility. Therefore the annual average yield on state debt was higher than the economic growth.

The above analysis is an important starting point for considering in which way general conditions of public finance squeezed the credibility of the main debtor, and therefore confidence in the new state. During cyclical downturns these two factors influenced the depth and duration of the crisis. In 1887 a boom in the real estate market of Rome collapsed and brought to failure a lot of banks, but the decrease in the rent value was really a symptom of a general loss of confidence in the state and of the withdrawal of foreign capital. This event caused the second and last period of debt unsustainability before 1914 which implied a very severe

Chart 13.3: Primary Deficits or Surpluses on GDP, State Interest Burden on Revenues, and Average Interest Rate on Public Debt Minus GDP Rate of Growth, 1862–2000 (in percentages).[8]

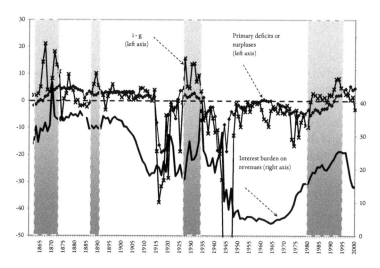

economic crisis and a deep political turmoil that overwhelmed the whole liberal ruling class.

During the liberal era, governments had adapted their fiscal policies to the Ricardian equivalence between extraordinary taxation and debt. This choice was strengthened by an international order constraint and by a national element of consensus-seeking. The payment of interest on a high national debt distressed the country and people feared a fiscal crisis in the state. Budgetary equilibrium is a golden rule consistent with monetary convertibility and with exchange rate parity. Sound money requires a solvent and reliable public finance system. Since taxation for redeeming the debt was not a viable solution, because taxpayers could not tolerate a heavier burden, liberal governments directed their efforts principally towards a large acceptance of the public debt. In this way they laid the foundations of an internal embryonic financial market.

In the nineteenth century the fiscal state maintained a strong tie between debt reputation, fiscal tolerance and political responsibility. This tie was strengthened through an intergenerational solidarity that implicitly acknowledged the principle of debt sustainability. The fiscal illusion in particular, based on issuing a reliable debt as a wealthy asset, could not bring about a monetary illusion that could discharge this debt through an inflationary tax. It was socially inconsistent in an agrarian country as Italy was: the land value depended on the purchasing power of rents, and a government which opted for an inflationary policy would have damaged these interests. In the liberal era the ruling classes were legitimized by a suffrage system which was limited to few wealthy voters. Of course they were the major taxpayers on whose shoulders a large part of the yield of taxation was burdened. The fiscal illusion was only partially feasible since the taxation, sooner or later, always hit the same family estates and properties.

However, a moderate transfer effect onto other social groups, and also onto other regional groups, was carried out in two different ways: an indirect taxation, that made the government unpopular; and a forced monetary circulation, which allowed a partial monetization of the public borrowing requirement, over many years. As important as it was, the last method was nothing more than a fiscal device. The destabilizing potential of a large state debt was defused only at the beginning of the twentieth century, when the economy grew very fast and the interest rates were falling.

Public Debt and Social Conflicts in a Mass Society

The first rifts in this social pact emerged as a consequence of industrial development and of the mass organizations in labour relations. In the nineteenth century, governments clung to a non-agenda rule: i.e. to avoid every kind of distortion in distributional mechanisms. After the beginning of the twentieth century some interventions concerned social policies, such as forced insurance schemes, political rights and universal male suffrage in 1912. However, the main change occurred with World War I, which swept away the liberal ruling class and its fiscal pact. Every attempt to restore it through the taxation of war profits contributed further to its downfall. The war finance transformed the fiscal state into a huge redistribution mechanism, which operated especially through money illusion. All fixed revenues lost a large part of their purchasing power, and many property values did not keep up with the inflation rate. In this situation, the highest debtors, such as the state, gained in a few years through the unburdening of their obligations. Fascism was able to benefit from this social situation and it was favourably welcomed by the middle classes and the rentiers for its aura of revenge and compensation.

During World War I, state indebtedness grew enormously until a peak in 1920 and 1921, both because of the lira's devaluation and because nearly half of all debt was external (Chart 13.1).[9] This situation did not jeopardize debt sustainability until 1927 (Chart 13.2). Interest payments were not a problem and primary deficits did not cause rising risks until inflation continued (Chart 13.3). Only when Mussolini decided to stabilize the lira and prices deflated was the situation reversed, in spite of the budgetary equilibrium, and the settlement of war debts was cancelled as well as all external indebtedness.[10] These events came about after the so-called liberalistic policies of first fascist governments. At last those favourable conditions were offset by the rise in interest rates and by an economic slowdown that weighed down the burden of debt. In these years the convergence index closely correlated with the price index (Chart 13.2). From this time onwards, Italian fascism abandoned its liberalistic guideline and adopted a corporative ideology consonant with its totalitarianism in politics which resulted in the repression of social rights. In its fiscal policy the new wave aimed to build up an authoritarian social state administered in a sort of a political patronage toward each social group, production category or individual.

It is very difficult to suppose where this system could have led in terms of debt: World War II arrived and simultaneously marked the end of the fascist regime and shifted the debt adjustment problem onto the post-war democratic ruling classes. Between 1941 and 1948 high inflation rates removed every fiscal problem created by debt.

So democratic and republican Italy inherited a very low debt ratio, about 44 per cent in 1948 descending to 33 per cent in 1964 (Chart 13.1). Until the second oil shock of 1979 the sustainability index remained very stable. But this can be situated in a different institutional context compared to other phases. First of all, public expenses rose continuously. Taxation had a similar trend, even if it covered only a small percentage of expenses, except during some years when governments were forced to adopt corrective measures. This was the reason why the debt ratio rose after the middle of the 1960s. Another factor which determined the rise of the debt ratio was the deep social transformation caused by the economic development which led Italy to be the seventh or sixth great industrialized country. This growth allowed the absorption of budgetary deficits and the smoothing of the public debt rise.

These conditions changed when pressing social needs emerged and the social state – which was just a rearrangement of the former authoritarian one established during the interwar period – was not able to face up the new social needs. A strong push in that direction was given at the beginnings of 1960s when the Italian economic boom weakened. Industrial labour conflicts arose claiming wage adjustment to productivity. Centrist governments gave way first to a centre-Left coalition with a social programme in schooling, health care and social security and a commitment to redressing the unbalance of regional latecomers. Until then the national income growth and relatively low interest rates were successful in maintaining current expenses without producing heavy burdens of debt. However, from 1973 high inflation rates led to an increasing debt that quickly accumulated into larger current deficits (Chart 13.3). Thus, up to 1980 we can observe a parallel course between the annual variation of prices and the index of convergence, as we have just seen during the interwar period (Chart 13.2).

Only after the second oil shock did economic, tax and budget policies change. This was also a result of the Italian adhesion to the European monetary system and of the adoption of a monetarist approach to policy-making in 1979 by the

Federal Reserve. In Italy, the so-called 'divorce' in treasury and central bank rela-tions shifted the operating instrument of monetary policy from interest rates to monetary aggregates. This important shift in policy marked the beginning of the disinflation effort that, some years after, reduced inflation from the double digit levels of the 1970s. During the disinflation period, the most important conse-quence was a very fast rise in interest rates and an increase in budget deficits. Whereas before this had been financed from the central bank, now it was financed by issuing debt at increasing yields (and state payments for interest). Tax receipts as a share of GDP remained roughly constant during the 1980s, equalling 37.2 per cent of GDP in 1982 and 41.9 per cent of GDP in 1989. In the same years, expenditures rose from 48.5 to 51.8 per cent. But whether lower taxes or higher spending 'caused' the deficit depends on the perspective from which we observe the phenomenon. The key question is why the deficit increased. Our perspective is focused on social consensus and so it highlights the growing loss of political cohe-sion in coalition governments. This fact hindered cooperation between monetary and fiscal policies. The latter delayed some essential adjustments needed to sup-port European financial integration and to meet the parameters of Maastricht in order to enter in the European Monetary Union.

The disinflation process, begun in 1980, had a reverse effect on the sustain-ability of the debt, getting the public budget into trouble (Chart 13.2). This was worsened by other factors such as the deceleration and the stagnation of economic growth rates (also in real terms) and the rising of real interest rates and, consequently, of interest expenditures, which grew from 16 per cent of tax receipts in 1980 to 25 per cent in the first years of the 1990s (Chart 13.3).

This path of the history of public debt after World War II is traced by three principal facts: a liberal-democratic republic governed by coalitions of parties, an increase in the size of governments and a process of economic transformation carried out by industrialization. The republic was built up on a pact that legiti-mated the state to intervene in income distribution in order to strengthen social cohesion.

Fiscal Illusion, Monetary Illusion and Social Consensus: A Historical View

Until now we have simply highlighted some historical evidence from each of the three eras under discussion and outlined some characteristics of their finan-cial and economic development. In order to analyse these dynamics it is worth comparing some typical situations and brief transitions from a situation of debt unsustainability to one of debt sustainability, or vice versa.

The schematic representation of Table 13.1 makes it easier to read the structure of my argument and the dynamics developed in each historical fiscal state era. I am essentially dealing with four kinds of financial situation that I have summarized in the following two-by-two table in order to offer them in a simple and symmetrical way. Each of these dynamics relates to a condition of debt sustainability and to a condition of consensus, showing the corresponding main tendencies of the fiscal policy and of its general social feeling. The situation in quadrant 1 is opposite to the one represented in quadrant 3, and the one represented in quadrant 2 is opposite to the one in 4. Every movement from one quadrant to another is admissible, but some movements are more likely to happen if we agree that governments have a little comprehension of their contemporary situation.

In general, if the social consensus towards the fiscal policy of the political ruling class is high and the public debt tends to be sustainable, it is probably in the interests of governments to maintain a prudent fiscal policy, as in quadrant 1, since the taxpayers, or the more influential social groups, are unlikely to exert any pressure in order to improve their conditions. It is very difficult to lose consensus without a change in the fiscal pressure and in the fiscal tolerance. This can be the case, for example, after a political decision of rising taxation (or reducing expenditures). Sage and prudent politicians refrain from making too many changes without reasons. In the Italian debt history we have no remarkable cases to illustrate this.

Table 13.1: Social Consensus and Public Debt Sustainability.

		Public Debt	
		Sustainable	Unsustainable
Social and Political Consensus	High	1 prudent and conservative fiscal policies	2 fiscal instability and consensus risks
	Low	4 insufficient consensus but sufficient credibility	3 potential fiscal crisis of the state

It is very important to establish how a government might move from one situation to another, and how it might return. In several cases the paths may not be direct. For example, a first step might be in the direction of quadrant 2. As we have already said, governments tend to grow their expenditures and to cover the expansion by borrowing capital. Generally, they levy taxes only when they judge that they have a high consensus margin. Social conflicts can push governments to make use of the fiscal illusion for fear of a loss of consensus. Thus, the situation will probably lead to rising debt unsustainability, moving towards quadrant 2. The fiscal illusion is a political choice used to gain time and preserve the assed of consensus, and in this sense it can be judged as a fiscal irresponsibility which leads to an uncertainty zone after leaving a safety zone.

In the new situation of quadrant 2, the loss of social consensus can be easy. A little change in some of the parameters of the equation discussed earlier push make the budget out of control with the consequence of compelling governments to adopt some recovery actions. These require sacrifices and at the same time they repel consensus rather than attract it. A virtuous and severe fiscal policy can be tied to very optimistic expectations.

Then the situation can slide towards that of quadrant 3. Fiscal disillusion arises from the incapability of the ruling class to fulfil its tasks. The government's actions are smothered by limited resources and by the fear that it will be very difficult to reverse the situation. This is a very dangerous level because the system is very close to a fiscal crisis and a break in social order. Falling consensus can be a consequence of the same fiscal instability. The ruling classes do not have enough instruments to regain consensus. With a large public debt fiscal disillusion is the other side of the loss of consensus. In order to recover a share of its social legitimization, a government can attempt hazardous fiscal policies because they offer a chance of automatic financial improvement. The fiscal crisis of the state hangs over government credibility and over the public debt solvency when a serious loss of control takes place in government finance. If the ruling class wants to responsibly govern the social conflict in this case it is compelled to restore the public accounts.

From the latter situation, a government can move towards quadrant 4 (or 1, if it is lucky). A successful fiscal policy brings back debt sustainability, but it might not be able to reverse the consensual mood of taxpayers. In this case, it is possible to use another policy without any increase of the fiscal burden, so the fiscal illusion can be newly exploited by a politically weak ruling class. Obviously such a policy, instead of leading to a situation like that of quadrant 1, can turn back into that of quadrant 3, or even in quadrant 2. The direction depends on many factors which are not submitted to very strict political control. It also depends on other factors like a more virtuous and orthodox fiscal policy, which should be implemented in order to avoid many of the distributive effects of fiscal illusion, and in order to reabsorb debt through ordinary fiscal instruments.

If we move through Italian debt history this change looks like a pendulum swing. In 1861, the financial situation of the new state was similar to the one of quadrant 4. This means that the political elite felt the narrowness of their consensus base, but they could manage the further difficulties (deriving from a recent independence war and from the production of a state apparatus) by issuing new debts. These debts could be held by land owners or by foreign bankers and investors. The fiscal illusion led the situation very close to the one in quadrant 3. The Right-wing governments tried to avoid a crash in state credibility. Those of the Left took advantage of the parliamentary fall of the Right, and the fiscal parity gave the Left the opportunity to gain a larger consensus. But some fundamental risk factors were not completely removed. In fact the restored international credibility was still subject to hectic waves in the capital markets. In the late 1880s the debt crisis marked the beginning of the so-called 'black years' of the Italian economy when the liberal era was hit by a long political and institutional crisis.

From the late 1890s the annual fiscal situation moved from quadrant 3 to 1. Liberal governments were able to reap an increasing consent by successfully managing social conflicts. Before 1914, the debt ratio decreased slowly, from 80 per cent in 1898 to 66 per cent in 1907. The sustainability index took advantage of a strong sloping downward trend in the ratio between interest payments and revenues and from a growing economy. The main element of this virtuous situation was a level of spending and taxation below 10 per cent of GDP and in equilibrium.

During the whole liberal era debt credibility could be based on an intergenerational pact. This pact prevented an expansion of the fiscal illusion and a reduction of debt burden via monetary illusion. The whole national debt was created at the beginning. But it was not reduced by means of debt repayment in spite of primary surpluses realized in many years. Liberal governments did not think that there were favourable conditions to reduce debt stock. In fact, neither a long period of economic growth occurred nor a social consensus was achieved in order to realize a gradual redemption. In the long run, liberal governments could not use all the fiscal tools available. Those governments did not have sufficient consensus in order to act as needed to; they were not strong enough to escape from the debt unsustainability zone as they would have hoped.

During the interwar years, governments had fewer obstacles to their actions. After World War I a growing fiscal disillusion was a financial threat for the ruling classes. A long inflationary process prevented a fiscal crisis, but it was an extraordinary propellant for social discontent increased also by other political and social diseases. All these factors led to a regime crisis. On the basis of fiscal rebalancing, fascism built up its own consensus. From 1926 the fascist government moved from a very conservative fiscal policy to a less bridled one. However until the mid-1930s the monetary order, which was settled by fascism in order to strengthen its power, represented an obstacle to the government acting freely.

After 1948 the democratic republic could begin without fiscal or debt burdens. Governments tended to incur escalating deficits because the state stimulated economic growth through increased spending, but resisted raising taxes in order to preserve its legitimacy. In a mass society, the rise of the welfare state was also a rule for governing a democracy and for managing social consent. In spite of that, until the mid-1960s governments could follow some prudent fiscal policies thanks to high economic growth rates and low debt costs. However, the rise of social conflicts and labour union pressures weakened the distributional equilibrium and the consensus. So the democratic state tried to free itself from its fiscal ties. From the mid-1960s fiscal illusion was viable (approaching quadrant 2). Between the late 1960s and the early 1970s the representative system was brought into question. During this period double digit inflation maintained the public debt in a sustainability zone. This inflationary process found domestic support in a large social protest, during a period of turbid conspiracies and terrorist attacks against democratic institutions. Thus the distributive effects of fiscal illusion could continue. As we have seen, this situation changed from 1979–80 when inflation was curbed. Now a high public debt led towards an unsustainability zone. This problem in turn led to fiscal irresponsibility in coalition governments. The increasing competition between parties focused on fiscal devices. Increasing public expenditures supported the growth of a patronage system. The opposition parties blamed the deficit spending policies of government parties, but they were ready to practise fiscal laxness too, once they won elections.

At the beginnings of 1990s, when fiscal tolerance was at its lowest level, all traditional mass parties were overwhelmed by the social protest and by a growing political apathy. The fiscal protest gave rise to new political movements that followed anti-centralistic programmes based on fiscal federalism and administrative isolationism. On the other side, the process of European integration was begun in order to impose an orthodox fiscal rule and to stop lax fiscal practices. Nevertheless, it was very difficult for fiscal orthodoxy to find supporters in any political party.

From the 1990s the political fragmentation of old mass parties opened another field of political fights. The predominant opinion was that through an administrative and fiscal decentralization taxpayers would have a more direct perception of the advantages of expenditure, and of the related tax burdens. It would have been the institutional solution to join consensus to fiscal responsibility. Besides, it would have been the way to take care of the widespread fiscal discontent and, at the same time, to reassemble the disrupted old party apparatus. From this perspective regional or local fiscal federalism can be seen as a means for relaxing and moving the debt frontiers.

In the late twentieth century the domestic situation seemed to be similar to that of the liberal era. There was slow economic growth and interest rates were not sufficiently low. In these conditions, only the realization of a series of primary surpluses could reduce public debt. But in this period the ruling classes were not motivated to follow responsible policies because there existed only a weak fiscal intergenerational pact.

From a historical perspective, high and persistent public debt levels are not only a problem in a mass democratic system. In fact the traditional Italian liberal system, which had a very narrow electoral base, also had problems reducing a large public debt. In this case, once indebted, the state would take considerable trouble to reduce the debt, especially when the social consensus crumbled. The inclination of the fiscal state to debt, both in a classical liberal system and in a mass democracy system, may be a question of social consensus more than of fiscal conditions. The difference between the two systems lies in debt stock deceleration rather than in debt stock acceleration. According to the above, inflation tax would not be tolerated in the first system, and only in the second one when favourable conditions did not permit a continuous economic growth and low interest rates.

In a mass democracy, various political parties competing for consensus use 'fiscal marketing' as a weapon with which to promise the greatest advantages with the smallest sacrifice. Fiscal marketing programmes try to show public debt as a kind of wealth (fiscal illusion). All governments aim to maintain fiscal credibility. This means that governments can never repudiate their debts. All political parties, in government and also in opposition, have to make a choice between two methods aimed to redeem public debt: inflation tax or sharing fiscal burdens in more balanced ways. Every other choice is a mix between these methods.

From 1970s a large part of Italian public debt has been held by Italian householders. Thus small savers have much to lose from inflation tax. In the 1980s, high inflation rates were supported less by working classes and by middle- and low-income individuals after the repeal of the indexed wage scale. Furthermore, it was not possible to use a capital levy in order to repay debts. In fact this would have dried up the financial assets of the middle classes. This social group can be used like a 'human shields' from the upper classes, as wealthy people and large security holders, or credit institutions and industrial groups, try to discourage governments from putting a progressive taxation on rental incomes or on capital stocks. Nowadays, only very few people can be ranked with the old affluent and idle rentiers. Thus the same welfare state becomes a bone of contention in political debates from 1980s onwards. In this way, the social and political contest brings into question the basis of the intergenerational pact, which is broken by an exchange of consensus: a present one for a future one. In order to preserve the integrity of the contract and to defend some vested interests, in the medium and long term the main difficulty seems to be how to convince future generations to pay a debt which was made to fund the welfare state of past generations. So future generations will pay a higher cost compared to the reduced services of the poorer welfare state they will inherit.

14 TIMES OF WASTEFUL ABUNDANCE: THE APOGEE OF THE FISCAL STATE IN THE FEDERAL REPUBLIC OF GERMANY FROM THE 1960S TO THE 1980S

Hans-Peter Ullmann

'Germans are getting poorer' – under this title, the news magazine *Der Spiegel* published a series of articles in the summer of 1982, shortly before the fall of the social-liberal coalition government. The author, Renate Merklein, took issue with the fiscal policies of the Brandt and Schmidt administrations. According to Merklein, these policies were based on the 'belief' that the state 'could do and know everything better, that it knew what was best for its citizens – even better than they themselves –, and that it was also capable of getting everything that was wished for, promptly and inexpensively'.[1] The controversial journalist thus reproached a wasting of public funds that she traced back to the 1960s and 1970s. In these two decades, it had often been debated whether there should be 'more state' or not; at the same time, public expenditures and state responsibilities had increased slowly at first, then accelerated. Growing deficits, more lending and increasing public debt were the consequences. Did the Federal Republic sink into a 'swirl of exorbitance', or was this development part of a trend among states of the Organisation for Economic Co-operation and Development (OECD)?

1

Beginning in the late 1950s, politicians, scholars and the general public intensely discussed what role the state should play in economics and society. These debates were framed by an international context that included the 'liberal consensus' in the United States of America, the *Planification* in France, the initiatives of the Labour government in Great Britain, and first attempts to harmonize economic and fiscal policies in the European Economic Community. With the popular phrases 'public poverty' and 'private wealth', the American economist John K. Galbraith caught the mood of the times. Moreover, his argument found resonance across the political spectrum. After the Social Democratic Party (SPD) gave up its Marxist traditions and its ideas of planned economy in the Godesberg Program of 1959, the SPD and its related unions pleaded for a globally regulated market economy that would delegate many tasks to the state. Coming from another direction, Alfred Müller-Armack's ideas for a second phase of the Social Market Economy and Ludwig Erhard's proposal for a 'formed society' came to similar conclusions: the reconstruction of the private economy had dominated the 1950s, but now it was time for the state to take up long-neglected 'social tasks'.[2]

The idea that the state should provide more public funds and services to satisfy the 'collective demands of the affluent society'[3] gained popularity at a time of economic uncertainty. On the one hand, economic growth was losing its dynamic, which, according to many, called for state intervention. On the other hand, the Gross Domestic Product (GDP) was still rising at the real growth rate of 7 per cent per year, with only a short interruption during the recession of 1966–7. The 'dream of eternal prosperity'[4] optimistically projected this growth well into the future. It appeared that there was enough financial manoeuvrability to allow for the increase of both social welfare and state investment. Fiscal policy had delivered the required instruments as well as the necessary legitimization for a more decided break with the ideal of a balanced budget, which also rested on the willingness to take on more debts. Additionally, the optimism of these years in regard to government financial planning made what Hansmeyer called 'the extension of state activities'[5] – essentially an increase in the government spending ratio – seem plausible.[6]

Still, the consensus to give the public hand more responsibilities remained partial and unstable. The demand for 'more state' unified politicians across the spectrum as well as divergent party factions, businessmen and unionists, scholars and journalists. At the same time, 'more state' could be interpreted in a variety of ways; it could describe a moderate expansion, or what Sturm called a 'primitive Keynesianism'[7] according to the motto that 'expenditures are good', or a 'politics of structural change' as was asked for by the New Left within the SPD.[8]

Nevertheless, long-term developments in terms of public expenditure show that this alliance, although heterogeneous, was practically unbeatable. By the 1960s, the government spending ratio (total expenditures as percentage of the GDP) had reached 39 per cent, after vacillating between 30 and 35 per cent in the 1950s. During the first half of the 1970s, it jumped to almost 50 per cent. While the figures sunk to 48 per cent over the next five years, they climbed up to nearly 50 per cent again in the early 1980s. Governments on all levels – federal, state and local – were responsible for this growth in spending. For instance, state governments increased their expenditures by an average rate of 13.5 per cent in every year from 1970 to 1975. The federal government and local communities followed, both with a rate of 12.3 per cent. During the second half of the 1970s these growth rates declined. However, they still remained somewhere between the federal rate of 6.3 per cent and a rate of 7.5 per cent on the local level.[9]

The advent of the social-liberal coalition brought a hefty increase in federal spending. In his first government statement, Chancellor Willy Brandt proposed a catalogue of domestic reforms, prompting what essentially became a competition among the ministries to carry out these measures. However, the coalition did not coordinate these individual projects into a medium- or long-term plan with clear priorities. As a result, only a handful of reforms were tackled, even fewer accomplished, and among those undertaken, most were basically watered down to the distribution of expensive benefits. Because the coalition's parliamentary majority was in jeopardy, it was not only looking for political success with its *Ostpolitik*, but also by extra spending for popular measures. Thus, reforms pushed up expenditures in the early 1970s. After 1975, however, the so-called 'Stagflation' became responsible for the rise in public spending. As in other countries, the two oil crises and the recession of 1974–5 ended the 'Golden Age' of post-war prosperity in West Germany. 'Crisis Decades'[10] followed, with slow economic growth and high levels of inflation and unemployment. The government tried to ease these problems with both restrictive and expansive measures. On the one hand, it sought to stabilize fiscal policies and to consolidate the budget; on the other, it issued more investment programmes. Though such programmes could not solve the economy's structural problems, they nevertheless burdened the budget with extra costs.[11]

On the state level, expenditure increased even faster. While the federal government's spending grew from 88 billion Deutschmarks in 1970 to 245 billion in 1982, or by a rate of 178 per cent, spending by the state governments rose by 218 per cent, from 77 to 218 billion. Local and district governments also increased their expenditures. While they spent 57 billion Deutschmarks in 1970, they gave out 153 billion in 1982, an increase of 168 per cent. Local finance reforms in 1969 made possible what Petzina has referred to as this 'boom-like development of local expenditures'.[12]

However, spending within the social insurance system managed to top even that of federal, state and local governments. Its costs soared from 88 billion Deutschmarks in 1970 to 311 billion in 1982, or by 250 per cent. Thus the social security transfers ratio (social security expenditures as a percentage of the Gross National Product (GNP)) rose from 27 to 33 per cent. In the early 1970s, this was caused by a social policy that was based on highly optimistic forecasts about the financial future of social insurance. As a result, the number of recipients grew, welfare payments increased, and more was spent on preventive measures. Although a tendency towards more restrictive policies emerged in the second half of the 1970s, economic problems and the cumulative effects of earlier social reforms continued to push up welfare costs.[13]

2

As a booming economy kept prices, wages and taxes on the rise, the general expansion of the state did not cause any major financial problems in the early 1970s. This changed, however, after the recession of 1974–5. Yet, the government did not slow down the process of increasing the state's spending ratio, or even try to coordinate tax revenues and the growing need for public goods by securing a gain in sustainable income. Rather, calls for a redistribution of wealth won out in financial politics. Consequently, the tax reform of 1974–5 was primarily responsible for the small increase in the tax ratio (taxes as a percentage of the GDP) from 24 to 25 per cent. At the same time, the tax and social security transfers ratio (taxes and social security transfers as a percentage of GDP) jumped from 37 to 43 per cent. More than anything else, this growth was caused by rising contributions to the social security system. From 1970 to 1975, social security spending climbed from 85 to 167 billion Deutschmarks, and continued to rise to 284 billion in 1982, barely checked by the first cuts into the social net. In sum, it rose by a rate of 235 per cent after 1970, or from 13 to 18 per cent of the GDP.[14]

A slowly increasing tax ratio and a fast rising spending ratio meant that the state's revenues could not keep pace with its expenditures; consequently, deficits in all budgets at federal, state and local levels grew. During the 1960s, deficits on average vacillated around 4.4 per cent of expenditures. While they had risen to 5.7 per cent during the first half of the 1970s, they jumped to 11.3 per cent over the next five years. For the most part, this was due to the federal state, whose budget balance soared by 15.6 per cent, but also the states (8.5 per cent) took their share; less so the local communities (3.8 per cent).[15]

Parallel to the negative budget balances, net lending grew. Between 1965 and 1969 it remained below 8 billion Deutschmarks per year on average. In the first five years of the 1970s, it increased to 14 billion; over the next five, it rose to 43 billion and reached 64 billion in the early 1980s. Again, the federal state was mainly responsible. Its lending ratio amounted to 15 per cent during the second half of the 1970s, while the states and local communities indebted themselves at lower rates of 8 per cent and 4 per cent of their expenditures, respectively. Financing by loans led to the rapid growth of public debt. Debt had been rising at a constant rate since the beginning of the 1960s, and this trend continued until the early 1970s, but changed after 1973. The mountain of debt within public budgets increased from 126 billion Deutschmarks in 1970 to 256 billion in 1975 and further up to 615 billion Deutschmarks in 1982; the debts multiplied almost five-fold over the period. While the debt to GDP ratio (debt as a percentage of the GDP) climbed from 17 per cent to 20 per cent during the 1960s, it doubled to nearly 39 per cent by 1982. State debts grew the fastest. Between 1970 and 1982 they increased from 28 to 191 billion Deutschmarks, or by a rate of 580 per cent. Next in line were federal debts, with a growth rate of more than

440 per cent, in actual terms a rise from 58 to 314 billion. In comparison, local debts rose at a relatively moderate rate of 175 per cent, or from 40 to 110 billion Deutschmarks.[16]

3

Did this 'breaking of the taboo'[17] against public debts cause the Republic's finances to lose direction? Was there the threat of a 'debt trap' or even a state bankruptcy? Was the economy's growth in danger? Scholars, politicians and the media hotly debated these issues at the beginning of the 1980s. These debates were not only about the limits or dangers of public deficits, but also they passed judgement on the fiscal policies of the social-liberal coalition. Ultimately, they tried yet again to define the role that the state should play in economy and society. Should the 'golden age of public sector intervention' continue or should it be ended?[18]

The steep rise of the government spending ratio, especially in the late 1960s and early 1970s, was unprecedented in the Republic's history, and thus could not fail to cause concern. While this ratio increased in other OECD member states, West Germany topped all other major OECD countries with a jump from 32 per cent in 1960 to 49 per cent in 1975, or an increase of 17 percentage points. Ten of these percentage points were added in the short time between 1968 and 1975. By 1975, the government spending ratio was larger than that of any other OECD country, with the exception of the Netherlands and Sweden. However, in the second half of the 1970s, some efforts to move towards financial consolidation were felt in the Federal Republic. With only 0.5 per cent, West Germany produced the slowest growth rate of major OECD states between 1975 and 1982, and kept well under the average of all OECD countries.[19]

Moreover, the Federal Republic's 'extension of state activities' was not paid for by a higher tax ratio. There was only a moderate increase in this rate after the end of the 1960s. Its growth remained below the OECD average, and while the West German ratio had been higher throughout the 1960s, by the beginning of the 1980s it fell below the average of all OECD members. Social security transfers, however, rose disproportionately. In the early 1970s, only France and Italy held a higher social security transfers ratio than the Federal Republic. If these expenditures are included in the tax ratio, West Germany found itself among average OECD countries. It thus remained a part of the 'Christian democratic tax family of continental Europe',[20] which was characterized by broad taxation, a comparatively low income tax, and a high level of social security transfers.[21]

In addition to a growing social security transfers ratio, the price to be paid for 'more state' was a quickly rising deficit. Admittedly, at the beginning of 1980s West Germany, with a rate of nearly 20 per cent, had the lowest net debt ratio (net public debts as a percentage of the GNP) among major OECD countries, alongside the United States of America and France. Moreover, of the smaller states, only Finland, Sweden, Norway and Spain had lower ratios. Thus, it was not the actual amount of public debts that was unusual, but rather its change. In the late 1960s and early 1970s the Federal Republic and Italy, for example, were the only states within the OECD whose net debt ratio did not decline but rose. Furthermore, West Germany, followed by Italy and Canada, led the major OECD countries with a growth of nearly 19 per cent from the mid-1970s to the early 1980s. Among the smaller member states, only Sweden, Denmark and Ireland had higher rates.

To sum up the comparison: West Germany did not sink into a 'swirl of abundance'. However, it experienced an 'expansion of state activities' unequalled in its history and whose dynamics stand out in international comparison. This process was fuelled by a broad consensus of diverse forces who hoped to find a solution to the problems facing the Federal Republic in the post-war period. The consequences of this willingness to accept 'more state' proved to be far-reaching and decisive. Although these effects were numerous and multifaceted, they were all tied together by the growth of public debts. During the 1980s this growth could only be slowed down, but not stopped, and in the 1990s it increased again considerably. For a short time, then, public expenditures could be increased without raising taxes or risking political conflicts over who should pay. Over the long term, however, this 'debt illusion' dissolved as the growing mountain of debts limited financial manoeuvrability at the federal, state and local levels, which in turn blocked expenditures in education or scientific research and placed an increasingly heavy burden on public finances. Thus, in order to find the decisions which led to the present fiscal problems of the Federal Republic of Germany, one must first examine the 1960s and 1970s.[22]

CONCLUSION: FINAL REMARKS

David Stasavage

The papers presented in this volume and in the International Economic History Congress (IEHC) session that preceded it constitute an important contribution to the study of governments, debts and financial markets in Europe. They point to the usefulness of studying these phenomena in comparative perspective, both across a broad set of states and over a lengthy time span. The papers also suggest the importance of drawing insights from historical cases and episodes that are often overlooked in general histories of the evolution of public credit in Europe. My concluding remarks for this volume will draw on those presented in the 2006 IEHC session. They represent observations by a political scientist who is grateful for the opportunity to comment on work by a respected group of historians and economists. There are many issues upon which these papers shed light. One of the most important, and that upon which I will focus my remarks, involves the following puzzle – why, given that long-term borrowing has obvious advantages for states, do we observe so much variation between states in terms of the date at which a long-term date was created? Likewise, why, once states have created a debt, do we also observe such considerable variation in the terms on which they borrowed, or more generally in their subsequent success at obtaining access to credit?

Economic Growth and the Imperatives of War

A first logical place to look for an answer to this puzzle is with a simple story emphasizing the imperatives of war and the effect of economic growth. Demand for war finance prompted states to develop mechanisms for borrowing long term, and it will surprise few readers to see that the imperatives of war were crucial to the development of a public debt in many of the cases considered in this volume. The varying intensity of inter-state competition in different European regions might help to explain why some states established long-term debts earlier than others. Numerous scholars have observed that, from the sixteenth century, a revolution in military technology and a period of intensified inter-state competition, especially on the

Italian peninsula, drove many states to create long-term debts. In addition, we also see clear evidence in these papers that borrowing depended upon the presence of a pool of potential lenders, a condition which was in turn favoured by economic growth and the accumulation of wealth. So, for example, Giuseppe De Luca demonstrates how Philip II was able to use the State of Milan as a source of finance because it was experiencing a period of renewed economic growth. The papers in this volume point to similar phenomena elsewhere in Europe.

While the papers for this volume provide important insights about both demand for credit by states and the supply of credit from lenders, in reading these contributions I was struck by the extent to which recent historical work seems to have made significant progress in uncovering evidence on the former issue while knowledge with regard to the supply of credit has proceeded less rapidly. It would be interesting for future work to explore more micro-evidence involving decisions made by potential lenders within these states. We learn significant facts about the social composition of creditors from De Luca's study. It would be interesting to see this sort of evidence for more states, as well as evidence showing why investors were purchasing government debt. Motivations may have been quite different if a creditor was a widow looking for a safe return, as opposed to a Genoese investor looking to invest abroad to obtain higher returns (albeit with greater risk) than could be obtained on the home market. The availability of different types of potential investors may have heavily influenced the ability of states that were relatively high- or low-risk borrowers to obtain access to credit.

Ultimately, while the expansion of debt in European states may have depended on both military imperatives and the availability of potential lenders, the ability of governments to gain access to credit also undoubtedly depended on the existence of an expectation that governments would be both willing and able to service their debts. In other words, explanations based on the demand for credit and its potential supply can take us only so far. This raises the question of what underlying conditions might create such an expectation. In what follows I will consider three existing explanations focusing on the importance of technical innovation, the development of a broad class of borrowers and on the role of representative institutions. After arguing that the evidence in the papers presented here raises questions about each of these explanations, I will then propose an alternative explanation that emphasizes the difference in underlying political conditions between city-states and territorial states in Europe.

The Importance of Technical Innovation

One possibility is that the relative success or failure of governments in gaining access to long-term credit at low interest rates depended on technical innovations. In other words, there were some states that innovated and others that failed to innovate. This could involve the establishment of efficient institutions for collecting and managing revenues, as well as efficient mechanisms for pricing, issuing and managing debt. This idea has been emphasized by Epstein who argues, in a broad comparative investigation, that European states that borrowed at low rates of interest were able to do so because they had efficient fiscal and administrative structures.[1] These institutions limited the likelihood that a government would be unable to service its debts. The papers in this volume provide some empirical support for this contention. Patrick O'Brien's contribution, as well as his important previous work, demonstrates how the post-1688 'revolution' in English public borrowing depended on a prior set of institutional reforms to rationalize tax collection. Likewise, Andreas Ranft's consideration of Hanseatic cities points to the sophisticated character of their public financial management, something that may have characterized many financially successful city-states in Europe.

To my mind, the contributions to this volume also raise important questions about the extent to which we can think of technical innovation as an underlying explanation for the successful development of a public debt. Technical innovations to rationalize revenue collection and improve revenue management depend on the presence of good ideas (what might in current terms be referred to as 'best practice'). A number of the papers presented here seem to suggest that good ideas were not in short supply, even in states that are not typically seen as success cases in the area of public borrowing. One of the reasons for this may have been that ideas for innovations were often supplied by 'foreign experts', as was the case with Jean Orry and the Spanish Crown as described by Anne Dubet in her chapter, or by domestic experts, as was the case with the Paris brothers as described by François Velde in his paper on French public finances between 1683 and 1726. Velde's contribution is particularly interesting because it recounts a little-known episode of financial reforms in France during the Regency that involved revolutionary changes to the government accounting system. The problem was that after a short period of successful operation, the institutional changes instituted by the Paris brothers were dismantled following the fall of the Duke of Bourbon in 1726. This episode in some respects resembles Jean Orry's fall from power in Spain, though in that case the reversal of institutional reforms was far less complete. What the French case demonstrates then is not that technical innovation was lacking but that it was not sufficiently durable. The question then becomes what underlying conditions might ensure that reforms actually take root. I will return to this question below. Two other papers also suggest why the existence of technical innovations may be insufficient to guarantee financial success. The paper by Fausto Piola Caselli on public debt in the Papal States demonstrates that, despite having highly sophisticated and transparent financial institutions, a state could nonetheless acquire an undeservedly poor reputation in the area of public credit. José Ignacio Andrès Ucendo observes with regard to Castile in the seventeenth century and its system of borrowing indirectly via the city of Madrid, that this system also was hardly lacking in technical sophistication. These contributions constitute further evidence that technical innovation was not always sufficient to earn either a good reputation or to commit a state to servicing its debt.

Development of a Broad Class of Creditors

While many scholars highlight the importance of technical innovation in the development of public debt, a second explanation would focus on the importance of creating a broad class of creditors within a state.[2] According to the argument, when debt ownership becomes widespread among citizens, then rulers are more likely to feel compelled to honour their debts, and consequently we may observe that rulers will develop institutions that ensure they can keep these promises. There is a clear problem with disentangling causality here. One does not know to what extent it is the existence of broad debt ownership that prompts a government to repay, or, alternatively, whether broad ownership simply reflects the fact that a government already has a good reputation with regard to debt servicing. Nonetheless, it is interesting to ask, in light of the papers presented here, whether we do observe in practice that those states that were the most successful in raising debt finance were also those where debt was held most widely. There is some evidence in the papers to support this assertion. Luciano Pezzolo's chapter reviews evidence on debt ownership in Florence, where the obligatory nature of lending no doubt helped to increase the breadth of debt ownership, as well as in Genoa. More generally, however, the evidence is mixed.

A good example is provided by François Velde's paper, which raises the interesting question of why John Law's System in France did not succeed in creating a sort of 'shareholder democracy' that would align interests of the king with those of taxpayers. Law's experiment was financed by a broad class of investors, representing a drastic expansion in the fraction of the French population that could benefit from the state respecting its engagements. The end result, however, is well known. Interestingly, the British case actually represents almost the exact opposite pattern as the government established a reputation for debt servicing, yet prior to 1750 the circle of British citizens holding debt remained very small and limited to London and, as O'Brien notes in his chapter, the British system of finance throughout the eighteenth century relied on a very small number of intermediaries to facilitate new debt issues. It is also worth noting here that in several northern European city-states that were successful in gaining access to long-term credit it is known that the pattern of debt ownership was highly concentrated.

The Importance of Representative Government

If having a broad circle of borrowers was neither necessary nor sufficient to prompt a state to service its debt obligations, then a third potential explanation is that what really matters is the extent to which creditors have political representation. Following the well-known argument of North and Weingast,[3] in states where rulers are constrained by the presence of representative assemblies that have strong prerogatives in the area of finance, then we will be less likely to see arbitrary actions like default on debts. In states where such institutions are absent, there will be fewer constraints on actions by rulers, and therefore governments will find it more difficult to gain access to credit in the first place. The evidence from the papers presented here provides some support for this hypothesis. So, for example, perhaps the problem with Law's System of shareholder democracy in France was that it did not simultaneously provide for a true system of shareholder representation, whereas in Great Britain parliamentary supremacy served precisely this function. Likewise we also know that political institutions in the republican city-states reviewed by Pezzolo also, in effect, provided for creditor representation.

What is particularly interesting, however, is that three of the papers included here also present clear evidence of how states elsewhere on the Italian peninsula that lacked republican political institutions also eventually gained access to long-term credit. This was the case with the State of Milan, as analysed by De Luca, with the Kingdom of Naples, as analysed by Gaetano Sabatini, and with the Papal States, as considered by Piola Caselli. Neither of these three states had strong representative assemblies during the period considered here. It is an open question to what extent these cases constitute evidence against the representative institutions hypothesis. It is true that all three states borrowed significantly during a period of warfare beginning in the sixteenth century, and they each also succeeded in attracting a relatively broad base of lenders. The cases of Milan, Naples and the Papal States are actually indicative of a broader European phenomenon at this time whereby states without strong national representative institutions moved to create long-term debts. In the case of the Italian states, however, we might also ask why these states did not create long-term debts at an earlier date – more than two centuries elapsed between the date at which these principalities and the city republics described by Pezzolo created long-term debts. If we consider the interest rates reported by De Luca for the debt of the State of Milan, these also seem to be significantly higher than those paid by the city republics considered by Pezzolo. One final contribution that raises particularly interesting questions about the impact of political representation is that of Andrès Ucendo. Castile in the seventeenth century actually did have a representative assembly, the Cortes, that played a prominent role with regard to taxation. However, the Castilian monarchy voluntarily bypassed the Cortes in order to borrow directly from the city of Madrid. As a consequence, Castile's representative assembly was actually considered to be something of an obstacle to raising debt finance.

City-States versus Territorial States

The overall picture from the above discussion can be described as follows. First, technical innovation seems to have been critical for successful access to credit, but it does not constitute an explanation in itself because it was generally the ability to implement good ideas in a durable fashion that was lacking, not the ideas themselves. Second, successful access to credit was often associated with the presence of a broad class of creditors, but having such a broad class was neither a necessary nor a sufficient condition. Finally, we see some evidence of the importance of strong representative institutions, but the papers also raise important questions in this regard. Ultimately, one of the clearest contributions of a set of papers like this is to demonstrate that no single simple explanation provides a satisfying account of the varieties of state experience in the area of public credit. With this said, I would like to suggest one possibility that may not have received sufficient recent emphasis, and which does appear consistent with the evidence from these papers. It involves the difference in financial and political development between city-states and larger territorial states in Europe.

In a recent publication that represents part of an ongoing project, I have documented the extent to which city-states in Europe established long-term debts at earlier dates, on average, than did territorial states, and in addition they also tended to borrow on more favourable terms.[4] One observes this difference even after attempting to control for other potential sources of difference between these two types of states, such as the extent of urbanization in a region. Evidence of early access to credit by city-states can also be seen in the papers presented here, in particular by comparing the descriptions of Italian city-states by Pezzolo and Hanseatic cities by Ranft with the significantly later development of long-term borrowing by territorial states like France, Castile or the Kingdom of Naples.

If city-states in Europe had a financial advantage over territorial states, then we might ask why this was the case. One simple possibility is that city-states obtained earlier access to credit because these were places where capital was abundant. A second possibility is that city-states found it easier to collect revenue and thus they could borrow more. The problem with both of these conditions is that they characterized cities that were independent political entities, but these characteristics also applied to the cities that were major commercial hubs within larger territorial entities like France or Castile. We also know that in many cases when territorial states in Europe moved to create long-term public debts, from the sixteenth century onwards, they often did so by attempting to borrow indirectly via municipal organizations in their capital cities. This was the case with both France and Castile. The latter case is considered in Andrès Ucendo's fascinating study for this volume. As a consequence, it would seem difficult to explain the apparent financial advantage of city-states by referring exclusively to economic factors involving the potential supply of credit and ease of collecting revenue.

Given the insufficiency of strictly economic explanations, I would like to suggest that differences in political conditions between city-states and territorial states may ultimately provide a better explanation for the observed financial advantage of the former group of European states. If access to debt finance was facilitated by the existence of institutions that gave representation to government creditors, then it is interesting to note that in medieval and early modern Europe such institutions emerged almost exclusively in city-states. Whether one considers city-states in Italy, as have been examined here by Pezzolo, German cities as reviewed by Ranft, or for that matter city-states in Switzerland, or the Low Countries, one observes a pattern whereby representative assemblies had strong prerogatives in the area of public finance, they met frequently so as to engage in active monitoring of state finances, and crucially, the members of these assemblies themselves often owned government debt. One should be careful not to automatically associate these conditions with nascent democracy. The situation in many European city-states would be better characterized as one of governance by a merchant oligarchy, combined with very high levels of wealth inequality. Nonetheless, there are abundant indications that political institutions in city-states were singularly successful in facilitating access to public credit. The situation in most territorial states could not have been more different. Representative assemblies in territorial states – when they existed – tended to have few prerogatives in the area of public finance, and they also tended to meet infrequently, which weakened their ability to play a role in active monitoring of state finances. Finally, in most cases government creditors were relatively poorly represented within territorial state assemblies. The two major exceptions to this pattern among territorial states involved the United Provinces after 1572 and Great Britain after 1688.

At a first glance, we might think that because city-states had strong representative institutions while territorial states did not, this provides support for the representative institutions hypothesis referred to above. Ultimately, however, if city-states had such institutions while territorial states did not, this divergence is not something that happened by accident. The development of strong representative institutions in city-states was arguably favoured by two underlying conditions. First, their small size made it feasible to hold frequent meetings of a representative assembly, allowing government creditors to actively monitor public finances. The importance of polity size as a determinant of representative activity in medieval and early modern Europe has been emphasized by Wim Blockmans.[5] Second, a significant fraction of the political elite in city-states held liquid wealth that could be easily invested in public debt, and they had an incentive to invest in debt to diversify out of commercial activities. The political position of these elites in city-states was fundamentally different from that of merchant groups in the large cities of territorial states.

We can also suggest that if most territorial states lacked strong representative institutions within which creditors played a prominent role, then this too was not an accidental outcome. The large size of territorial states like France, Castile or even the Kingdom of Naples created significant obstacles for maintaining an active representative assembly that would serve as an effective monitor of public finance. Likewise, within territorial states a much smaller section of the political elite held liquid wealth that could be easily invested in debt, given the importance of land ownership. What this suggests then is that access to credit and strong representative institutions were each outcomes driven by two underlying conditions involving geographic size and the wealth composition of the political elite. The implication of the above argument is that representative institutions may have mattered for access to credit, but they were not its underlying cause.

My argument about underlying conditions that led simultaneously to the development of representative institutions and to access to credit is offered as one way of placing some of the evidence from the papers in this volume in comparative perspective, and as a potential idea to stimulate future research. In the end, however, it should be emphasized that the contributions to this volume already constitute a very significant advance on our knowledge of governments, debts and financial markets in Europe.

NOTES

1 Ranft, 'The Financial Administration of North Hanseatic Cities in the Late Middle Ages'

1. This is, in essence the text of my lecture with only a few essential notes added.
2. See the clearly-explained, illustrated book by H. Boockmann, *Die Stadt im späten Mittelalter* (München: Beck-Verlag, 1986). For the North German sector, see, among others, J. Schildhauer, *Die Hanse. Geschichte und Kultur* (Stuttgart: Verlag Kohlhammer, 1984), and the rather boldly-titled N. Zazke and R. Zaske, *Kunst in Hansestädten* (Leipzig: Verlag Koehler & Amelang Leipzig, 1985).
3. An exemplary text in this context is K. Schreiner, 'Die Stadt in Webers Analyse und Deutung des okzidentalen Rationalismus', in J. Kocka (ed.) *Max Weber, der Historiker*, Kritische Studien der Geschichtswissenschaft 73 (Göttingen: Verlag Vandenhoeck & Ruprecht Göttingen, 1986), pp. 119–50. Also see the excellent synopsis in E. Isenmann, *Die deutsche Stadt im Spätmittelalter* (Stuttgart: Ulmer Verlag, 1988), especially pp. 19–25, with additional literature.
4. An instructive text with a detailed analysis is R. S. Elkar and G. Fouquet, 'Und sie bauten einen Turm ... Bemerkungen zur materiellen Kultur des Alltags in einer kleinen deutschen Stadt des Spätmittelalters', in R. S. Elkar, G. Fouquet and U. Dirlmeier (eds), *Öffentliches Bauen in Mittelalter und früher Neuzeit* (Siegen: Scripta Mercaturae-Verlag St Katharinen, 1992), pp. 293–328.
5. For the specific legal development, see W. Ebel, *Bürgerliches Rechtsleben zur Hansezeit in Lübecker Ratsurteilen* (Göttingen, Frankfurt am Main and Berlin: Musterschmidt-Verlag, 1990), pp. 46–59.
6. In terms of the history of science, see L. Schorn-Schütte, 'Stadt und Staat. Zum Zusammenhang von Gegenwartsverständnis und historischer Erkenntnis in der Stadtgeschichtsschreibung der Jahrhundertwende', *Die alte Stadt*, 10 (1983), pp. 228–66.
7. Isenmann, *Die deutsche Stadt im Spätmittelalter*, p. 78; for Lüneburg, see K. Friedland, *Der Kampf der Stadt Lüneburg mit ihren Landesherren. Stadtfreiheit und Fürstenhoheit im 16. Jahrhundert* (Hildesheim: Buchdruckerei August Lax, 1953); for Lübeck among others, see E. Hoffmann, 'Lübeck im Hoch und Spätmittelalter:

die große Zeit Lübecks', in A. Graßmann (ed.), *Lübeckische Geschichte* (Lübeck: Schmidt-Römhild Verlag, 1988), pp. 103–32.

8. Cf. for the German situation, see Isenmann, *Die deutsche Stadt im Spätmittelalter*, pp. 177–81. See also W. Kuppers, *Die Stadtrechnungenvon Geldern 1386–1423* (Geldern: Johannes Keuck, 1993), p. 56.

9. For the German towns in general, see B. Kuske, 'Das Schuldenwesen der deutschen Städte im Mittelalter', *Zeitschrift für die gesamten Staatswissenschaften, Ergänzungsheft*, 12 (1904); Isenmann, *Die deutsche Stadt im Spätmittelalters*, pp. 174–78; for Hamburg and Cologne, see H. Reincke, 'Die alte Hamburger Staatsschuld der Hansezeit (1300–1563), in A. von Brandt and Wilhelm Koppe (eds), *Städtewesen und Bürgertum als geschichtliche Kräfte* (Lübeck: Schmidt-Römhild Verlag, 1953), pp. 489–511; and R. Knipping, 'Das Schuldenwesen der Stadt Köln im 14. und 15. Jahrhundert', in *Westdeutsche Zeitschrift für Geschichte und Kunst*, 13 (1894), pp. 340–97.

10. This includes the period from 1385 to 1416 and registers most of the bonds in the period from 1388, where the attack on Celle was unsuccessful following the defeat near Winsen/Aller, to 1393, the first administration year of *Sate*. For Lüneburg's point of view, see W. Reinecke, *Geschichte der Stadt Lüneburg*, 2 vols (1933; Lüneburg: Heinrich Heine Buchhandlung Neubauer, 1977), vol. 1, pp. 123–44.

11. Cf. A. Ranft, *Der Basishaushalt der Stadt Lüneburg in der Mitte des 15. Jahrhunderts. Zur Struktur der städtischen Finanzen im Spätmittelalter*, Veröffentlichungen des Max-Planck-Instituts für Geschichte 84 (Göttingen: Verlag Vandenhoeck & Ruprecht Göttingen, 1987).

12. Stadtarchiv Lüneburg, AB 561 (hereafter StA Lüneburg).

13. The *vorschoß* was a kind of minimum tax or capitation for every inhabitant and a kind of pre-tax for taxable property (*c.* 0.5 %).

14. U. Dirlmeier and G. Fouquet, 'Eigenbetriebe niedersächsischer Städte im Spätmittelalter', in C. Meckseper (ed.) *Stadt im Wandel. Kunst und Kultur des Bürgertums in Norddeutschland 1150–1650*, 3 vols (Stuttgart and Bad Cannstatt: Cantz-Verlag, 1985), vol. 3, pp. 157–279.

15. This research shows that only the analysis of many cashboxes can make the urban household accessible. See also O. Fahlbusch, *Die Finanzverwaltung der Stadt Braunschweig seit dem großen Aufstand im Jahre 1374 bis zum Jahre 1425. Eine städtische Finanzreform im Mittelater* (1913; Aalen: Scientia Verlag, 1970).

16. StA Lüneburg AB 183.

17. StA Lüneburg AB 197.

18. StA Lüneburg AB 175.

19. H. Witthöft, 'Struktur und Kapazität der Lüneburger Saline seit dem 12. Jahrhundert', *Vierteljahrsschrift für Sozial und Wirtschaftsgeschichte*, 63 (1976), pp. 1–117.

20. Cf. L. Schönberg, *Die Technik des Finanzhaushalts der deutschen Städte im Mittelalter* (Stuttgart and Berlin: J. G. Cotta'sche Buchhandlung Nachfolger, 1910), especially pp. 21–6.

21. In general, see ibid.; and R. Knipping, *Die Kölner Stadtrechnungen des Mittelalters, mit einer Darstellung der Finanzverwaltung*, 2 vols (Bonn: Behrendt-Verlag, 1897–8).

22. For a typical town budget, see P. Huber, *Der Haushalt der Stadt Hildesheim am Ende des 14. Jahrhunderts und in der ersten Hälfte des 15. Jahrhunderts* (Leipzig: Jäh & Schunke, 1901); for an exceptional town budget, see J. Rosen, 'Der Staatshaushalt [*sic*] Basels von 1360 bis 1535', in H. Kellenbenz (ed.), *Öffentliche Finanzen und privates Kapital im späten Mittelalter und in der ersten Hälfte des 19. Jahrhunderts* (Stuttgart: Fischer Verlag, 1971), pp. 24–38.

23. See the collected studies of J. Rosen, *Finanzgeschichte Basels im späten Mittelalter* (Wiesbaden: Steiner Verlag Wiesbaden, 1989), with a side glance to Frankfurt; or B. Kirchgässner, 'Währungspolitik, Stadthaushalt und soziale Fragen südwestdeutscher Reichsstädte im Spätmittelalter. Menschen und Kräfte zwischen 1360 und 1460', *Jahrbuch für Geschichte der oberdeutschen Reichsstädte*, 11 (1965), pp. 90–127.

24. This example clearly helps to demonstrate the overall coherence of the books. W. Reinecke, 'Die drei ältesten Kämmereirechnungen ([1322], 1331, 133[5], 1337)', *Lüneburger Museumsblätter*, 2, (1928), pp. 309–37; G. Winter (ed.), 'Die ältesten Lüneburger Kämmereirechnungen', *Lüneburger Blätter*, 2 (1951), pp. 2–26. Besides Ranft, *Der Basishaushalt der Stadt Lüneburg*, pp. 24–6.

25. Cf. also W. Reinecke, 'Des Bürgermeisters Claus Stöterogge Denkbüchlein über die Ratsämter', in *Lüneburger Museumsblätter*, 2 (1912), pp. 349–83.

26. J. Ellermeyer, *Stade 1300–1399. Liegenschaften und Renten in Stadt und Land. Untersuchungen zur Wirtschafts und Sozialstruktur einer hansischen Landstadt im Spätmittelalter* (Stade: Selbstverlag des Stader Geschichts- und Heimatsvereins, 1975), pp. 42–5.

27. Fahlbusch, *Die Finanzverwaltung der Stadt Braunschweig*, p. 12; R. Sprandel, 'Der städtische Rentenmarkt in Nordwestdeutschland im Spätmittelalter', in Kellenbenz (ed.), *Öffentliche Finanzen und privates Kapital*, pp. 14–23, on p. 20.

28. H.-J. Wenner, *Handelskonjunkturen und Rentenmarkt am Beispiel der Stadt Hamburg um die Mitte des 14. Jahrhunderts* (Hamburg: Christians, 1972), p. 91.

29. Sprandel, 'Der städtische Rentenmarkt in Nordwestdeutschland', p. 20. For connections between Lübeck und Lüneberg, see G. Franke, *Lübeck als Geldgeber Lünebergs* (Neumünster: K. Wachholtz, 1935).

30. J. Bohmbach, 'Umfang und Struktur des Braunschweiger Rentenmarkts 1300–1350', *Niedersächsisches Jahrbuch für Landesgeschichte*, 41:2 (1969–70), p. 121.

31. Sprandel, 'Der städtische Rentenmarkt in Nordwestdeutschland', p. 19.

32. Reincke, 'Die alte Hamburger Staatsschuld der Hansezeit (1300–1563)', p. 500.

33. Ranft, *Der Basishaushalt der Stadt Lüneberg*, esp. pp. 228–31, 258–60.

34. Similar situations were to be found in other salt-towns: see W. Freitag, 'Die Salzstadt – Alteuropäische Strukturen und frühmoderne Innovation. Eine Einführung', in W. Freitag (ed.), *Die Salzstadt: Alteuropäische Strukturen und frühmoderne Innovation*, Studien zur Regionalgeschichte 19 (Bielefeld: Verlag für Regionalgeschichte, 2004), pp. 9–37; M. Hecht, 'Geburtsstand oder Funktionselite? Ueberlegungen zum 'Salzpatrizitat' im Zeitraum von 1400 bis 1700', in Freitag (ed.), *Die Salzstadt*, pp. 83–116.

35. Reinecke, *Geschichte der Stadt Lüneberg*, vol. 1, pp. 180–6.

36. The *Sotmeister* was the head of the saltworks, elected from the ranks of the council members.

2 Pezzolo, 'Government Debts and Credit Markets in Renaissance Italy'

1.   G. Luzzatto, *Le origini dell'organizzazione finanziaria dei comuni italiani* (Urbino: QuattroVenti, 1990), pp. 88ff. I wish to thank Julius Kirshner and Bepi Tattara, who read an earlier version of this paper and provided me with useful comments.

2.   See, for example, W. Bowsky, *Le finanze del comune di Siena 1287–1355* (Firenze: La Nuova Italia, 1975), pp. 449ff. (Appendix 12); D. Balestracci, *La zappa e la retorica. Memorie familiari di un contadino toscano del Quattrocento* (Siena: Salimbeni, 1984), pp. 144, 147–8; C. Meek, *Lucca 1369–1400. Politics and Society in an Early Renaissance City-State* (Oxford: Oxford University Press, 1978), p. 48; L. Pezzolo, *Il fisco dei veneziani. Finanza pubblica ed economia tra XV e XVII secolo* (Verona: Cierre, 2003), pp. 21–2.

3.   M. Del Treppo, 'Il re e il banchiere. Strumenti e processi di razionalizzazione dello stato aragonese di Napoli', in G. Rossetti (ed.), *Spazio, società, potere nell'Italia dei Comuni* (Napoli: Liguori, 1986), pp. 229–304, on p. 269. See also A. Ryder, 'Cloth and Credit: Aragonese War Finance in the mid Fifteenth Century', *War and Society*, 2 (1984), pp. 1–21.

4.   A. Barbero, *Un'oligarchia urbana. Politica ed economia a Torino fra tre e quattrocento* (Roma: Viella, 1995), pp. 217–18, 231ff.

5.   H. L. Root, *The Fountain of Privilege. Political Foundations of Markets in Old Regime France and England* (Berkeley, CA: University of California Press, 1994).

6.   Ryder, 'Cloth and Credit', p. 13; R. Goldthwaithe, 'Lorenzo Morelli, Ufficiale del Monte, 1484–88: interessi privati e cariche pubbliche nella Firenze laurenziana', *Archivio Storico Italiano*, 154 (1996), pp. 605–33, on pp. 613, 617, 630.

7.   For the sake of brevity, see especially M. Ginatempo, *Prima del debito. Finanziamento della spesa pubblica e gestione del deficit nelle grandi città toscane (1200–1350 ca.)* (Firenze: Olschki, 2001).

8.   L. Martines, *Power and Imagination. City-States in Renaissance Italy* (New York: Vintage Books, 1979), p. 175.

9.   Source: author's database. The sources of these data will be presented more extensively in a forthcoming monograph. For 1650, see J. Macdonald, *A Free Nation Deep in Debt. The Financial Roots of Democracy* (New York: Farrar, Straus and Giroux, 2003), p. 152.

10.   C. Tilly, *L'oro e la spada. Capitale, guerra e potere nella formazione degli stati europei 990–1990* (Firenze: Ponte alle Grazie, 1991).

11.   A. Michielin and G. M. Varanini, 'Nota introduttiva', in A. Michielin (ed.), *Mutui e risarcimenti del comune di Treviso (secolo XIII)* (Roma: Viella, 2003), pp. lxxvii, lxxx; F. Scarmoncin (ed.), *I documenti del Comune di Bassano dal 1259 al 1295* (Padova: Antenore, 1989).

12.   P. Grillo, 'L'introduzione dell'estimo e la politica fiscale del comune di Milano alla metà del secolo XIII (1240–1260)', in P. Mainoni (ed.), *Politiche finanziarie e fiscali nell'Italia settentrionale (secoli XIII–XV)* (Milano: Unicopli, 2001), pp. 11–37, on pp. 22–3, 35–6; G. Barbieri, *Origini del capitalismo lombardo. Studi e documenti sull'economia milanese del periodo ducale* (Milano: Giuffrè, 1961), pp. 15–16, 31–2.

13. It seems that the backwardness of the financial market in preindustrial China was due above all to the lack of state credit demand: see J. L. Rosenthal and B. Wong, 'Another Look at Credit Markets and investment in China and Europe before the Industrial Revolution', unpublished Yale Economic History Workshop paper, 2005, <http://www.econ.yale.edu/seminars/echist/eh05-06/paper_Wong.doc>. For the French case, see P. T. Hoffman, G. Postel-Vinay and J.-L. Rosenthal, *Priceless Markets. The Political Economy of Credit in Paris, 1660–1870* (Chicago, IL: University of Chicago Press, 2000).

14. See ibid., p. 289.

15. H. Sieveking, *Studio sulle finanze genovesi nel medioevo e in particolare sulla Casa di S. Giorgio*, 2 vols (Genova: Società Ligure di Storia Patria, 1905–6), vol. 1, p. 206.

16. F. Chabod, *Storia di Milano nell'età di Carlo V* (Torino: Einaudi, 1971), pp. 353–4; and, for a later example, R. Villari, *La rivolta antispagnola a Napoli. Le origini (1585–1647)* (Roma-Bari: Laterza, 1967), p. 148.

17. On the misleading use of the term negotiability in the early phase of the Florentine Monte, see the subtle pages of J. Kirshner, 'Encumbering Private Claims to Public Debt in Renaissance Florence', in V. Piergiovanni (ed.), *The Growth of the Bank as Institution and the Development of Money-Business Law* (Berlin: Duncker & Humblot, 1993), pp. 19–75.

18. Goldthwaite, 'Lorenzo Morelli'; S. Tognetti, *Il banco Cambini. Affari e mercati di una compagnia mercantile-bancaria nella Firenze del XV secolo* (Firenze: Olschki, 1999), pp. 258, 261; A. Molho, *Florentine Public Finances in the Early Renaissance, 1400–1433* (Cambridge, MA: Harvard University Press, 1971), pp. 153, 164, 170,176; A. Molho, 'Lo stato e la finanza pubblica. Un'ipotesi basata sulla storia tardomedievale di Firenze', in G. Chittolini, A. Molho and P. Schiera (eds), *Origini dello stato. Processi di formazione statale in Italia fra medioevo e età moderna* (Bologna: Il mulino, 1994), pp. 225–80.

19. R. C. Mueller, *The Venetian Money Market. Banks, Panics and Public Debt, 1200–1500* (Baltimore, MD: Johns Hopkins University Press, 1997), pp. 425ff.

20. Ryder, 'Cloth and Credit', pp. 12–13; A. Silvestri, 'Sull'attività bancaria napoletana durante il periodo aragonese', *Bollettino dell'Archivio Storico del Banco di Napoli*, 6 (1953), pp. 3–57.

21. F. Piola Caselli, 'Aspetti del debito pubblico nello stato pontificio: gli uffici vacabili', *Annali della Facoltà di Scienze Politiche dell'Università di Perugia*, 11 (1970–72), pp. 3–74. For the decision to allow the constitution of investors' companies, see W. von Hofmann, *Forschungen zur Geschichte der kurialen Behörden von Schisma bis zur Reformation*, 2 vols (Rom: Loescher, 1914), vol. 1, pp. 188–9.

22. C. Bauer, 'Die Epochen der Papstfinanz. Ein Versuch', *Historische Zeitschrift*, 138 (1928), pp. 457–503, on p. 488.

23. F. Litva, 'L'attività finanziaria della Dataria durante il periodo tridentino', *Archivum historiae pontificiae*, 5 (1967), pp. 79–174, on p. 135. For data on offices of third category sold between the fifteenth and sixteenth century, see Piola Caselli, 'Aspetti del debito pubblico', pp. 27, 30–1, 34.

24. Sources: B. Schimmelpfennig, 'Der Ämterhandel an der römischen Kurie von Pius II. bis zum Sacco di Roma (1458–1527)', in I. Mieck (ed.), *Ämterhandel im Spätmittelalter und im 16. Jahrhundert* (Berlin: Colloquium Verlag, 1984), pp. 3–41,

on pp. 39–41; T. Frenz, *Die Kanzlei der Päpste der Hochrenaissance (1471–1 527)*, (Tübingen: Niemeyer, 1986), pp. 204 ff.; Piola Caselli, 'Aspetti del debito pubblico', pp. 40, 63–5.

25. A. Esposito, 'Note sulle *societates officiorum* alla corte di Roma nel pontificato di Sisto IV', in B. Flug, M. Matheus and A. Rehberg (eds), *Kurie und Region. Festschrift für Brigide Schwarz zum 65. Geburtstag* (Stuttgart: Steiner, 2005), pp. 197–207; R. Ago, *Economia barocca. Mercato e istituzioni nella Roma del seicento* (Roma: Donzelli, 1998), pp. 192–3; R. Ago, 'Norme e regole: i ceti urbani davanti al notaio', in *Disuguaglianze: stratificazione e mobilità sociale nelle popolazioni italiane (dal sec. XIV agli inizi del secolo XX)*, 2 vols (Bologna: Cleup, 1997), vol. 2, pp. 540–1.

26. H. J. Gilomen, 'La prise de décision en matière d'emprunts dans les villes suisses au XVe siècle', in M. Boone, K. Davids and P. Janssens (eds), *Urban Public Debts. Urban Government and the Market for Annuities in Western Europe (14th–18th Centuries)* (Turnhout: Brepols, 2003), pp. 127–48, on pp. 137, 139.

27. R. Barducci, 'Le riforme finanziarie nel tumulto dei Ciompi', in *Il Tumulto dei Ciompi; Un momento di storia fiorentina ed europa* (Firenze: Olschki, 1981), pp. 95–102.

28. Sieveking, *Studio sulle finanze genovesi*, vol. 1, p. 126; S. A. Epstein, *Genoa and the Genoese, 958–1528* (Chapel Hill, NC: North Carolina University Press, 1996), pp. 204–5; G. Felloni, 'Introduzione', in G. Felloni (ed.), *Inventario dell'Archivio del Banco di San Giorgio (1407–1805)*, 4 vols (Roma: Ministero dei Beni Culturali, 1989–2001), vol. 4, part 1, p. 18, n. For a similar episode in Bâle, see Gilomen, 'La prise de décision', p. 131.

29. See the remarks of J. Kirshner, '*Civitas sibi faciat civem*: Bartolus of Sassoferrato's Doctrine on the Making of a Citizen', *Speculum*, 48 (1973), pp. 694–713, on pp. 699–701; as well as P. Costa, *Civitas. Storia della cittadinanza in Europa*, 4 vols (Roma-Bari: Laterza, 1999–2001), vol. 1, pp. 14ff.

30. I am referring to the model put forward by J. L. van Zanden and M. Prak, 'Towards an Economic Interpretation of Citizenship: The Dutch Republic between Medieval Communes and Modern-States', *European Review of Economic History*, 10 (2006), pp. 111–45.

31. See, for example, J. Kirshner, 'Angelo degli Ubaldi and Bartolomeo da Saliceto on Priviliged Risk: Investments of Luchino Novello Visconti in the Public Debt (Monte Comune) of Florence', *Rivista internazionale di diritto comune*, 14 (2003), pp. 83–117.

32. J. Kirshner, 'Papa Eugenio IV e il Monte Comune. Documenti su investimento e speculazione nel debito pubblico di Firenze', *Archivio Storico Italiano*, 127 (1969), pp. 339–82, on pp. 341–3, 344.

33. Ibid., p. 352.

34. Sieveking, *Studio sulle finanze genovesi*, vol. 2, p. 29.

35. See, for Florence, R. Barducci, 'Politica e speculazione finanziaria a Firenze dopo la crisi del primo trecento (1343–1358)', *Archivio storico italiano*, 137 (1979), pp. 177–219, on p. 204.

36. G. Brucker, *Dal comune alla signoria. La vita pubblica a Firenze nel primo rinascimento* (Bologna: il Mulino, 1981), p. 61. By 1380 it seems that there were about 5,000 creditors. See also R. Ninci, 'La politica finanziaria della Repubblica fiorentina dopo il Tumulto dei Ciompi (1380–1425): Un tentativo di 'Programmazione'?', in

R. Ninci (ed.), *La società fiorentina nel Basso medioevo: Per Elio Conti* (Roma: Istituto Storico Italiano per il Medio Evo, 1995), pp. 151–67.

37. Sieveking, *Studio sulle finanze genovesi*, vol. 1, pp. 205–6; J. Heers, *Gênes au XVe siècle* (Paris: Sevpen, 1961), p. 175. It is interesting to recall that the British loan of 1694, which gave life to the Bank of England, was underwritten by 1,268 people: P. G. M. Dickson, *The Financial Revolution in England. A Study in the Development of Public Credit 1688–1756* (London and New York: St. Martin's, 1967; Aldershot: Gregg Revivals, 1993), p. 254.

38. I have estimated the Genoese population in 1460 at 40,000 and in 1500 at 50,000: see G. Felloni, *Scritti di storia economica*, 2 vols (Genova: Società ligure di storia patria, 1999), vol. 2, pp. 1177–215.

39. Unfortunately, there are only a few works, mostly on Florence, on this crucial aspect. Sieveking, *Studio sulle finanze genovesi*, vol. 1, p. 57; and B. Barbadoro, *Le finanze della repubblica fiorentina. Imposta diretta e debito pubblico fino all'istituzione del Monte* (Firenze: Olschki, 1929), pp. 652–4, have noticed this phenomenon. For recent analyses, see A. Molho, 'Créanciers de Florence en 1347. Un aperçu statistique du quartier de Santo Spirito', in *La Toscane et les Toscans autour de la Renaissance. Cadre de vie, société, croyances. Mélanges offerts à Charles-M. de La Roncière* (Aix-en-Provence: Publications de l'Université de Provence, 1999), pp. 79–93.

40. Source: D. Herlihy, 'Family and Property in Renaissance Florence', in D. Herlihy, *Cities and Society in Medieval Italy* (London: Variorum, 1980), essay 13, p. 8.

41. A. Molho, *Marriage Alliance in Late Medieval Florence* (Cambridge, MA: Harvard University Press, 1994), pp. 80ff. Data refers to the Dowry Fund.

42. See Molho, 'Créanciers de Florence', pp. 83, 88; J. Kirshner and J. Klerman, 'The Seven Percent Fund of Renaissance Florence', in *Banchi pubblici, banchi private e monti di pietà nell'Europa preindustriale. Amministrazione, tecniche operative e ruoli economici* (Genova: Società ligure di storia patria, 1991), pp. 367–98, on p. 396. It is likely that in Venice and Genoa the upward concentration was lower than in Florence.

43. Sieveking, *Studio sulle finanze genovesi*, vol. 2, pp. 37–8; M. Sanudo, *Diari*, ed. R. Fulin et al., 58 vols (Venezia: Deputazione di storia patria, 1879–1903), vol. 52, col. 302.

44. Much information can be drawn from Florentine material. See, for some examples, U. di N. Martelli, *Ricordanze dal 1433 al 1483*, ed. F. Pezzarossa (Roma: Ed. di storia e letteratura, 1989); F. di M. Castellani, *Ricordanze*, ed. G. Ciappelli, 3 vols (Firenze: Olschki, 1992–5) vol. 1; G. C. da San Miniato, *Le ricordanze*, ed. M. T. Sillano (Milano: FrancoAngeli, 1984).

45. Source: L. Pezzolo, 'Bonds and Government Debt in Italian City States, 1250–1650', in W. Goetzman and G. Rouwenhorst (eds), *Origins of Value. Financial Innovations in History* (New York: Oxford University Press, 2005), pp. 145–63, on p. 154.

46. See E. Conti, *L'imposta diretta a Firenze nel quattrocento (1427–1494)* (Roma: Istituto Storico Italiano per il Medio Evo, 1984), pp. 30–1, 39, 128.

47. L. Pezzolo, 'The Venetian Government Debt, 1350–1650', in Boone et al. (eds), *Urban Public Debts*, pp. 61–74, on p. 62.

48. L. Neal, 'How it All Began: The Monetary and Financial Architecture of Europe during the First Global Capital Markets, 1648–1815', *Financial History Review*, 7 (2000), pp. 117–40.

49. Heers, *Gênes au XVe siècle*, pp. 163ff., 260–3; J.-G. da Silva, 'Le sconto à Gênes. A propos d'un croquis', *Annales*, 13 (1958), pp. 150–3; and J. Kirshner, 'The Moral Problem of Discounting Genoese *Paghe*, 1450–1550', *Archivum Fratrum Praedicatorum*, 47 (1977), pp. 109–67.

50. Heers, *Gênes au XVe siècle*, p. 166.

51. See data in R. C. Mueller, 'Foreign Investment in Venetian Government Bonds and the Case of Paolo Guinigi, Lord of Lucca, Early Fifteenth Century', in H. Diederiks and D. Reeder (eds), *Cities of Finance* (Amsterdam: Koninklijke Nederlandse Akademie van Wetenschappen, 1996), pp. 69–90, on p. 82.

52. A. Petrucci (ed.), *Il libro di ricordanze dei Corsini (1362–1457)* (Roma: Istituto Storico Italiano per il Medio Evo, 1965), pp. 7–8, 62, 113; Balestracci, *La zappa e la retorica*, p. 143.

53. O. Gelderblom and J. Jonker, 'Probing a Virtual Market. Interest Rates and the Trade in Government Bonds in the Dutch Republic', paper presented at the seminar on The Origins and Development of Financial Markets and Institutions, Urbana, IL, 27–9 April 2006, p. 20. See also W. Fritschy, 'A "Financial Revolution" Reconsidered: Public Finance in Holland during the Dutch Revolt, 1568–1648', *Economic History Review*, 56:1 (2003), pp. 57–89, on p. 64.

54. See some examples in J. H. Munro, 'The Medieval Origins of the Financial Revolution: Usury, *Rentes*, and Negotiability', *International History Review*, 25 (2003), pp. 505–615.

55. Ibid.; H. van der Wee, *The Low Countries in the Early Modern World* (Aldershot: Variorum, 1993), pp. 145ff.

56. Gelderblom and Jonker, 'Probing a Virtual Market'.

57. Pezzolo, 'The Venetian Government Debt', p. 67. The coercive character of Genoese loans, however, is not always evident.

58. Unfortunately quantitative data is lacking, but it is sufficient to look through G. Luzzatto's 'Introduzione' to *I prestiti della repubblica di Venezia* (Padove: A. Draghi, 1929); and Mueller, *The Venetian Money Market*, to get some evidence.

59. For a comparison between the two systems, see L. Pezzolo, 'Government Debts and Trust. French Kings and Roman Popes as Borrowers, 1520–1660', *Rivista di Storia Economica*, 15:3 (1999), pp. 233–61. A revaluation of the royal bonds is put forward by M. Moulin, 'Les rentes sur l'hôtel de ville de Paris sous Louis XIV', *Histoire, Economie, Société*, 17 (1998), pp. 623–48.

60. D. C. North and B. R. Weingast, 'Constitutions and Commitment: The Evolution of Institutions Governing Public Choice in Seventeenth-Century England', *Journal of Economic History*, 49:4 (1989), pp. 803–32.

61. R. La Porta, F. Lopez de Silanes, A. Shleifer and R. Vishny, 'Legal Determinants of External Finance', *Journal of Finance*, 52 (1997), pp. 1131–50.

62. G. Clark, 'The Political Foundations of Modern Economic Growth: Britain, 1540–1800, *Journal of Interdisciplinary History*, 26 (1996), pp. 563–88; N. Sussman and Y. Yafeh, 'Constitutions and Commitment: Evidence on the Relation Between Institutions and the Cost of Capital', *CEPR Discussion Papers* (June 2004), n. 4404.

63. D. Stasavage, *Public Debt and the Birth of the Democratic State. France and Great Britain, 1688–1789* (Cambridge: Cambridge University Press, 2003), pp. 68ff.; but see also B. G. Carruthers, *Politics and Markets in the English Financial Revolution*

(Princeton: Princeton University Press, 1996); A. Dixit and J. Londregan, 'Political Power and the Credibility of Government Debt', *Journal of Economic Theory*, 94 (2000), pp. 80–105.

64. P. T. Hoffman and K. Norberg (eds), *Fiscal Crises, Liberty, and Representative Government, 1450–1789* (Stanford, CA: Stanford University Press, 1994).

65. J. Brewer, *The Sinews of Power. War, Money and the English State, 1688–1783* (New York: Alfred A. Knopf, 1989); P. K. O'Brien, 'The Political Economy of British Taxation, 1660–1815', *Economic History Review*, 41:1 (1988), pp. 1–32; Fritschy, 'A "Financial Revolution" Reconsidered'.

66. D. C. North, *Institutions, Institutional Change and Economic Performance* (Cambridge: Cambridge University Press, 1990), p. 69.

67. See the data published by S. R. Epstein, *Freedom and Growth. The Rise of States and Markets in Europe, 1300–1750* (London: Routledge, 2000), pp. 20–3; and the discussion of D. Stasavage, 'Cities, Constitutions, and Sovereign Borrowing in Europe, 1274–1785', *International Organization*, 61 (2007), pp. 489–525.

68. Molho, *Florentine Public Finances*, p. 164.

69. Sources: Barbadoro, *Le finanze della repubblica*, pp. 534ff.; A. Sapori, *Studi di storia economica*, 3rd edn, 2 vols (Firenze: Sansoni, 1982), vol. 1, p. 197. Interest rates are on medium- and long-term loans.

70. B. Dini, *Manifattura, commercio e banca nella Firenze medievale* (Firenze: Nardini, 2001), p. 94, argues that Monte loans had a pegging effect on the private market.

71. M. B. Becker, 'Economic Change and the Emerging Florentine Territorial State', *Studies in the Renaissance*, 13 (1966), pp. 7–39; M. B. Becker, 'Problemi della finanza pubblica fiorentina nella seconda metà del Trecento e nei primi del Quattrocento', *Archivio Storico Italiano*, 123 (1965), pp. 433–66.

72. J. D. Tracy, 'On the Dual Origins of Long-Term Urban Debt in Medieval Europe', in Boone et al. (eds), *Urban Public Debts*, pp. 13–24.

73. J. M. Poterba, 'Annuities in Early Modern Europe', in Goetzman and Rouwenhorst (eds), *Origins of Value*, pp. 207–24. But in the period 1397–1402 some Burgundian cities issued life annuities at interest rates linked to the age of investors: W. P. Blockmans, 'Le crédit public dans les Pays-Bas méridionaux au bas moyen âge', in H. Dubois (ed.), *Local and International Credit in the Middle Ages and the 16th Century* (Bern: Ninth International Economic History Congress, 1986), pp. 3–8, on p. 4.

74. Pezzolo, 'Bonds and Government Debt in Italian City States', p. 156.

75. O. Gelderblom and J. Jonker, 'Amsterdam as the Cradle of Modern Futures and Options Trading, 1550–1650', in Goetzman and Rouwenhorst (eds), *Origins of Value*, pp. 189–205, on p. 194.

3 Alonso García, 'Government Debts and Financial Markets in Castile between the Fifteenth and Sixteenth Centuries'

1. M. Á. Ladero Quesada, *Castilla y la conquista del reino de Granada* (Granada: Diputación Provincial de Granada, 1987). There is a wealth of material for Charles V's time. Some of the latest studies are highlighted here: I. Pulido Bueno, *La corte, las*

Cortes y los mercaderes. Política imperial y desempeño de la hacienda real en la España de los Austrias (Huelva: for the author, 2002), pp. 13–62; J. D. Tracy, *Emperor Charles V, Impresario of War. Campaign Strategy, International Finance, and Domestic Politics* (Cambridge: Cambrige University Press, 2002); see also an interesting review of this book, H. G. Koenigsberger, *The International History Review*, 25 (3 September 2003), pp. 646–8.

2.   D. A. García, *Fisco, poder y monarquía en los albores de la Modernidad. Castilla, 1504–1525* (Phd dissertation, Universidad Complutense, Madrid, 2007), <http://www.ucm.es/BUCM/tesis/ghi/ucm-t27728.pdf>.

3.   P. Toboso Sánchez, *La deuda pública castellana durante el Antiguo Régimen (juros) y su liquidación en el siglo XIX* (Madrid: Instituto de Estudios Fiscales, 1987).

4.   W. M. Ormrod, 'Urban Communities and Royal Finance in England during the Later Middle Ages', in *Actes. Colloqui Corona, Municipis i fiscalitat a la Baixa Edad Mitjana*, (Lleida: Institut d'Estudis Ilerdencs, 1995), pp. 45–60.

5.   Munro, 'The Medieval Origins of the Financial Revolution'.

6.   D. A. García, 'La configuración de lo ordinario en el sistema fiscal de la Monarquía. Una o dos ideas', *Studia Historica. Historia Moderna*, 21 (1999), pp. 117–52; D. A. García, 'El sistema fiscal castellano (1503–1536). Elementos de análisis, palabras de discusión', in F. J. Guillamón Álvarez, J. D. Muñoz Rodríguez and D. Centenero de Arce (eds), *Entre Clío y Casandra. Poder y sociedad en la Monarquía Hispánica durante la Edad Moderna* (Murcia: Universidad de Murcia, 2005), pp. 235–55.

7.   Source: D. A. García, *El erario del reino. Fiscalidad en Castilla a principios de la Edad Moderna (1504–1525)* (Valladolid: Junta de Castilla y León, 2007).

8.   D. A. García, 'Entre Granada y Castilla. La familia Fuente y la hacienda real a comienzos de la Edad Moderna', *Investigaciones Históricas*, 25 (2005), pp. 11–30.

9.   Archivo General de Simancas, Escribanía Mayor de Rentas (hereafter AGS, EMR), leg. 100–1. For further information about Pedro de Santa Cruz, see M. Diago Hernando, 'Arrendadores arandinos al servicio de los Reyes Católicos', *Historia. Instituciones. Documentos*, 18 (1991), pp. 71–95.

10.   Source: García, 'La configuración de lo ordinario', p. 129.

11.   D. A. García, 'Dinero en Castilla. Notas sobre el pago de guardas en 1523', *Tiempos Modernos*, 8 (2003), pp. 1–18, <http://www.tiemposmodernos.org>.

12.   Valladolid, AGS, EMR, leg. 175. García, *El erario del reino*.

13.   Source: ibid., pp. 139–40.

14.   Such as Juan de Almansa and Diego de Bruselas. See R. Carande, *Carlos V y sus banqueros*, 3 vols (Barcelona: Crítica, 1990).

15.   AGS, EMR, leg. 145.

16.   Diago Hernando, 'Arrendadores arandinos'.

17.   C. J. Mathers, 'Relations between the City of Burgos and the Crown, 1506–1556' (Phd dissertation, Michigan University, MI, 1973).

18.   AGS, EMR, leg. 157–1A. For further information about the Santa María family, see M. Basas Fernández, 'Banqueros burgaleses del siglo XVI', *Boletín de la Institución Fernán González*, 163 (1964), pp. 314–32, on p. 322.

19.   On Beltrán, see J. Martínez Millán (ed.), *La Corte de Carlos V*, 5 vols (Madrid: Sociedad Estatal para la Conmemoración de los Centenarios de Felipe II y Carlos V, 2000), vol. 2, pp. 62–6.

20. F. Ruiz Martín, 'La banca en España hasta 1782', in *El banco de España. Una historia económica* (Madrid: Banco de España, 1970), pp. 1–196, on p. 29.
21. Toboso Sánchez, *La deuda pública castellana*; F. Ruiz Martín, 'Crédito y banca, comercio y transportes en la etapa del capitalismo mercantil', in *Actas de las I Jornadas de Metodología Aplicada de las Ciencias Históricas. III. Metodología de la Historia Moderna. Economía y Demografía* (Santiago de Compostela: Universidad de Santiago de Compostela, 1975), pp. 725–49.
22. García, *El erario del reino.*
23. C. J. de Carlos Morales, *Carlos V y el crédito de Castilla. El tesorero general Francisco de Vargas y la Hacienda Real entre 1516 y 1524* (Madrid: Sociedad Estatal para la Conmemoración de los Centenarios de Felipe II y Carlos V, 2000), pp. 56ff.
24. D. A. García, 'Tras la muerte de la reina: Isabel I y la Hacienda Real de Castilla en la crisis dinástica de 1504–1507', in M. V. López-Cordón and G. Franco (eds), *La reina Isabel y las reinas de España: realidad, modelos e imagen historiográfica. Actas de la VIII Reunión Científica de la Fundación Española de Historia Moderna* (Madrid: Fundación Española de Historia Moderna, 2005), pp. 203–17, on p. 217.
25. Carlos Morales, *Carlos V y el crédito de Castilla*, p. 56.
26. H. Kellenbenz, *Los Fugger en España y Portugal hasta 1560* (Salamanca: Junta de Castilla y León, 2000), pp. 193–212.
27. A. Rodríguez Villa, *El emperador Carlos V y su corte según las cartas de don Martín de Salinas, embajador del infante don Fernando (1522–1559)* (Madrid: Fortanet, 1903), p. 53.
28. AGS, EMR, leg. 174.
29. Source: Archivo Histórico Nacional, Dirección General de la Deuda, Madrid, 641/27 and 32.
30. Carande, *Carlos V y sus banqueros*, vol. 3, pp. 126–8.
31. See note 29 above.
32. F. Ruiz Martín, 'Un expediente financiero entre 1560 y 1575. La hacienda de Felipe II y la Casa de la Contratación de Sevilla', *Moneda y Crédito*, 92 (1965), pp. 3–58.
33. A. Marcos Martín, 'Deuda pública, fiscalidad y arbitrios en la Corona de Castilla', in C. Sanz and B. García (eds), *Banca, crédito y capital. La Monarquía Hispánica y los antiguos Países Bajos (1505–1700)* (Madrid: Fundación Carlos de Amberes, 2006), pp. 345–75, on p. 353; M. Körner, 'Public Credit', in R. Bonney (ed.), *Economic Systems and State Finance* (Oxford: Oxford University Press, 1995), pp. 515–48, on p. 521.
34. At the beginning of sixteenth century, the office of *corredor mayor de ventas de juros y seguros* was created, specializing in selling bonds. E. F. de Pinedo, 'La deuda pública y los juristas laicos (1550–1650)', in A. M. Bernal (ed.), *Dinero, moneda y crédito en la Monarquía Hispánica* (Madrid: Marcial Pons-Fundación ICO, 2000), pp. 805–24.
35. Ibid.
36. M. S. Anderson, *The Rise of Modern Diplomacy, 1450–1919* (London: Logman, 1993). On Spanish Embassies, see M. Á. Ochoa Brun, *Historia de la diplomacia española* (Madrid: Ministerio de Asuntos Exteriores, 1999); M. Rivero Rodríguez, *Diplomacia y relaciones exteriores en la Edad Moderna, 1453–1794* (Madrid: Alianza Editorial, 2000).

37. A. Pacini, *La Genova di Andrea Doria nell'Impero di Carlo V* (Firenze: Leo S. Olschki, 1999), esp., pp. 239ff. See B. Caunedo del Potro, *Mercaderes castellanos en el golfo de Vizcaya (1475–1492)* (Madrid: Universidad Autónoma de Madrid, 1983), pp. 11ff.

38. García, *El erario del reino*.

39. AGS, Estado-Castilla (hereafter E-C), leg. parts 1 and 2, num. 400.

40. 'In Valladolid, 23 December 1514 His Majesty gave order to bachelor Vargas to pay Bautista de Negro or the company or the person who had his licence, sixty-eight thousand three hundred and thirty five *maravedíes* as payment for seventy-three *ducados* of gold that Antonio de Serón (the Ambassador's Secretary) had received in Rome as his salary from Micer Andrea Gentil and Company, at an exchange rate of 395 [*maravedíes*] to one *ducado* as stated in the bill of exchange sent to the bachelor and signed in Rome on the 12 August 1514'. See AGS, E-C, leg. parts 1 and 2, num. 409.

41. AGS, E-C, leg. parts 1 and 2, nums 408 and 410.

42. AGS, E-C, leg. parts 1 and 2, nums 400 and 411.

43. Real Academia de la Historia, Salazar y Castro, K–4, num. 544, f. 236 r.; see Duque de Berwick y de Alba, *Correspondencia de Gutierre Gómez de Fuensalida* (Madrid: Real Academia de la Historia, 1907).

44. AGS, E-C, leg. parts 1 and 2, nums 400 and 411.

45. García, *El erario del reino*. See also A. Rodríguez Villa, *Don Francisco de Rojas, embajador de los Reyes Católicos* (Madrid: Fortanet, 1896).

46. M. Á. Solinís Estalló, *La alcabala del rey, 1474–1504. Fiscalidad en el partido de las Cuatro Villas cántabras y las merindades de Campoo y Campos con Palencia* (Santander: Universidad de Cantabria, 2003), p. 109.

47. AGS, Consejo Real, leg. 102, num. 23, f. 11 r. For further information about Pedro del Alcázar, see D. A. García, 'Poder financiero y arrendadores de rentas reales en Castilla a principios de la Edad Moderna', *Cuadernos de Historia Moderna*, 31 (2006), pp. 117–38.

48. AGS, Consejo Real, leg. 102, num. 23, f. 11 r.

49. On Spanish fiscal institutions during the sixteenth century, see M. Á. Ladero Quesada, *La Hacienda Real de Castilla en el siglo XV* (La Laguna: Universidad de La Laguna, 1973); E. Hernández-Esteve, *Creación del Consejo de Hacienda de Castilla (1523–1525)* (Madrid: Banco de España, 1983); E. Hernández-Esteve, 'Estructuras y atribuciones del Consejo de Hacienda durante su proceso constituyente', *Cuadernos de Investigación Histórica*, 8 (1984), pp. 35–64; T. García-Cuenca, 'El Consejo de Hacienda (1576–1803)', in M. Artola (ed.), *La economía española al final del Antiguo Régimen. IV. Instituciones* (Madrid: Alianza and Banco de España, 1982), pp. 405–502; M. Cuartas Rivero, 'El Consejo de Hacienda: su primera época', *Hacienda Pública Española*, 74 (1982), pp. 255–66; R. Pérez Bustamante, 'Del sistema de contadurías al Consejo de Hacienda, 1433–1525 (una perspectiva institucional), in *Historia de la Hacienda Española (épocas antigua y medieval)* (Madrid: Instituto de Estudios Fiscales, 1982), pp. 681–738; J. L. de las Heras, 'La jurisdicción del Consejo de Hacienda en tiempos de los Austrias', in C. M. Cremades Griñán, (ed.), *Estado y fiscalidad en el Antiguo Régimen* (Murcia: Universidad de Murcia, 1989), pp. 117–27; J. E. Gelabert, 'Sobre la fundación del Consejo de Hacienda', in J. I. Fortea Pérez and C. M. Cremades Griñán (eds), *Política y hacienda en el Antiguo Régimen. II Reunión*

Científica de la Asociación de Historia Moderna (Murcia: Universidad de Murcia, 1992), pp. 83–95; C. J. de Carlos Morales, 'El Consejo de Hacienda de Castilla en el reinado de Carlos V (1523–1556)', *Anuario de Historia del Derecho Español*, 69 (1989), pp. 49–159; C. J. de Carlos Morales, *El Consejo de Hacienda de Castilla, 1523–1602. Patronazgo y clientelismo en el gobierno de las finanzas reales durante el siglo XVI* (Valladolid: Junta de Castilla y León, 1996).

50. This tendency has also been shown in France and Flanders. See P. Hamon, *'Messieurs des finances'. Les grands officiers de finance dans la France de la Renaissance* (París, Comité pour l'histoire économique et financière de la France, 1999); P. Stabel and J. Haemers, 'From Bruges to Antwerp. International Commercial Firms and Government's Credit in Late 15th Century and Early 16th Century', in Sanz and García (eds), *Banca, crédito y capital*, pp. 21–38.

51. D. A. García, 'Le gouvernment des finances royales au début de l'époque moderne (1504–1523)', in A. Dubet (ed.), *Administrer les finances royales dans la monarchie espagnole (XVIe–XIXe siècles)* (Rennes: Presses Universitaires de Rennes, forthcoming).

52. A. Esteban Estríngana, *Guerra y finanzas en los Países Bajos católicos. De Farnesio a Spínola (1592–1630)* (Madrid: Ediciones del Laberinto, 2002).

53. C. Álvarez-Nogal, 'El factor general del rey y las finanzas de la monarquía hispánica', *Revista de Historia Económica*, 17:3 (1999), pp. 507–39.

54. Rodríguez Villa, *El emperador Carlos V*.

55. P. Rauscher, 'La casa de Austria y sus banqueros alemanes', in J. L. Castellano and F. Sánchez-Montes (eds), *Carlos V. Europeísmo y universalidad*, 5 vols (Madrid: Sociedad Estatal para la Conmemoración de los Centenarios de Felipe II y Carlos V, 2001), vol. 3, pp. 411–28.

56. D. A. García, 'Ducados entre dos dinastías. La circulación de capital entre Castilla y Flandes a comienzos del siglo XVI', in Sanz and García (eds), *Banca, crédito y capital*, pp. 85–104.

57. I. A. A. Thompson, 'Money, Money and Yet More Money! Finance, the Fiscal-State, and the Military Revolution', in C. J. Rogers (ed.), *The Military Revolution Debate: Readings on the Military Transformation of Early Modern Europe* (Boulder, CO: Westview Press, 1995), pp. 273–98.

58. J. D. Tracy, *A Financial Revolution in the Habsburg Netherlands: Renten and Renteniers in the County of Holland, 1515–1565* (Berkeley, CA: University of California Press, 1985); see also W. Fritschy, 'A "Financial Revolution" Reconsidered'. For Spain, see C. J. de Carlos Morales, '¿Una revolución financiera en tiempos de Felipe II? Dimensiones y evolución de los fundamentos de la Hacienda Real de Castilla, 1556–1598', in E. Belenguer (ed.), *Felipe II y el Mediterráneo*, 4 vols (Madrid: Sociedad Estatal para la Conmemoración de los Centenarios de Felipe II y Carlos V, 1999), vol. 1, pp. 473–504.

59. On this tendency, see R. Bonney and W. M. Ormrod, 'Introduction', in W. M. Ormrod, M. Bonney and R. Bonney, *Crises, Revolutions and Self-Sustained Growth. Essays in European Fiscal History, 1130–1830*, (Stanford, CA: Shaun Tyas, 1999), pp. 1–21.

60. H. van der Wee and I. Blanchard, 'The Habsburgs and the Antwerp Money Market: the Exchange Crises of 1521 and 1522–1523', in I. Blanchard, A. Goodman and J.

Newman (eds), *Industry and Finance in Early Modern History. Essays Presented to George Hammersley on the Occasion of his 74th Birthay* (Stuttgart: Franz Steiner Verlag, 1992), pp. 27–57.

4 De Luca, 'Government Debt and Financial Markets'

1. This paper gathers the main results of the second session of the Congress 'Debito pubblico e mercati finanziari in Italia fra età moderna e contemporanea', that took place in Bergamo, 25–7 May 2006, organized by CIRSFI (Centro interuniversitario di ricerca per la storia finanziaria italiana). The session, focused on northern Italy, presented the following essays: C. Marsilio, 'La frammentazione del network finanziario delle fiere di cambio genovesi (1621–1640 circa)'; G. De Luca, 'Debito pubblico, mercato finanziario ed economia reale nel Ducato di Milano e nella Repubblica di Venezia tra XVI e XVII secolo'; E. Stumpo, 'Città, stato e mercato finanziario: il diverso ruolo del debito pubblico in Piemonte e in Toscana'; and G. L. Podestà, 'Finanza pubblica nel Ducato di Parma e Piacenza in età farnesiana', now published in G. De Luca and A. Moioli (eds), *Debito pubblico e mercati finanziari in Italia. Secoli XIII–XX* (Milano: FrancoAngeli, 2007).
2. 'Per la nota de reddituari, 1559', 27 October 1559, Archivio di Stato, Milan (hereafter ASM), finanze reddituari, cart. 1.
3. L. Pezzolo, 'Elogio della rendita. Sul debito pubblico degli Stati italiani nel Cinque e Seicento', *Rivista di storia economica*, 12:3 (1995), pp. 284–330, on p. 309; E. Stumpo, *Finanza e stato moderno nel Piemonte del Seicento* (Roma: Istituto storico per l'età moderna e contemporanea, 1979), p. 265.
4. Source: ASM, rogiti camerali, cart. 809–19.
5. Sources: a and b: L. Pezzolo, *Una finanza d'ancien régime. La Repubblica veneta tra XV e XVIII secolo* (Napoli: Edizioni Scientifiche Italiane, 2006), p. 88; c: G. Felloni, 'Stato genovese, finanza pubblica e ricchezza privata: un profilo storico', in Felloni, *Scritti di storia economica*, vol. 1, pp. 275–95, on pp. 284, 288; d: Stumpo, *Finanza e stato moderno*, pp. 310–12.
6. 'Carichi ovvero interessi assentati sopra lo Stato di Milano all'entrate ordinarie, 1559', Bibliothèque Nationale de Paris, MSS italiani, P 239, f. 66; 28 febbraio 1536, Archivo General de Simancas (hereafter AGS), Estado, leg. 1181.
7. Cf. A. Castillo Pintado, 'Los juros de Castilla. Apogeo y fin de un instrumento de *crédito*', *Hispania*, 23:89 (1963), pp. 43–70; Tracy, *A Financial Revolution in the Habsburg Netherlands*; A. Calabria, *The Cost of Empire. The Finances of the Kingdom of Naples in the Time of Spanish Rule* (Cambridge: Cambridge University Press, 1991); G. Muto, 'The Spanish System: Centre and Periphery', in Bonney (ed.), *Economic Systems and State Finance*, pp. 231–59, on pp. 251–9.
8. Cf. G. Aleati and C. M. Cipolla, 'Aspetti e problemi dell'economia milanese nei secoli XVI e XVII', in *Storia di Milano*, 17 vols (Milano: Fondazione Treccani degli Alfieri, 1953–66), vol. 11, pp. 377–99; G. Vigo, *Fisco e società nella Lombardia del Cinquecento* (Bologna: Il Mulino, 1979); G. De Luca, *Commercio del denaro e crescita economica a Milano fra Cinquecento e Seicento* (Milano: Il Polifilo, 1996); S. D'Amico,

'Crisis and Trasformation: Economic Reorganization and Social Structures in Milan, 1570–1610', *Social History*, 25:1 (2000), pp. 1–21.

9. ASM, rogiti camerali, cart. 811, year 1556.

10. Cf. C. M. Cipolla, *Le avventure della lira* (Milano: Edizioni di Comunità, 1958), p. 117; G. Felloni, 'Finanze statali, emissioni monetarie ed alterazioni della moneta di conto in Italia nei secoli XVI–XVIII', in Felloni, *Scritti di storia economica*, vol. 1, pp. 471–96, on p. 485.

11. Cf. Chabod, *Storia di Milano*, pp. 313–19.

12. Cf. ASM, rogiti camerali, cart. 811, year 1553; and 'Rellatione della intrata ... dell'anno 1553', AGS, Estado, leg. 1204.

13. Cf. 'Carichi ovvero interessi assentati sopra lo Stato di Milano all'entrate ordinarie, 1559' and 'Relatione del sommario dell'entrata ordinaria dell'Estato di Milano dell'anno 1559', AGS, Consejo y Juntas de Hacienda, leg. 24, n. 435.

14. Cf. ASM, rogiti camerali, cart. 811, year 1560; S. Pugliese, *Condizioni economiche e finanziarie della Lombardia nella prima metà del secolo XVIII* (Torino: Bocca, 1924), p. 339; G. Muto, 'Il governo della *Hacienda* nella Lombardia spagnola', in P. Pissavino and G. Signorotto (eds), *Lombardia borromaica Lombardia spagnola. 1554–1659*, 2 vols (Roma: Bulzoni, 1995), vol. 1, pp. 265–302, on p. 287.

15. Ibid., pp. 289–91.

16. Cf. ASM, rogiti camerali, cart. 811–13; and Muto, 'Il governo della *Hacienda*', p. 289.

17. ASM, rogiti camerali, cart. 815, year 1619.

18. Cf. Pugliese, *Condizioni economiche e finanziarie della Lombardia*, p. 343; and Muto, 'Il governo della *Hacienda*', pp. 290–3, 301.

19. Cf. Pugliese, *Condizioni economiche e finanziarie della Lombardia*, pp. 346–51; A. Cova, 'Banchi e monti pubblici a Milano tra interessi privati e pubbliche necessità', in Pissavino and Signorotto (eds), *Lombardia borromaica Lombardia spagnola*, vol. 1, pp. 363–81, on pp. 368–77.

20. C. G. Cavazzi della Somaglia, *Nuova inventione certissima, e facilissima per liberare la città di Milano e le provincie dello Stato da loro debiti senza cagionare alcuna Gravezza ma ben sì evidente, ed universale utilità* (Milano: Filippo Ghidolfi, [1648]), in Biblioteca Nazionale Braidense, Milano, 14. 16 C. 11/6.

21. Cf. Muto, 'Il governo della *Hacienda*', pp. 291–4.

22. ASM, rogiti camerali, cart. 819–20.

23. Cf. Chart 4.1; for the total amuont of revenues at the end of the Spanish age, see S. Agnoletto, *Lo Stato di Milano al principio del Settecento. Finanza pubblica, sistema fiscale e interessi locali* (Milano: FrancoAngeli, 2000), p. 184. Pugliese, *Condizioni economiche e finanziarie della Lombardia*, p. 339, says that at the end of the seventeenth century the alienated revenues of the Duchy amounted to 32,304,810 lire.

24. Cf. Pezzolo, *Una finanza d'ancien régime*, pp. 86–9.

25. Ibid., pp. 89–92.

26. Cf. Mueller, *The Venetian Money Market*, pp. 623–4.

27. Cf. Pezzolo, *Una finanza d'ancien régime*, pp. 94–101.

28. Cf. G. Felloni, *Genoa and the History of Finance: A Series of First?* (Genova: Banco di San Giorgio, 2005).

29. Cf. Felloni, 'Stato genovese', pp. 275–87.

30. Ibid., pp. 291–5.
31. Cf. Stumpo, 'Città, stato e mercato finanziario', pp. 12–15.
32. Cf. Stumpo, *Finanza e stato moderno*, pp. xviii, 308–19.
33. Ibid., pp. 308–14.
34. Cf. Podestà, 'Finanza pubblica nel Ducato di Parma e Piacenza'.
35. Sources: for the revenues of the Duchy of Milan, see Agnoletto, *Lo Stato di Milano al principio del Settecento*, p. 184; Pezzolo, *Una finanza d'ancien régime*, p. 88; Stumpo, *Finanza e stato moderno*, pp. 310–12; Felloni, 'Stato genovese', pp. 284, 288.
36. Revenues alienation of 2 September 1557, ASM, rogiti camerali, cart. 811.
37. Sources: ASM, rogiti camerali, cart. 809–13.
38. M. Tabarrini (ed.), 'Relazione inedita dello Stato di Milano di G.B. Guarini', *Archivio Storico Italiano*, 5:1 (1867), pp. 3–34, on p. 15.
39. ASM, rogiti camerali, cart. 809–13. For Caterina Porta, see her will in deeds of 14 and 15 July 1623, ASM, notarile, cart. 25522, notary Francesco Girolamo Giusti q. Giovanni.
40. P. Prodi, 'Operazioni finanziarie presso la corte romana di un uomo d'affari milanese nel 1562–63', *Rivista storica italiana*, 73:3 (1961), pp. 641–59, on p. 657.
41. Cf. Calabria, *The Cost of Empire*, pp. 106ff.; L. Pezzolo, 'Government Debt and Trust', pp. 236ff.
42. See the case of the community of Vimercate in 'memoriale del Magistrato', 18 May 1602, ASM, finanze reddituari, cart. 293 (fasc. Carcassola). For the issue of tax shifting in the Kingdom of Naples, see G. Sabatini, *Proprietà e proprietari a L'Aquila e nel contado. Le rilevazioni catastali in età spagnola* (Napoli: Edizioni Scientifiche Italiane, 1995), pp. 289ff.
43. 'Memoria degli abitanti di Vimodrone', 25 August 1645, Archivio Visconti di Modrone, Istituto di storia economica e sociale Mario Romani, Università Cattolica del S. Cuore, Milano, b. B 58.
44. 'Memoria di Bernardo Molina', 24 May 1572, ASM, finanze reddituari, cart. 3.
45. Cf. De Luca, *Commercio del denaro e crescita economica a Milano*, pp. 13–49.
46. Revenues alienation, 10 April 1579, ASM, rogiti camerali, cart. 811.
47. 'Memoriale de' Mercanti di Milano', 18 January 1592, Archivio Storico della Camera di Commercio di Milano (hereafter ACCM), scatola 32, fasc. 1. In general for the Milanese brokers, see G. De Luca, 'Tra funzioni di tutela e istanze di controllo del mercato urbano: i sensali milanesi durante l'età moderna', in P. Massa and A. Moioli (eds), *Dalla corporazione al mutuo soccorso. Organizzazione e tutela del lavoro tra XVI e XX secolo* (Milano, FrancoAngeli, 2004), pp. 191–204; for their collegues in Bologna and Rome, see B. Farolfi, 'Brokers and Brokerage in Bologna from the Sixteenth to the Nineteenth Century', in A. Guenzi, P. Massa and F. Piola Caselli, *Guilds, Markets and Work Regulations in Italy, 16th–19th Centuries* (Aldershot: Ashgate, 1998), pp. 306–22; F. Colzi, '"Per maggiore facilità del commercio". I sensali e la mediazione mercantile e finanziaria a Roma nei secoli XVI–XIX', *Roma*, 6:3 (1998), pp. 397–425.
48. For example, the delays in interest payments to subscribers, which the tax farmer Pelegro Doria and some others were responsible for, were harshly stigmatized and carefully worked out by the authority, see the order to Pelegro Doria of 23 July 1601, ASM, finanze reddituari, cart. 3.

49. See a letter of 31 October 1550, ASM, finanze reddituari, cart. 1; and A. Terreni, "'Sogliono tutti i forastieri, i quali vanno a negotiare nelle città d'altri Dominii, essere favoriti et privilegiati". La concessione della "civilitas mediolanensis" ai mercanti-banchieri genovesi nel XVI secolo', in C. Donati (ed.), *Alle frontiere della Lombardia. Politica, guerra e religione nell'età moderna* (Milano: FrancoAngeli, 2006), pp. 105–22. When the military needs were strictly urgent, foreigners were allowed to buy bonds without any restriction, see the order of Philip II of 19 March 1594, ASM, finanze reddituari, cart. 1.

50. The same occurred in the Amsterdam bonds market, see M. 't Hart, 'Money and Trust. Amsterdam Moneylenders and the Rise of the Modern State, 1478–1794', paper presented at the XIVth International Economic History Congress, Helsinki, 26 August 2006, <http://www.helsinki.fi/iehc2006/papers1/Hart13.pdf> [accessed 31 January 2007].

51. ASM, rogiti camerali, cart. 809–13.

52. Deed of 8 June 1599, Madrid, Archivo Histórico de Protocolos de Madrid, notary Luis Erviar, cart. 2812, f. 598.

53. Cf. Muto, 'Il governo della *Hacienda*', pp. 288–93. The habit of paying bondholders only ten months of interest became common from 1635, see 'Li ragionati generali della Regia duc. Camera dello Stato di Milano', 4 April 1635, ASM, finanze reddituari, cart. 10; from 1639 the interests were paid only for nine month, see 'Li ragionati generali della Regia duc. Camera dello Stato di Milano', 13 January 1639, ASM, finanze reddituari, cart. 12.

54. Cf. Cova, 'Banchi e monti pubblici a Milano'.

55. Cf. ASM, finanze reddituari, cart. 622 (fasc. Emilio Omodei); and A. Borlandi, "'Al Real Servitio di S. Maestà". Genova e la Milano del Seicento', in *'Millain the Great'. Milano nelle brume del Seicento* (Milano: Cariplo, 1989), p. 53.

56. In 1712 the Real Committee – created by the Austrians, to check all the contracts between the Real Chamber and private buyers – noted that in 1646 Turconi got bonds for an annual 48,444 lire whose principal counted for 954,906 lire; of this sum he lent only 69,891 lire to the Chamber in cash while the rest was previous debts the state had; but these debts were calculated in money that had a major nominal value instead of the real one, according to which the true credit amounted to 823,959 lire, see Committee reports of 12, 15 and 29 January 1712, ASM, finanze parte antica, cart. 91.

57. Cf. G. Felloni, *Gli investimenti finanziari genovesi in Europa tra il Seicento e la Restaurazione* (Milano: Giuffrè, 1971), p. 214.

58. Quoted in Pugliese, *Condizioni economiche e finanziarie della Lombardia*, p. 183.

59. Cf. Pezzolo, *Il fisco dei veneziani*, pp. 215–17.

60. Cf. Pezzolo, *Una finanza d'ancien régime*, pp. 94–6.

61. Ibid., p. 103.

62. Ibid., pp. 101–3.

63. Cf. Pezzolo, *Il fisco dei veneziani*, pp. 215–16.

64. Cf. Felloni, 'Stato genovese', pp. 277–87.

65. Cf. Sieveking, *Studio sulle finanze genovesi*, vol. 1, p. 33.

66. Cf. G. Felloni, 'Il Banco di San Giorgio e il suo archivio: una memoria a più valenze', in Felloni, *Scritti di storia economica*, vol. 1, pp. 461–8, on pp. 465–6.

67. S. J. Woolf, 'Sviluppo economico e struttura sociale nel Piemonte da Emanuele Filiberto a Carlo Emanuele III', *Nuova Rivista Storica*, 46:3–4 (1962), pp. 1–57.

68. Cf. Stumpo, 'Città, stato e mercato finanziario', pp. 18–19.

69. Ibid., pp. 19–20; E. Stumpo, 'La distribuzione sociale degli acquirenti dei titoli del debito pubblico in Piemonte nella seconda metà del Seicento', in *La fiscalité et ses implications sociales en Italie et en France aux XVIIe et XVIIIe siècles* (Rome: École française de Rome, 1980), pp. 113–124, on pp. 116–24.

70. Cf. Stumpo, *Finanza e stato moderno*, p. 347.

71. Ibid., pp. 314–48.

72. Cf. Marsilio, 'La frammentazione del network finanziario'.

73. Cf. De Luca, *Commercio del denaro e crescita economica a Milano*, pp. 61–71; D'Amico, 'Crisis and Trasformation', pp. 4–21.

74. Cf. J. Delumeau, *Vie économique et sociale de Rome dans la seconde moitié du XVIe siècle*, 2 vols (Paris: De Boccard, 1959), vol. 2, pp. 870–3; L. Alonzi, 'I censi consegnativi nel XVI e XVII secolo tra "finzione" e "realtà"', *L'Acropoli*, 6:1 (2005), pp. 86–102.

75. Sources: for the public bonds, see ASM, rogiti camerali, cart. 809–13; for the *censi consegnativi*, see ASM, notarile, cart. 13092–102 (1576–88), notaio Rolando Mazza; 13710–11 (1575–7), Giovanni Battista Bombelli; 13880–95 (1575–97), Dionigi Oldoni; 14776–84 (1575–94), Ambrogio Ferni; 14922–9 (1591–8), Ventura Solari; 14937–44 (1575–84), Ottaviano Castelletti; 15432–41 (1575–91), Giacomo Filippo Cattaneo Vaiani; 15505–15 (1575–1601), Cesare Borsani; 15505–15 (1575–1607), Cesare Borsani; 16296–300 (1575–1607), Bernardo Quarantini; 16471–83 (1575–98), Giovanni Giacomo Fedeli; 16612–23 (1575–1606), Cesare Guidi; 16939–58 (1575–1607), Francesco Massarola; 17030–1 (1573–1608), Polidoro Mantelli; 17569–81 (1575–92), Giovanni Paolo Pellizzari; 17676–83 (1575–1607), Girolamo Martini; 17782–7 (1575–1607), Benedetto Barbavara; 18928–38 (1575–1607), Paolo Girolamo Fontana; 19594–603 (1578–1607), Giovanni Battista Baruffi; 20651–67 (1583–1611), Giuseppe Martignone; 23715–19 (1597–1611), Dionigi Capra; 23821–4 (1597–1604), Pietro Luigi Merlato; 23950–6 (1598–1611), Francesco Rugginelli; 23982–91 (1598–1611), Giovanni Ambrogio Caccia; 24779–80 (1603–11), Francesco Brofferio; *ad vocem censo*.

76. Cf. C. M. Cipolla, *Mouvement Monétaires dans l'Etat de Milan (1580–1700)* (Paris: Armand Colin, 1952), pp. 42–7, 90; E. García Guerra, *Carlo V e il sistema finanziario milanese. 2. La coniazione delle monete*, in M. Fantoni (ed.), *Carlo V e l'Italia* (Roma, Bulzoni, 2000), pp. 245–55.

77. Cf. G. Vigo, 'Manovre monetarie e crisi economica nello Stato di Milano (1619–1622)', *Studi storici*, 17:4 (1976), pp. 101–26, on pp. 113–26.

78. 'Attestato de' signori negozianti della Piazza di Milano', 6 December 1663, ACCM, scatola 2, fasc. 42.

79. Cf. De Luca, *Commercio del denaro e crescita economica a Milano*, pp. 50–60.

80. 'Attestato della Camera de Mercanti di Milano', 9 July 1572, ACCM, scatola 2, fasc. 9.

81. O. Gelderblom and J. Jonker, 'Exploring the Market for Government Bonds in the Dutch Republic (1600–1800)', paper presented at the Séminaires d'histoire économique Atelier François Simiand, Campus Paris-Jordan, 18 December 2006,

<http://www.paris-jordan.ens.fr/depot/semin/texte0607/GEL2006EXP.pdf>, pp. 1–26, on p. 3 [accessed 31 January 2007].

82. Cf. D. Sella, *L'economia lombarda durante la dominazione spagnola* (Bologna: Il Mulino, 1982), pp. 119–20.

83. Cf. Stumpo, *Finanza e stato moderno*, pp. 264–8.

84. Cf. A. Moioli, 'The Changing Role of the Guilds in the Reorganization of the Milanese Economy throughout the Sixteenth and the Eighteenth Centuries', in Guenzi et al., *Guilds, Markets and Work Regulations in Italy*, pp. 32–55.

85. Cf. Pezzolo, *Il fisco dei veneziani*, pp. 205–17.

86. See the legation of the Milanese Vicario di provvisione Lodovico Moresini to Charles V, in 1538, at Nice, in A. Salomoni (ed.), *Memorie storico-diplomatiche degli Ambasciatori, Incaricati d'affari, Corrispondenti, e Delegati, che la città di Milano inviò a diversi suoi principi dal 1500 al 1796* (Milano: Tipografia Pulini al Bocchetto, 1806), p. 84.

87. Cf. Calabria, *The Cost of Empire*, pp. 128–9.

88. ASM, rogiti camerali, cart. 816, year 1639.

89. Cf. G. Signorotto, 'Stabilità politica e trame antispagnole nella Milano del Seicento', in Y. M. Bercé and E. Fasano Guarini (eds), *Complots et conjurations dans l'Europe moderne: actes du colloque international organisé par l'École française de Rome, l'Institut de recherches sur les civilisations de l'occident moderne de l'Université de Paris-Sorbonne et le Dipartimento di storia moderna e contemporanea dell'Università degli studi di Pisa* (Rome: Ecole française de Rome, 1996), pp. 721–45.

90. Starting from the first decades of the sixteenth century, many communities of the Duchy directly lent huge amounts of money to the Milanese treasury by the *censi*, see L. Faccini, *La Lombardia fra '600 e '700: riconversione economica e mutamenti sociali* (Milano: FrancoAngeli, 1988), pp. 54–63; M. C. Giannini, 'Un caso di stabilità politica nella monarchia asburgica: comunità locali, finanza pubblica e clero nello Stato di Milano durante la prima metà del Seicento', in F. J. Guillamón Álvarez and J. J. Ruiz Ibáñez (eds), *Lo conflictivo y lo consensual en Castilla. Sociedad y poder político 1521–1715* (Murcia: Universidad de Murcia, 2001), pp. 99–162.

5 Andrés Ucendo, 'Government Policies and the Development of Financial Markets'

1. This paper has been written thanks to a research project funded by the Spanish Education Ministry. The title of the project is 'Fisco, moneda y depression económica en la Castilla del siglo XVII: límites y riesgos del estado fiscal en la España Moderna', HUM 2005-02334/HIST.

2. F. Piola Caselli, *Il buon governo. Storia della finanza pubblica nell'Europa preindustriale* (Torino: Giappichelli, 1997); Bonney (ed.), *Economic Systems and State Finance*; R. Bonney (ed.), *The Rise of the Fiscal State in Europe c. 1200–1815* (Oxford: Oxford University Press, 1999).

3. Fritschy, 'A "Financial Revolution" Reconsidered'; M. 't Hart, *The Making of a Bourgeois State. War, Politics and Finance during the Dutch Revolt* (Manchester and New York: Manchester University Press, 1993). M. 't Hart, 'The United Provinces,

1597–1806', in Bonney, (ed), *The Rise of the Fiscal State in Europe*, pp. 309–25. For the English case, see North and Weingass, 'Constitutions and Commitment'.

4. A. Domínguez Ortiz, *Política y Hacienda de Felipe IV*, (Madrid: Editorial de derecho financiero, 1960). J. E. Gelabert, *La bolsa del rey* (Barcelona: Crítica, 1997); and J. I. Andrés Ucendo, 'Castile's Fiscal System in the Seventeenth Century', *Journal of European Economic History*, 30 (2001), pp. 597–621.

5. North and Weingass, 'Constitutions and Commitment'.

6. Andrés Ucendo, 'Castile's Fiscal System in the Seventeenth Century', p. 614.

7. J. A. Sánchez Belén, *La política fiscal en Castilla durante el reinado de Carlos II* (Madrid: Siglo XXI, 1996), pp. 201–48.

8. Domínguez Ortiz, *Política y Hacienda de Felipe IV*, pp. 97–101.

9. C. Sanz Ayán, *Los banqueros de Carlos II* (Valladolid: Universidad, 1988), p. 479; and Álvarez-Nogal, 'El factor general del rey', p. 530.

10. F. Ruiz Martín, *Las finanzas de la Monarquía Hispánica en tiempos de Felipe II* (Madrid: Real Academia de la Historia, 1990) p. 22; Álvarez-Nogal, 'El factor general del rey', p. 524; and C. Álvarez-Nogal, 'Los problemas del vellón en el siglo XVII', *Revista de Historia Económica*, Extraodinary Number (2001), pp. 17–37, on p. 32. Gelabert, *La bolsa del rey*, p. 224.

11. Madrid's City Archives (hereafter AVM), Secretaría, 2–447–48, 3–297–31.

12. A. Domínguez Ortiz, 'La población de Sevilla a mediados del siglo XVII', *Archivo Hispalense*, 221:71 (1989), pp. 3–15, on p. 10.

13. AVM, Secretaría, 3–297–31.

14. On the *millones*, see J. I. Andrés Ucendo, *La fiscalidad en Castilla en el siglo XVII: los servicios de millones, 1601–1700* (Lejona: Universidad del País Vasco, 1999).

15. Domínguez Ortiz, *Política y Hacienda de Felipe IV*, p. 226.

16. Ibid., p. 226. Spanish National Library (hereafter BN), MSS 6,579, fols 55–6; BN, MSS 18.206, fols 152ff.

17. H. Peñasco de la Fuente, *Las sisas de Madrid* (Madrid, 1890), pp. 43–4.

18. The second column shows the value of the *donativos* awarded on the transfer of the *servicios de millones*; the third shows the value of the *donativos* pledged on municipal taxes; the fourth shows the *donativos* awarded on the pledge of *servicios de millones*; the fifth show *donativos* awarded on unspecified pledges; and the sixth shows *donativos* awarded on the tobacco monopoly. Source: AVM, Secretaría, 2–447–48, 3–297–31.

19. P. Madoz, *Diccionario Geográfico-Estadístico de España y de sus posesiones de ultramar*, Vol. 1 (Madrid, 1848), p. 494.

20. Spanish National Archive (hereafter AHN), Consejos, leg. 10,108.

21. AVM, Secretaría, 4–319–5, 3–264–10.

22. The same pattern was followed in other cases. For example, Madrid obtained in 1657 the *servicio de los tres millones*, after a 150,000 ducat *donativo*, but this amount increased to 1.21 million ducats after further *donatives* in the 1660s and 70s. Madoz, *Diccionario Geográfico Estadístico de España*, p. 494; AVM, Secretaría, 3–297–31, 2–447–48.

23. AVM, Secretaría, 3–297–61, 3–267–4; Peñasco de la Fuente, *Las sisas de Madrid*, p. 43.

24. AVM, Secretaría, 3–259–2, 3–255–1.

25. AVM, Secretaría, 3–264–5, 2–350–17.
26. In these two cases the authorities took good care to redeem most parts of their debts in order to keep the payment of the interest at manageable levels. In the last years of the sixteenth century, around 30 per cent of the fiscal revenue of the Republic of Venice was devoted to servicing its public debt. L. Pezzolo, *L'oro dell Stato. Società, finanza e fisco nella Republicca Veneta del secondo '500* (Venecia: Il Cardo, 1990), p. 189. This percentage seems to have been higher in the province of Holland in 1640 and in 1668 (around 50–60 per cent), but even here the differences with Madrid are remarkable. J. De Vries and A. van der Woude, *The First Modern Economy* (Cambridge: Cambridge University Press, 1997), p. 115.
27. M. F. Carbajo Isla, *La población de la villa de Madrid desde mediados del siglo XVI hasta mediados del siglo XIX* (Madrid: Siglo XXI, 1987), p. 227.
28. Around 1746 the global value of the capital borrowed by the city was 18.5 million ducats. This seems to suggest that the level of the city's debt had stabilized, in nominal terms, at the levels reached arround 1680. BN, MS 12,348.
29. For the fiscal and monetary reforms of these years, see E. Hamilton, *Guerra y precios en España* (Madrid: Alianza, 1988), pp. 48–63; and Sánchez Belén, *La política fiscal en Castilla*, pp. 225–48.
30. AVM, Secretaría, 3–492–25.
31. AVM, Secretaría, 3–255–1.
32. AVM, Secretaría, 3–267–4, 4–33–18; AHN, Consejos, leg. 10,108, lib. 3,467.
33. AVM, Secretaría, 4–333–18.
34. AVM, Secretaría, 3–256–1.
35. AVM, Secretaria, 3–297–73.
36. See, to quote a few examples, the cases of the Republic of Genoa during the Middle Ages and the Duchy of Milán in the early modern period. G. Felloni, 'Ricchezza privata, credito e banche: Genova e Venezia nei sec. XII–XV', *Genova, Venezia. Il Levante nei secoli XII–XV* (Genova: Societaú ligure di storia patria, 2001), pp. 295–318, on pp. 301–2; Agnoletto, *Lo Stato di Milano al pricipio del Settecento*, pp. 61–7.
37. A. Domínguez Ortiz, 'Juros y censos en la Castilla del Sesicientos: una sociedad de rentistas', in Bernal (ed.), *Dinero, moneda y crédito en la Monarquía Hispánica*, pp. 789–807, on pp. 793–4.
38. The Crown had resorted to these measures in 1625, 1629 and 1630. With the introduction in 1634 of the Media Annata, the cuts in the sums paid to the *juristas* became a consistent fiscal policy. The Media Annata was theorically a 50 per cent cut in the interest paid to the *juristas* by the Crown every year. Although the discounts could vary, the Media Annata soon became one of the most important revenues of the Royal Treasury. Domínguez Ortiz, *Política y Hacienda de Felipe IV*, pp. 299–330; Toboso Sánchez, *La deuda pública castellana*, pp. 176–8.
39. Pinedo, 'La deuda pública y los juristas laicos', pp. 810–11.
40. Ibid., pp. 815–21.
41. Ibid., p. 820.
42. As has been previously mentioned, in 1669 and 1679, 83 per cent and 94 per cent respecitvely of Madrid's revenue was invested in the payment of their interest to the *efectistas*, while in 1706 this percentage was nearly 80 per cent. Madoz, *Diccionario Geográfico-Estadístico de España*, pp. 479–80.

43. See, for example, Fritschy, 'A "Financial Revolution" Reconsidered', pp. 79–80; L. Neal, 'The Monetary, Financial and Political Architecture of Europe, 1648–1815', in L. Prados de la Escosura (ed.), *Exceptionalism and Industrialisation. Britain and its European Rivals* (Cambridge: Cambridge University Press, 2004), pp. 173–89, on pp. 179–81; O. Gelderblom and J. Jonker, 'Completing a Financial Revolution: The Finance of the Dutch East Indian Trade and the Rise of the Amsterdam Capital Market, 1597–1621', *Journal of Economic History*, 64:3 (2004), pp. 641–72, on pp. 653–63.

44. Ibid., pp. 653–9; and Neal, 'The Monetary, Financial and Political Architecture of Europe', p. 181.

45. This traffic was centered around the *cartas de pago* of the *efectos*. These *cartas* were coupons issued by the town council to the *efectistas* and signed by Madrid's accountants (*contadores*). The *efectistas* had to present these *cartas* to the city's authorities to receive their interests.

46. For example, the *efectos* were used to provide a safe source of income for religious institutions such as the *capellanías*.

47. Many thanks to the data of Martín Aceña, see P. Martín Aceña, 'Los precios en Europa durante los siglos XVI y XVII. Estudio comparativo', *Revista de Historia Económica*, 3, (1992), pp. 359–95, p. 364.

48. Madoz, *Diccionario geográfico-estadístico de España*, p. 475.

49. AHN, Consejos, leg. 6772–6. According to Madoz this *valimiento* was introduced in 1710. Madoz, *Diccionario geográfico-estadístico de España*, p. 476.

50. This amount would have risen to 4.1 million ducats if we had included the value of the *donativos* awarded during the period.

51. On Madrid's indebtedness, see Peñasco de la Fuente, *Las sisas de Madrid*; and C. de la García, 'La reforma de la Hacienda madrileña en la época de Carlos III', in *Equipo Madrid, Carlos III, Madrid y la Ilustración. Contradicciones de un proyecto reformista* (Madrid: Siglo XXI, 1988), pp. 77–101.

52. See North and Weingast, 'Constitutions and Commitment'.

6 Álvarez-Nogal, 'The Role Played by Short-Term Credit in the Spanish Monarchy's Finances'

1. A previous version of this paper was presented at the Workshop in Comparative Politics and Historical Analysis and the Workshop in Social and Economic History at Stanford University and at the Economic History Seminar at Universidad Carlos III, Madrid. It has received funding from a Spanish Education Ministry project: HUM 2005-02334/HIST.

2. Carande, *Carlos V y sus banqueros*; Domínguez Ortiz, *Política y Hacienda de Felipe IV*; M. Ulloa, *La Hacienda Real de Castilla en el reinado de Felipe II*, 3rd edn (Madrid: Fundación Universitaria Española, 1986); M. Artola, *La Hacienda del Antiguo Régimen*, (Madrid: Alianza Editorial, 1982); Ruiz Martín, 'La banca en España hasta 1782'; J. C. Boyajian, *Portuguese Bankers at the Court of Spain 1626–1650* (New Brunswick, NJ: Rutgers University Press, 1983); A. Maddalena and H. Kellenbenz

(eds), *La Repubblica internazionale del denaro tra XV e XVII secolo* (Bologna: Il Mulino, 1986).

3. North and Weingast, 'Constitutions and Commitment'; North, *Institutions, Institutional Change and Economic Performance*; Hoffman and Norberg (eds), *Fiscal Crises*.

4. J. Bulow and K. Rogoff, 'A Constant Reconstructing Model of Sovereign Debt', *Journal of Political Economy*, 102:5 (1989), pp. 155–78; J. Eaton, M. Gersovitz and J. E. Stiglitz, 'The Pure Theory of Country Risk', *European Economic Review: International Seminar on Macroeconomics*, 30:3 (1986), pp. 481–514.

5. H. Grossman and J. B. Van Huyck, 'Sovereign Debt as a Contingent Claim: Excusable Default, Repudiation, and Reputation', *American Economic Review*, 78:5 (1988), pp. 1088–97; A. Atkeson, 'International Lending with Moral Hazard and Risk of Repudiation', *Econometrica*, 59:4 (1991), pp. 1069–89.

6. J. Conklin, 'The Theory of Sovereign Debt and Spain under Philip II', *Journal of Political Economy*, 106:3 (1998), pp. 483–513.

7. B. R. Weingast, 'The Political Foundations of Limited Government: Parliament and Sovereign Debt in 17th and 18th Century England', in J. Drobak and J. Nye (eds), *The Frontiers of the New Institutional Economics* (San Diego, CA: Academic Press, 1997), pp. 213–46. His model explains how the institutional change following the Glorious Revolution in England allowed a dramatic increase in the government's credit limit. He concludes that a limited sovereign would have more opportunities to obtain larger amounts of credit than an absolutist, because the English parliament helped lenders to coordinate in order to punish the king in the event of default. A credible penalty and coordination are crucial.

8. C. Álvarez-Nogal, *El crédito de la Monarquía Hispánica durante el reinado de Felipe IV* (Valladolid: Junta de Castilla y León, 1997).

9. A. Greif, P. Milgrom and B. R. Weingast, 'Coordination, Commitment, and Enforcement: The Case of the Merchant Guild', *Journal of Political Economy* 102:4 (1994), pp. 745–76.

10. North and Weingast, 'Constitutions and Commitment'.

11. Artola, *La Hacienda del Antiguo Régimen*, pp. 67–8.

12. Carande, *Carlos V y sus banqueros*, vol. 3, pp. 22–35. According to Carande, with time credit costs went up from 17.6 to 48.8 per cent, although loans and *asientos* were not the same. *Asientos* became more expensive because of increases in the exchange rate and other costs involving intermediaries and negotiations, while interest rates did not change.

13. Boyajian, *Portuguese Bankers at the Court of Spain*, p. 168.

14. 'The exchange rate, in most *asientos*, specifically in the case of international *asientos* from the year 1540 onwards, became the most expensive factor of the loan ... This tax or rate of exchange which initially, and for some time, did not exceed 7 per cent, rose progressively to reach a peak of 30 per cent at critical moments.' Carande, *Carlos V y sus banqueros*, vol. 3, p. 12.

15. F. Ruiz Martín, 'Las Finanzas del Rey', in *Felipe II. Un monarca y su época* (San Lorenzo de El Escorial: Fundación ICO, 1998), pp. 387–408, on p. 404. The new fairs of Piacenza were almost blocked.

16. B. Hernández, 'Hombres de negocios y finanzas públicas en la Cataluña de Felipe II', *Revista de Historia Económica*, 15:1 (1997), pp. 65–81, on p. 77.

17. See details in Weingast, 'The Political Foundations of Limited Government'.

18. C. Álvarez-Nogal, 'Las compañías bancarias genovesas en Madrid a comienzos del siglo XVII', *Hispania*, 65–1:219 (2005), pp. 67–90.

19. Weingast, 'The Political Foundations of Limited Government'. The king will cooperate when the penalty is greater than the payment: P>M (1+i).

20. Bulow and Rogoff, 'A Constant Reconstructing Model', pp. 155–78.

21. Greif et al., 'Coordination, Commitment, and Enforcement'.

22. A. Greif, 'Contract Enforceability and Economic Institutions in Early Trade: The Maghribi Traders' Coalition', *American Economic Review*, 83:3 (1993), pp. 525–48.

23. G. Doria, 'Conoscenza del mercato e sistema informativo: il know-how dei mercanti-finanzieri genovesi nei secoli XVI e XVII', in Maddalena and Kellenbenz (eds), *La Repubblica internazionale del denaro*, pp. 57–122, on p. 69. This common strategy had one of its best moments between 1598 and 1609 with the Genoese group when these financiers signed 88 per cent of the total number of *asientos*. However, this does not mean that the monarchy was bargaining with one group only because they had to compete with others: Spaniards, Germans or other Italians.

24. This group became the masters of the financial system of the Habsburg dynasty. German bankers had participated to a large extent in public financing with their own capital, unlike the Genoese, who had not committed themselves to the same extent and had participated using borrowed funds. As a result, the Genoese withstood the different crises over time much better. H. van der Wee, 'Monetary, Credit and Banking Systems', in E. E. Rich and C. H. Wilson (eds), *The Cambridge Economic History of Europe, Vol. 5: The Economic Organization of Early Modern Europe* (Cambridge: Cambridge University Press, 1977), pp. 290–393, on p. 371.

25. R. Canosa, *Banchieri genovesi e sovrani spagnoli tra Cinquecento e Seicento* (Roma: Sapere 2000, 1998), p. 167.

26. F. Ruiz Martín, *'Pequeño capitalismo, gran capitalismo. Simón Ruiz y sus negocios en Florencia* (Barcelona: Crítica, 1990), p. 19.

27. H. Lapeyre, *Simón Ruiz et les asientos de Philippe II* (Paris: A. Colin, 1953). It has been shown that they were only able to lend small amounts of money and usually in Castile.

28. 'Consulta', 17 August 1626, Archivo General de Simancas (hereafter AGS), Consejo y Juntas de Hacienda (hereafter CJH), 621. There had been negotiations with Portuguese merchant bankers since at least 1622. Boyajian, *Portuguese Bankers at the Court of Spain*, p. 17.

29. 'Cédula', 31 January 1627, AGS, CJH, 656.

30. 'Consulta', 17 August 1626, AGS, CJH, 621.

31. 'Consulta', 12 November 1633, AGS, CJH, 701.

32. 'Letter written by Conde de Siruela', Génova, 15 February 1638, AGS, Estado, 3347.

33. Ruiz Martín, *Las finanzas de la Monarquía Hispánica*, pp. 60–1.

34. I. A. A. Thompson, 'Castile: Polity, Fiscality, and Fiscal Crisis', in Hoffman and Norberg (eds), *Fiscal Crises*, pp. 140–81, on p. 160.

35. In part, the financial problems of the Fugger in the 1630s were caused by the accumulation of arrears of more than a million ducats, especially from the *millones*, one of the best payments that a banker could receive. The problem was that the Crown used the revenue to promise more payments than the money that could be collected from it.

36. C. Sanz Ayán, 'La estrategia de la Monarquía en la suspensión de pagos del 96 y su "Medio General"', in *Congreso Internacional Las Sociedades Ibéricas y el Mar a finales del siglo XVI*, 6 vols ([Madrid]: Sociedad Estatal Lisboa, 1998), vol. 2, pp. 81–95, on p. 90. This *Medio General* was a good deal for the bankers and many of them were able to recover a large part of their old debts, so they entered credit negotiations with the Spanish monarchy again.

37. The king would not be able to renegotiate the old debt in the *Medio General* if the monarchy did not have a credible credit alternative for some period. An example of this happened during the suspension of payments of 1596. Immediately after the bankruptcy, the monarchy excluded the Fugger in order to get their credit during the hard year of negotiations with the rest of the bankers affected by the default. The Fugger provided one million *escudos* in Milan in July 1597. They were the most important creditors until the *Medio General* of February 1598. Sanz Ayán, 'La estrategia de la Monarquía', p. 87.

38. 'Consulta', 10 December 1626, AGS, CJH, 622.

39. Álvarez-Nogal, *El crédito de la Monarquía Hispánica*, p. 125.

40. Source: J. E. Gelabert, 'The King's Expenses: The Asientos of Philip III and Philip IV of Spain, 1598–1650', in Ormrod et al., *Crises, Revolutions and Self-Sustained Growth*, pp. 224–49, on p. 231.

41. Source: 'Contaduría', Archivo General de Indias, 362A–2.

42. The difference up to 41 per cent was also paid in the Casa de la Contratación but using money from a different source. The same happened with Duarte Fernández and Manuel de Paz. Every banker received the same proportion on his payment.

43. Eaton et al., 'The Pure Theory of Country Risk', p. 488.

7 Sabatini, 'From Subordination to Autonomy'

1. This contribution arises from a paper presented during the session on Southern Italy in the Early Modern Age at the conference on Public Debt and Financial Markets in Italy from Early Modern Times to the Contemporary Age, held at Bergamo on 25–6 May 2006: G. Sabatini, 'Nel sistema imperiale spagnolo: considerazioni sul debito pubblico napoletano nella prima età moderna', in De Luca and Moioli (eds), *Debito pubblico e mercanti finanziari in Italia*. The comments received, the debates during the session and in particular the reading of the papers presented there by M. C. Ermice and I. Zilli have led me to rewrite and broaden my paper. See I. Zilli, 'Il debito pubblico del Regno di Napoli fra '600 e '700: bilanci e prospettive' and M. C. Ermice, 'Le origini del Gran Libro del debito pubblico del Regno di Napoli e l'emergere di nuovi gruppi sociali (1806–1815)', both in De Luca and Moioli (eds), *Debito pubblico e mercanti finanziari in Italia*.

2. See J. Vicens Vives, *Aproximación a la istoria de España* (Barcelona: Universidad de Barcelona, 1952); and J. H. Elliott, 'A Europe of Composite Monarchies', *Past and*

Present, 137 (1992), pp. 48–71; more recently, A. Marcos Martín, *España en los siglos XVI, XVII y XVIII. Economía y sociedad* (Barcelona: Critica, 2000); B. Yun Casalilla, *Marte contra Minerva. El precio del Imperio español c. 1450–1600* (Barcelona: Critica, 2004); A. M. Bernal, *España, proyecto inacabado: los costes y beneficios del imperio* (Madrid: Marcial Pons, 2005).

3. G. Galasso, *Alla periferia dell'impero. Il Regno di Napoli nel periodo spagnolo (secc. XVI–XVII)* (Turin: Einaudi, 1994); A. Musi (ed.), *Nel sistema imperiale. L'Italia spagnola* (Naples: Edizioni Scientifiche Italiane, 1994).

4. For an updated bibliography on the subject, G. Sabatini, 'Gastos militares y finanzas publicas en el reino de Nápoles en el siglo XVII', in E. García Hernán and D. Maffi (eds), *Guerra y sociedad en la monarquía hispánica. Politica, estrategia y cultura en la Europa moderna, 1500–1700,* 2 vols (Madrid: CSIC, 2006), vol. 2, pp. 257–91.

5. For the meaning of this division into periods, see L. De Rosa, *Il Mezzogiorno spagnolo tra crescita e decadenza* (Milan: Il Saggiatore, 1987), pp. 12–37; R. Mantelli, 'Guerra, inflazione e recessione nella seconda metà del Cinquecento. Filippo II e le finanze dello Stato napoletano', in A. Di Vittorio (ed.), *La finanza pubblica in età di crisi* (Bari: Cacucci, 1993), pp. 213–44; G. Fenicia, *Il regno di Napoli e la difesa del Mediterraneo nell'età di Filippo II (1556–1598). Organizzazione e finanziamento* (Bari: Cacucci, 2003).

6. B. Hernández, *Fiscalidad de reinos y deuda pública en la Monarquía Hispanica del siglo XVI* (Cordoba: Universidad de Cordoba, 2002), esp. the reference to Naples on p.19; see also J. E. Gelabert, 'La Hacienda Real de Castilla, 1598–1652', in Bernal (ed.), *Dinero, moneda y crédito en la Monarquía Hispanica,* pp. 839–61; and J. E. Gelabert, 'Trafíco de oficios y gobierno de los pueblos en Castilla (1543–1643)', in L. A. Ribot García and L. De Rosa (eds), *Ciudad y mundo urbano en la época moderna* (Madrid: El Rio de Eráclito, 1997), pp. 157–86.

7. For the technical aspects of the formation process of the Neapolitan public debt in the modern age, see L. De Rosa, *Studi sugli arrendamenti: aspetti della distribuzione della ricchezza mobiliare nel Mezzogiorno continentale: 1649–1806* (Naples: L'Arte Tipografica, 1958); L. De Rosa, 'L'azienda e le finanze', in L. De Rosa and L. M. Inciso Recio (eds), *Spagna e Mezzogiorno d'Italia nell'età della transizione (1650–1760),* 2 vols (Naples: Edizioni Scientifiche Italiane, 1997), vol. 1, pp. 128–48.

8. I have tried to deal with this specific aspect in 'Collecteurs et fermiers des impôts dans les communautés du Royaume de Naples durant la période espagnole', *Mélanges de la Casa de Velázquez,* 34:2 (2004), pp. 141–59, a monograph edition on the 'Couronne espagnole et magistrature citadines à l'époque moderne'.

9. G. Muto, 'Modelli di organizzazione finanziaria nell'esperienza degli stati italiani della prima età moderna', in Chittolini et al. (eds), *Origini dello stato,* pp. 287–302; Muto, 'The Spanish System'. See also G. Muto, *Saggi sul governo dell'economia nel Mezzogiorno spagnolo* (Naples: Edizioni Scientifiche Italiane, 1992).

10. The subject of an 'Italian area' of the Spanish monarchy has been studied in depth, especially the period of the Messina War, in L. A. Ribot García, *La Monarquia de España y la Guerra de Mesina (1674–1678)* (Madrid: Actas, 2002), in particular pp. 339–40.

11. Muto, 'The Spanish System', p. 255.

12. Ibid., p. 257; see also Ulloa, *La Hacienda Real de Castilla,* pp. 820–26.

13. See L. De Rosa, 'Immobility and Change in Public Finance in the Kingdom of Naples, 1694–1806', *Journal of European Economic History*, 28:1 (1998), pp. 9–28; R. Mantelli, *Burocrazia e finanze pubbliche nel Regno di Napoli a metà del '500* (Naples: Pironti, 1981); R. Mantelli, *L'alienazione della rendita pubblica e i suoi acquirenti dal 1556 al 1583 nel Regno di Napoli* (Bari: Cacucci, 1997).

14. Calabria, *The Cost of Empire*, esp. ch. 5: 'The Creation of a Security Market in the Later Sixteenth Century', pp. 104–29.

15. Ibid., p.113.

16. Ibid., pp. 114ff. The reference to the financial revolution and to the case of Holland is from Tracy, *A Financial Revolution in the Habsburg Netherlands*; see also J. D. Tracy, *Holland under Habsburg Rule, 1506–1566. The Formation of a Body Politic* (Berkeley, CA: University of California Press, 1990); Dickson, *The Financial Revolution in England*; P. Kennedy, *The Rise and Fall of Great Power* (London: Fontana Press, 1988).

17. Calabria, *The Cost of Empire*, pp. 122–3.

18. Ibid., pp. 115–17, 125–7.

19. Ibid., p. 123, which deals with the Castile crisis and Elliott's interpretation of it; see also J. H. Elliott, 'The Decline of Spain', in T. Aston (ed.), *Crisis in Europe, 1550–1960. Essays from Past and Present* (London: Routledge & Kegan Paul, 1965), pp. 167–93, esp. pp. 185–6. See also A. Calabria, 'La finanza pubblica a Napoli nel primo Cinquecento', in Musi (ed.), *Nel sistema imperiale*, pp. 225–34.

20. See – also for the connections between the growth of the public debt and currency problems in Naples – L. De Rosa, 'Introduzione', in L. De Rosa (ed.), *Il Mezzogiorno agli inizi del Seicento* (Bari and Rome: Laterza, 1994), pp. i–lx.

21. A proposal regarding the global interpretation of this subject is to be found in M. Rizzo, J. J. Ruiz Ibañez and G. Sabatini, 'Introducción', in M. Rizzo, J. J. Ruiz Ibañez and G. Sabatini (eds), *Le forze del Principe. Recursos, instrumentos y limites en la pratica del poder soberano en los territorios de la Monarquía Hispanica*, 2 vols (Murcia: Universidad de Murcia, 2003), vol. 1, pp. 23–68.

22. De Rosa, *Studi sugli arrendamenti*, pp. 3–4.

23. Ibid., pp. 13–17.

24. Galasso, *Alla periferia dell'impero*, pp. 157–8: 'Le riforme del conte di Lemos e le finanze napoletane nella prima metà del Seicento'.

25. On this aspect, see I. Zilli, *Carlo di Borbone e la rinascita del Regno di Napoli. Le finanze pubbliche, 1734–42* (Naples: Edizioni Scientifiche Italiane, 1990), pp. 235–43.

26. De Rosa, *Studi sugli arrendamenti*, p. 13.

27. Ibid., pp. 19–32.

28. A. Di Vittorio, 'Il Banco di S. Carlo in Napoli ed il riformismo asburgico', *Rassegna economica*, 33:2 (1969), pp. 235–63, esp. pp. 235–42.

29. De Rosa, *Studi sugli arrendamenti*, pp. 26–32.

30. Ibid., pp. 44–5.

31. Ibid., pp. 45–53.

32. Ibid., p. 50.

33. I. Zilli, *Imposta diretta e debito pubblico nel Regno di Napoli, 1669–1737* (Naples: Edizioni Scientifiche Italiane, 1990).

34. V. D'Arienzo, *L'arrendamento del sale dei Quattro Fondaci* (Salerno: Eleapress, 1996); I. Zilli, *Lo Stato e i suoi creditori. Il debito pubblico del Regno di Napoli tra '600 e '700* (Naples: Edizioni Scientifiche Italiane, 1997); A. Montaudo, *L'olio nel Regno di Napoli nel sec. XVIII. Commercio, annona e arrendamenti* (Naples: Edizioni Scientifiche Italiane, 2005).

35. L. De Rosa, 'The Beginning of Paper-Money Circulation: The Neapolitan Public Banks, 1540–1650', *Journal of European Economic History*, 30:3 (2001), pp. 497–532.

36. M. C. Ermice, *Le origini del Gran Libro del debito pubblico nel Regno di Napoli e l'emergere di nuovi gruppi sociali, 1806–1815* (Naples: L'Arte Tipografica, 2005), pp. 43–55.

37. Ibid., pp. 97–111.

38. Ibid., pp. 113–25.

39. Ibid., pp. 131–46.

8 Piola Caselli, 'Public Debt in the Papal States'

1. In the last thirty years the literature on the public debt of the Papal States has expanded considerably, thanks to the research of several Italian and foreign scholars who have tapped into the vast body of available archival sources. Despite considerable progress, however, we are still lacking an accurate picture of the long-term evolution of papal debt and of the emerging financial market spurred by the trading of securities between the early sixteenth and the late eighteenth century. To fill this gap a team of scholars has chosen to start dealing in a coordinated fashion with a limited number of selected issues regarding the development of the papal public debt over a span of about three centuries. This paper outlines some of the main findings around major themes: origin and growth of papal debt – revenues to service the debt (Fausto Piola Caselli); debt efficiency and the formation of the Roman financial market (Francesco Colzi); investors in papal bonds (Paola Masini); looking at the periphery: the *Legazione* Bolognese (Mauro Carboni); investments in the papal debt in nineteenth-century Rome (Pia Toscano); the making of Rome's stock exchange (Donatella Strangio).

2. For the early start of papal debt in fifteenth century, as a sale of Chamber offices, see Piola Caselli, 'Aspetti del debito pubblico'.

3. For a keen view of public finances in the first period of the formation of the Papal States, see P. Partner, 'Papal Financial Policy in the Renaissance and Counter-Reformation', *Past and Present*, 88 (1980), pp. 17–62.

4. Archivio di Stato di Roma (hereafter ASR), Cam. II, 'Archivio della Camera', vol. 10.

5. Sources for Figures 8.1 and 8.2: F. Piola Caselli, 'Public Debt, State Revenue and Town Consumption in Rome (16th–18th Centuries)', in Boone et al. (eds), *Urban Public Debt*, pp. 93–105, on p. 95; and F. Piola Caselli, 'Evoluzione e finanziamento del debito pubblico pontificio tra XVII e XVIII secolo', in De Luca and Moioli (eds), *Debito pubblico e mercati finanziari in Italia*, pp. 221–42, on p. 227. Demographic data for the state and Roman population are recorded in K. J. Beloch, *Storia della popolazione d'Italia*, a cura della Società Italiana di Demografia Storica (Firenze: Le

Lettere, 1994), pp. 627–9, 263; H. Gross, *Rome in the Age of Enlightenment: The Post Tridentine Syndrome and the Ancient Regime* (Cambridge: Cambridge University Press, 1990), p. 64. For the silver coin debasement, see G. De Gennaro, *L'esperienza monetaria a Roma in età moderna* (Napoli: Edizioni Scientifiche Italiane, 1980); L. Londei, 'La monetazione pontificia e la zecca di Roma in età moderna (secc. XVI–XVIII)', *Studi Romani*, 38 (1990), pp. 311–18.

6. P. Partner, 'The Papacy and the Papal States', in Bonney (ed.), *The Rise of the Fiscal State in Europe*, pp. 359–80, on pp. 369, 363.

7. F. Braudel, *Civiltà e imperi nel Mediterraneo nell'età di Filippo II*, 2 vols (Torino: Einaudi, 1976), vol. 2, p. 738.

8. Archivio Segreto Vaticano, Arm. V, t. 258, fols 102,126, 165.

9. Transaction costs are mentioned in the *Costituzione* of Paolo V, signed 2 April 1615, in ASR, 'Bandi', b. 472.

10. For middlemen fees, see ASR, 'Bandi', b. 470.

11. ASR, Cam. I, 'Chirografi', coll. B, vol. 240.

12. Sources: R. Masini, *Il debito pubblico pontificio a fine Seicento. I monti camerali* (Città di Castello: Edimond, 2005), pp. 165–87.

13. Very similar percentages have been investigated in E. Stumpo, *Il capitale finanziario a Roma fra Cinque e Seicento, contributo alla storia della fiscalità pontificia in età moderna (1570–1660)* (Milano: Giuffrè, 1985), pp. 301–3.

14. Delumeau, *Vie économique et sociale de Rome*, vol. 2, p. 882; Felloni, *Gli investimenti finanziari genovesi*, p. 168.

15. Some balance sheets have been entirely published. For accounting techniques and public double-entry, see G. Perugino, *Il bilancio pontificio del 1657* (Napoli: Edizioni Scientifiche Italiane, 1999).

16. Sources: ASR, Cam. II, 'Dogane', vols 42, 127,44, 55–69.

17. ASR, Cam. II, 'Dogane', vol. 54.

18. G. Orlandelli, 'I Monti di pubbliche prestanze in Bologna', *Acta Italica*, 14 (1969), pp. ix–xxii; M. Carboni, *Il debito della città. Mercato del credito, fisco e società a Bologna fra Cinque e Seicento* (Bologna: Il Mulino, 1995), pp. 131–7; Archivio di Stato di Bologna (hereafter ASB), Monti di pubbliche prestanze, 'Monte Benedettino', taglioli 1765. Additional elaboration are based on ASB, Ambasciata Bolognese a Roma, 'Posizioni', 307, Francazioni di Monti di Bologna; ASB, Assunteria di Camera, 'Miscellanea antica', 11.

19. Orlandelli, 'I Monti di pubbliche prestanze', pp. xix–xxi.

20. Carboni, *Il debito della città*, pp. 131–37; ASB, 'Monti di pubbliche prestanze', Monte Benedettino, taglioli 1765.

21. A. Giacomelli, 'Conservazione e innovazione nell'assistenza bolognese del Settecento', in *Forme e soggetti dell'intervento assistenziale in una città d'antico regime* (Bologna: Istituto per la storia di Bologna, 1986), pp. 269–302.

22. Felloni, *Gli investimenti finanziari genovesi*, p. 179.

23. L. Laudanna, 'Le grandi ricchezze private di Roma agli inizi dell'Ottocento', *Dimensioni e problemi della ricerca storica*, 2 (1989), p. 137.

24. D. Strangio, *Il debito pubblico pontificio. Cambiamento e continuità nella finanza pontificia dal periodo francese alla restaurazione romana. 1798–1820* (Padova: Cedam, 2001), p. 157.

25. Sources: ASR, 'Amministrazione del Debito Pubblico', Trasferimento di titoli, vols 2744–54; Concambio di certificati nominativi in certificati al portatore, vols 2872–84.

26. ASR, 'Congregazione economica (1815–1830)', b. 134, Fogli anonimi presentati alla Segreteria di Stato sulla sistemazione della borsa, fol. 761.

27. Ibid., fol. 763.

28. Ibid., fol. 795. See also D. Strangio, '*Facilitare al Governo il mezzo di conoscere, e di soddisfare i veri bisogni del commercio, e delle arti.* La disciplina della Borsa di Roma nella prima metà del XIX secolo', *Studi Storici Luigi Simeoni*, 56 (2006), pp. 389–404.

29. Sources: *Cracas, Diario di Roma* (1821–47). Information has been collated by Donatella Strangio.

9 Dubet, 'Towards a New Public Credit Policy in Eighteenth-Century Spain'

1. This paper has been funded by a research project granted by Spanish Education Ministry, HUM 2005-06628.

2. Carlos Morales, *Carlos V y el crédito de Castilla*.

3. H. Kamen, *La Guerra de Sucesión en España, 1710–1715* (Barcelona, Buenos Aires and México DF: Grijalbo, 1974), pp. 213–14; S. Madrazo, *Estado débil y ladrones poderosos en la España del siglo XVIII. Historia de un peculado en el reinado de Felipe V* (Madrid: Catarata, 2000); J.-P. Dedieu, 'La Nueva Planta en su contexto. Las reformas del aparato del Estado en el reinado de Felipe V', *Manuscrits*, 18 (2000), pp. 113–39; T. Nava Rodríguez, '"Nervios de bóveda": las tesorerías centrales de la hacienda borbónica (1716–1743)', in E. Martínez Ruiz (ed.), *III seminario hispanovenezolano. Vínculos y sociabilidades en España et Iberoamérica. Siglos XVI–XX* (Ciudad Real: Ediciones Puertollano, 2004), pp. 111–31, p. 119.

4. Ibid.; A. González Enciso, 'El coste de la guerra y su gestión: las cuentas del tesorero del ejército en la guerra con Portugal de 1762', in A. Guimerá and V. Peralta (eds), *El Equilibrio de los Imperios: De Utrecht a Trafalgar. Actas de la VIIIᵃ Reunión Científica de la Fundación Española de Historia Moderna (Madrid, 2–4 de junio de 2004)* (Madrid: Fundación Española de Historia Moderna, Consejo Superior de Investigaciones Científicas, Universidad Complutense, Sociedad Estatal de Conmemoraciones Culturales, 2005), pp. 551–64.

5. Kamen, *La Guerra de Sucesión en España*; M. Ibáñez Molina, 'Notas sobre la introducción de los intendentes en España', *Anuario de Historia Contemporánea*, no. 9, 1982, pp. 5–27; F. Abbad and D. Ozanam, *Les intendants espagnols du XVIIIe siècle* (Madrid: Casa de Velázquez, 1992); Didier Ozanam, 'La restauration de l'État espagnol au début du règne de Philippe V (1700–1724): le problème des hommes', in *Philippe V d'Espagne et l'Art de son temps. Actes du colloque des 7, 8 et 9 juin 1993 à Sceaux sous la haute autorité scientifique du Professeur Yves Bottineau* (Paris: Musées de l'Ile de France, 1995), vol. 2, pp. 79–89; and Didier Ozanam, 'Les intendants espagnols de la première moitié du XVIIIe siècle, 1711–1749', in R. Descimon, J.-F. Schaub and B. Vincent (eds), *Les figures de l'administrateur. Institutions, réseaux, pou-*

voirs en Espagne, en France et au Portugal, 16ᵉ–19ᵉ siècle (Paris: Editions de l'EHESS, 1997), pp. 181–99, on p. 183; Nava Rodríguez, '"Nervios de bóveda"'.

6. F. Andújar Castillo, *Consejo y Consejeros de Guerra en el siglo XVIII* (Granada: Universidad de Granada, 1996); J.-P. Dedieu and J. I. Ruiz Rodríguez, 'Tres momentos en la historia de la Real Hacienda', *Cuadernos de Historia Moderna*, 15 (1994), pp. 77–98; C. de Castro, *A la sombra de Felipe V. José de Grimaldo, ministro responsable (1703–1726)* (Madrid, Marcial Pons, 2004); Nava Rodríguez, '"Nervios de bóveda"'.

7. Ozanam, 'La restauration de l'État espagnol'; J.-P. Dedieu, 'Dinastía y élites de poder en el reinado de Felipe V', in P. F. Albaladejo ed., *Los Borbones. Dinastía y memoria denación en la España del siglo XVIII* (Madrid: Marcial Pons Historia, Casa de Velázquez, 2002), pp. 381–99, on p. 392. C. Sanz Ayán, in 'Administration and Resources for the Mainland War in the First Phases of the War of the Spanish Succession', in H. V. Bowen and A. González Enciso, *Mobilising Resources for War: Britain and Spain at Work During the Early Modern Period* (Pamplona: EUNSA, 2006), pp. 135–58, studies the evolution of payments and funds of the Tesorería Mayor de Guerra during the first two battles of Moriana, but not its relations with others institutions.

8. S. Aquerreta, 'La participación de los financieros nacionales en la Guerra de Sucesión: el abastecimiento de víveres al ejército', in R. Torres Sánchez (ed.), *Capitalismo mercantil en la España del siglo XVIII* (Pamplona: EUNSA, 200), pp. 273–314; S. Aquerreta, *Negocios y finanzas en el siglo XVIII: la familia Goyeneche* (Pamplona, EUNSA, 2001); S. Aquerreta, '"De su cuenta y riesgo y por vía de asiento": trayectoria y negocios de Francisco Mendinueta', in S. Aquerreta (ed.), *Francisco Mendinueta: Finanzas y mecenazgo en la España del siglo XVIII* (Pamplona: EUNSA, 2002), pp. 77–99; A. González Enciso and R. Torres Sánchez (eds), *Tabaco y economía en el siglo XVIII* (Pamplona: EUNSA, 1999); C. Sanz Ayán, 'Financieros holandeses de Felipe en la Guerra de Sucesión. Huberto Hubrecht', in A. Crespo Solana and M. Herrero Sánchez (eds), *España y las 18 provincias de los Países Bajos. Una revisión historiográfica* (Córdoba: Universidad de Córdoba, Ministerio de Asuntos Exteriores, Fundación Carlos de Amberes, 2002), pp. 563–81; C. Sanz Ayán, *Estado, Monarquía y Finanzas. Estudios de Historia financiera en tiempos de los Austrias* (Madrid: Centro de Estudios Políticos y Constitucionales, 2004), chs 8, 9; R. Torres Sánchez, '"Servir al rey", más una comisión. El fortalecimiento de los asentistas en la corona española durante la segunda mitad del siglo XVIII', in P. F. Albaladejo (ed.), *Monarquía, imperio y pueblos en la España moderna. Actas de la IV Reunión Científica de la Asociación Española de Historia Moderna. Alicante, 27–30 de mayo de 1996* (Alicante: Caja de Ahorros del Mediterráneo, Universidad de Alicante, AEHM, 1997), pp. 149–67; R. Torres Sánchez, 'Cuando las reglas del juego cambian. Mercados y privilgio en el abastecimiento del ejército español en el siglo XVIII', *Revista de Historia Moderna*, 20 (2002), pp. 487–512. See also other works by the same authors and by Hernández Escayola listed in this paper.

9. Nava Rodríguez, '"Nervios de bóveda"'.

10. On Jean Orry, see Denise Ozanam, 'Jean Orry, munitionnaire du Roi', *Etudes et documents*, 5 (1993), pp. 123–56; and G. Hanotin, 'Jean Orry, un homme des finances

royales entre France et Espagne (1652–1705)' (unpublished thesis, Université Paris-Sorbonne, 2003).

11. Ministère des Affaires Etrangères, Paris, Correspondance Politique Espagne (hereafter MAE, CPE), 122, fol. 241.

12. MAE, CPE, 119, Letter from Orry to Torcy, 17 May 1703.

13. On this project, see MAE, CPE, 119, fols 357–67; CPE, 124, fols 459v.–66v.; CPE, 124, fols 493–502; CPE, 119, fols 384–411; CPE, 124, fols 514–17; CPE, 119, fols 412–14; CPE, 120, fols 106–8; Archivo General de Simancas (hereafter AGS), Dirección General del Tesoro, Inv. 4, leg. 10; AGS, Secretaría de Estado, lib. 496; Archivo Histórico Nacional, Madrid (hereafter AHN), Estado, lib. 279, fol. 8; AHN, Fondos Contemporáneos-Ministerio de Hacienda (hereafter FC-MH), lib. 7924, fols 263–4.

14. MAE, CPE, 119, fols 449–56; Service Historique de la Défense (old Service Historique de l'Armée de Terre (SHAT, Vincennes), general correspondence, old fund (hereafter SHD, A[1]), 1696, no. 21.

15. AHN, Estado, leg. 262–2.

16. AGS, Dirección General del Tesoro, Inv. 4, leg. 10; AHN, Estado, lib. 279, fols 10–11; AHN, Estado, leg. 744, no. 124; AHN, FC-MH, lib. 7924, fols 264–6.

17. MAE, CPE, 120, fols 78–78v.; CPE, 125, fol. 168; SHD, A[1], 1696, no. 35; C. de Castro, 'El Estado español en el siglo XVIII: su configuración durante los primeros años del reinado de Felipe V', *Historia y política. Ideas, procesos y movimientos sociales*, 4 (2000), pp. 137–69; Castro, *A la sombra de Felipe V*, p. 72.

18. See note 16 above.

19. MAE, CPE, 120, fols 113–17; SHD, A[1], 1696, no. 45.

20. MAE, CPE, 139, fols 70–1, 73, 65–6.

21. M. V. López Cordón Cortezo, 'Instauración dinástica y reformismo administrativo: la implantación del sistema ministerial', *Manuscrits*, 18 (2000), pp. 93–111; Castro, *A la sombra de Felipe V*.

22. MAE, CPE, 120, fols 260–1.

23. MAE, CPE, 119, fols 384–412; MAE, CPE, 120, fols 106–10; AGS, Tribunal Mayor de Cuentas, leg. 1689.

24. AGS, Tribunal Mayor de Cuentas, leg. 1689; Dirección General del Tesoro, Inv. 39, leg. 2.

25. AGS, Secretaría de Estado, lib. 399, fol. 5; AHN, Estado, leg. 469, 871.

26. SHD, A[1], 1976, no. 202; 1886, no. 61; 1976, no. 29–30.

27. AHN, Estado, leg. 262, 744, 871.

28. AGS, Secretaría de Estado, lib. 496; AHN, FC-MH-Tesorería, lib. 1, passim. See also the works quoted in note 15 above.

29. On the methods implemented by the Crown to audit the royal armies, see Esteban Estríngana, *Guerra y finanzas en los Países Bajos católicos*; and A. Esteban Estríngana, 'Autopsia del despacho financiero. Ejecución y control de pagos en el tesoro militar del ejército de Flandes (siglo XVII)', *Obradoiro de historia moderna*, 12 (2003), pp. 47–78.

30. MAE, CPE, 120, fols 248–80.

31. AHN, FC-MH, lib. 7924, fol. 281; SHD, A[1], 1885, no. 168; AHN, Estado, leg. 269–71.

32. A. Dubet, *Jean Orry et le gouvernement de l'Espagne (1701–1706)* (Clermont-Ferrand: Presses Universitaires Blaise Pascal, forthcoming), chs 6, 9.
33. AHN, FC-MH, lib. 7926, fols 11–12.
34. This is the case of the *beneficios* of the sale of *oficios*. Dubet, *Jean Orry*, chs 4.4, 4.6.1, 5.1.2, 6.1.1, 9.2; Sanz Ayán, 'Administration and resources for the Mainland War', p. 155; F. Andújar Castillo, *Tiempo de necesidad, tiempo de venalidad. España e Indias, 1705–1711* (forthcoming).
35. Andújar Castillo, 'La reforma militar en el reinado de Felipe V', in M. A. Bel Bravo, J. M. Delgado Barrado and J. Fernández García (eds), *El cambio dinástico y sus repercusiones en la España del siglo XVII* (Jaén: Universidad de Jaén, 2000), pp. 617–40, on pp. 631–32; Castro, *A la sombra de Felipe V*; and Dubet, 'La reforma en acción: gobernar la hacienda militar al principio de la Guerra de Sucesión (1701–1706)', *IX Reunión Científica de la FEHM – Málaga, 7 a 9 junio 2006* (forthcoming).
36. For this, see Dubet, *Jean Orry*; A. Dubet, '¿La importación de un modelo francés? Acerca de algunas reformas de la administración española a principios del siglo XVIII', in J. G. Castaño and J. Muñoz Rodríguez (eds), *El conflicto sucesorio, 1700–1715*, special issue of *Revista de Historia Moderna*, 25 (2007), pp. 207–33; A. Dubet, '¿Francia en España? La elaboración de los proyectos de reformas político-administrativas de Felipe V (1701–1703)', in A. Álvarez-Ossorio Alvariño and B. J. García (eds), *La pérdida de Europa. La Guerra de Sucesión por la Monarquía de España* (Madrid: Fundación Carlos de Amberes – Universidad Autónoma de Madrid 2007), pp. 293–311.
37. A. Dubet, 'L'autorité royale et ses limites: les projets de Jean Orry pour l'administration des finances espagnole au début du XVIIIe siècle', in P. Fournier, J.-P. Luis, L. Martín and N. Planas (eds), *Institutions et représentations du politique. Espagne – France – Italie, XVIIe–XXe siècles* (Clermont-Ferrand: Presses Universitaires Blaise Pascal, 2006), pp. 81–96.
38. Castro, 'El Estado español en el siglo XVIII'; Castro, *A la sombra de Felipe V*; and Dubet, *Jean Orry*, chs 6.2, 8.1.3.
39. Dubet, 'La reforma en acción'.
40. Sanz Ayán, 'Administration and Resources for the Mainland War', studies the accounting of the Tesorero Mayor de Guerra presented to the Contaduría Mayor de Cuentas during those years.
41. SHD, A¹, 1786, no. 293.
42. MAE, CPE, 120, fols 113–17; SHD, A¹, 1696, no. 45.
43. On Orry's plans, see Dubet, 'L'autorité royale et ses limites'.
44. MAE, CPE, 125, fols 43–8; 120, fols 113–17; SHD, A¹, 1696, no. 45.
45. See note 40 above.
46. MAE, CPE, 120, fols 121–4; CPE, 125, fols 521–34v.; SHD, A¹, 1696, no. 74; 1787, no. 87.
47. MAE, CPE, 119, fol. 149.
48. Toboso Sánchez, *La deuda pública castellana*.
49. MAE, CPE, 120, fols 111–17; SHD, A¹, 1696, nos 44–5; AHN, FC-MH-Tesorería, lib. 1, fol. 318.
50. MAE, CPE, 123, fols 5–9.
51. MAE, CPE, 120, fols 181–214; SHD, A¹, 1696, no. 74.

52. SHD, A¹, 1787, nos 104–6.
53. However, contrary to Kamen's belief, double-entry accounting was not imported. Kamen, *La Guerra de Sucesión en España*, pp. 226–8.
54. AHN, Estado, leg. 873; SHD, A¹, 1786, no. 307; AHN, Estado, leg. 846; SHD, A¹, 1786, no. 182, fols 182, 234–5, 244, 247–8, 281, 301–6.
55. AHN, Estado, leg. 262, 274, 280–1, 744, 816.
56. See notes 44 and 52 above.
57. MAE, CPE, fols 292–7; CPE, 119, fols 306–8; 120, fols 324–71; SHD, A¹, 1696, no. 125–31.
58. M. C. Hernández Escayola, 'Los últimos arrendatarios del tabaco en Navarra (1700–1717)', in González Enciso and Torres Sánchez (eds), *Tabaco y economía en el siglo XVIII*, pp. 355–89; M. C. Hernández Escayola, *De tributo para la Iglesia a negocio para mercaderes: el arrendamiento de las rentas episcopales en la diócesis de Pamplona (siglo XVIII)* (Pamplona: EUNSA, 2000); M. C. Hernández Escayola, 'Las posibilidades de hacer negocios en Navarra a principios del siglo XVIII: el caso de Juan Mendinueta', in Aquerreta (ed.), *Francisco Mendinueta*, pp. 31–76. See also the works of Aquerreta, Dedieu and Ruiz Rodríguez, González Enciso and Torres Sánchez listed in this paper.
59. Dubet, *Jean Orry*, ch. 1; and Dubet, '¿Francia en España?'.
60. MAE, CPE, 119, fols 12, 143–4, 160–70, 180–1.
61. MAE, CPE, 119, fol. 438; SHD, A¹, 1696, no. 20.
62. MAE, CPE, 120, fols 443–50.
63. MAE, CPE, 125, fols 10–11; 119, fols 437–48; SHD, A¹, 1696, no. 20; MAE, CPE, 119, p. 457; SHD, A¹, 1696, no. 24; MAE, CPE, 119, fols 443–50.
64. MAE, CPE, 120, fols 62–77; SHD, A¹, 1696, no. 34.
65. MAE, CPE, 107, fols 110–18.
66. S. Aquerreta, 'Financiar la Guerra de Sucesión: asentistas y compañías al servicio de Felipe V', in *La Guerra de Sucesión en España y América. Actas X Jornadas Nacionales de Historia Militar. Sevilla, 13–17 de noviembre de 2000* (Madrid: Deimos, 2001), pp. 569–82; González Enciso, 'Las finanzas reales y los hombres de negocios en el siglo XVIII', in Dubet (ed.), *Administrer les finances royales dans la monarchie espagnole*.
67. A. Dubet, 'Administrar los gastos de la guerra: Juan Orry y las primeras reformas de Felipe V (1703–1705)' en Agustín Guimerá y Víctor Peralta (coord.), *El Equilibrio de los Imperios: De Utrecht a Trafalgar. Actas de la VIIIª Reunión Científica de la Fundación Española de Historia Moderna (Madrid, 2–4 de junio de 2004)* (Madrid: Fundación Española de Historia Moderna, Consejo Superior de Investigaciones Científicas, Universidad Complutense, Sociedad Estatal de Conmemoraciones Culturales, 2005), pp. 483–501; Dubet, *Jean Orry*, ch. 6.4.
68. Sanz Ayán, *Los banqueros de Carlos II*, p. 424. I would like to thank Jean-Pierre Dedieu for allowing me unrestricted use of his well-known database (J.-P. Dedieu, 'Un instrumento para la historia social: la base de datos Ozanam', *Cuadernos de Historia Moderna*, 24 (2000), pp. 185–205).
69. Aquerreta, 'Financiar la Guerra de Sucesión'.
70. In the accounting of Moriana, Juan de Goyeneche is present as a provider of bills of exchange (AGS, Tribunal Mayor de Cuentas, leg. 1869).

71. M. C. Hernández Escayola, *Negocio y servicios: finanzas públicas y hombres de negocios en Navarra en la primera mitad del siglo XVIII* (Pamplona: EUNSA, 2004), pp. 192–4.

10 Velde, 'French Public Finance between 1683 and 1726'

1. Paper prepared for the XIVth International Economic History Congress, Helsinki 2006.
2. North and Weingast, 'Constitutions and Commitment'.
3. Dickson, *The Financial Revolution in England*; Brewer, *The Sinews of Power*.
4. A. E. Murphy, *John Law: Economic Theorist and Policy-Maker* (Oxford: Clarendon Press, 1997).
5. Extensive genealogical information can be found in P. Laroche, *Moirans en Dauphiné: vingt siècles d'histoire* (Moirans: Association Moirans recherche historique, 1992).
6. She was born Antoinette Poisson, the daughter of an employee of the Paris brothers; at her birth in 1721, Jean Paris was her godfather and Antoinette Paris, daughter of Antoine and wife of Jean, was her godmother.
7. Two lasting legacies of this second career, apart from financing the War of the Austrian Succession and Seven Years War, were the foundation of the École militaire in 1751 and launching the career of the writer Beaumarchais.
8. Or part of the establishment more generally, since one daughter of Paris La Montagne married a Choiseul in 1734 and Paris de Monmartel married a Béthune in 1746. The family links with the financier establishment persisted throughout the eighteenth century. Paris Duverney's only, and illegitimate, daughter married a receiver general of finances, and their daughter married the future finance minister Calonne. The Paris brothers had a sister, Marthe, who married a receiver of the tailles: of her three children the son became receiver general of finances and the daughters each married a farmer general.
9. At least five copies are known: Bibliothèque municipale de Grenoble, MS 1049; Bibliothèque de l'Arsenal, Paris, 4494; Archives Nationales de France, Paris (hereafter AN), KK 1005D; Bibliothèque Méjanes, Aix-en-Provence, MSS 616; University of Chicago, IL, MSS 1026. Two other memoirs to justify their conduct are in AN, K885. This manuscript was the main basis for J. P. L. Luchet, *Histoire de Messieurs Paris: Ouvrage dans lequel ou montre comment un royaume peut passer dans l'espace de cinq années de l'état le plus déplorable à l'état le plus florissant* (Lausanne: n.p, 1776). Aside from R. Dubois-Corneau, *Paris de Monmartel (Jean) banquier de la cour, receveur des rentes de la ville de Paris 1690–1766: origine et vie des frères Paris, munitionnaires des vivres et financiers; les logis de Monmartel* (Paris: E. Jean-Fontaine, 1917), there is still no study of their career and policies.
10. In terms of fiscal revenues, the French monarchy's tradition of levying relatively lower taxes on the newly-conquered provinces meant that the gains to the treasury from annexations were actually lower. The territorial gains up to 1789 were about 15 per cent (whether in area or population); but using numbers from C. J. Panckouke (ed.), *Encyclopédie méthodique: Finances, 2 vols* (Paris: Panckouke, 1784–5), vol. 2, p. 683, I find that the tax revenues from the new provinces amounted to 52 million *livres*

(about 10 per cent of total revenues) or, for the provinces conquered before 1715, 41 million *livres*. This means that the wars of Louis XIV, at a cost of nearly 6 billion *livres*, yielded a paltry 0.7 per cent rate of return.

11. Bibliothèque Nationale de France, Paris (hereafter BN), Clairambault 529, fols 297ff.

12. Sources: J. R. Mallet, *Comptes rendus de l'administration des finances du royaume de France* (London: Buisson, 1789); A. M. Boislisle, *Correspondance des contrôleurs généraux des finances avec les intendants des provinces, publiée par ordre du ministre des finances d'après les documents conservés aux Archives nationales* (Paris: Imprimerie Nationale, 1874–97); F. V. D. de Forbonnais, *Recherches et considérations sur les finances de France, depuis l'année 1595 jusqu'à l'année 1721, 6 vols* (Liege: n.p., 1758), vol. 5, p. 212; Ministère des Affaires Étrangères, Mémoires et Documents, France (hereafter MAE, M&D), 1258, fols 200–4.

13. In practice, of course, the king did not start from scratch every year, but updated the previous year's assessments depending on the local conditions in each province for the current year.

14. In some cases, such as Brittany, Franche-Comté and Flanders, a tax on beverages made up part of the revenue.

15. BN, Fr 7771, fol. 100.

16. The numbers are based on series published by three historians whose coverage varies: Mallet, *Comptes rendus de l'administration des finances,* 1662–95; Boislisle, *Correspondance des contrôleurs généraux des finances,* 1683–1707; and Forbonnais, *Recherches et considérations sur les finances de France,* 1682–1716. The series themselves are available on Richard J. Bonney's European State Finance Database, <http://www.le.ac.uk/hi/bon/ESFDB> [accessed June 2002], datasets: rjb/boislisl, rjb/forbon, rjb/frmalet. Roughly, I use Mallet's numbers until 1695 and then Forbonnais's numbers, complemented with Boislisle's numbers.

17. Noailles, the finance minister, wrote in 1717 that the kingdom's greatest splendour had been reached under Colbert (BN, Fr 7769). The banker Jacques Necker, who would be the last great reformer of the monarchy's finances, wrote *Éloge de Jean-Baptiste Colbert, discour qui a remporté le prix de l'Académie Françoise, en 1773* (Paris: n.p., 1773) to establish his credentials as a statesman.

18. The *abonnement* (Panckouke (ed.), *Encyclopédie méthodique*, vol. 1, p. 1) was a practice whereby a region, a town, a community or a corporation could win an exemption from a particular tax in exchange for an annual payment. The term applied properly to indirect taxes, and the general farmers were free to enter into any such arrangement they saw fit. Often, this was done for taxes which involved high collection costs. With direct taxes, the *abonnement* was obtained by the clergy as a whole, and by those provinces annexed after the creation of the *taille* in the fifteenth century and which had negotiated to collect the *taille* by themselves (the so-called *pays d'État*). See M. Del Negro, F. Perri and F. Schivardi, *Tax Buyouts. Working Paper* (New York: New York University, 2006), for theoretical arguments in favour of the practice.

19. M. Kwass, *Privilege and the Politics of Taxation in Eighteenth-Century France: liberté, égalité, fiscalité* (Cambridge: Cambridge University Press, 2000).

20. F. R. Velde and D. R. Weir, 'The Financial Market and Government Debt Policy in France, 1746–1793', *Journal of Economic History*, 52 (1992), pp. 1–39.

21. E. N. White, 'From Privatized to Government-Administered Tax Collection: Tax Farming in Eighteenth-Century France', *Economic History Review*, 57:4 (2004), pp. 636–63.

22. Velde and Weir, 'The Financial Market and Government Debt Policy in France'.

23. Forbonnais, *Recherches et considérations sur les finances de France*.

24. See D. R. Weir, 'Tontines, Public Finance and Revolution in France and England, 1688–1789', *Journal of Economic History*, 49:1 (1989), pp. 95–124.

25. The lottery tickets in principle bore the name of the lender/purchaser, but it was possible to inscribe instead a motto or phrase by which the owner could identify himself; this made the tickets into easily-traded bearer instruments.

26. F. R. Velde, 'Chronicle of a Deflation Unforetold', working paper 12 (Chicago, IL: Federal Reserve Bank of Chicago, 2006).

27. See T. J. Sargent and F. R. Velde, *The Big Problem of Small Change* (Princeton, NJ: Princeton University Press, 2002).

28. In practice, the old coins were also given a temporary legal tender value of 1+y during the exchange period, so that they were worth the same in circulation and at the mint. After the exchange period ended, the old coins ceased to be legal tender, and were only worth the mint price of their content.

29. E. Dutot, *Réflexions politiques sur les finances et le commerce, 2 vols* (1738; Paris: E. Droz, 1935), vol. 2, p. 241, provides additional quotations from March to August 1715.

30. Sussman and Y. Yafeh, 'Constitutions and Commitment'.

31. Sources: *Gazette d'Amsterdam*, *Amsterdamse Courant*, AN, G/7/1122, Bibliothèque municipale de Reims MSS 2086.

32. AN, K900 contains a summary history.

33. AN, G/7/728-735; BN, Fr 7759.

34. AN, E* 886, fol. 309.

35. AN, MC XXXVIII/309, 6 November 1739.

36. It is no doubt to such demonstrated talents that Brehamel later owed his appointment as chief accountant of the Visa of 1721 by the Paris brothers.

37. BN, Fr 7769, fols 401–3.

38. The more recent works include P. Harsin, *Les doctrines monétaires et financières en France du XVIe au XVIIIe siècle* (Paris: F. Alcan, 1928); P. Harsin, *Crédit public et banque d'état en France du XVIe au XVIIIe siècle* (Paris: E. Droz, 1933); E. Faure, *La Banqueroute de Law* (Paris: Gallimard, 1977); L. Neal, *The Rise of Financial Capitalism: International Capital Markets in the Age of Reason* (Cambridge: Cambridge University Press, 1990); Murphy, *John Law;* Hoffman et al., *Priceless Markets*; see also F. R. Velde, 'Government Equity and Money: John Law's System in 1720 France', working paper 31 (Chicago, IL: Federal Reserve Bank of Chicago, 2003).

39. See, for example, C. A. Sims, 'Fiscal Consequences for Mexico of Adopting the Dollar', *Journal of Money, Credit and Banking* 33:2 (2001), pp. 597–616.

40. See the excellent description in Y. Lemarchand, 'Introducing Double-Entry Bookkeeping in Public Finance: A French Experiment at the Beginning of the Eighteenth Century', *Accounting, Business and Financial History*, 9:2 (1999), pp. 225–54.

41. BN, Fr 11101: 'Controlle de la Caisse commune de l'administration des recettes générales, du premier juillet au dernier décembre 1716, tiré des livres tenus en parties doubles', 1717; BN Fr 7742: 'Administration des recouvremens dans les vingt généralités. Billan des six derniers mois 1716'; AN, U 2486–7: 'Journal de la caisse commune', 17 January 1718–15 January 1719, copy of the finance minister; Bibliothèque de l'Assemblée Nationale, 1010–11, 'administration du recouvrement des impositions dans les 20 généralités: bilan', 15 January 1718 and 17 January 1718–15 January 1719. A memoir of 1722 in MAE, M&D, 1253, fols 216–23 describes the importance of the reforms.

42. MAE, M&D, 1252, fol. 76r.

43. The Visa of 1721 was to some degree foreshadowed by the Visa of 1716, which required owners of government paper to certify how they had acquired them, and which also provided a matrix to determine the reduction rate, as a function of the type of paper; but the other criterion was the rank and profession of the owner. The scale of the operation was much smaller: it lasted only six weeks (BN, Fr 7769, pp. 209–17). As we know from the case of Brehamel, some of the personnel of the 1716 Visa found employment in the 1721 Visa.

44. Musée Dubois Corneau, Brunoy (France), Lettres sur le Visa (1732), fichier 731. The author was François Michel Chrétien Deschamps (1688–1747), who wrote several tragedies and is also given as the author of J. Paris Duverney, *Examen du livre intitulé Réflexions politiques sur les finances et le commerce* (The Hague: V. & N. Prevôt, 1740) by C. Parfaict and F. Parfaict, *Histoire du théâtre françois depuis son origine jusqu'à présent, 15 vols* (Amsterdam: n.p, 1735–49), vol. 15, p. 195. The manuscript itself is silent on the author, but a letter from Antoine Paris to Cardinal Dubois (MAE, M&D, 1252, fol. 138) as well as Deschamps's own interrogation in December 1726 (Bibliothèque de l'Arsenal, Paris, 10949, fol. 290) confirm his authorship.

45. The original documents of the trial are in Bibliothèque de l'Arsenal, Paris, MSS 2848–9; and Bibliothèque du Sénat, Paris, MSS 138–40; see also M. Antoine, *Le Conseil du roi sous le règne de Louis XV* (Geneva: Droz, 1970), p. 266; Y. Combeau, *Le comte d'Argenson (1696–1764), ministre de Louis XV* (Paris: École des Chartes, 1999), pp. 232–5.

46. Paris Duverney, *Examen du livre intitulé Réflexions politiques sur les finances*.

47. M. Marion, *Histoire financière de la France, 6 vols* (Paris: Arthur Rousseau, 1914–31), vol. 1, p. 474.

48. Sources: *Gazette d'Amsterdam*, BN, Fr 13771; J. Buvat, *Journal de la Régence (1715–1723)* (Paris: H. Plon, 1865); M. Marais, *Journal de Paris* (Saint-Étienne: Saint-Étienne University Press, 2004).

49. As far as I know they have disappeared, except perhaps the treatise on revenues and expenditures in AN, KK 1005C, attributed to Paris la Montagne by Lemarchand, 'Introducing Double-Entry Bookkeeping in Public Finance'. One manuscript dated 1724, in the Bibliothèque de l'Assemblée Nationale, 1141–2, bound to the arms of the finance minister Dodun, is possibly their history of the perpetual annuities, although it is signed 'M.D.C.'.

50. Boislisle, *Correspondance des contrôleurs généraux des finances*.

51. They did, however, note at one point the fact that the core provinces of France, the *pays d'élection*, paid 2.5 times more taxes than the more recently conquered provinces

of France, the *pays d'Etat* (recently meaning since the fifteenth century!). They note that equalizing the burden would allow them to either raise more revenue overall or else reduce taxes for some (BN, Fr 7771, fols 100–1).

52. AN, G/7/1176, 'Mémoire sur la proposition de faire des fermes générales et des sou-fermes'; based on its contents it was written between 1724 and 1726. Volume 5 of Malézieu's *Histoire des fermes* of 1746 (BN, NAF 2565) also compares in great detail the two systems. For a contrary opinion, see Desmarets's evaluation of 1717 (MAE, M&D, 137, fols 3–5).

53. It was also argued, in the case of the receivers general, that they had an incentive to smooth short-term fluctuations in taxes, and ease tax collections when necessary (MAE, M&D, 137, fols 3–5).

54. AN G/7/1175, a 'Projet pour un bail des fermes à remise', from around 1722, pro-poses to add to the *régisseurs'* wages 10 per cent of the difference (positive or negative) of the net product of the *régie* over a target of 60 million. It also proposes as a variant a non-convex function, of 5 per cent on the first million, 7.5 per cent on the second, 10 per cent on the third, 12.5 per cent on the fourth through sixth millions, 15 per cent on the seventh through ninth and 20 per cent above. In the end, the linear function was adopted on 15 March 1723, centred on a lower threshold of 57 million; the farm-ers had enough cheek to ask that this bonus apply to the previous years (BN, NAF 2564, p. 70).

55. BN, NAF 2564, pp. 68–9.

56. Sources: *Gazette d'Amsterdam*, Bibliothèque Historique de la Ville de Paris, MS 712; Bibliothèque de l'Arsenal, Paris, 10155–6; BN, Fr 13771 and NAF 4287.

57. Velde, 'Chronicle of a Deflation Unforetold'.

58. S. L. Kaplan, 'The Paris Bread Riot of 1725', *French Historical Studies*, 14:1 (1985), pp. 23–56.

59. As part of the peace treaties that concluded the War of Spanish Succession, Louis XIV's grandson was allowed to remain King of Spain on condition that he renounced his right to the French throne. But he was also the closest heir to Louis XV, and did not feel bound by his renunciation. Should Louis XV die childless, the King of Spain would certainly press his claim, provoking a succession war.

60. A memo by the elder Paris sent to the Duke of Bourbon at his request in May 1726, shortly before his fall, condemns the diminutions (MAE, M&D, 1259, fol. 61r.). There were contemporary rumours of an estrangement between Paris Duverney, who became an intimate of the Duke of Bourbon, and his brothers (Marais, *Journal de Paris*, p. 760).

61. MAE, M&D, 1259, fols 100–4.

62. BN, NAF 2560, fol. 7.

63. MAE, M&D, 1259, fols 205–15.

64. Paris La Montagne admits that it was initially difficult to find the personnel they needed, and they had to bring skilled clerks from the Netherlands, Spain, Italy and the main commercial centres of France; and even they had to be trained in the accounts of public finance. But he claimed that by 1726 they had trained a large number of very able individuals. According to the 1725 budget, the cost was 309,520 *livres* (BN, Fr 7771, fol. 110).

65. The leader of the competing syndicate was Durand de Mézy, who had been a farmer under the Paris brothers; see details in BN, NAF 2564, fols 126ff., and Fr 11099 (written by Durand de Mézy); AN G/7/1175-6.

66. Fleury did use the competing bid to demand from the farmers an additional 6 million per year to fund a lottery reimbursing annuities, but after a year and a half the fund was used instead to buy back shares in the Indies Company.

67. Marion, *Histoire financière de la France*, vol. 1, pp. 147-9.

68. The franc was made heavier by 1.25 per cent to make its specifications round numbers in the metric system.

69. Spending is computed in constant silver units. The exchange rate used is 23 *livres* per £1. The period of suspension in Britain from 1798 to 1816 is deflated to account for fiat money inflation.

11 Chamley, 'Long-Term War Loans and Market Expectations in England, 1743-50'

1. Discussions with Gilles Postel-Vinay, François Velde and participants at the 2006 Oxford Finance Summer Symposium were very helpful.

2. The study by Dickson, *The Financial Revolution in England*, 1st edn, on the growth of public deficit financing, remains the only detailed description for the period before 1750. See also R. Barro, 'Government Spending, Interest Rates, Prices, and Budget Deficits in the United Kingdom, 1701-1918', *Journal of Monetary Economics*, 20 (1987), pp. 221-47; H. Roseveare, *The Financial Revolution, 1660-1760* (London: Longmans, 1991).

3. For example, 'war expenses were paid for in short-term paper debt, which was then exchanged for perpetual debt, mainly after peace was restored'. Velde and Weir, 'The Financial Market and Government Debt Policy in France'.

4. For the slow decrease of interest rates after 1688, see Stasavage, *Public Debt and the Birth of the Democratic State*; D. Stasavage, 'Partisan Politics and Public Debt: The Importance of the Whig Supremacy for Britain's Financial Revolution', *European Review of Economic History*, 11 (2007), pp. 123-53; Sussman and Yafeh, 'Constitutions and Commitment'.

5. The impact of the callable feature on the effective cost of borrowing has been emphasized by C. K. Harley, 'Goschen's Conversion of the National Debt and the Yield on Consols', *Economic History Review*, 29 (1976), pp. 101-6; J. T. Klovland, 'Pitfalls in the Estimation of the Yield on British Consols, 1850-1914', *Journal of Economic History*, 54 (1994), pp. 164-87. For the computation of the long-term rate at the end of the nineteenth century, when the government exercised the call and lowered the interest rate to 2.75 per cent first, and then to 2.5 per cent, the rate in effect today, Harley does not use any model but makes assumptions about the call. Klovland evaluates critically these assumptions and rejects some of them by comparing the ex post mean returns of the redeemable and the non-redeemable debt for some time intervals.

6. Dickson, *The Financial Revolution in England*. See also the references given in notes 2-5 above.

7. J. J. Grellier, *The Terms of All the Loans Which Have Been Raised for the Public Service*, 3rd edn (London: John and J. M. Richardson, 1812), p. 75.
8. The accounts do not show the refinancing of a short-term debt after the Seven Years War. Short-term debt accumulated during the War of American Independence and was refinanced after the Peace of Versailles, but it did not represent the major part of debt financing in that war.
9. Sources: United Kingdom Parliamentary Papers, *History of the Funded Debt from 1694 to 1786*, LII (1898), J. J. Grellier, *A History of the National Debt* (London: John Richardson, 1810); Grellier, *The Terms of All the Loans*.
10. The financial instruments of all the loans are easy to trace thanks to a commission of the British parliament in the late nineteenth century. Grellier, *The Terms of All the Loans* (see also his *A History of the National Debt*) provides a number of details on the specifics of the loans, and consolidated data on the British debt in some years. The actual liability of a new loan could be slightly higher than the face value reported in the second column of Table 11.1 and depended on its provisions.
11. Velde and Weir, 'The Financial Market and Government Debt Policy in France'.
12. Dickson, *The Financial Revolution in England*.
13. United States government callable bonds were available until 1995. Municipal bonds are often callable. Callable corporate bonds are redeemable in the stock of the company.
14. Grellier, *The Terms of All the Loans*.
15. As mentioned above, the French government, which was financing the other side of the same wars, relied overwhelmingly on life annuities, which were expensive. The higher borrowing cost for France has been mechanically assigned to a lower credibility of the government, but the types of financial instruments and markets may have been more important. An investigation of interactions between financial instruments, markets and institutions in eighteenth-century France remains to be done.
16. See the accounts in Grellier, *The Terms of All the Loans*, pp. 215–21; and Dickson, *The Financial Revolution in England*, 1st edn, pp. 231–41.
17. Ibid., pp. 228–45.
18. The plan was certainly discussed publicly before November 1749. Pelham was against secrecy in the determination of the terms of the interest reduction.
19. See C. Chamley, 'Contingent Government Liabilities against Private Expectations in England 1743–49' (mimeo: Boston University, 2007).
20. For a descriptive narration, see R. S. Browning, *The War of the Austrian Succession* (New York: St. Martin's Press, 1993).
21. Source: *The Gentleman's Magazine*, various issues since 1737. All prices are adjusted ex-dividend. The prices are weekly averages of daily quotes. The consol refers to the 3 per cent annuity and the bond to the 4 per cent annuity. Different periods (which are reported by the dates) are represented by different symbols. The price points for 1746 are joined by a dashed line to keep track of their sequence.
22. Chamley, 'Contingent Government Debt in 18th Century England'.
23. If the government had used standard (non inflation-linked) bonds, it would have had to pay an average ex post real return of 7.7 per cent in the fifteen years after 1982 (while the average inflation rate had been 4.3 per cent). On the inflation-linked bonds the government paid only 2.8 per cent.

12 O'Brien, 'Mercantilist Institutions for the Pursuit of Power with Profit'

1. Dickson, *The Financial Revolution in England*.
2. J. R. Jones, *Britain and the World, 1649–1815* (Brighton: Harvester Press, 1980); K. J. Holsti, *Peace and War. Armed Conflicts and International Order, 1648–1989* (Cambridge: Cambridge University Press, 1991); L. Colley, *Britons Forging the Nation, 1707–1837* (New Haven, CT: Yale University Press, 1992).
3. N. Gordon, *Political Economy in Parliament* (London: Macmillan, 1976); B. Hilton, *Corn, Cash and Commerce* (Oxford: Oxford University Press, 1977).
4. L. Gomes, *Foreign Trade and the National Economy* (Basingstoke: Macmillan, 1987); L. Stone, *An Imperial State at War. Britain from 1689 to 1815* (London: Routledge, 1994); J. G. Black, *A System of Ambition? British Foreign Policy, 1660–1793* (London: Longman, 1991).
5. D. Baugh, 'Great Britain's Blue Water Policy, 1689–1815', *International History Review*, 10:2 (1988), pp. 33–58; C. Tilly, *Capital, Coercion and European States, 990–1990* (Oxford: Blackwell, 1990); N. Ferguson, *The Cash Nexus. Money and Power in the Modern World, 1700–2000* (London: Allen Lane, 2001).
6. O'Brien 'The Political Economy of British Taxation'; Brewer, *The Sinews of Power*; Roseveare, *The Financial Revolution*; M. J. Braddick, *The Nerves of State: Taxation and Financing of the English State, 1558–1714* (Manchester: Manchester University Press, 1996); P. K. O'Brien and P. A. Hunt, 'The Rise of a Fiscal State in England, 1485–1915', *Historical Research*, 66:2 (1993), pp. 129–76; P. K. O'Brien and P. A. Hunt, 'England 1485–1815', in Bonney (ed.), *The Rise of the Fiscal State in Europe*, pp. 53–100; P. K. O'Brien, 'Fiscal Exceptionalism: Great Britain and its European Rivals from Civil War to Triumph at Trafalgar and Waterloo', in D. Winch and P. K. O'Brien (eds), *The Political Economy of British Historical Experience, 1688–1914* (Oxford: Oxford University Press, 2002), pp. 245–67; W. Ashworth, *Customs and Excise: Trade Production and Consumption in England* (Oxford: Oxford University Press, 2003).
7. North and Weingast, 'Constitutions and Commitment'; Stasavage, *Public Debt and the Birth of the Democratic State*.
8. P. K. O'Brien, 'The Hanoverian State and the Defeat of Napoleon's Continental System', in M. Lundahl and H. Lingren, *Eli F. Heckscher 1879–1952. A Celebratory Symposium* (Boston: MIT Press, 2007).
9. O'Brien and Hunt, 'The Rise of a Fiscal State in England'.
10. O'Brien 'The Political Economy of British Taxation'.
11. Brewer, *The Sinews of Power*; Stone, *An Imperial State at War*.
12. J. Hoppit, 'Checking the Leviathan, 1688–1832', in Winch and O'Brien (eds), *The Political Economy of British Historical Experience*, pp. 267–94; M. Daunton, 'Trusting Leviathan: The Politics of Taxation, 1815–1914', in Winch and O'Brien (eds), *The Political Economy of British Historical Experience*, pp. 319–50.
13. Baugh, 'Great Britain's Blue Water Policy'; N. Rodger, *The Command of the Ocean, 1649–1815* (London: Allen Lane, 2004).
14. Dickson, *The Financial Revolution in England*.

15. B. G. Carruthers, *Politics and Markets in the English Financial Revolution* (Princeton, NJ: Princeton University Press, 1996).

16. Neal, *The Rise of Financial Capitalism*.

17. Hoffman and Norberg (eds), *Fiscal Crises*; Stasavage, *Public Debt and the Birth of the Democratic State*; R. Bonney, 'Towards a Comparative Fiscal History of Britain and France During the "Long" Eighteenth Century', in Prados de la Escosura (ed.), *Exceptionalism and Industrialization*, pp. 191–215.

18. J. McArthur, *Financial and Political Facts of the Eighteenth Century*, 3rd edn (London: J. Wright, 1801); F. Crouzet, *L'Economie Britannique et le blocus continental*, 2nd edn, 2 vols (Paris: Economica, 1987), 'Introduction', vol. 1, pp. v–cxiv; Bonney, 'Towards a Comparative Fiscal History'.

19. Bonney (ed.), *Economic Systems and State Finance*; H. T. Dickinson (ed.), *Britain and the French Revolution* (Basingstoke: Macmillan, 1989).

20. P. Mandler, *Aristocratic Government in the Age of Reform* (Cambridge: Cambridge University Press, 1990); P. K. O'Brien, 'The Security of the Realm and the Growth of the Economy, 1688–1914', in P. Clarke and C. Trebilcock (eds), *Understanding Decline. Perceptions and Realities of British Economic Performance* (Cambridge: Cambridge University Press, 1997).

21. '14th Report of the Commissioners to Examine, Take and State the Public Accounts', *Journals of the House of Commons*, 41 (1786); 'Report from the Select Committee on Accounts and other Papers Related to the Public Income and Expenditure', *Reports from Committees of the House of Commons*, 11 (1786); R. Rayment, *The Income and Expenditure of Great Britain of the Last Seven Years*. (London: J. Debrett, 1791).

22. *Report from the Select Committee on Public Monies*, 9 (1857), pp. 488–534; E. Woods, *English Theories of Central Banking Control, 1819–58* (Cambridge, MA: Harvard University Press, 1939), pp. 60–2.

23. *Accounts of Public Income and Expenditure 1688–1869*, 35 (1868–9), pp. 710–12; E. L. Hargreaves, *The National Debt* (London: Arnold, 1930), pp. 98–100.

24. R. Peel, *The National Debt Productive of National Prosperity* (Warrington: J. Johnson, 1787); W. Playfair, *An Essay on the National Debt* (London: J. Debrett and G. G. J. and J. Robinson, 1787).

25. Lord W. W. Grenville, *Essay on the Supposed Advantages of the Sinking Fund* (London: J. Murray, 1828); J. E. D. Binney, *British Public Finance and Administration, 1774–92* (Oxford: Oxford University Press, 1958), pp. 112–14.

26. C. B. Cone, 'Richard Price and Pitt's Sinking Fund of 1786', *Economic History Review*, 4:2 (1951), pp. 243–51.

27. R. Price, *Appeal to the Public, on the Subject of the National Debt* (London: T. Cadell, 1772), pp. 312–15.

28. J. Ehrman, *The Younger Pitt: The Years of Acclaim* (London: Constable, 1969), pp. 66–73; *Accounts of Public Income and Expenditure*, pp. 711–12.

29. 'Papers of William Pitt the Younger, 1759–1800', National Archives (formerly Public Records Office), Kew, Surrey, Chatham Papers, Series 30/8/102-352 (hereafter Pitt Papers), p. 275.

30. J. Sinclair, *History of the Public Revenue of the British Empire*, 3rd edn, 3 vols (London: T. Cadell and W. Davies, 1803–4), pp. 486–7, 496, 499; Grenville, *Essay on the Supposed Advantages of the Sinking Fund*, pp. 59, 63.

31. W. Fairman, *An Account of the Public Funds Transferable at the Bank of England* (1815; 7th edn, London: J. Richardson, 1824), p. 182.

32. *Accounts of Public Income and Expenditure*, pp. 694–701; 'Accounts Relating to the Issue and Redemption of Exchequer Bills', Treasury Papers, 30/20, 35/27.

33. S. Campbell, 'Usury and Annuities in the Eighteenth Century', *Transactions of the Royal Historical Society*, 44 (1928), pp. 473–91; S. Campbell, 'The Economic and Social Effect of the Usury Laws in the Eighteenth Century', *Transactions of the Royal History Society*, 4:16 (1933), pp. 197–210, on pp. 192–8, 206.

34. *Report from the Select Committee Appointed to Consider the Effects of the Laws which Regulate or Restrain the Interest of Money*, 6 (1818), pp. 8, 11, 13, 20, 143, 162, 197; *Three Reports from the Committee of Secrecy on the Outstanding Demands of the Bank of England and on the Restriction of Payments in Cash 1797*, 3 (1826), p. 145; H. Thornton, *An Inquiry into the Nature and Effects of the Paper Credit of Great Britain* (London: J. Hatchard, 1802), pp. 286, 290–2, 310; D. M. Joslin, 'London Bankers in Wartime, 1739–84', in L. S. Pressnell (ed.), *Studies in the Industrial Revolution* (London: Athlone Press, 1960), pp. 156–77, on pp. 169, 171, 174.

35. *Three Reports from the Committee of Secrecy*, pp. 43, 57, 178, 180, 205, 212–16; Joslin, 'London Bankers in Wartime'; L. Pressnell, *Country Banking in the Industrial Revolution* (Oxford: Oxford University Press, 1956), pp. 287–8.

36. *Three Reports from the Committee of Secrecy*, p. 37, 43, 57, 180, 190, 192, 212, 215; W. Boyd, *A Letter to the Right Honourable William Pitt*, 2nd edn (London: J. Ridgway, 1811), pp. 2–5.

37. Pitt Papers, p. 183; *Reports from the Select Committee to whom the 10th and 11th Reports of the Commissioners of Naval Enquiry were Referred*, 2 (1805), p. 169; *Three Reports from the Committee of Secrecy*, pp. 191–2, 271–2; Anon., *Observations on the National Debt* (Norwich: J. March, 1797), p. 33.

38. Parliamentary Papers: *Report of the Select Committee Appointed to Examine what Regulations and Checks have been Established in order to Control the Several Branches of Public Expenditure*, 2 (1807), p. 951; *Report from the Select Committee on Funding Exchequer and Bills*, 3 (1810), p. 271; *Reports from Committees of the Lords and Commons to consider the State of the Bank of England with Reference to the Expediency of the Resumption of Cash Payments*, 3 (1819), pp. 11–12; J. D. Collier, *Life of Abraham Newland* (London: B. Crosby and Co., 1808), pp. 54–7.

39. *Three Reports from the Committee of Secrecy*, p. 50.

40. 'Report from the Committee Appointed to Enquire into the Circumstances of the Negotiation of the Loan', *Journals of the House of Commons*, 51 (1796), pp. 317–19.

41. Pitt Papers, p. 108; 'Papers of Nicholas Vansittart, Baron Bexley, 1766–1851', British Library, Additional Manuscripts (hereafter Vansittart Papers), 31231.

42. T. Mortimer, *Every Man his Own Broker*, 13th edn (London: W. J. and J. Richardson, 1801), p. 255.

43. Ibid., pp. 248–51; D. Macpherson, *Annals of commerce*, 4 vols (London: Nichols and Son, 1805), p. 264; Royal Commission on Historical Manuscripts, *The Manuscripts of J. B. Fortescue, Esq: Preserved at Dropmore*, 10 vols (London: HMSO, 1892–1927), vol. 2; H. Maxwell (ed.), *Creevy Papers*, 2 vols (London: 1904), p. 11.

44. Monthly bond prices were published in the *Annual Register* and *Monthly Magazine*.

45. 'Report from the Committee Appointed to Enquire into the Circumstances of the Negotiation of the Loan', p. 319.

46. *Reports from the Select Committee to whom the 10th and 11th Reports of the Commissioners of Naval Enquiry were Referred*, pp. 167–8.

47. Anon., *The Calumnious Aspersions contained in the Report of the Sub-Committee of the Stock Exchange* (London: Jones, 1814); and *Monthly Magazine* (February 1803), p. 98.

48. Mortimer, *Every Man his Own Broker*.

49. Vansittart Papers.

50. *Accounts of Public Income and Expenditure*, pp. 513–41; Sinclair, *History of the Public Revenue of the British Empire*, pp. 484–5, 503–5

51. C. Hales, *The Bank Mirror, or A Guide to the Funds* (London: W. Treppass, 1796); R. D. Rickards, *The Financial Policy of War* (London: J. Ridgway, 1855); Sinclair, *History of the Public Revenue of the British Empire*, p. 280.

52. Pitt Papers, pp. 102, 276.

53. 'Papers of William Huskisson, 1770–1830', British Library, Additional Manuscripts (hereafter Huskisson Papers), 38759; Pitt Papers, p. 183; *Parliamentary Debates*, 31 vols (London: n.p, 1803–15) [vols 1–23: *Cobbett's Parliamentary Debates*; vols 24–31: *Hansard's Parliamentary Debates*], vol. 2, pp. 144, 179, 880; vol. 10, p. 991; vol. 23, pp. 574, 582, 583, 1203–9.

54. Ibid., vol. 10, p. 991; vol. 11, p. 13; vol. 16, p. 1045.

55. 'Reports of the Facts and Proceedings related to Negotiations for Loans and Funding Operations', 1793–1815, Bank of England, Committee of the Treasury (hereafter Bank of England Reports), 8 March 1809, 9 May, 1809, 4 March 1812.

56. Bank of England Reports, 1793–1815 passim.

57. *Report from the Select Committee on Public Monies*.

58. J. R. McCulloch, *A Treatise on the Principles and Practical Influence of Taxation and the Funding System* (London: Longman, Brown, Green, and Longmans, 1845), pp. 448, 465, 475; Rickards, *The Financial Policy of War*, pp. 32–5, 76, 79, 80, 82; Hargreaves, *The National Debt*, pp. 121–2.

59. Rickards, *The Financial Policy of War*, pp. 79–80.

60. *Accounts of Public Income and Expenditure*, pp. 513–15, 523–8, 537–41; Sinclair, *History of the Public Revenue of the British Empire*, pp. 484–5; Fairman, *An Account of the Public Funds* pp. 22, 162.

61. G. Rose, *Observations Respecting the Public Expenditure, and the Influence of the Crown* (London: T. Cadell and W. Davies, 1810) p. 27.

62. Grellier, *Terms of all the Loans*, pp. 33–56; Hales, *The Bank Mirror*, p. 34.

63. *Cobbett's Parliamentary History*, 36 vols (London: n.p., 1806–20), vol. 22, pp. 1052–64; vol. 23, pp. 767–96; vol. 24, pp. 1018–34; Rose, *Observations Respecting the Public Expenditure*, p. 27; Sinclair, *History of the Public Revenue of the British Empire*, p. 281; J. Norris, *Shelburne and Reform* (London: Macmillan, 1963), p. 105.

64. S. Douglas, *On the Principle of Free Competition* (1791); *Cobbett's Parliamentary History*, vol. 32, p. 792.

65. Sinclair, *History of the Public Revenue of the British Empire*, p. 280; Hales, *The Bank Mirror*, p. 35.

66. Sinclair, *History of the Public Revenue of the British Empire*, pp. 281–5.

67. *Parliamentary Debates*, vol. 3, p. 549; vol. 6, p. 569; vol. 13, p. 535.

68. See the speeches of politicians including Fox, Tierney and Sheridan before the House of Commons and Lauderdale and King to the House of Lords. Outside parliament the debate can be surveyed in that favoured eighteenth-century mode of communication – the pamphlet. The Goldsmith's Library of Economic Literature of the University of London holds literally hundreds of pamphlets concerned with the national debt.

69. Nearly every budget speech opened with a statement by the chancellor that the economy was flourishing and the country possessed the resources required to prosecute war. His assurances are echoed in pamphlet after pamphlet in the Goldsmith's collections of pamphlets in political economy.

70. Dickson, *The Financial Revolution in England*.

71. See Grellier, *The Terms of All the Loans*; and W. Newmarch, *On the Loans Raised by Mr. Pitt during the First French War, 1793–1801* (London: Effingham Wilson, 1855). See also parliamentary papers for 1796–8, 1805, 1807, 1810, 1821, 1826, 1868–9; Bank of England Reports and Minutes; statemen's papers (Pitt, Auckland, Huskisson, Vansittart, Liverpool, Dacres-Adams) deposited at the Public Record Office and the British Library; departmental records (Admiralty, War Office, Treasury and Inland Revenue); as well as debates in parliament (*Parliamentary History, Parliamentary Debates*); newspapers (*Times, Morning Chronicle*); magazines (*Monthly Magazine, Annual Register*).

72. P. K. O'Brien, *Government Revenue 1793–1815. A Study in Fiscal and Financial Policy in the Wars against France* (Oxford: Oxford University Press, 1967), pp. 99–168. This long section of the thesis endeavours to reconstruct conditions in the London capital year by year 1793–1815.

73. See O'Brien, *Government Revenue*; Ehrman, *The Younger Pitt: The Consuming Struggle*; O'Brien, 'Fiscal Exceptionalism'; O'Brien, 'The Hanoverian State and the Defeat of Napoleon's Continental System'. Monetary policy formed the subject of three reports to parliament (*Three Reports from the Committee of Secrecy*; and *Report of the Lords Committee of Secrecy to Enquire into the Causes which Produced the Order in Council of 26ᵗʰ February 1797*, 3 (1810)) and the whole debate is covered by in J. Ehrman, *The Younger Pitt: The Consuming Struggle* (London: Constable, 1996), O'Brien, *Government Revenue*; P. K. O'Brien, 'Merchants and Bankers as Patriots or Speculators. Foreign Commerce and Monetary Policy in War Time, 1793–1815', in J. McCusker and K. Morgan (eds), *The Early Modern Atlantic Economy* (Cambridge: Cambridge University Press, 2000).

74. Departmental administration connected to the budgetary process was investigated by select committees on finance and is covered in thirty-five reports to the House of Commons in 1797–8 (see *Reports from the Committees of the House of Commons*, 11–13); by commissioners' select committees on the expenditures of the armed forces in *Reports from the Select Committee to whom the 10th and 11th Reports of the Commissioners of Naval Enquiry were Referred*. The administration, collection and despatch of tax revenues were investigated long after the war, see numerous parliamentary papers from 1820 to 1828.

75. O'Brien, 'Merchants and Bankers as Patriots or Speculators'.

76. *Three Reports from the Committee of Secrecy.*

77. *Report of the Lords Committee of Secrecy.*

78. O'Brien, *Government Revenue.*

79. W. Morgan, *An Appeal the People of Great Britain on the Present Alarming State of Public Finances* (London: J. Debrett, 1797), pp. 11–12, 16, 21, 31–3, 42; *Parliamentary Debates*, vol. 2, p. 244; vol. 22, pp. 1203–4, 1209; H. James *State of the Nation: Causes and Effects of the Rise and Fall in the Value of Property* (London: Saunders & Otley, 1835), pp. 20–1.

80. O'Brien, *Government Revenue*, pp. 148–68.

81. *Report together with Minutes of and Accounts from the Select Committee on the High Price of Gold Bullion*, 3 (1810); and F.W. Fetter, 'The Politics of the Bullion Report' *Economica*, 26:102 (1959), pp. 99–103.

82. *Reports from the Select Committee to whom the 10th and 11th Reports of the Commissioners of Naval Enquiry were Referred.*

83. Newmarch, *On the Loans Raised by Mr. Pitt.*

84. Grellier, *Terms of all the Loans.*

85. *Parliamentary Debates*, vol. 26, p. 576; vol. 27, pp. 107–8, 629.

86. 'Minutes of the Committee of the Treasury', 1793–1815, Bank of England, Committee of the Treasury (hereafter Bank of England Minutes), 1812–15 passim; Anon., 'Inquiries with respect to the Influence of National Debts and Taxes', *Edinburgh Review*, 47 (1828), pp. 75–83; F. Silver, *Observations on Vansittart's Plan of Finance* (London: n.p., 1813).

87. O'Brien, *Government Revenue*, pp. 148–68.

88. D. Ricardo, *On the Principles of Political Economy and Taxation* (London: J. Murray, 1819); McCulloch, *A Treatise on the Principles and Practical Influence of Taxation.*

89. Anon., 'Inquiries with respect to the Influence of National Debts and Taxes'.

90. Hargreaves, *The National Debt.*

91. Grenville, *Essay on the Supposed Advantages of the Sinking Fund*; J. E. Cookson, *Lord Liverpool's Administration* (Edinburgh: Edinburgh University Press, 1975).

92. O'Brien, *Government Revenue*, pp. 99–168; Silver, *Observations on Vansittart's Plan of Finance.*

93. *Report from the Select Committee on Public Monies.*

94. W. Morgan, *Facts Addressed to the Serious Attention of the People of Great Britain* (London: J. Debrett, 1796), pp. 15–17; Morgan, *An Appeal the People of Great Britain*, p. 24; Anon., *Observations on the National Debt*, p. 73–4; Sinclair, *History of the Public Revenue of the British Empire*, p. 457; F. P. Eliot, *Demonstration, or Financial Remarks* (London: John Cawthorne, 1807), p. 23; R. Hamilton, *An Inquiry concerning the Rise and Progress, the Redemption and Present State, and the Management of the National Debt of Great Britain* (Edinburgh: Oliphant, Waugh and Innes, 1814), pp. 245–55.

95. Anon., 'Inquiries with respect to the Influence of National Debts and Taxes', pp. 75–9; T. Hopkins, *Great Britain for the Last Forty Years* (London: Simpkin and Marshall, 1834), pp. 72–6; McCulloch, *A Treatise on the Principles and Practical Influence of Taxation*, pp. 448, 465, 474; Rickards, *The Financial Policy of War*, pp. 32–5, 76, 79, 80–2; Hargreaves, *The National Debt*, pp. 97, 108, 109, 111, 121.

96. S. Parker, *An Attempt to Ascertain a Theory for Determining the Value of Funded Property* (London: M. Richardson, 1809), p. 6.

97. Bank of England Reports, 25 March 1806.

98. Huskisson Papers, 38759.

99. Pitt Papers, p. 183.

100. Eliot, *Demonstration, or Financial Remarks*, p. 10.

101. O'Brien, *Government Revenue*, pp. 100–68.

102. Bank of England Minutes, 1797–1815.

103. Ricardo, *On the Principles of Political Economy and Taxation*.

104. *Accounts of Public Income and Expenditure*, pp. 794–5.

105. McCulloch, *A Treatise on the Principles and Practical Influence of Taxation*, p. 574.

106. Ricardo, *On the Principles of Political Economy and Taxation*, p. 184.

107. Bond prices are from the *Annual Register*.

108. Anon., 'Inquiries with Respect to the Influence of National Debts and Taxes', p. 83.

109. McCulloch, *A Treatise on the Principles and Practical Influence of Taxation*, p. 474.

110. 'Commissioners for the Sinking Fund Annual Reports', *House of Commons Journals* (1792–1815); *Report of the Comptroller General for the National Debt Commissioners on their Proceedings Since 1786*, 48 (1890–1).

111. *Accounts of Public Income and Expenditure*, pp. 710–15; Hamilton, *An Inquiry concerning the Rise and Progress*.

112. McCulloch, *A Treatise on the Principles and Practical Influence of Taxation*, p. 482; T. Doubleday, *Financial, Monetary and Statistical History of the United Kingdom, 1688–1847* (London: Effingham Wilson, 1847), p. 177; Grenville, *Essay on the Supposed Advantages of the Sinking Fund*, p. 7; Newmarch, *On the Loans Raised by Mr. Pitt*, p. 25.

113. Hargreaves, *The National Debt*, pp. 110, 121, 148; A. W. Acworth, *Financial Reconstructions in England, 1815–22* (London: P. S. King, 1925), pp. 42–4; J. F. Rees, *A Short Fiscal and Financial History of England, 1815–1918* (London: Methuen, 1921), pp. 16–17.

114. Hamilton, *An Inquiry concerning the Rise and Progress*.

115. Cone, 'Richard Price and Pitt's Sinking Fund of 1786', p. 244; Hargreaves, *The National Debt*, pp. 91–5, 97, 101, 104.

116. Hamilton, *An Inquiry concerning the Rise and Progress*, pp. 188–9.

117. Anon., *Considerations on the Annual Million Bill* (London: T. Payne and Son, J. Sewell, and W. Debrett, 1787), pp. 404, 408.

118. Hargreaves, *The National Debt*, pp. 104, 112.

119. *Cobbett's Parliamentary History*, vol. 33, p. 1052; vol. 34, p. 997; *Parliamentary Debates*, vol. 11, p. 264.

120. *Cobbett's Parliamentary History*, vol. 33, p. 1041; vol. 34, p. 1059.

121. Pitt Papers, p. 187; Ehrman, *The Younger Pitt: The Years of Acclaim*, pp. 76–87.

122. *Cobbett's Parliamentary History*, vol. 34, p. 1060.

123. Ehrman, *The Younger Pitt: The Years of Acclaim*, pp. 76–87; *Accounts of Public Income and Expenditure*, pp. 711–12.

124. N. Vansittart, *An Inquiry into the State of the Finances of Great Britain* (London: J. Owen, 1796); Hamilton, *An Inquiry concerning the Rise and Progress*, pp. 144, 199; *Accounts of Public Income and Expenditure*, p. 712.

125. G. Rose, *A Brief Examination into the Increase of Revenue, Commerce and Navigation of Great Britain* (London: J. Hatchard, 1806), p. 21; 'Papers of W. Dacres-Adams, 1775–1862', National Archives (formerly Public Records Office), Kew, Surrey, 30/8/6,7,8, on 7.

126. Fairman, *An Account of the Public Funds*, p. 180.

127. McCulloch, *A Treatise on the Principles and Practical Influence of Taxation*, p. 487; Ricardo, *On the Principles of Political Economy and Taxation*, pp. 152, 175.

128. Hamilton, *An Inquiry concerning the Rise and Progress*, p. 205, Grenville, *Essay on the Supposed Advantages of the Sinking Fund*; D. Wakefield, *Observations on the Credit and Finances of Great Britain* (London: F. and C. Rivington, 1797), p. 32.

129. Ehrman, *The Younger Pitt: The Consuming Struggle*; *Cobbett's Parliamentary History*, vol. 36, pp. 451, 890–5.

130. 'Papers of William Eden, Lord Auckland, 1744–1814', British Library, Additional Manuscripts (hereafter Auckland Papers), 34457; *Parliamentary Debates*, vol. 9, pp. 427, 813–15; Eliot, *Demonstration, or Financial Remarks*, pp. 47–9.

131. *Parliamentary Debates*, vol. 11, p. 262.

132. 'Papers of Charles and Robert Banks Jenkinson. 1st 1727–1808 and 2nd 1770–1826, Earls of Liverpool', British Library, Additional Manuscripts (hereafter Liverpool Papers), 38363.

133. *Parliamentary Debates*, vol. 24, p. 1083; vol. 25, p. 766.

134. Silver, *Observations on Vansittart's Plan of Finance*, pp. 315–18; W. Huskisson, *Substance of a Speech* (London: J. Murray, 1813), pp. 20–2, 25–35.

135. *Parliamentary Debates*, vol. 24, pp. 1102, 1096; vol. 25, pp. 352, 769.

136. *Parliamentary Debates*, vol. 24, p. 1086.

137. Huskisson, *Substance of a Speech*, pp. 208–11, 231, 241–7.

138. *Parliamentary Debates*, vol. 8, p. 579.

139. Grenville, *Essay on the Supposed Advantages of the Sinking Fund*, pp. 18–20; W. Morgan *A Comparative View of Public Finances* (London: J. Debrett, 1801), p. 32; Binney, *British Public Finance and Administration*, pp. 113–14; Hamilton, *An Inquiry concerning the Rise and Progress*, p. 91.

140. Sinclair, *History of the Public Revenue of the British Empire*, pp. 496–9.

141. Grenville, *Essay on the Supposed Advantages of the Sinking Fund*, p. 59; *Cobbett's Parliamentary History*, vol. 30, pp. 560, 1259; vol. 36, p. 459; *Parliamentary Debates*, vol. 6, p. 6.

142. Ehrman, *The Younger Pitt: The Years of Acclaim*; Rose, *A Brief Examination into the Increase of Revenue*, pp. 21–4; Hamilton, *An Inquiry concerning the Rise and Progress*, p. 141; Huskisson, *Substance of a Speech*, p. 20.

143. W. Frend, *The National Debt in its True Colours* (London: J. Mawman, 1817), p. 17.

144. H. Bird, *Proposals for Paying Off the Whole of the Present National Debt* (London: F. and C. Rivington, J. Stockdale, and W. J. and J. Richardson, 1799), p. 16; Wakefield *Observations on the Credit and Finances of Great Britain*, p. 60.

145. D. Wakefield, *Facts of Importance relative to the Present State of Great Britain* (London: F. and C. Rivington, J. Wright, and Bye and Law, 1800), p. 33.

146. Pitt Papers, pp. 107, 275; Huskisson Papers, 38759, 38760; Liverpool Papers, 38256, 38363, 38366; Vansittart Papers, 31237; Auckland Papers, 34457.

147. *Cobbett's Parliamentary History*, vol. 33, pp. 1052–3; vol. 34, p. 977; vol. 36, pp. 890–5; *Parliamentary Debates*, vol. 3, p. 528; vol. 8, p. 574.
148. 'Commissioners for the Sinking Fund Annual Report' (1797), p. 217.
149. Pitt Papers, p. 197; *Cobbett's Parliamentary History*, vol. 31, p. 1314; Ehrman, *The Younger Pitt: The Consuming Struggle*.
150. *Parliamentary Debates*, vol. 6, p. 626.
151. Anon., *A Letter to the Right Hon. W. Pitt on his Conduct with Respect to the Loan Concluded on 25th November 1796* (London: J. Debrett, 1796), p. 50; Grenville, *Essay on the Supposed Advantages of the Sinking Fund*, p. 9; Hamilton, *An Inquiry concerning the Rise and Progress*, pp. 110–11.
152. Ricardo, *On the Principles of Political Economy and Taxation*, p. 171.
153. *Cobbett's Parliamentary History*, vol. 31, p. 1314; *Parliamentary Debates*, vol. 3, p. 528; vol. 6, 657; vol. 11, p. 262; Vansittart, *An Inquiry into the State of the Finances of Great Britain*, p. 30; Huskisson, *Substance of a Speech*, pp. 223–34.
154. Hamilton, *An Inquiry concerning the Rise and Progress*, p. 193.
155. Ricardo, *On the Principles of Political Economy and Taxation*, p. 171.
156. *Parliamentary Debates*, vol. 28, pp. 66–8.
157. *Report of the Select Committee Appointed to Examine what Regulations and Checks have been Established*, p. 100; *House of Commons Journals* (1793–1815), Sinclair, *History of the Public Revenue of the British Empire*, p. 530.
158. *Cobbett's Parliamentary History*, vol. 32, pp. 805–6; 'Commissioners for the Sinking Fund Annual Reports'.
159. *Report of the Comptroller General*, p. 39; Vansittart, *An Inquiry into the State of the Finances of Great Britain*, p. 34.
160. Ricardo, *On the Principles of Political Economy and Taxation*, p. 172; 'Commissioners for the Sinking Fund Annual Report' (1828), p. 566.
161. Acworth, *Financial Reconstructions in England*; Gordon, *Political Economy in Parliament*.
162. O'Brien, 'The Security of the Realm and the Growth of the Economy'; B. Porter, *Britannia's Burden: The Political Evolution of Modern Britain* (London: Edward Arnold, 1994); M. Daunton, *Trusting Leviathan* (Cambridge: Cambridge University Press, 2003).
163. B. Porter, *Britain, Europe and the World: Delusions of Grandeur* (London: Unwin-Hyman, 1983).
164. Porter, *Britannia's Burden*; O'Brien 'The Political Economy of British Taxation'.

13 Conti, 'Italian Government Debt Sustainability in the Long Run, 1861–2000'

1. This is founded on the seminal works of R. Goldscheid, *Staatssozialismus oder Staatekapitalismus* (Wien: Anzengruber, 1917); R. Goldscheid, 'A Sociological Approach to Problems of Public Finance' (1925), in R. A., Musgrave and A. T. Peacock (eds), *Classics in the Theory of Public Finance* (London and New York: Macmillan, 1958), pp. 202–13; and J. A. Schumpeter, 'The Crisis of the Tax State' (1918), in A. Peacock et al (eds), *International Economic Papers*, vol. 4 (London: Macmillan, 1954), pp. 5–38.

Puviani is a very original fiscal theorist who introduced many arguments of fiscal sociology, see A. Puviani, *Teoria della illusione finanziaria* (1903; Milano: Isedi, 1973).

2. Sources: R. Artoni and S. Biancini, 'Il debito pubblico dall'Unità ad oggi', in P. Ciocca and G. Toniolo (eds), *Storia economica d'Italia*, 2 vols (Roma-Bari: Laterza, 2003), vol. 2, pp. 269–380; S. Fenoaltea, *L'economia italiana dall'unità alla grande guerra* (Roma-Bari: Laterza, 2006); N. Rossi, A. Sorgato and G. Toniolo, 'I conti economici italiani: una ricostruzione statistica, 1890–1990', *Rivista di storia economica*, n.s. 10:1 (1993), pp. 1–47; Istat, *Annuario statistico italiano* (Roma: Istat, various years); Ragioneria generale dello Stato, *Il bilancio dello Stato italiano dal 1862 al 1967* (Roma: Poligrafico dello Stato, 1969); V. Zamagni, 'Il debito pubblico italiano 1861–1946: ricostruzione della serie storica', *Rivista di storia economica*, 14:3 (1998), pp. 207–42.

3. F. Chabod, *Storia della politica estera italiana dal 1870 al 1896* (Roma-Bari: Laterza, 1951), p. 491.

4. Sources: see note 2 above.

5. We make reference to P. Sylos Labini, *Torniamo ai classici. Produttività del lavoro, progresso tecnico e sviluppo economico* (Roma-Bari: Laterza, 2004) pp. 124–9; L. Pasinetti, 'European Union at the End of 1997: Who is Within the Public Finance "Sustainability" Zone?', in *BNL Quarterly Review*, 51:204, (1998), pp. 17–36; and L. Pasinetti, 'The Myth (or Folly) of the 3% Deficit/GDP Maastricht "Parameter"', *Cambridge Journal of Economics*, 22:1 (1998), pp. 103–16.

6. Zamagni, 'Il debito pubblico italiano 1861–1946', table A.

7. V. A. Muscatelli and F. Spinelli, 'Gibson's Paradox and Policy Regimes: A Comparison of the Experience in the US, UK and Italy', *Scottish Journal of Political Economy*, 43:4 (1996), pp. 468–92, do not find evidences for this paradox from the end of nineteenth century until 1914.

8. Sources: see note 2 above.

9. Zamagni, 'Il debito pubblico italiano 1861–1946'.

10. G. Salvemini and V. Zamagni, 'Finanza pubblica e indebitamento tra le due guerre mondiali: il finanziamento del settore statale', in F. Cotula (ed.), *Problemi di finanza pubblica tra le due guerre, 1919–1939*, Ricerche per la storia della Banca d'Italia, 2 (Roma-Bari: Laterza, 1993), pp. 139–283.

14 Ullmann, 'Times of Wasteful Abundance'

1. R. Merklein, *Die Deutschen werden ärmer: Staatsverschuldung, Geldentwertung, Markteinbußen, Arbeitsplatzverluste* (Reinbek bei Hamburg: Rowohlt Taschenbuch Verlag, 1982), pp. 7, 142.

2. J. Angster, *Konsensliberalismus und Sozialdemokratie. Die Westernisierung von SPD und DGB* (München: Oldenbourg Wissenschaftsverlag, 2003); J. K. Galbraith, *Gesellschaft im Überfluß* (München: Droemersche Verlags-Anstalt, 1958), pp. 267ff.; R. Parker, *John Kenneth Galbraith: His Life, His Politics, His Economics* (New York: Farrar, 2005), pp. 273ff.; D. Grimm (ed.), *Staatsaufgaben* (Frankfurt: Suhrkamp Verlag, 1996); V. Tanzi and L. Schuknecht, *Public Spending in the 20th Century: A Global Perspective* (Cambridge: Cambridge University Press, 2000),

pp. 10ff.; G. Metzler, 'Am Ende aller Krisen? Politisches Denken und Handeln in der Bundesrepublik der sechziger Jahre', *Historische Zeitschrift*, 275 (2002), pp. 57–103; M. Görtemaker, *Geschichte der Bundesrepublik: Von der Gründung bis zur Gegenwart* (München: Verlag C. H. Beck, 1999), pp. 328ff.; T. Ellwein, *Krisen und Reformen: Die Bundesrepublik seit den sechziger Jahren*, 2nd edn (München: Deutscher Taschenbuch-Verlag, 1993); A. Schildt, D. Siegfried and K. C. Lammers (eds.), *Dynamische Zeiten: Die sechziger Jahre in beiden deutschen Gesellschaften* (Hamburg: Hans Christians Verlag, 2000); M. Frese, J. Paulus and K. Teppe (eds), *Demokratisierung und gesellschaftlicher Aufbruch: Die sechziger Jahre als Wendezeit der Bundesrepublik* (Paderborn: Schöningh Verlag, 2003); H.-G. Haupt and J. Requate, *Aufbruch in die Zukunft: Die 1960er Jahre zwischen Planungseuphorie und kulturellem Wandel* (Weilerswist: Velbrück Wissenschaft, 2004); C. Führ and C.-L. Furck (eds), *Handbuch der deutschen Bildungsgeschichte*, vol. 6 (München: Verlag C. H. Beck, 1998); H. G. Hockerts, 'Metamorphosen des Wohlfahrtsstaats', in M. Broszat (ed.), *Zäsuren nach 1945: Essays zur Periodisierung der deutschen Nachkriegsgeschichte* (München: Oldenbourg Verlag, 1990), pp. 35–46.

3.   W. Kitterer, 'Öffentliche Finanzen und Notenbank', in Deutsche Bundesbank (ed.), *Fünfzig Jahre Deutsche Mark: Notenbank und Währung in Deutschland seit 1948* (München: Verlag C. H. Beck, 1998), pp. 199–256, on p. 219.

4.   B. Lutz, *Der kurze Traum der immerwährenden Prosperität: Eine Neuinterpretation der industriell-kapitalistischen Entwicklung im Europa des 20. Jahrhunderts*, 2nd edn (Frankfurt: Campus-Verlag, 1989), p. 3.

5.   R. Caesar and K. H. Hansmeyer, 'Die finanzwirtschaftliche Entwicklung', in K. G. A. Jeserich (ed.), *Deutsche Verwaltungsgeschichte*, vol. 5 (Stuttgart: Deutsche Verlags-Anstalt, 1988), pp. 919–45, on p. 937.

6.   J. M. Buchanan and R. E. Wagner, *Democracy in Deficit: The Political Legacy of Lord Keynes* (New York: Academic Press, 1977); D. Duwendag (ed.), *Der Staatssektor in der sozialen Marktwirtschaft: Vorträge und Diskussionsbeiträge der 43. Staatswissenschaftlichen Forschungstagung 1975 der Hochschule für Verwaltungswissenschaften Speyer* (Berlin: Duncker & Humblot, 1976); K. Littmann, 'Bundesrepublik Deutschland', in F. Neumark (ed.), *Handbuch der Finanzwissenschaft*, vol. 3, 3rd edn (Tübingen: J. C. B. Mohr Verlag, 1981), pp. 1011–64; W. Abelshauser, *Deutsche Wirtschaftsgeschichte seit 1945* (München: Verlag C. H. Beck, 2004), pp. 275ff.

7.   R. Sturm, *Staatsverschuldung* (Opladen: Leske & Budrich Verlag, 1993), p. 39.

8.   W. Jäger, 'Die Innenpolitik der sozial-liberalen Koalition 1969–1974', in K. D. Bracher, W. Jäger and W. Link, *Republik im Wandel 1969–1974* (Stuttgart: Deutsche Verlags-Anstalt, 1986), pp. 15–160.

9.   W. Ehrlicher, 'Finanzwirtschaft, öffentliche II: Die Finanzwirtschaft der Bundesrepublik Deutschland', in W. Albers and A. Zottmann (eds), *Handwörterbuch der Wirtschaftswissenschaft*, vol. 3 (Stuttgart: UTB für Wissenschaft bei Vandenhoeck & Ruprecht, 1988), pp. 164–95; Caesar and Hansmeyer, 'Die finanzwirtschaftliche Entwicklung'; K. Littmann, *Definition und Entwicklung der Staatsquote: Abgrenzung, Aussagekraft und Anwendungsbereiche unterschiedlicher Typen von Staatsquoten* (Göttingen: Schwartz Verlag, 1975); Sachverständigenrat zur Begutachtung der gesamtwirtschaftlichen Entwicklung, *Vor weitreichenden Entscheidungen. Jahresgutachten 1998/99* (Stuttgart: Metzler-Poeschel Verlag, 1998),

table 33*; Caesar and Hansmeyer, 'Die finanzwirtschaftliche Entwicklung', p. 936; Bundesministerium der Finanzen (ed.), *Die finanzwirtschaftliche Entwicklung von Bund, Ländern und Gemeinden seit 1970* (Bonn: Bundesministerium der Finanzen, 1985), p. 6; Bundesministerium der Finanzen (ed.), *Finanzbericht 1985* (Bonn: Bundesministerium der Finanzen, 1985), p. 227.

10. E. Hobsbawm, *Das Zeitalter der Extreme* (München: Carl Hanser Verlag, 1995), p. 503.

11. Caesar and Hansmeyer, 'Die finanzwirtschaftliche Entwicklung', p. 940; Görtemaker, *Geschichte der Bundesrepublik*, pp. 563ff.; Jäger, 'Die Innenpolitik der sozial-liberalen Koalition', pp. 27ff.; A. Rödder, *Die Bundesrepublik Deutschland 1969–1990* (München: Oldenbourg Wissenschaftsverlag, 2004), pp. 43ff.; A. Baring and M. Görtemaker, *Machtwechsel: Die Ära Brandt-Scheel*, 4th edn (Stuttgart: Deutsche Verlags-Anstalt, 1993), pp. 650ff.; J. Hohensee, *Der erste Ölpreisschock, 1973/74: Die politischen und gesellschaftlichen Auswirkungen der arabischen Erdölpolitik auf die Bundesrepublik Deutschland und Westeuropa* (Stuttgart: Franz Steiner Verlag, 1996); H. K. Giersch, H. Paque and H. Schmieding, *Fading Miracle: Four Decades of Market Economy in Germany* (Cambridge: Cambridge University Press, 1992), pp. 150ff.; N. Kloten, 'Erfolg und Mißerfolg der Stabilisierungspolitik (1969–1974)', in Deutsche Bundesbank (ed.), *Währung und Wirtschaft 1876–1975* (Frankfurt: Knapp Verlag, 1976), pp. 643–90; A. Ehrlicher, *Die Finanzpolitik im Spannungsfeld zwischen konjunkturpolitischen Erfordernissen und Haushaltskonsolidierung* (Berlin: Duncker & Humblot, 1991); M. Hanswillemenke and B. Rahmann, *Zwischen Reformen und Verantwortung für Vollbeschäftigung: Die Finanzpolitik der sozial-liberalen Koalition 1969–1982* (Frankfurt: Lang Verlag, 1997); H. Scherf, *Enttäuschte Hoffnungen – vergebene Chancen: Die Wirtschaftspolitik der sozial-liberalen Koalition 1969–1982* (Göttingen: Vandenhoeck & Ruprecht, 1986), pp. 34ff.

12. D. Petzina, 'Zwischen Reform und Krise', in D. Petzina and J. Reulecke (eds), *Bevölkerung, Wirtschaft, Gesellschaft seit der Industrialisierung: Festschrift für Wolfgang Köllmann zum 65. Geburtstag* (Dortmund: Gesellschaft für Westfälische Wirtschaftsgeschichte, 1990), pp. 261–77, p. 269. See also W. Renzsch, *Finanzverfassung und Finanzausgleich: Die Auseinandersetzungen um ihre politische Gestaltung in der Bundesrepublik Deutschland zwischen Währungsreform und deutscher Vereinigung (1948–1990)* (Bonn: Verlag J. H. W. Dietz Nachf, 1991), pp. 261ff.; Bundesministerium der Finanzen, *Die finanzwirtschaftliche Entwicklung von Bund*, pp. 18ff.; K. Geppert et al., *Die wirtschaftliche Entwicklung der Bundesländer in den siebziger und achtziger Jahren: Eine vergleichende Analyse* (Berlin: Duncker & Humblot, 1987), pp. 146ff.; H. Zimmermann, *Kommunalfinanzen: Eine Einführung in die finanzwissenschaftliche Analyse der kommunalen Finanzwirtschaft* (Baden-Baden: Nomos-Verlagsgesellschaft, 1999); P. Marcus, *Das kommunale Finanzsystem der Bundesrepublik Deutschland* (Darmstadt: Wissenschaftliche Buchgesellschaft, 1987); H. Elsner, *Gemeindehaushalte, Konjunktur und Finanzausgleich: Die Notwendigkeit einer wirtschafts-, zentralitäts- und aufgabenpolitischen Fortsetzung der Gemeindefinanzreform* (Baden-Baden: Nomos-Verlagsgesellschaft, 1978).

13. Caesar and Hansmeyer, 'Die finanzwirtschaftliche Entwicklung', pp. 935–6; Sachverständigenrat, *Vor weitreichenden Entscheidungen*, table 33*; Bundesministerium für Arbeit und Sozialordnung (ed.), *Sozialbericht 1993* (Bonn:

Bundesministerium für Arbeit und Sozialordnung, 1994), p. 244. M. G. Schmidt, *Sozialpolitik in Deutschland: Historische Entwicklung und internationaler Vergleich*, 2nd edn (Opladen: Leske & Budrich Verlag, 1998), pp. 75ff.; M. G. Schmidt (ed.), *Geschichte der Sozialpolitik in Deutschland seit 1945*, vol. 7 (Baden-Baden: Nomos-Verlagsgesellschaft, 2005), pp. 63ff.

14. Sachverständigenrat, *Vor weitreichenden Entscheidungen*, tables 21*, 33*; T. Sarrazin, 'Die Finanzpolitik des Bundes 1970 bis 1982', *Finanzarchiv*, n.s. 41 (1983), pp. 373–87; Ehrlicher, *Die Finanzpolitik im Spannungsfeld*, pp. 16ff.; K. Franzen, *Die Steuergesetzgebung der Nachkriegszeit in Westdeutschland (1945–1961)* (Bremen: Kamloth Verlag, 1994), pp. 224ff.; J. Muscheid, *Steuerpolitik in der Bundesrepublik Deutschland 1949–1982* (Berlin: Duncker & Humblot, 1986), pp. 67ff.; Sachverständigenrat, *Vor weitreichenden Entscheidungen*, table 33*.

15. Ibid., tables 33*, 34*.

16. Ibid., tables 37*, 21*; Sturm, *Staatsverschuldung*, pp. 33ff.

17. R. Caesar, 'Öffentliche Verschuldung in Deutschland seit der Weltwirtschaftskrise', in D. Petzina (ed.), *Probleme der Finanzgeschichte des 19. und 20. Jahrhunderts* (Berlin: Duncker & Humblot, 1990), pp. 9–55, on p. 25.

18. U. Wagschal, *Staatsverschuldung* (Opladen: Leske & Budrich Verlag, 1996); E. Nowotny (ed.), *Öffentliche Verschuldung* (Stuttgart: S. Fischer Verlag, 1979); D. B. Simmert and K.-D. Wagner (eds), *Staatsverschuldung kontrovers* (Köln: Verlag Wissenschaft und Politik, 1981); E. Lang and W. A. S. Koch, *Staatsverschuldung – Staatbankrott?* (Würzburg: Physica-Verlag, 1980); K. Diehl and P. Mombert, *Das Staatsschuldenproblem* (Frankfurt: Ullstein-Verlag, 1980).

19. OECD, *Economic Outlook. Historical Statistics 1960–1985* (Paris: OECD, 1987), p. 64. For comparative studies, see R. J. Franzese, *Macroeconomic Policies of Developed Democracies* (Cambridge: Cambridge University Press, 2002); M. Hallerberg, *Domestic Budgets in a United Europe: Fiscal Governance from the End of Bretton Woods to EMU* (Ithaca, NY: B&T, 2004); U. Wagschal, *Steuerpolitik und Steuerreformen im internationalen Vergleich* (Münster: Literatur-Verlag, 2005), pp. 52ff., 105ff.; OECD, *Economic Outlook*, p. 63; OECD, *Revenue Statistics 1965–2001* (Paris: OECD, 2002), pp. 73ff.

20. Wagschal, *Steuerpolitik und Steuerreformen*, p. 107.

21. D. G. Skilling, *Policy Coordination, Political Structure and Public Debt: The Political Economy of Public Debt Accumulation in OECD Countries since 1960* (Ann Arbor, MI: University of Michigan Press, 2001); Franzese, *Macroeconomic Policies of Developed Democracies*, pp. 22ff., 126ff.; G. Corsetti and N. Roubini, 'Fiscal Deficits, Public Debt, and Government Solvency: Evidence from OECD Countries', *Journal of the Japanese and International Economies*, 5 (1991), pp. 354–80, on table 5; J.-C. Chouraqui, B. Jones and R. B. Montador, *Public Debt in a Medium-Term Context and its Implications for Fiscal Policy* (Paris: OECD, 1986), pp. 9–10; W. Leibfritz, D. Roseveare and P. Van Den Noord, *Fiscal Policy, Government Debt and Economic Performance* (Paris: OECD, 1994), pp. 80–1.

22. H.-P. Ullmann, *Der deutsche Steuerstaat: Geschichte der öffentlichen Finanzen vom 18. Jahrhundert bis heute* (München: Verlag C. H. Beck, 2005), pp. 205ff.

Stasavage, 'Conclusion'

1. Epstein, *Freedom and Growth*, ch. 2.
2. This is an argument that has been emphasized by Macdonald, *A Free Nation Deep in Debt*, though he simultaneously emphasizes the importance of democratic political institutions.
3. North and Weingast, 'Constitutions and Commitment'.
4. Stasavage 'Cities, Constitutions, and Sovereign Borrowing in Europe'.
5. W. P. Blockmans, 'Representation since the Thirteenth Century', in R. Mckitterick (ed.) *The New Cambridge Medieval History* (Cambridge: Cambridge University Press, 1997), pp. 29–64.

BIBLIOGRAPHY

United Kingdom Parliamentary Papers

'14th Report of the Commissioners to Examine, Take and State the Public Accounts', *Journals of the House of Commons*, 41 (1786).

'Report from the Select Committee on Accounts and other Papers Related to the Public Income and Expenditure', *Reports from Committees of the House of Commons*, 11 (1786).

'Commissioners for the Sinking Fund Annual Reports', *House of Commons Journals* (1792–1815).

'Report from the Committee appointed to Enquire into the Circumstances of the Negotiation of the Loan', *Journals of the House of Commons*, 51 (1796).

Parliamentary Debates, 31 vols (London: n.p, 1803–15) [vols 1–23: *Cobbett's Parliamentary Debates*; vols 24–31: *Hansard's Parliamentary Debates*].

Reports from the Select Committee to whom the 10th and 11th Reports of the Commissioners of Naval Enquiry were Referred, 2 (1805).

Cobbett's Parliamentary History, 36 vols (London: n.p., 1806–20).

Report of the Select Committee Appointed to Examine what Regulations and Checks have been Established in order to Control the Several Branches of Public Expenditure, 2 (1807).

Report together with Minutes of and Accounts from the Select Committee on the High Price of Gold Bullion, 3 (1810).

Report from the Select Committee on Funding Exchequer and Bills, 3 (1810).

Report of the Lords Committee of Secrecy to Enquire into the Causes which Produced the Order in Council of 26ᵗʰ February 1797, 3 (1810).

Report from the Select Committee Appointed to Consider the Effects of the Laws which Regulate or Restrain the Interest of Money, 6 (1818).

Reports from Committees of the Lords and Commons to Consider the State of the Bank of England with Reference to the Expediency of the Resumption of Cash Payments. 3 (1819).

Three Reports from the Committee of Secrecy on the Outstanding Demands of the Bank of England and on the Restriction of Payments in Cash 1797, 3 (1826).

Report from the Select Committee on Public Monies, 9 (1857).

Accounts of Public Income and Expenditure 1688–1869, 35 (1868–9).

Report of the Comptroller General for the National Debt Commissioners on their Proceedings Since 1786, 48 (1890–1).

History of the Funded Debt from 1694 to 1786, LII (1898).

Published Works

Abbad, F., and D. Ozanam, *Les intendants espagnols du XVIIIe siècle* (Madrid: Casa de Velázquez, 1992).

Abelshauser, W., *Deutsche Wirtschaftsgeschichte seit 1945* (München: Verlag C. H. Beck, 2004).

Acworth, A. W., *Financial Reconstructions in England, 1815–22* (London: P. S. King, 1925).

Agnoletto, S., *Lo Stato di Milano al principio del Settecento. Finanza pubblica, sistema fiscale e interessi locali* (Milano: FrancoAngeli, 2000).

Ago, R., 'Norme e regole: i ceti urbani davanti al notaio', in *Disuguaglianze: stratificazione e mobilità sociale nelle popolazioni italiane (dal sec. XIV agli inizi del secolo XX)*, 2 vols (Bologna: Cleup, 1997), vol. 2, pp. 540–1.

—, *Economia barocca. Mercato e istituzioni nella Roma del seicento* (Roma: Donzelli, 1998).

Aleati, G., and C. M. Cipolla, 'Aspetti e problemi dell'economia milanese nei secoli XVI e XVII', in *Storia di Milano*, 17 vols (Milano: Fondazione Treccani degli Alfieri, 1953–66), vol. 11, pp. 377–99.

Alonzi, L., 'I censi consegnativi nel XVI e XVII secolo tra "finzione" e "realtà"', *L'Acropoli*, 6:1 (2005), pp. 86–102.

Álvarez-Nogal, C., *El crédito de la Monarquía Hispánica durante el reinado de Felipe IV* (Valladolid: Junta de Castilla y León, 1997).

—, 'El factor general del rey y las finanzas de la monarquía hispánica', *Revista de Historia Económica*, 17:3 (1999) pp. 507–39.

—, 'Los problemas del vellón en el siglo XVII', *Revista de Historia Económica*, Extraodinary Number (2001), pp. 17–37.

—, 'Las compañías bancarias genovesas en Madrid a comienzos del siglo XVII', *Hispania*, 65–1:219 (2005), pp. 67–90.

Anderson, M. S., *The Rise of Modern Diplomacy, 1450–1919* (London: Logman, 1993).

Andrés Ucendo, J. I., *La fiscalidad en Castilla en el siglo XVII: los servicios de millones, 1601–1700* (Lejona: Universidad del País Vasco, 2000).

—, 'Castile's Fiscal System in the Seventeenth Century', *Journal of European Economic History*, 30 (2001), pp. 597–621.

Andújar Castillo, F., *Consejo y Consejeros de Guerra en el siglo XVIII* (Granada: Universidad de Granada, 1996).

—, 'La reforma militar en el reinado de Felipe V', in M. A. Bel Bravo, J. M. Delgado Barrado and J. Fernández García (eds), *El cambio dinástico y sus repercusiones en la España del siglo XVII* (Jaén: Universidad de Jaén, 2000), pp. 617–40.

—, *Tiempo de necesidad, tiempo de venalidad. España e Indias, 1705–1711* (forthcoming).

Angster, J., *Konsensliberalismus und Sozialdemokratie. Die Westernisierung von SPD und DGB* (München: Oldenbourg Wissenschaftsverlag, 2003).

Anon., *Considerations on the Annual Million Bill* (London: T. Payne and Son, J. Sewell, and W. Debrett, 1787).

—, *A Letter to the Right Hon. W. Pitt on his Conduct with respect to the Loan Concluded on 25th November 1796* (London: J. Debrett, 1796).

—, *Observations on the National Debt* (Norwich: J. March, 1797).

—, *The Calumnious Aspersions Contained in the Report of the Sub-Committee of the Stock Exchange* (London: Jones, 1814).

—, 'Inquiries with respect to the Influence of National Debts and Taxes', *Edinburgh Review*, 47 (1828), pp. 75–83.

Antoine, M., *Le Conseil du roi sous le règne de Louis XV* (Geneva: Droz, 1970).

Aquerreta, S., 'La participación de los financieros nacionales en la Guerra de Sucesión: el abastecimiento de víveres al ejército', in R. Torres Sánchez (ed.), *Capitalismo mercantil en la España del siglo XVIII* (Pamplona: EUNSA, 2000), pp. 273–314.

—, 'Financiar la Guerra de Sucesión: asentistas y compañías al servicio de Felipe V', in *La Guerra de Sucesión en España y América. Actas X Jornadas Nacionales de Historia Militar. Sevilla, 13–17 de noviembre de 2000* (Madrid: Deimos, 2001), pp. 569–82.

—, *Negocios y finanzas en el siglo XVIII: la familia Goyeneche* (Pamplona: EUNSA, 2001).

—, '"De su cuenta y riesgo y por vía de asiento": trayectoria y negocios de Francisco Mendinueta', in S. Aquerreta (ed.), *Francisco Mendinueta: Finanzas y mecenazgo en la España del siglo XVIII* (Pamplona: EUNSA, 2002), pp. 77–99.

Artola, M., *La Hacienda del Antiguo Régimen* (Madrid: Alianza Editorial, 1982).

Artoni, R., and S. Biancini, 'Il debito pubblico dall'Unità ad oggi', in P. Ciocca and G. Toniolo (eds), *Storia economica d'Italia*, 2 vols (Roma-Bari: Laterza, 2003), vol. 2, pp. 269–380.

Ashworth, W., *Customs and Excise: Trade Production and Consumption in England* (Oxford: Oxford University Press, 2003).

Atkeson, A., 'International Lending with Moral Hazard and Risk of Repudiation' *Econometrica*, 59:4 (1991), pp. 1069–89.

Balestracci, D., *La zappa e la retorica. Memorie familiari di un contadino toscano del Quattrocento* (Siena: Salimbeni, 1984).

Barbadoro, B., *Le finanze della repubblica fiorentina. Imposta diretta e debito pubblico fino all'istituzione del Monte* (Firenze: Olschki, 1929).

Barbero, A., *Un'oligarchia urbana. Politica ed economia a Torino fra tre e quattrocento* (Roma: Viella, 1995).

Barbieri, G., *Origini del capitalismo lombardo. Studi e documenti sull'economia milanese del periodo ducale* (Milano: Giuffrè, 1961).

Barducci, R., 'Politica e speculazione finanziaria a Firenze dopo la crisi del primo trecento (1343–1358)', *Archivio storico italiano*, 137 (1979), pp. 177–219.

—, 'Le riforme finanziarie nel tumulto dei Ciompi', in *Il Tumulto dei Ciompi; Un momento di storia fiorentina ed europa* (Firenze: Olschki, 1981), pp. 95–102.

Baring, A., and M. Görtemaker, *Machtwechsel: Die Ära Brandt-Scheel*, 4th edn (Stuttgart: Deutsche Verlags-Anstalt, 1993).

Barro, R., 'Government Spending, Interest Rates, Prices, and Budget Deficits in the United Kingdom, 1701–1918', *Journal of Monetary Economics*, 20 (1987), pp. 221–47.

Basas Fernández, M., 'Banqueros burgaleses del siglo XVI', *Boletín de la Institución Fernán González*, 163 (1964), pp. 314–32.

Bauer, C., 'Die Epochen der Papstfinanz. Ein Versuch', *Historische Zeitschrift*, 138 (1928), pp. 457–503.

Baugh, D., 'Great Britain's Blue Water Policy, 1689–1815', *International History Review*, 10:2 (1988), pp. 33–58.

Becker, M. B., 'Problemi della finanza pubblica fiorentina nella seconda metà del Trecento e nei primi del Quattrocento', *Archivio Storico Italiano*, 123 (1965), pp. 433–66.

—, 'Economic Change and the Emerging Florentine Territorial State', *Studies in the Renaissance* 13 (1966), pp. 7–39.

Beloch, K. J., *Storia della popolazione d'Italia*, a cura della Società Italiana di Demografia Storica (Firenze: Le Lettere, 1994).

Bernal, A. M., *España, proyecto inacabado: los costes y beneficios del imperio* (Madrid: Marcial Pons, 2005).

Berwick y de Alba, Duque de, *Correspondencia de Gutierre Gómez de Fuensalida* (Madrid: Real Academia de la Historia, 1907).

Binney, J. E. D., *British Public Finance and Administration, 1774–92* (Oxford: Oxford University Press, 1958).

Bird, H., *Proposals for Paying Off the Whole of the Present National Debt* (London: F. and C. Rivington, J. Stockdale, and W. J. and J. Richardson, 1799).

Black, J. G., *A System of Ambition? British Foreign Policy, 1660–1793* (London: Longman, 1991).

Blockmans, W. P., 'Le crédit public dans les Pays-Bas méridionaux au bas moyen âge', in H. Dubois (ed.), *Local and International Credit in the Middle Ages and the 16th Century* (Bern: Ninth International Economic History Congress, 1986), pp. 3–8.

—, 'Representation since the Thirteenth Century', in R. Mckitterick (ed.) *The New Cambridge Medieval History* (Cambridge: Cambridge University Press, 1997), pp. 29–64.

Bohmbach, J., 'Umfang und Struktur des Braunschweiger Rentenmarkts 1300–1350', *Niedersächsisches Jahrbuch für Landesgeschichte*, 41:2 (1969–70), p. 121.

Boislisle, A. M., *Correspondance des contrôleurs généraux des finances avec les intendants des provinces, publiée par ordre du ministre des finances d'après les documents conservés aux Archives nationales* (Paris: Imprimerie Nationale, 1874–97).

Bonney, R. (ed.), *Economic Systems and State Finance* (Oxford: Oxford University Press, 1995).

—, *The Rise of the Fiscal State in Europe c. 1200–1815* (Oxford: Oxford University Press, 1999).

—, 'Towards a Comparative Fiscal History of Britain and France during the "Long" Eighteenth Century', in L. Prados de la Escosura (ed.), *Exceptionalism and Industrialization. Britain and its European Rivals 1688–1815* (Cambridge: Cambridge University Press, 2004), pp. 191–215.

Bonney, R., and W. M. Ormrod, 'Introduction', in W. M. Ormrod, M. Bonney and R. Bonney, *Crises, Revolutions and Self-Sustained Growth. Essays in European Fiscal History, 1130–1830* (Stanford, CA: Shaun Tyas, 1999), pp. 1–21.

Boockmann, H., *Die Stadt im späten Mittelalter* (München: Beck-Verlag, 1986).

Borlandi, A., '"Al Real Servitio di S. Maestà". Genova e la Milano del Seicento', in *'Millain the Great'. Milano nelle brume del Seicento* (Milano: Cariplo, 1989).

Bowsky, W., *Le finanze del comune di Siena 1287–1355* (Firenze: La Nuova Italia, 1975).

Boyajian, J. C., *Portuguese Bankers at the Court of Spain 1626–1650* (New Brunswick, NJ: Rutgers University Press, 1983).

Boyd, W., *A Letter to the Right Honourable William Pitt*, 2nd edn (London: J. Ridgway, 1811).

Braddick, M. J., *The Nerves of State: Taxation and Financing of the English State, 1558–1714* (Manchester: Manchester University Press, 1996).

Braudel, F., *Civiltà e imperi nel Mediterraneo nell'età di Filippo II*, 2 vols (Torino: Einaudi, 1976).

Brewer, J. W., *The Sinews of Power: War, Money and the English State, 1688–1783* (New York: Alfred A. Knopf, 1989).

Browning, R. S., *The War of the Austrian Succession* (New York: St. Martin's Press, 1993).

Brucker, G., *Dal comune alla signoria. La vita pubblica a Firenze nel primo rinascimento* (Bologna: il Mulino, 1981).

Buchanan, J. N., and R. E. Wagner, *Democracy in Deficit: The Political Legacy of Lord Keynes* (New York: Academic Press, 1977).

Bulow, J., and K. Rogoff, 'A Constant Reconstructing Model of Sovereign Debt', *Journal of Political Economy*, 102:5 (1989), pp. 155–78.

Bundesministerium der Finanzen (ed.), *Die finanzwirtschaftliche Entwicklung von Bund, Ländern und Gemeinden seit 1970* (Bonn: Bundesministerium der Finanzen, 1985).

—, *Finanzbericht 1985* (Bonn: Bundesministerium der Finanzen, 1985).

Bundesministerium für Arbeit und Sozialordnung (ed.), *Sozialbericht 1993* (Bonn: Bundesministerium für Arbeit und Sozialordnung, 1994).

Buvat, J., *Journal de la Régence (1715–1723)* (Paris: H. Plon, 1865).

Caesar, R., 'Öffentliche Verschuldung in Deutschland seit der Weltwirtschaftskrise', in D. Petzina (ed.), *Probleme der Finanzgeschichte des 19. und 20. Jahrhunderts* (Berlin: Duncker & Humblot, 1990), pp. 9–55.

Caesar, R., and K. H. Hansmeyer, 'Die finanzwirtschaftliche Entwicklung', in K. G. A. Jeserich (ed.), *Deutsche Verwaltungsgeschichte*, vol. 5 (Stuttgart: Deutsche Verlags-Anstalt, 1988), pp. 919–45.

Calabria, A., *The Cost of Empire. The Finances of the Kingdom of Naples at the Time of Spanish Rule* (Cambridge: Cambridge University Press, 1991).

—, 'La finanza pubblica a Napoli nel primo Cinquecento', in A. Musi (ed.), *Nel sistema imperiale. L'Italia spagnola* (Naples: Edizioni Scientifiche Italiane, 1994), pp. 225–34.

Campbell, S., 'Usury and Annuities of the Eighteenth Century', *Law Quarterly Review*, 44 (1928), pp. 473–91.

—, 'The Economic and Social Effect of the Usury Laws in the Eighteenth Century', *Transactions of the Royal History Society*, 4:16 (1933), pp. 197–210.

Canosa, R., *Banchieri genovesi e sovrani spagnoli tra Cinquecento e Seicento* (Roma: Sapere 2000, 1998).

Carande, R., *Carlos V y sus banqueros*, 3 vols (Madrid: Crítica, 1990).

Carbajo Isla, M. F., *La población de la villa de Madrid desde mediados del siglo XVI hasta mediados del siglo XIX* (Madrid: Siglo XXI, 1987).

Carboni, M., *Il debito della città. Mercato del credito, fisco e società a Bologna fra Cinque e Seicento* (Bologna: Il Mulino, 1995).

Carlos Morales, C. J. de, 'El Consejo de Hacienda de Castilla en el reinado de Carlos V (1523–1556)', *Anuario de Historia del Derecho Español*, 69 (1989), p. 49–159.

—, *El Consejo de Hacienda de Castilla, 1523–1602. Patronazgo y clientelismo en el gobierno de las finanzas reales durante el siglo XVI* (Valladolid: Junta de Castilla y León, 1996).

—, '¿Una revolución financiera en tiempos de Felipe II? Dimensiones y evolución de los fundamentos de la Hacienda Real de Castilla, 1556–1598', in E. Belenguer (ed.), *Felipe II y el Mediterráneo*, 4 vols (Madrid: Sociedad Estatal para la Conmemoración de los Centenarios de Felipe II y Carlos V, 1999), vol. 1, pp. 473–504.

—, *Carlos V y el crédito de Castilla. El tesorero general de Francisco de Vargas y la Hacienda Real entre 1516 y 1524* (Madrid: Sociedad Estatal para la Conmemoración de los Centenarios de Felipe II y Carlos V, 2000).

Carruthers B. G., *Politics and Markets in the English Financial Revolution* (Princeton, J: Princeton University Press, 1996).

Castellani, F. di M., *Ricordanze*, ed. G. Ciappelli, 3 vols (Firenze: Olschki, 1992–5).

Castillo Pintado, A., 'Los juros de Castilla. Apogeo y fin de un instrumento de *crédito*', *Hispania*, 23:89 (1963), pp. 43–70.

Castro, C. de., 'El Estado español en el siglo XVIII: su configuración durante los primeros años del reinado de Felipe V', *Historia y política. Ideas, procesos y movimientos sociales*, 4 (2000), pp. 137–69.

—, *A la sombra de Felipe V. José de Grimaldo, ministro responsable (1703–1726)* (Madrid: Marcial Pons, 2004).

Caunedo del Potro, B., *Mercaderes castellanos en el golfo de Vizcaya (1475–1492)* (Madrid: Universidad Autónoma de Madrid, 1983).

Cavazzi della Somaglia, C. G., *Nuova inventione certissima, e facilissima per liberare la città di Milano e le provincie dello Stato da loro debiti senza cagionare alcuna Gravezza ma ben sì evidente, ed universale utilità* (Milano: Filippo Ghidolfi, [1648]).

Chabod, F., *Storia della politica estera italiana dal 1870 al 1896* (Bari, Laterza: 1951).

—, *Storia di Milano nell'età di Carlo V* (Torino: Einaudi, 1971).

Chamley, C., 'Contingent Government Liabilities against Private Expectations in England 1743–49' (mimeo: Boston University, 2007).

Chouraqui, J.-C., B. Jones and R. B. Montador, *Public Debt in a Medium-Term Context and its Implications for Fiscal Policy* (Paris: OECD, 1986).

Cipolla, C. M., *Mouvement Monétaires dans l'Etat de Milan (1580–1700)* (Paris: Armand Colin, 1952).

—, *Le avventure della lira* (Milano: Edizioni di Comunità, 1958).

Clark, G., 'The Political Foundations of Modern Economic Growth: Britain, 1540–1800, *Journal of Interdisciplinary History*, 26 (1996), pp. 563–88.

Colley, L., *Britons Forging the Nation, 1707–1837* (New Haven, CT: Yale University Press, 1992).

Collier, J. D., *Life of Abraham Newland* (London: B. Crosby and Co., 1808).

Colzi, F., '"Per maggiore facilità del commercio". I sensali e la mediazione mercantile e finanziaria a Roma nei secoli XVI–XIX', *Roma*, 6:3 (1998), pp. 397–425.

Combeau, Y., *Le comte d'Argenson (1696–1764), ministre de Louis XV* (Paris: École des Chartes, 1999).

Cone, C. B., 'Richard Price and Pitt's Sinking Fund of 1786', *Economic History Review*, 4:2 (1951), pp. 243–51.

Conklin, J., 'The Theory of Sovereign Debt and Spain under Philip II', *Journal of Political Economy*, 106:3 (1998), pp. 483–513.

Conti, E., *L'imposta diretta a Firenze nel quattrocento (1427–1494)* (Roma: Istituto Storico Italiano per il Medio Evo, 1984).

Cookson, J. E., *Lord Liverpool's Administration* (Edinburgh: Edinburgh University Press, 1975).

Corsetti, G., and N. Roubini, 'Fiscal Deficits, Public Debt and Government Solvency: Evidence from OECD Countries', *Journal of the Japanese and International Economies*, 5 (1991), pp. 354–80.

Costa, P., *Civitas. Storia della cittadinanza in Europa*, 4 vols (Roma-Bari: Laterza, 1999–2001).

Cova, A., 'Banchi e monti pubblici a Milano tra interessi privati e pubbliche necessità', in P. Pissavino and G. Signorotto (eds), *Lombardia borromaica Lombardia spagnola. 1554–1659*, 2 vols (Roma: Bulzoni, 1995), vol. 1, pp. 363–81.

Crouzet, F., *L'économie britannique et le blocus continental*, 2nd edn, 2 vols (Paris: Economica, 1987), 'Introduction', vol. 1, pp. v–cxiv.

Cuartas Rivero, M., 'El Consejo de Hacienda: su primera época', *Hacienda Pública Española*, 74 (1982), pp. 255–66.

D'Amico, S., 'Crisis and Trasformation: Economic Reorganization and Social Structures in Milan, 1570–1610', *Social History*, 25:1 (2000), pp. 1–21.

D'Arienzo, V., *L'arrendamento del sale dei Quattro Fondaci* (Salerno: Eleapress, 1996).

Da Silva, J. G., 'Le sconto à Gênes. A propos d'un croquis', *Annales*, 13 (1958), pp. 150–3.

Daunton, M., 'Trusting Leviathan: The Politics of Taxation, 1815–1914', in D. Winch and P. K. O'Brien (eds), *The Political Economy of British Historical Experience, 1688–1914* (Oxford, Oxford University Press, 2002), pp. 319–50.

—, *Trusting Leviathan* (Cambridge: Cambridge University Press, 2003)

De Gennaro, G., *L'esperienza monetaria a Roma in età moderna* (Napoli: Edizioni Scientifiche Italiane, 1980).

De Luca, G., *Commercio del denaro e crescita economica a Milano fra Cinquecento e Seicento* (Milano: Il Polifilo, 1996).

—, 'Tra funzioni di tutela e istanze di controllo del mercato urbano: i sensali milanesi durante l'età moderna', in P. Massa and A. Moioli (eds), *Dalla corporazione al mutuo soccorso. Organizzazione e tutela del lavoro tra XVI e XX secolo* (Milano, FrancoAngeli, 2004), pp. 191–204.

— 'Debito pubblico, mercato finanziario e cicli economici nel Ducato di Milano e nella Repubblica veneta durante l'età moderna', in G. De Luca and A. Moioli (eds), *Debito pubblico e mercati finanziari in Italia. Secoli XIII–XX* (Milano, FrancoAngeli, 2007).

De Luca, G., and A. Moioli (eds), *Debito pubblico e mercati finanziari in Italia. Secoli XIII–XX* (Milano: FrancoAngeli, 2007).

De Rosa, L., *Studi sugli arrendamenti: aspetti della distribuzione della ricchezza mobiliare nel Mezzogiorno continentale: 1649–1806* (Napoli: L'Arte Tipografica, 1958).

—, *Il Mezzogiorno spagnolo tra crescita e decadenza* (Milano: Il Saggiatore, 1987).

—, 'Introduzione', in L. De Rosa (ed.), *Il Mezzogiorno agli inizi del Seicento* (Bari and Rome: Laterza, 1994), pp. i–lx.

—, 'L'azienda e le finanze', in L. De Rosa and L. M. Enciso Recio (eds), *Spagna e Mezzogiorno d'Italia nell'età della transizione (1650–1760)*, 2 vols (Napoli: Edizioni Scientifiche Italiane, 1997), vol. 1, pp. 128–48.

—, 'Immobility and Change in Public Finance in the Kingdom of Naples, 1694–1806', *The Journal of European Economic History*, 28:1 (1998), pp. 9–28.

—, 'The Beginning of Paper-Money Circulation: The Neapolitan Public Banks, 1540–1650', *Journal of European Economic History*, 30:3 (2001), pp. 497–532.

De Vries, J., and A. M. van der Woude, *The First Modern Economy* (Cambridge: Cambridge University Press, 1997).

Dedieu, J. P., 'Un instrumento para la historia social: la base de datos Ozanam', *Cuadernos de Historia Moderna* 24 (2000), pp. 185–205.

—, 'La Nueva Planta en su contexto. Las reformas del aparato del Estado en el reinado de Felipe V', *Manuscrits*, 18 (2000), pp. 113–39.

—, 'Dinastía y élites de poder en el reinado de Felipe V', in P. F. Albaladejo (ed.), *Los Borbones. Dinastía y memoria denación en la España del siglo XVIII* (Madrid: Marcial Pons Historia, Casa de Velázquez, 2002), pp. 381–99.

Dedieu, J. P., and J. I. Ruiz Rodríguez, 'Tres momentos en la historia de la Real Hacienda', *Cuadernos de Historia Moderna*, 15 (1994), pp. 77–98.

Del Negro, M., F. Perri and F. Schivardi, *Tax Buyouts. Working Paper* (New York: New York University, 2006).

Del Treppo, M., 'Il re e il banchiere. Strumenti e processi di razionalizzazione dello stato aragonese di Napoli', in G. Rossetti (ed.), *Spazio, società, potere nell'Italia dei Comuni* (Napoli: Liguori, 1986), pp. 229–304.

Delumeau, J., *Vie économique et sociale de Rome dans la seconde moitié du XVIe siècle*, 2 vols (Paris: Boccard, 1957).

Di Vittorio, A., 'Il Banco di S. Carlo in Napoli ed il riformismo asburgico', *Rassegna economica*, 33:2 (1969), pp. 235–63.

Diago Hernando, M., 'Arrendadores arandinos al servicio de los Reyes Católicos', *Historia. Instituciones. Documentos*, 18 (1991), pp. 71–95.

Dickinson, H. T. (ed.), *Britain and the French Revolution* (Basingstoke: Macmillan, 1989).

Dickson, P. G. M. *The Financial Revolution in England. A Study in the Development of Public Credit, 1688–1756* (London and New York: St. Martin's, 1967; 2nd edn, Aldershot: Gregg Revivals, 1993).

Diehl, K., and P. Mombert, *Das Staatsschuldenproblem* (Frankfurt: Ullstein-Verlag, 1980).

Dini, B., *Manifattura, commercio e banca nella Firenze medievale* (Firenze: Nardini, 2001).

Dirlmeier, U. and G. Fouquet, 'Eigenbetriebe niedersächsischer Städte im Spätmittelalter', in C. Meckseper (ed.), *Stadt im Wandel. Kunst und Kultur des Bürgertums in Norddeutschland 1150–1650*, 3 vols (Stuttgart and Bad Cannstatt: Cantz-Verlag, 1985), vol. 3, pp. 157–279.

Dixit, A., and J. Londregan, 'Political Power and the Credibility of Government Debt', *Journal of Economic Theory*, 94 (2000).

Domínguez Ortiz, A., *Política y Hacienda de Felipe IV* (Madrid: Editorial de derecho financiero, 1960).

—, 'La población de Sevilla a mediados del siglo XVII', *Archivo Histórico Hispalense*, 221:71 (1989), pp. 3–15.

—, 'Juros y censos en la Castilla del Seiscientos: una sociedad de rentistas', in A. M. Bernal (ed.), *Dinero, moneda y crédito en la Monarquía Hispánica* (Madrid: Marcial Pons-ICO, 2000), pp. 789–807.

Doria, G., 'Conoscenza del mercato e sistema informativo: il know-how dei mercanti-finanzieri genovesi nei secoli XVI e XVII', in A. Maddalena and H. Kellenbenz (eds), *La Repubblica internazionale del denaro tra XV e XVII secolo* (Bologna: Il Mulino, 1986), pp. 57–122.

Doubleday, T., *Financial, Monetary and Statistical History of the United Kingdom, 1688–1847* (London: Effingham Wilson, 1847).

Douglas, S., *On the Principle of Free Competition* (1791).

Dubet, A., 'Administrar los gastos de la guerra: Juan Orry y las primeras reformas de Felipe V (1703–1705)', in A. Guimerá and V. Peralta (eds), *El Equilibrio de los Imperios: De Utrecht a Trafalgar. Actas de la VIII^a Reunión Científica de la Fundación Española de Historia Moderna (Madrid, 2–4 de junio de 2004)* (Madrid: Fundación Española de Historia Moderna, Consejo Superior de Investigaciones Científicas, Universidad Complutense, Sociedad Estatal de Conmemoraciones Culturales, 2005), pp. 483–501.

—, 'L'autorité royale et ses limites: les projets de Jean Orry pour l'administration des finances espagnole au début du XVIIIe siècle', in P. Fournier, J. P. Luis, L. Martín and N. Planas (eds), *Institutions et représentations du politique. Espagne – France – Italie, XVIIe–XXe siècles* (Clermont-Ferrand: Presses Universitaires Blaise Pascal, 2006), pp. 81–96.

—, '¿La importación de un modelo francés? Acerca de algunas reformas de la administración española a principios del siglo XVIII', in J. G. Castaño and J. Muñoz Rodríguez (eds), *El conflicto sucesorio, 1700–1715*, special issue of *Revista de Historia Moderna*, 25 (2007), pp. 207–33.

—, '¿Francia en España? La elaboración de los proyectos de reformas político-administrativas de Felipe V (1701–1703)', in A. Álvarez-Ossorio Alvariño and B. J. García (eds),

La pérdida de Europa. La Guerra de Sucesión por la Monarquía de España (Madrid: Fundación Carlos de Amberes – Universidad Autónoma de Madrid, 2007), pp. 293–311.

—, *Jean Orry et le gouvernement de l'Espagne (1701–1706)* (Clermont-Ferrand: Presses Universitaires Blaise Pascal, forthcoming).

—, 'La reforma en acción: gobernar la hacienda militar al principio de la Guerra de Sucesión (1701–1706)', *IX Reunión Científica de la FEHM – Málaga, 7 a 9 junio 2006* (forthcoming).

Dubois-Corneau, R., *Paris de Monmartel (Jean) banquier de la cour, receveur des rentes de la ville de Paris 1690–1766: origine et vie des frères Paris, munitionnaires des vivres et financiers; les logis de Monmartel* (Paris: E. Jean-Fontaine, 1917).

Dutot, E., *Réflexions politiques sur les finances et le commerce, 2 vols (*1738; Paris: E. Droz, 1935).

Duwendag, D. (ed.), *Der Staatssektor in der sozialen Marktwirtschaft: Vorträge und Diskussionsbeiträge der 43. Staatswissenschaftlichen Forschungstagung 1975 der Hochschule für Verwaltungswissenschaften Speyer* (Berlin: Duncker & Humblot, 1976).

Eaton, J., M. Gersovitz and J. E. Stiglitz, 'The Pure Theory of Country Risk', *European Economic Review: International Seminar on Macroeconomics*, 30:3 (1986), pp. 481–514.

Ebel, W., *Bürgerliches Rechtsleben zur Hansezeit in Lübecker Ratsurteilen* (Göttingen, Frankfurt am Main and Berlin: Musterschmidt-Verlag, 1990).

Ehrlicher, A., *Die Finanzpolitik im Spannungsfeld zwischen konjunkturpolitischen Erfordernissen und Haushaltskonsolidierung* (Berlin: Duncker & Humblot, 1991).

Ehrlicher, W., 'Finanzwirtschaft, öffentliche II: Die Finanzwirtschaft der Bundesrepublik Deutschland', in W. Albers and A. Zottmann (eds), *Handwörterbuch der Wirtschaftswissenschaft*, vol. 3 (Stuttgart: UTB für Wissenschaft bei Vandenhoeck & Ruprecht, 1988), pp. 164–95.

Ehrman, J., *The Younger Pitt: The Years of Acclaim* (London: Constable, 1969).

—, *The Younger Pitt: The Consuming Struggle* (London: Constable, 1996).

Eliot, F. P., *Demonstration, or Financial Remarks* (London: John Cawthorne, 1807).

Elkar, R. S., and G. Fouquet, 'Und sie bauten einen Turm ... Bemerkungen zur materiellen Kultur des Alltags in einer kleinen deutschen Stadt des Spätmittelalters', in R. S. Elkar, G. Fouquet and U. Dirlmeier (eds), *Öffentliches Bauen im Mittelalter und früher Neuzeit* (Siegen: Scripta Mercaturae-Verlag St Katharinen, 1992), pp. 293–328.

Ellermeyer, J., *Stade 1300–1399. Liegenschaften und Renten in Stadt und Land. Untersuchungen zur Wirtschafts und Sozialstruktur einer hansischen Landstadt im Spätmittelalter* (Stade: Selbstverlag des Stader Geschichts- und Heimatsvereins, 1975).

Elliott, J. H., 'The Decline of Spain', in T. Aston (ed.), *Crisis in Europe, 1550–1960. Essays from Past and Present* (London: Routledge & Kegan Paul, 1965), pp. 167–93.

—, 'A Europe of Composite Monarchies', *Past and Present*, 137 (1992), pp. 48–71.

Ellwein, T., *Krisen und Reformen: Die Bundesrepublik seit den sechziger Jahren*, 2nd edn (München: Deutscher Taschenbuch-Verlag, 1993).

Elsner, H., *Gemeindehaushalte, Konjunktur und Finanzausgleich: Die Notwendigkeit einer wirtschafts-, zentralitäts- und aufgabenpolitischen Fortsetzung der Gemeindefinanzreform* (Baden-Baden: Nomos-Verlagsgesellschaft, 1978).

Epstein, S. A., *Genoa and the Genoese, 958–1528* (Chapel Hill, NC: North Carolina University Press, 1996).

Epstein, S. R., *Freedom and Growth. The Rise of States and Markets in Europe, 1300–1750* (London: Routledge, 2000).

Ermice, M. C., *Le origini del Gran Libro del debito pubblico nel Regno di Napoli e l'emergere di nuovi gruppi sociali, 1806–1815* (Napoli: L'Arte Tipografica, 2005).

—, 'Le origini del Gran Libro del debito pubblico del Regno di Napoli e l'emergere di nuovi gruppi sociali (1806–1815)', in G. De Luca and A. Moioli (eds), *Debito pubblico e mercati finanziari in Italia. Secoli XIII–XX* (Milano: FrancoAngeli, 2007).

Esposito, A., 'Note sulle *societates officiorum* alla corte di Roma nel pontificato di Sisto IV', in B. Flug, M. Matheus and A. Rehberg (eds), *Kurie und Region. Festschrift für Brigide Schwarz zum 65. Geburtstag* (Stuttgart: Steiner, 2005), pp. 197–207.

Esteban Estríngana, A., *Guerra y finanzas en los Países Bajos católicos. De Farnesio a Spínola (1592–1630)* (Madrid: Ediciones del Laberinto, 2002).

—, 'Autopsia del despacho financiero. Ejecución y control de pagos en el tesoro militar del ejército de Flandes (siglo XVII)', *Obradoiro de historia moderna*, 12 (2003), pp. 47–78.

Faccini, L., *La Lombardia fra '600 e '700: riconversione economica e mutamenti sociali* (Milano: FrancoAngeli, 1988).

Fahlbusch, O., *Die Finanzverwaltung der Stadt Braunschweig seit dem großen Aufstand im Jahre 1374 bis zum Jahre 1425. Eine städtische Finanzreform im Mittelalter* (1913; Aalen: Scientia Verlag, 1970).

Fairman, W., *An Account of the Public Funds Transferable at the Bank of England* (1815; 7th edn, London: J. Richardson, 1824).

Farolfi, B., 'Brokers and Brokerage in Bologna from the Sixteenth to the Nineteenth Century', in A. Guenzi, P. Massa and F. Piola Caselli, *Guilds, Markets and Work Regulations in Italy, 16th–19th Centuries* (Aldershot: Ashgate, 1998), pp. 306–22.

Faure, E., *La Banqueroute de Law* (Paris: Gallimard, 1977).

Felloni, G., *Gli investimenti finanziari genovesi in Europa tra il Seicento e la Restaurazione* (Milano: Giuffré, 1971).

—, 'Introduzione', in G. Felloni (ed.), *Inventario dell'Archivio del Banco di San Giorgio (1407–1805)*, 4 vols (Roma: Ministero dei Beni Culturali, 1989–2001), vol. 4, part 1.

—, 'Finanze statali, emissioni monetarie ed alterazioni della moneta di conto in Italia nei secoli XVI–XVIII', in G. Felloni, *Scritti di storia economica*, 2 vols (Genova: Società ligure di storia patria, 1999), vol. 1, pp. 471–96.

—, 'Il Banco di San Giorgio e il suo archivio: una memoria a più valenze', in G. Felloni, *Scritti di storia economica*, 2 vols (Genova: Società ligure di storia patria, 1999), vol. 1, pp. 461–8.

—, *Scritti di storia economica*, 2 vols (Genova: Società ligure di storia patria, 1999).

—, 'Stato genovese, finanza pubblica e ricchezza privata: un profilo storico', in G. Felloni, *Scritti di storia economica*, 2 vols (Genova: Società ligure di storia patria, 1999), vol. 1, pp. 275–95.

—, 'Ricchezza privata, credito e banche: Genova e Venezia nei sec. XII–XV', in *Genova, Venezia. Il Levante nei secoli XII–XV* (Genova : Società ligure di storia patria, 2001), pp. 295–318.

—, *Genoa and the History of Finance: A Series of First?* (Genova: Banco di San Giorgio, 2005).

Fenicia, G., *Il regno di Napoli e la difesa del Mediterraneo nell'età di Filippo II (1556–1598). Organizzazione e finanziamento* (Bari: Cacucci, 2003).

Fenoaltea, S., *L'economia italiana dall'unità alla grande guerra* (Roma-Bari: Laterza, 2006).

Ferguson, N., *The Cash Nexus. Money and Power in the Modern World, 1700–2000* (London: Allen Lane, 2001).

Fetter, F. W., 'The Politics of the Bullion Report', *Economica*, 26:102 (1959), pp. 99–103.

Forbonnais, F. V. D. de, *Recherches et considérations sur les finances de France, depuis l'année 1595 jusqu'à l'année 1721, 6 vols* (Liege: n.p., 1758).

Franke, G., *Lübeck als Geldgeber Lünebergs* (Neumünster: K. Wachholtz, 1935).

Franzen, K., *Die Steuergesetzgebung der Nachkriegszeit in Westdeutschland (1945–1961)* (Bremen: Kamloth Verlag, 1994).

Franzese, R. J., *Macroeconomic Policies of Developed Democracies* (Cambridge: Cambridge University Press, 2002).

Freitag, W., 'Die Salzstadt – Alteuropäische Strukturen und frühmoderne Innovation. Eine Einführung', in W. Freitag (ed.), *Die Salzstadt: Alteuropäische Strukturen und frühmoderne Innovation*, Studien zur Regionalgeschichte 19 (Bielefeld: Verlag für Regionalgeschichte, 2004), pp. 9–37.

Frend, W., *The National Debt in its True Colours* (London: J. Mawman, 1817).

Frenz, T., *Die Kanzlei der Päpste der Hochrenaissance (1471–1527)* (Tübingen: Niemeyer, 1986).

Frese, M., J. Paulus and K. Teppe (eds), *Demokratisierung und gesellschaftlicher Aufbruch: Die sechziger Jahre als Wendezeit der Bundesrepublik* (Paderborn: Schöningh Verlag, 2003).

Friedland, K., *Der Kampf der Stadt Lüneburg mit ihren Landesherren. Stadtfreiheit und Fürstenhoheit im 16. Jahrhundert* (Hildesheim: Buchdruckerei August Lax, 1953).

Fritschy, W., 'A "Financial Revolution" Reconsidered: Public Finance in Holland during the Dutch Revolt, 1568–1648', *Economic History Review*, 56:1 (2003), pp. 57–89.

Führ, C. and C. L. Furck (eds), *Handbuch der deutschen Bildungsgeschichte*, vol. 6 (München: Verlag C. H. Beck, 1998).

Galasso, G., *Alla periferia dell'impero. Il Regno di Napoli nel periodo spagnolo (secc. XVI–XVII)* (Torino: Einaudi, 1994).

Galbraith, J. K., *Gesellschaft im Überfluß* (München: Droemersche Verlags-Anstalt, 1958).

García, C. de la, 'La reforma de la Hacienda Madrileña en la época de Carlos II', *Equipo Madrid, Carlos III, Madrid y la Ilustración. Contradicciones de un proyecto reformista* (Madrid: Siglo XXI, 1988), pp. 77–101.

García, D. A., 'La configuración de lo ordinario en el sistema fiscal de la Monarquía. Una o dos ideas', *Studia Historica. Historia Moderna*, 21 (1999), pp. 117–52.

—, 'Dinero en Castilla. Notas sobre el pago de guardas en 1523', *Tiempos Modernos*, 8 (2003), pp. 1–18, <http://www.tiemposmodernos.org>.

—, 'El sistema fiscal castellano (1503–1536). Elementos de análisis, palabras de discusión', in F. J. Guillamón Álvarez, J. D. Muñoz Rodríguez and D. Centenero de Arce (eds), *Entre Clío y Casandra. Poder y sociedad en la Monarquía Hispánica durante la Edad Moderna* (Murcia: Universidad de Murcia, 2005), pp. 235–55.

—, 'Entre Granada y Castilla. La familia Fuente y la hacienda real a comienzos de la Edad Moderna', *Investigaciones Históricas*, 25 (2005), pp. 11–30.

—, 'Tras la muerte de la reina: Isabel I y la Hacienda Real de Castilla en la crisis dinástica de 1504–1507', in M. V. López-Cordón and G. Franco (eds), *La reina Isabel y las reinas de España: realidad, modelos e imagen historiográfica. Actas de la VIII Reunión Científica de la Fundación Española de Historia Moderna* (Madrid: Fundación Española de Historia Moderna, 2005), pp. 203–17.

—, 'Ducados entre dos dinastías. La circulación de capital entre Castilla y Flandes a comienzos del siglo XVI', in C. Sanz and B. García (eds), *Banca, crédito y capital. La Monarquía Hispánica y los antiguos Países Bajos (1505–1700)* (Madrid: Fundación Carlos de Amberes, 2006), pp. 85–104.

—, 'Poder financiero y arrendadores de rentas reales en Castilla a principios de la Edad Moderna', *Cuadernos de Historia Moderna*, 31 (2006), pp. 117–38.

—, *El erario del reino. Fiscalidad en Castilla a principios de la Edad Moderna (1504–1525)* (Valladolid: Junta de Castilla y León, 2007).

—, 'Fisco, poder y monarquía en los albores de la Modernidad. Castilla, 1504–1525' (Phd dissertation, Universidad Complutense, Madrid, 2007), <http://www.ucm.es/BUCM/tesis/ghi/ucm-t27728.pdf>.

—, 'Le gouvernment des finances royales au début de l'époque moderne (1504–1523)', in A. Dubet (ed.), *Administrer les finances dan la monarchie espagnole (XVI-XIX) siècle* (Clermont-Ferrand: Presses Universitaires Blaise-Pascal, forthcoming).

García-Cuenca, T., 'El Consejo de Hacienda (1576–1803)', in M., Artola (ed.), *La economía española al final del Antiguo Régimen. IV. Instituciones* (Madrid: Alianza and Banco de España, 1982), pp. 405–502.

García Guerra, E., *Carlo V e il sistema finanziario milanese. 2. La coniazione delle monete*, in M. Fantoni (ed.), *Carlo V e l'Italia* (Roma, Bulzoni, 2000), pp. 245–55.

Gelabert, J. E., 'Sobre la fundación del Consejo de Hacienda', in J. I. Fortea Pérez and C. M. Cremades Griñán (eds), *Política y hacienda en el Antiguo Régimen. II Reunión Científica de la Asociación de Historia Moderna* (Murcia: Universidad de Murcia, 1992), pp. 83–95.

—, *La bolsa del rey* (Barcelona: Crtítica, 1997).

—, 'Tráfico de oficios y gobierno de los pueblos en Castilla (1543–1643)', in L. A. Ribot García and L. de Rosa (eds), *Ciudad y mundo urbano en la época moderna* (Madrid: El Rio de Eráclito, 1997), pp. 157–86.

—, 'The King's Expenses: The Asientos of Philip III and Philip IV of Spain, 1598–1650', in W. M. Ormrod, M. Bonney and R. Bonney, *Crises, Revolutions and Self-Sustained Growth* (Stamford, CA: Shaun Tyas, 1999), pp. 224–49.

—, 'La Hacienda Real de Castilla, 1598–1652', in A. M. Bernal (ed.), *Dinero, moneda y crédito en la Monarquía Hispanica* (Madrid: Marcial Pons, 2000), pp. 839–61.

Gelderblom, O. and J. Jonker, 'Completing a Finacial Revolution: The Finance of the Dutch East Indian Trade and the Rise of the Amsterdam Capital Market, 1596–1621', *Journal of Economic History*, 64:3 (2004), pp. 641–72.

—, 'Amsterdam as the Cradle of Modern Futures and Options Trading, 1550–1650', in W. Goetzman and G. Rouwenhorst (eds), *Origins of Value. Financial Innovations in History* (New York: Oxford University Press, 2005), pp. 189–205.

—, 'Probing a Virtual Market. Interest Rates and the Trade in Government Bonds in the Dutch Republic', paper presented at the seminar on The Origins and Development of Financial Markets and Institutions, Urbana, IL, 27–9 April 2006.

—, 'Exploring the Market for Government Bonds in the Dutch Republic (1600–1800)', paper presented at the Séminaires d'histoire économique Atelier François Simiand, Campus Paris-Jordan, 18 December 2006, <http://www.paris-jordan.ens.fr/depot/semin/texte0607/GEL2006EXP.pdf>, pp. 1–26 [accessed 31 January 2007].

Geppert, K., et al., *Die wirtschaftliche Entwicklung der Bundesländer in den siebziger und achtziger Jahren: Eine vergleichende Analyse* (Berlin: Duncker & Humblot, 1987).

Giacomelli, G., 'Conservazione e innovazione nell'assistenza bolognese del Settecento', in *Forme e soggetti dell'intervento assistenziale in una città d'antico regime* (Bologna: Istituto per la storia di Bologna, 1986), pp. 269–302.

Giannini, M. C., 'Un caso di stabilità politica nella monarchia asburgica: comunità locali, finanza pubblica e clero nello Stato di Milano durante la prima metà del Seicento', in F. J. Guillamón Álvarez and J. J. Ruiz Ibáñez (eds), *Lo conflictivo y lo consensual en Castilla. Sociedad y poder político 1521–1715* (Murcia: Universidad de Murcia, 2001), pp. 99–162.

Giersch, H. K., H. Paque and H. Schmieding, *The Fading Miracle: Four Decades of Market Economy in Germany* (Cambridge: Cambridge University Press, 1992).

Gilomen, H. J., 'La prise de décision en matière d'emprunts dans les villes suisses au XVe siècle', in M. Boone, K. Davids and P. Janssens (eds), *Urban Public Debts. Urban*

Government and the Market for Annuities in Western Europe (14th–18th Centuries) (Turnhout: Brepols, 2003), pp. 127–48.

Ginatempo, M., *Prima del debito. Finanziamento della spesa pubblica e gestione del deficit nelle grandi città toscane (1200–1350 ca.)* (Firenze: Olschki, 2001).

Goldscheid, R., *Staatssozialismus oder Staatekapitalismus* (Wien: Anzengruber, 1917).

—, 'A Sociological Approach to Problems of Public Finance' (1925), in R. A. Musgrave and A. T. Peacock (eds), *Classics in the Theory of Public Finance* (London and New York: Macmillan, 1958), pp. 202–13.

Goldthwaithe, R., 'Lorenzo Morelli, Ufficiale del Monte, 1484–88: interessi privati e cariche pubbliche nella Firenze laurenziana', *Archivio Storico Italiano*, 154 (1996), pp. 605–33.

Gomes, L., *Foreign Trade and the National Economy* (Basingstoke: Macmillan, 1987).

González Enciso, A., 'El coste de la guerra y su gestión: las cuentas del tesorero del ejército en la guerra con Portugal de 1762', in A. Guimerá and V. Peralta (eds), *El Equilibrio de los Imperios: De Utrecht a Trafalgar. Actas de la VIIIª Reunión Científica de la Fundación Española de Historia Moderna (Madrid, 2–4 de junio de 2004)* (Madrid : Fundación Española de Historia Moderna, Consejo Superior de Investigaciones Científicas, Universidad Complutense, Sociedad Estatal de Conmemoraciones Culturales, 2005), pp. 551–64.

—, 'Las finanzas reales y los hombres de negocios en el siglo XVIII', in A. Dubet (ed.), *Administrer les finances royales dans la monarchie espagnole (XVIe–XIXe siècles)* (Rennes: Presses Universitaires de Rennes, forthcoming).

González Enciso, A., and R. Torres Sánchez (eds), *Tabaco y economía en el siglo XVIII* (Pamplona: EUNSA, 1999).

Gordon, N., *Political Economy in Parliament* (London: Macmillan, 1976).

Görtemaker, M., *Geschichte der Bundesrepublik: Von der Gründung bis zur Gegenwart* (München: Verlag C. H. Beck, 1999).

Greif, A., 'Contract Enforceability and Economic Institutions in Early Trade: The Maghribi Traders' Coalition', *American Economic Review*, 83:3 (1993), pp. 525–48.

Greif, A., P. Milgrom and B. R. Weingast, 'Coordination, Commitment, and Enforcement: The Case of the Merchant Guild', *Journal of Political Economy*, 102:4 (1994), pp. 745–76.

Grellier, J. J., *A History of the National Debt* (London: John Richardson, 1810).

—, *The Terms of All the Loans Which Have Been Raised for the Public Service*, 3rd edn (London: John and J. M. Richardson, 1812).

Grenville, Lord W. W., *Essay on the Supposed Advantages of the Sinking Fund* (London: J. Murray, 1828).

Grillo, P., 'L'introduzione dell'estimo e la politica fiscale del comune di Milano alla metà del secolo XIII (1240–1260)', in P. Mainoni (ed.), *Politiche finanziarie e fiscali nell'Italia settentrionale (secoli XIII-XV)* (Milano: Unicopli, 2001), pp. 11–37.

Grimm, D. (ed.), *Staatsaufgaben* (Frankfurt: Suhrkamp Verlag, 1996).

Gross, H., *Rome in the Age of Enlightenment: The Post Tridentine Syndrome and the Ancient Regime* (Cambridge: Cambridge University Press, 1990).

Grossman H., and J. B. Van Huyck, 'Sovereign Debt as a Contingent Claim: Excusable Default, Repudiation and Reputation', *American Economic Review*, 78:5 (1988), pp. 1088–97.

Hales, C., *The Bank Mirror, or A Guide to the Funds* (London: W. Treppass, 1796).

Hallerberg, M., *Domestic Budgets in a United Europe: Fiscal Governance from the End of Bretton Woods to EMU* (Ithaca, NY: B&T, 2004).

Hamilton, E., *Guerra y precios en España* (Madrid: Alianza, 1988).

Hamilton, R., *An Inquiry concerning the Rise and Progress, the Redemption and Present State, and the Management of the National Debt of Great Britain* (Edinburgh: Oliphant, Waugh and Innes, 1814).

Hamon, P., *'Messieurs des finances'. Les grands officiers de finance dans la France de la Renaissance* (París, Comité pour l'histoire économique et financière de la France, 1999).

Hanotin, G., 'Jean Orry, un homme des finances royales entre France et Espagne (1652–1705)' (unpublished thesis, Université Paris-Sorbonne, 2003).

Hanswillemenke, M., and B. Rahmann, *Zwischen Reformen und Verantwortung für Vollbeschäftigung: Die Finanzpolitik der sozial-liberalen Koalition 1969–1982* (Frankfurt: Lang Verlag, 1997).

Hargreaves, E. L., *The National Debt* (London: Arnold, 1930).

Harley, C. K., 'Goschen's Conversion of the National Debt and the Yield on Consols', *Economic History Review*, 29 (1976), pp. 101–6.

Harsin, P., *Les doctrines monétaires et financières en France du XVIe au XVIIIe siècle* (Paris: F. Alcan, 1928).

—, *Crédit public et banque d'état en France du XVIe au XVIIIe siècle* (Paris: E. Droz, 1933).

Hart, M. 't, *The Making of a Bourgeois State. War, Politics and Finance during the Dutch Revolt* (Manchester and New York: Manchester University Press, 1993).

—, 'The United Provinces, 1579–1806', R. Bonney (ed.), *The Rise of the Fiscal State in Europe c. 1200–1815* (Oxford: Oxford University Press, 1999), pp. 309–25.

—, 'Money and Trust. Amsterdam Moneylenders and the Rise of the Modern State, 1478–1794', paper presented at the XIVth International Economic History Congress, Helsinki, 26 August 2006, <http://www.helsinki.fi/iehc2006/papers1/Hart13.pdf>, pp. 1–25.

Haupt, H.-G., and J. Requate, *Aufbruch in die Zukunft: Die 1960er Jahre zwischen Planungseuphorie und kulturellem Wandel* (Weilerswist: Velbrück Wissenschaft, 2004).

Hecht, M., 'Geburtsstand oder Funktionselite? Ueberlegungen zum 'Salzpatriziat' im Zeitraum von 1400 bis 1700', in W. Freitag (ed.), *Die Salzstadt: Alteuropäische*

Strukturen und frühmoderne Innovation, Studien zur Regionalgeschichte 19 (Bielefeld: Verlag für Regionalgeschichte, 2004), pp. 83–116.

Heers, J., *Gênes au XVe siècle* (Paris: Sevpen, 1961).

Heras, J. L. de las, 'La jurisdicción del Consejo de Hacienda en tiempos de los Austrias', in C. M. Cremades Griñán (ed.), *Estado y fiscalidad en el Antiguo Régimen* (Murcia: Universidad de Murcia, 1989), pp. 117–27.

Herlihy, D., 'Family and Property in Renaissance Florence', in D. Herlihy, *Cities and Society in Medieval Italy* (London: Variorum, 1980), essay 13.

Hernández, B., 'Hombres de negocios y finanzas públicas en la Cataluña de Felipe II', *Revista de Historia Económica*, 15:1 (1997), pp. 65–81.

—, *Fiscalidad de reinos y deuda pública en la Monarquía Hispanica del siglo XVI* (Cordoba: Universidad de Cordoba, 2002).

Hernández Escayola, M. C., 'Los últimos arrendatarios del tabaco en Navarra (1700–1717)', in A. González Enciso and R. Torres Sánchez (eds), *Tabaco y economía en el siglo XVIII* (Pamplona: EUNSA, 1999), pp. 355–89.

—, *De tributo para la Iglesia a negocio para mercaderes: el arrendamiento de las rentas episcopales en la diócesis de Pamplona (siglo XVIII)* (Pamplona: EUNSA, 2000).

—, 'Las posibilidades de hacer negocios en Navarra a principios del siglo XVIII: el caso de Juan Mendinueta', in S. Aquerreta (ed.), *Francisco Mendinueta: Finanzas y mecenazgo en la España del siglo XVIII* (Pamplona: EUNSA, 2002), pp. 31–76.

—, *Negocio y servicios: finanzas públicas y hombres de negocios en Navarra en la primera mitad del siglo XVIII* (Pamplona: EUNSA, 2004).

Hernández-Esteve, E., *Creación del Consejo de Hacienda de Castilla (1523–1525)* (Madrid: Banco de España, 1983).

—, 'Estructuras y atribuciones del Consejo de Hacienda durante su proceso constituyente', *Cuadernos de Investigación Histórica*, 8 (1984), pp. 35–64.

Hilton, B., *Corn, Cash and Commerce* (Oxford: Oxford University Press, 1977).

Hobsbawm, E., *Das Zeitalter der Extreme* (München: Carl Hanser Verlag, 1995).

Hockerts, H. G., 'Metamorphosen des Wohlfahrtsstaats', in M. Broszat (ed.), *Zäsuren nach 1945: Essays zur Periodisierung der deutschen Nachkriegsgeschichte* (München: Oldenbourg Verlag, 1990), pp. 35–46.

Hoffman, P. T., and K. Norberg (eds), *Fiscal Crises, Liberty and Representative Government, 1450–1789* (Stanford, CA: Stanford University Press, 1994).

Hoffman, P. T., G. Postel-Vinay and J.-L. Rosenthal, *Priceless Markets. The Political Economy of Credit in Paris, 1660–1870* (Chicago, IL: University of Chicago Press, 2000).

Hoffmann, E., 'Lübeck im Hoch und Spätmittelalter: die große Zeit Lübecks', in A. Graßmann (ed.), *Lübeckische Geschichte* (Lübeck: Schmidt-Römhild Verlag, 1988), pp. 103–32.

Hofmann, W. von, *Forschungen zur Geschichte der kurialen Behörden von Schisma bis zur Reformation*, 2 vols (Rom: Loescher, 1914).

Hohensee, J., *Der erste Ölpreisschock, 1973/74: Die politischen und gesellschaftlichen Auswirkungen der arabischen Erdölpolitik auf die Bundesrepublik Deutschland und Westeuropa* (Stuttgart: Franz Steiner Verlag, 1996).

Holsti, K. J., *Peace and War. Armed Conflicts and International Order, 1648–1989* (Cambridge: Cambridge University Press, 1991).

Hopkins, T., *Great Britain for the last Forty Years* (London: Simpkin and Marshall, 1834).

Hoppit, J., 'Checking the Leviathan, 1688–1832', in D. Winch and P. K. O'Brien (eds), *The Political Economy of British Historical Experience, 1688–1914* (Oxford: Oxford University Press, 2002), pp. 267–94.

Huber, P., *Der Haushalt der Stadt Hildesheim am Ende des 14. Jahrhunderts und in der ersten Hälfte des 15. Jahrhunderts* (Leipzig: Jäh & Schunke, 1901).

Huskisson, W., *Substance of a Speech* (London: J. Murray, 1813).

Ibáñez Molina, M., 'Notas sobre la introducción de los intendentes en España', *Anuario de Historia Contemporánea*, 9 (1982), pp. 5–27.

Isenmann, E., *Die deutsche Stadt im Spätmittelalter* (Stuttgart: Ulmer Verlag, 1988).

Jäger, W., 'Die Innenpolitik der sozial-liberalen Koalition 1969–1974', in K. D. Bracher, W. Jäger and W. Link, *Republik im Wandel 1969–1974* (Stuttgart: Deutsche Verlags-Anstalt, 1986), pp. 15–160.

James, H., *State of the Nation: Causes and effects of the rise and fall in the Value of Property* (London: Saunders & Otley, 1835).

Jones, J. R., *Britain and the World, 1649–1815* (Brighton: Harvester Press, 1980).

Joslin, D. M., 'London Bankers in Wartime, 1739–84', in L. S. Pressnell (ed.), *Studies in the Industrial Revolution* (London: Athlone Press, 1960), pp. 156–77.

Kamen, H., *La Guerra de Sucesión en España, 1710–1715* (Barcelona, Buenos Aires and México DF: Grijalbo, 1974).

Kaplan, S. L., 'The Paris Bread Riot of 1725', *French Historical Studies*, 14:1 (1985), pp. 23–56.

Kellenbenz, H., *Los Fugger en España y Portugal hasta 1560* (Salamanca: Junta de Castilla y León, 2000).

Kennedy, P., *The Rise and Fall of Great Power* (London: Fontana Press, 1988).

Kirchgässner, B., 'Währungspolitik, Stadthaushalt und soziale Fragen südwestdeutscher Reichsstädte im Spätmittelalter. Menschen und Kräfte zwischen 1360 und 1460', *Jahrbuch für Geschichte der oberdeutschen Reichsstädte*, 11 (1965), pp. 90–127.

Kirshner, J., 'Papa Eugenio IV e il Monte Comune. Documenti su investimento e speculazione nel debito pubblico di Firenze', *Archivio Storico Italiano*, 127 (1969), pp. 339–82.

—, '*Civitas sibi faciat civem*: Bartolus of Sassoferrato's Doctrine on the Making of a Citizen', *Speculum*, 48 (1973), pp. 694–713.

—, 'The Moral Problem of Discounting Genoese *Paghe*, 1450–1550', *Archivum Fratrum Praedicatorum*, 47 (1977), pp. 109–67.

—, 'Encumbering Private Claims to Public Debt in Renaissance Florence', in V. Piergiovanni (ed.), *The Growth of the Bank as Institution and the Development of Money-Business Law* (Berlin: Duncker & Humblot, 1993), pp. 19–75.

—, 'Angelo degli Ubaldi and Bartolomeo da Saliceto on Priviliged Risk: Investments of Luchino Novello Visconti in the Public Debt (Monte Comune) of Florence', *Rivista internazionale di diritto comune*, 14 (2003), pp. 83–117.

Kirshner, J., and J. Klerman, 'The Seven Percent Fund of Renaissance Florence', in *Banchi pubblici, banchi private e monti di pietà nell'Europa preindustriale. Amministrazione, tecniche operative e ruoli economici* (Genova: Società ligure di storia patria, 1991), pp. 367–98.

Kitterer, W., 'Öffentliche Finanzen und Notenbank', in Deutsche Bundesbank (ed.), *Fünfzig Jahre Deutsche Mark: Notenbank und Währung in Deutschland seit 1948* (München: Verlag C. H. Beck, 1998), pp. 199–256.

Kloten, N., 'Erfolg und Mißerfolg der Stabilisierungspolitik (1969–1974)', in Deutsche Bundesbank (ed.), *Währung und Wirtschaft 1876–1975* (Frankfurt: Knapp Verlag, 1976), pp. 643–90.

Klovland, J. T., 'Pitfalls in the Estimation of the Yield on British Consols, 1850–1914', *Journal of Economic History*, 54 (1994), pp. 164–87.

Knipping, R., 'Das Schuldenwesen der Stadt Köln im 14. und 15. Jahrhundert', in *Westdeutsche Zeitschrift für Geschichte und Kunst*, 13 (1894), pp. 340–97.

—, *Die Kölner Stadtrechnungen des Mittelalters, mit einer Darstellung der Finanzverwaltung*, 2 vols (Bonn: Behrendt-Verlag, 1897–8).

Koenigsberger, H. G., Review of J. D. Tracy, 'Emperor Charles V, Impresario of War. Campaign Strategy, International Finance and Domestic Politics', *International History Review*, 25 (3 September 2003), pp. 646–8.

Körner, M., 'Public Credit', in R. Bonney (ed.), *Economic Systems and State Finance* (Oxford: Oxford University Press, 1995), pp. 515–48.

Kuppers, W., *Die Stadtrechnungenvon Geldern 1386–1423* (Geldern: Johannes Keuck, 1993).

Kuske, B., 'Das Schuldenwesen der deutschen Städte im Mittelalter', *Zeitschrift für die gesamten Staatswissenschaften, Ergänzungsheft*, 12 (1904).

Kwass, M., *Privilege and the Politics of Taxation in Eighteenth-Century France: liberté, égalité, fiscalité* (Cambridge: Cambridge University Press, 2000).

La Porta, R., F. Lopez de Silanes, A. Shleifer and R. Vishny, 'Legal Determinants of External Finance', *Journal of Finance*, 52 (1997), pp. 1131–50.

Ladero Quesada, M. A., *La Hacienda Real de Castilla en el siglo XV* (La Laguna: Universidad de La Laguna, 1973).

—, M. A., *Castilla y la conquista del reino de Granada* (Granada: Diputación Provincial de Granada, 1987).

Lang, E., and W. A. S. Koch, *Staatsverschuldung – Staatbankrott?* (Würzburg: Physica-Verlag, 1980).

Lapeyre, H., *Simón Ruiz et les asientos de Philippe II* (Paris: A. Colin, 1953).

Laroche, P., *Moirans en Dauphiné: vingt siècles d'histoire* (Moirans: Association Moirans recherche historique, 1992).

Laudanna, L., 'Le grandi ricchezze private di Roma agli inizi dell'Ottocento', *Dimensioni e problemi della ricerca storica*, 2 (1989), pp. 104–52.

Leibfritz, W., D. Roseveare and P. Van Den Noord, *Fiscal Policy, Government Debt and Economic Performance* (Paris: OECD, 1994).

Lemarchand, Y., 'Introducing Double-Entry Bookkeeping in Public Finance: A French Experiment at the Beginning of the Eighteenth Century', *Accounting, Business and Financial History*, 9:2 (1999), pp. 225–54.

Littmann, K., *Definition und Entwicklung der Staatsquote: Abgrenzung, Aussagekraft und Anwendungsbereiche unterschiedlicher Typen von Staatsquoten* (Göttingen: Schwartz Verlag, 1975).

—, 'Bundesrepublik Deutschland', in F. Neumark (ed.), *Handbuch der Finanzwissenschaft*, vol. 3, 3rd edn (Tübingen: J. C. B. Mohr Verlag, 1981), pp. 1011–64.

Litva, F., 'L'attività finanziaria della Dataria durante il periodo tridentino', *Archivum historiae pontificiae*, 5 (1967), pp. 79–174.

Londei, L., 'La monetazione pontificia e la zecca di Roma in età moderna (secc. XVI–XVIII)', *Studi Romani*, 38 (1990), pp. 311–18.

López Cordón Cortezo, M. V., 'Instauración dinástica y reformismo administrativo: la implantación del sistema ministerial', *Manuscrits*, 18 (2000), pp. 93–111.

Luchet, J. P. L., *Histoire de Messieurs Paris: Ouvrage dans lequel ou montre comment un royaume peut passer dans l'espace de cinq années de l'état le plus déplorable à l'état le plus florissant* (Lausanne: n.p, 1776).

Lutz, B., *Der kurze Traum der immerwährenden Prosperität: Eine Neuinterpretation der industriell-kapitalistischen Entwicklung im Europa des 20. Jahrhunderts*, 2nd edn (Frankfurt: Campus-Verlag, 1989).

Luzzatto, G., *I prestiti della repubblica di Venezia* (Padove: A. Draghi, 1929).

—, *Le origini dell'organizzazione finanziaria dei comuni italiani* (Urbino: QuattroVenti, 1990).

McArthur, J., *Financial and Political Facts of the Eighteenth Century*, 3rd edn (London: J. Wright, 1801).

McCulloch, J. R., *A Treatise on the Principles and Practical Influence of Taxation and the Funding System* (London: Longman, Brown, Green, and Longmans, 1845).

Macdonald, J., *A Free Nation Deep in Debt. The Financial Roots of Democracy* (New York: Farrar, Straus and Giroux, 2003).

Macpherson, D., *Annals of commerce*, 4 vols (London: Nichols and Son, 1805).

Maddalena, A., and H. Kellenbenz (eds), *La Repubblica internazionale del denaro tra XV e XVII secolo* (Bologna: Il Mulino, 1986).

Madoz, P., *Diccionario Geográfico-Estadístico de España y de sus posesiones de ultramar, Vol. 1* (Madrid, 1848).

Madrazo, S., *Estado débil y ladrones poderosos en la España del siglo XVIII. Historia de un peculado en el reinado de Felipe V* (Madrid: Catarata, 2000).

Mallet, J. R., *Comptes rendus de l'administration des finances du royaume de France* (London: Buisson, 1789).

Mandler, P., *Aristocratic Government in the Age of Reform* (Cambridge: Cambridge University Press, 1990).

Mantelli, R., *Burocrazia e finanze pubbliche nel Regno di Napoli a metà del '500* (Napoli: Pironti, 1981).

—, 'Guerra, inflazione e recessione nella seconda metà del Cinquecento. Filippo II e le finanze dello Stato napoletano', in A. Di Vittorio (ed.), *La finanza pubblica in età di crisi* (Bari: Cacucci, 1993), pp. 213–44.

—, *L'alienazione della rendita pubblica e i suoi acquirenti dal 1556 al 1583 nel Regno di Napoli* (Bari: Cacucci, 1997).

Marais, M., *Journal de Paris* (Saint-Étienne: Saint-Étienne University Press, 2004).

Marcos Martín, A., *España en los siglos XVI, XVII y XVIII. Economía y sociedad* (Barcelona: Critica, 2000).

—, 'Deuda pública, fiscalidad y arbitrios en la Corona de Castilla', in C. Sanz and B. García (eds), *Banca, crédito y capital. La Monarquía Hispánica y los antiguos Países Bajos (1505–1700)* (Madrid: Fundación Carlos de Amberes, 2006), pp. 345–75.

Marcus, P., *Das kommunale Finanzsystem der Bundesrepublik Deutschland* (Darmstadt: Wissenschaftliche Buchgesellschaft, 1987).

Marion, M., *Histoire financière de la France, 6 vols* (Paris: Arthur Rousseau, 1914–31).

Marsilio, C., 'La frammentazione del network finanziario delle fiere di cambio genovesi (1621–1640 circa)', in G. De Luca and A. Moioli (eds), *Debito pubblico e mercati finanziari in Italia. Secoli XIII–XX* (Milano: FrancoAngeli, 2007).

Martelli, U. di N., *Ricordanze dal 1433 al 1483*, ed. F. Pezzarossa (Roma: Ed. di storia e letteratura, 1989).

Martín Aceña, P., 'Los precios en Europa durante los siglos XVI y XVII. Estudio comparativo', *Revista de Historia Económica*, 3 (1992), pp. 359–95.

Martines, L., *Power and Imagination. City-States in Renaissance Italy* (New York: Vintage Books, 1979).

Martínez Millán, J. (ed.), *La Corte de Carlos V*, 5 vols (Madrid: Sociedad Estatal para la Conmemoración de los Centenarios de Felipe II y Carlos V, 2000).

Masini, R., *Il debito pubblico pontificio a fine Seicento. I monti camerali* (Città di Castello: Edimond, 2005).

Mathers, C. J., 'Relations between the City of Burgos and the Crown, 1506–1556' (Phd dissertation, Michigan University, MI, 1973).

Meek, C., *Lucca 1369–1400. Politics and Society in an Early Renaissance City-State* (Oxford: Oxford University Press, 1978).

Merklein, R., *Die Deutschen werden ärmer: Staatsverschuldung, Geldentwertung, Markteinbußen, Arbeitsplatzverluste* (Reinbek bei Hamburg: Rowohlt Taschenbuch Verlag, 1982).

Metzler, G., 'Am Ende aller Krisen? Politisches Denken und Handeln in der Bundesrepublik der sechziger Jahre', *Historische Zeitschrift*, 275 (2002), pp. 57–103.

Michielin, A., and G. M. Varanini, 'Nota introduttiva', in A. Michielin (ed.), *Mutui e risarcimenti del comune di Treviso (secolo XIII)* (Roma: Viella, 2003).

Moioli, A., 'The Changing Role of the Guilds in the Reorganization of the Milanese Economy throughout the Sixteenth and the Eighteenth Centuries', in A. Guenzi, P. Massa and F. Piola Caselli, *Guilds, Markets and Work Regulations in Italy, 16th–19th Centuries* (Aldershot: Ashgate, 1998), pp. 32–55.

Molho, A., *Florentine Public Finances in the Early Renaissance, 1400–1433* (Cambridge, MA: Harvard University Press, 1971).

—, 'Lo stato e la finanza pubblica. Un'ipotesi basata sulla storia tardomedievale di Firenze', in G. Chittolini, A. Molho and P. Schiera (eds), *Origini dello stato. Processi di formazione statale in Italia fra medioevo e età moderna* (Bologna: Il mulino, 1994), pp. 225–80.

—, *Marriage Alliance in Late Medieval Florence* (Cambridge, MA: Harvard University Press, 1994).

—, 'Créanciers de Florence en 1347. Un aperçu statistique du quartier de Santo Spirito', in *La Toscane et les Toscans autour de la Renaissance. Cadre de vie, société, croyances. Mélanges offerts à Charles-M. de La Roncière* (Aix-en-Provence: Publications de l'Université de Provence, 1999), pp. 79–93.

Montaudo, A., *L'olio nel Regno di Napoli nel sec. XVIII. Commercio, annona e arrendamenti* (Napoli: Edizioni Scientifiche Italiane, 2005).

Morgan, W., *Facts Addressed to the Serious Attention of the People of Great Britain* (London: J. Debrett, 1796).

—, *An Appeal the People of Great Britain on the Present Alarming State of Public Finances* (London: J. Debrett, 1797).

—, *A Comparative view of Public Finances* (London: J. Debrett, 1801).

Mortimer, T., *Every Man his Own Broker*, 13th edn (London: W. J. and J. Richardson, 1801).

Moulin, M., 'Les rentes sur l'hôtel de ville de Paris sous Louis XIV', *Histoire, Economie, Société*, 17 (1998), pp. 623–48.

Mueller, R. C., 'Foreign Investment in Venetian Government Bonds and the Case of Paolo Guinigi, Lord of Lucca, Early Fifteenth Century', in H. Diederiks and D. Reeder (eds), *Cities of Finance* (Amsterdam: Koninklijke Nederlandse Akademie van Wetenschappen, 1996).

—, *The Venetian Money Market. Banks, Panics and Public Debt, 1200–1500* (Baltimore, MD: Johns Hopkins University Press, 1997).

Munro, J. H. 'The Medieval Origins of the Financial Revolution: Usury, *Rentes* and Negociability', *The International History Review*, 25 (3 September 2003), pp. 505–615.

Murphy, A. E., *John Law: Economic Theorist and Policy-Maker* (Oxford: Clarendon Press, 1997).

Muscatelli, V. A., and F. Spinelli, 'Gibson's Paradox and Policy Regimes: A Comparison of the Experience in the US, UK and Italy', *Scottish Journal of Political Economy*, 43:4 (1996), pp. 468–92.

Muscheid, J., *Steuerpolitik in der Bundesrepublik Deutschland 1949–1982* (Berlin: Duncker & Humblot, 1986).

Musi, A. (ed.), *Nel sistema imperiale. L'Italia spagnola* (Napoli: Edizioni Scientifiche Italiane, 1994).

Muto, G., *Saggi sul governo dell'economia nel Mezzogiorno spagnolo* (Napoli: Edizioni Scientifiche Italiane, 1992).

—, 'Modelli di organizzazione finanziaria nell'esperienza degli stati italiani della prima età moderna', in G. Chittolini, A. Molho and P. Schiera (eds), *Origini dello Stato moderno. Processi di formazione statale in Italia fra medioevo ed età moderna* (Bologna: Il Mulino, 1994), pp. 287–302.

—, 'Il governo della *Hacienda* nella Lombardia spagnola', in P. Pissavino and G. Signorotto (eds), *Lombardia borromaica Lombardia spagnola. 1554–1659*, 2 vols (Roma: Bulzoni, 1995), vol. 1, pp. 265–302.

—, 'The Spanish System: Centre and Periphery', in R. Bonney (ed.), *Economic Systems and State Finance* (Oxford: Oxford University Press, 1995), pp. 231–59.

Nava Rodríguez, T., '"Nervios de bóveda": las tesorerías centrales de la hacienda borbónica (1716–1743)', in E. Martínez Ruiz (ed.), *III seminario hispanovenezolano. Vínculos y sociabilidades en España et Iberoamérica. Siglos XVI–XX* (Ciudad Real: Ediciones Puertollano, 2000), pp. 111–31.

Neal, L., *The Rise of Financial Capitalism: International Capital Markets in the Age of Reason* (Cambridge: Cambridge University Press, 1990).

—, 'How it All Began: The Monetary and Financial Architecture of Europe during the First Global Capital Markets, 1648–1815', *Financial History Review*, 7 (2000), pp. 117–40.

—, 'The Monetary, Financial and Political Architecture of Europe, 1648–1815', in L. Prados de la Escosura (ed.), *Exceptionalism and Industrialisation. Britain and its European Rivals* (Cambridge: Cambridge University Press, 2004), pp. 173–89.

Necker, J., *Éloge de Jean-Baptiste Colbert, discour qui a remporté le prix de L'Académie Françoise, en 1773* (Paris: n.p., 1773).

Newmarch, W., *On the Loans Raised by Mr. Pitt during the First French War, 1793–1801* (London: Effingham Wilson, 1855).

Ninci, R., 'La politica finanziaria della Repubblica fiorentina dopo il Tumulto dei Ciompi (1380–1425): Un tentativo di 'Programmazione'?', in R. Ninci (ed.), *La società fiorentina nel Basso medioevo: Per Elio Conti* (Roma: Istituto Storico Italiano per il Medio Evo, 1995), pp. 151–67.

Norris, J., *Shelburne and Reform* (London: Macmillan, 1963).

North, D. C., *Institutions, Institutional Change and Economic Performance* (Cambridge: Cambridge University Press, 1990).

North, D. C., and B. Weingast, 'Constitutions and Commitment: The Evolution of Institutions Governing Public Choice in Seventeenth-Century England', *Journal of Economic History*, 49:4 (1989), pp. 803–32.

Nowotny, E. (ed.), *Öffentliche Verschuldung* (Stuttgart: S. Fischer Verlag, 1979).

O'Brien, P. K., *Government Revenue 1793–1815. A Study in Fiscal and Financial Policy in the Wars against France* (Oxford: Oxford University Press, 1967).

—, 'The Political Economy of British Taxation, 1660–1815', *Economic History Review*, 41:1 (1988), pp. 1–32.

—, 'The Security of the Realm and the Growth of the Economy, 1688–1914', in P. Clarke and C. Trebilcock (eds), *Understanding Decline. Perceptions and Realities of British Economic Performance* (Cambridge: Cambridge University Press, 1997).

—, 'Merchants and Bankers as Patriots or Speculators. Foreign Commerce and Monetary Policy in War Time, 1793–1815', in J. McCusker and K. Morgan (eds), *The Early Modern Atlantic Economy* (Cambridge: Cambridge University Press, 2000).

—, 'Fiscal Exceptionalism: Great Britain and its European Rivals from Civil War to Triumph at Trafalgar and Waterloo', in D. Winch and P. K. O'Brien (eds), *The Political Economy of British Historical Experience, 1688–1914* (Oxford: Oxford University Press, 2002), pp. 245–67.

—, 'The Hanoverian State and the Defeat of Napoleon's Continental System', in M. Lundahl and H. Lingren, *Eli F. Heckscher 1879–1952. A Celebratory Symposium* (Boston: MIT Press, 2007).

O'Brien, P. K., and P. A. Hunt, 'The Rise of a Fiscal State in England, 1485–1915', *Historical Research*, 66:2 (1993), pp. 129–76.

—, 'England 1485–1815', in R. Bonney (ed.), *The Rise of the Fiscal State in Europe, c. 1200–1915* (Oxford: Oxford University Press, 1999), pp. 53–100.

Ochoa Brun, M. A., *Historia de la diplomacia española* (Madrid: Ministerio de Asuntos Exteriores, 1999).

OECD, *Economic Outlook. Historical Statistics 1960–1985* (Paris: OECD, 1987).

—, *Revenue Statistics 1965–2001* (Paris: OECD, 2002).

Orlandelli, G., 'I Monti di pubbliche prestanze in Bologna', *Acta Italica*, 14 (1969), pp. ix–xxii.

Ormrod, W. M. 'Urban Communities and Royal Finance in England during the Later Middle Ages', in *Actes. Colloqui Corona, Municipis i fiscalitat a la Baixa Edad Mitjana* (Lleida: Institut d'Estudis Ilerdencs, 1995), pp. 45–60.

Ozanam, Denise, 'Jean Orry, munitionnaire du Roi', *Etudes et documents*, 5 (1993), pp. 123–56.

Ozanam, Didier, 'La restauration de l'État espagnol au début du règne de Philippe V (1700–1724): le problème des hommes', *Philippe V d'Espagne et l'Art de son temps. Actes du colloque des 7, 8 et 9 juin 1993 à Sceaux sous la haute autorité scientifique du Professeur Yves Bottineau*, (Paris: Musées de l'Ile de France, 1995), vol. 2, pp. 79–89.

—, 'Les intendants espagnols de la première moitié du XVIIIe siècle, 1711–1749', in R. Descimon, J. F. Schaub and B. Vincent (eds), *Les figures de l'administrateur. Institutions, réseaux, pouvoirs en Espagne, en France et au Portugal, 16–19ᵉ siècle* (Paris: Editions de l'EHESS, 1997), pp. 181–99.

Pacini, A., *La Genova di Andrea Doria nell'Impero di Carlo V* (Firenze: Leo S. Olschki, 1999).

Panckouke, C. J. (ed.), *Encyclopédie méthodique: Finances, 2 vols* (Paris: Panckouke, 1784–5).

Parfaict, C., and F. Parfaict, *Histoire du théâtre françois depuis son origine jusqu'à présent, 15 vols* (Amsterdam: n.p, 1735–49).

Paris Duverney, J., *Examen du livre intitulé Réflexions politiques sur les finances et le commerce* (The Hague: V. & N. Prevôt, 1740).

Parker, R., *John Kenneth Galbraith: His Life, His Politics, His Economics* (New York: Farrar, 2005).

Parker, S., *An Attempt to Ascertain a Theory for Determining the Value of Funded Property* (London: M. Richardson, 1809).

Partner, P., 'Papal Financial Policy in the Renaissance and Counter-Reformation', *Past and Present*, 88 (1980), pp. 17–62.

—, 'The Papacy and the Papal States', in R. Bonney (ed.), *The Rise of the Fiscal State in Europe c. 1200–1815* (Oxford: Oxford University Press, 1999), pp. 359–80.

Pasinetti, L., 'European Union at the End of 1997: Who is Within the Public Finance "Sustainability" Zone?', *BNL Quarterly Review*, 51:204 (1998), pp. 17–36.

—, 'The Myth (or Folly) of the 3% Deficit/GDP Maastricht "Parameter"', *Cambridge Journal of Economics*, 22:1 (1998), pp. 103–16.

Peel, R., *The National Debt Productive of National Prosperity* (Warrington: J. Johnson, 1787).

Peñasco de la Fuente, H., *Las sisas de Madrid* (Madrid, 1890).

Pérez Bustamante, R., 'Del sistema de contadurías al Consejo de Hacienda, 1433–1525 (una perspectiva institucional), in *Historia de la Hacienda Española (épocas antigua y medieval)* (Madrid: Instituto de Estudios Fiscales, 1982), pp. 681–738.

Perugino, G., *Il bilancio pontificio del 1657* (Napoli: Edizioni Scientifiche Italiane, 1999).

Petrucci, A. (ed.), *Il libro di ricordanze dei Corsini (1362–1457)* (Roma: Istituto Storico Italiano per il Medio Evo, 1965).

Petzina, D., 'Zwischen Reform und Krise', in D. Petzina and J. Reulecke (eds), *Bevölkerung, Wirtschaft, Gesellschaft seit der Industrialisierung: Festschrift für Wolfgang Köllmann zum 65. Geburtstag* (Dortmund: Gesellschaft für Westfälische Wirtschaftsgeschichte, 1990), pp. 261–77.

Pezzolo, L., *L´oro dello Stato. Società, finanza e fisco nella Republicc Veneta del secondo '500* (Venice: Il Cardo, 1990).

—, 'Elogio della rendita. Sul debito pubblico degli Stati italiani nel Cinque e Seicento', *Rivista di storia economica*, 12:3 (1995), pp. 284–330.

—, 'Government Debts and Trust. French Kings and Roman Popes as Borrowers, 1520–1660', *Rivista di Storia Economica*, 15:3 (1999), pp. 233–61.

—, *Il fisco dei veneziani. Finanza pubblica ed economia tra XV e XVII secolo* (Verona: Cierre, 2003).

—, 'The Venetian Government Debt, 1350–1650', in M. Boone, K. Davids and P. Janssens (eds), *Urban Public Debts. Urban Government and the Market for Annuities in Western Europe (14th–18th Centuries)* (Turnhout: Brepols, 2003), pp. 61–74.

—, 'Bonds and Government Debt in Italian City States, 1250–1650', in W. Goetzman and G. Rouwenhorst (eds), *Origins of Value. Financial Innovations in History* (New York: Oxford University Press, 2005), pp. 145–63.

—, *Una finanza d'ancien régime. La Repubblica veneta tra XV e XVIII secolo* (Napoli: Edizioni Scientifiche Italiane, 2006).

Pinedo, E. F. de, 'La deuda pública y los juristas laicos (1550–1650)', in A. M. Bernal (ed.), *Dinero moneda y crédito en la Monarquía Hispánica* (Madrid: Marcial Pons-Fundación ICO, 2000), pp. 805–24.

Piola Caselli, F., 'Aspetti del debito pubblico nello Stato Pontificio: gli uffici vacabili', *Annali della Facoltà di Scienze Politiche dell'Università degli Studi di Perugia*, 11 (1973), pp. 3–74.

—, *Il buon governo. Storia della finanza pubblica nell'Europa preindustriale* (Torino: Giappichelli, 1997).

—, 'Public Debt, State Revenue and Town Consumption in Rome (16th–18th Centuries)', in M. Boone, K. Davids and P. Jansenns (eds), *Urban Public Debt. Urban Government and the Market for Annuities in Western Europe (14th–18th centuries)* (Turnhout: Brepols, 2003), pp. 93–105.

—, 'Evoluzione e finanziamento del debito pubblico pontificio tra XVII e XVIII secolo', in G. De Luca and A. Moioli (eds), *Debito pubblico e formazione dei mercati finanziari in Italia. Secoli XIII–XX* (Milano: FrancoAngeli, 2007), pp. 221–42.

Playfair, W., *An Essay on the National Debt* (London: J. Debrett and G. G. J. and J. Robinson, 1787).

Podestà, G. L., 'Finanza pubblica nel Ducato di Parma e Piacenza in età farnesiana', in G. De Luca and A. Moioli (eds), *Debito pubblico e mercati finanziari in Italia. Secoli XIII–XX* (Milano: FrancoAngeli, 2007).

Porter, B., *Britain, Europe and the World: Delusions of Grandeur* (London: Unwin-Hyman, 1983).

—, *Britannia's Burden: The Political Evolution of Modern Britain* (London: Edward Arnold, 1994).

Poterba, J. M., 'Annuities in Early Modern Europe', in W. Goetzman and G. Rouwenhorst (eds), *Origins of Value. Financial Innovations in History* (New York: Oxford University Press, 2005), pp. 207–24.

Pressnell, L., *Country Banking in the Industrial Revolution* (Oxford: Oxford University Press, 1956).

Price, R., *Appeal to the Public, on the Subject of the National Debt* (London: T. Cadell, 1772).

Prodi, P., 'Operazioni finanziarie presso la corte romana di un uomo d'affari milanese nel 1562–63', *Rivista storica italiana*, 73:3 (1961), pp. 641–59.

Pugliese, S., *Condizioni economiche e finanziarie della Lombardia nella prima metà del secolo XVIII* (Torino: Bocca, 1924).

Pulido Bueno, I., *La corte, las Cortes y los mercaderes. Política imperial y desempeño de la hacienda real en la España de los Austrias* (Huelva: for the author, 2002).

Puviani, A., *Teoria della illusione finanziaria* (1903; Milano: Isedi, 1973).

Ragioneria generale dello Stato, *Il bilancio dello Stato italiano dal 1862 al 1967* (Roma: Poligrafico dello Stato, 1969).

Ranft, A., *Der Basishaushalt der Stadt Lüneburg in der Mitte des 15. Jahrhunderts. Zur Struktur der städtischen Finanzen im Spätmittelalter*, Veröffentlichungen des Max-Planck-Instituts für Geschichte 84 (Göttingen: Verlag Vandenhoeck & Ruprecht Göttingen, 1987).

Rauscher, P., 'La casa de Austria y sus banqueros alemanes', in J. L. Castellano and F. Sánchez-Montes (eds), *Carlos V. Europeísmo y universalidad*, 5 vols (Madrid: Sociedad Estatal para la Conmemoración de los Centenarios de Felipe II y Carlos V, 2001), vol. 3, pp. 411–28.

Rayment, R., *The Income and Expenditure of Great Britain of the Last Seven Years* (London: J. Debrett, 1791).

Rees, J. F., *A Short Fiscal and Financial History of England, 1815–1918* (London: Methuen, 1921).

Reincke, H., 'Die alte Hamburger Staatsschuld der Hansezeit (1300–1563)', in A. von Brandt and W. Koppe (eds), *Städtewesen und Bürgertum als geschichtliche Kräfte* (Lübeck: Schmidt-Römhild Verlag, 1953), pp. 489–511.

Reinecke, W., 'Des Bürgermeisters Claus Stöterogge Denkbüchlein über die Ratsämter', *Lüneburger Museumsblätter*, 2 (1912), pp. 349–83.

—, 'Die drei ältesten Kämmereirechnungen ([1322], 1331, 133[5], 1337)', *Lüneburger Museumsblätter*, 2 (1928), pp. 309–37.

—, *Geschichte der Stadt Lüneburg*, 2 vols (1933; Lüneburg: Heinrich Heine Buchhandlung Neubauer, 1977).

Renzsch, W., *Finanzverfassung und Finanzausgleich: Die Auseinandersetzungen um ihre politische Gestaltung in der Bundesrepublik Deutschland zwischen Währungsreform und deutscher Vereinigung (1948–1990)* (Bonn: Verlag J. H. W. Dietz Nachf, 1991).

Ribot García, L.A., *La Monarquia de España y la guerra de Mesina (1674–1678)* (Madrid: Actas, 2002).

Ricardo, D., *On the Principles of Political Economy and Taxation* (London: J. Murray, 1819).

Rickards, R. D., *The Financial Policy of War* (London: J. Ridgway, 1855).

Rivero Rodríguez, M., *Diplomacia y relaciones exteriores en la Edad Moderna, 1453–1794* (Madrid: Alianza Editorial, 2000).

Rizzo, M., J. J. Ruiz Ibañez and G. Sabatini, 'Introducción', in M. Rizzo, J. J. Ruiz Ibañez and G. Sabatini (eds), *Le forze del Principe. Recursos, instrumentos y limites en la pratica del poder soberano en los territorios de la Monarquia Hispanica*, 2 vols (Murcia: Universidad de Murcia, 2003), vol. 1, pp. 23–68.

Rödder, A., *Die Bundesrepublik Deutschland 1969–1990* (München: Oldenbourg Wissenschaftsverlag, 2004).

Rodger, N., *The Command of the Ocean, 1649–1815* (London: Allen Lane, 2004).

Rodríguez Villa, A., *Don Francisco de Rojas, embajador de los Reyes Católicos* (Madrid: Fortanet, 1896).

—, *El emperador Carlos V y su corte según las cartas de don Martín de Salinas, embajador del infante don Fernando (1522–1559)* (Madrid: Fortanet, 1903).

Root, H. L., *The Fountain of Privilege. Political Foundations of Markets in Old Regime France and England* (Berkeley, CA: University of California Press, 1994).

Rose, G., *A Brief Examination into the Increase of Revenue, Commerce and Navigation of Great Britain* (London: J. Hatchard, 1806).

—, *Observations Respecting the Public Expenditure, and the Influence of the Crown* (London: T. Cadell and W. Davies, 1810).

Rosen, J., 'Der Staatshaushalt [*sic*] Basels von 1360 bis 1535', in H. Kellenbenz (ed.), *Öffentliche Finanzen und privates Kapital im späten Mittelalter und in der ersten Hälfte des 19. Jahrhunderts* (Stuttgart: Fischer Verlag, 1971), pp. 24–38.

—, *Finanzgeschichte Basels im späten Mittelalter* (Stuttgart: Steiner Verlag Wiesbaden, 1989).

Rosenthal, J. L., and B. Wong, 'Another Look at Credit Markets and investment in China and Europe before the Industrial Revolution', unpublished Yale Economic History Workshop paper, 2005, <http://www.econ.yale.edu/seminars/echist/eh05-06/paper_Wong.doc>.

Roseveare, H., *The Financial Revolution, 1660–1760* (London: Longmans, 1991).

Rossi, N., A. Sorgato and G. Toniolo, 'I conti economici italiani: una ricostruzione statistica, 1890–1990', *Rivista di storia economica*, n.s. 10:1 (1993), pp. 1–47.

Royal Commission on Historical Manuscripts, *The Manuscripts of J. B. Fortescue, Esq: Preserved at Dropmore*, 10 vols (London: HMSO, 1892–1927).

Ruiz Martín, F., 'Un expediente financiero entre 1560 y 1575. La hacienda de Felipe II y la Casa de la Contratación de Sevilla', *Moneda y Crédito*, 92 (1965), pp. 3–58.

—, 'La banca en España hasta 1782', in *El banco de España. Una historia económica* (Madrid: Banco de España, 1970), pp. 1–196.

—, 'Crédito y banca, comercio y transportes en la etapa del capitalismo mercantil', in *Actas de las I Jornadas de Metodología Aplicada de las Ciencias Históricas. III. Metodología de la Historia Moderna. Economía y Demografía* (Santiago de Compostela: Universidad de Santiago de Compostela, 1975), pp. 725–49.

—, *Las finanzas de la Monarquía Hispánica en tiempos de Felipe IV (1621–1665)* (Madrid: Real Academia de la Historia, 1990).

—, *Pequeño capitalismo, gran capitalismo. Simón Ruiz y sus negocios en Florencia* (Barcelona: Crítica, 1990).

—, 'Las Finanzas del Rey', in *Felipe II. Un monarca y su época* (San Lorenzo de El Escorial: Fundación ICO, 1998), pp. 387–408.

Ryder, A., 'Cloth and Credit: Aragonese War Finance in the mid Fifteenth Century', *War and Society*, 2 (1984), pp. 1–21.

Sabatini, G., *Proprietà e proprietari a L'Aquila e nel contado. Le rilevazioni catastali in età spagnola* (Napoli: Edizioni Scientifiche Italiane, 1995).

—, 'Collecteurs et fermiers des impôts dans les communautés du Royaume de Naples durant la période espagnole', *Mélanges de la Casa de Velázquez*, 34:2 (2004), pp. 141–59.

—, 'Gastos militares y finanzas publicas en el reino de Nápoles en el siglo XVII', in E. García Hernán and D. Maffi (eds), *Guerra y sociedad en la monarquía hispánica. Política, estrategia y cultura en la Europa moderna, 1500–1700*, 2 vols (Madrid: CSIC, 2006), vol. 2, pp. 257–91.

—, 'Nel sistema imperiale spagnolo: considerazioni sul debito pubblico napoletano nella prima età moderna', in G. De Luca and A. Moioli (eds), *Debito pubblico e mercati finanziari in Italia. Secoli XIII–XX* (Milano: FrancoAngeli, 2007).

Sachverständigenrat zur Begutachtung der gesamtwirtschaftlichen Entwicklung, *Vor weitreichenden Entscheidungen. Jahresgutachten 1998/99* (Stuttgart: Metzler-Poeschel Verlag, 1998).

Salomoni, A. (ed.), *Memorie storico-diplomatiche degli Ambasciatori, Incaricati d'affari, Corrispondenti, e Delegati, che la città di Milano inviò a diversi suoi principi dal 1500 al 1796* (Milano: Tipografia Pulini al Bocchetto, 1806).

Salvemini, G., and V. Zamagni, 'Finanza pubblica e indebitamento tra le due guerre mondiali: il finanziamento del settore statale', in F. Cotula (ed.), *Problemi di finanza pubblica tra le due guerre, 1919–1939*, Ricerche per la storia della Banca d'Italia, 2 (Roma-Bari: Laterza, 1993), pp. 139–283.

Sánchez Belén, J. A., *La política fiscal en Castilla durante el reinado de Carlos II* (Madrid: Siglo XXI, 1996).

San Miniato, G. C. da, *Le ricordanze*, ed. M. T. Sillano (Milano: FrancoAngeli, 1984).

Sanudo, M., *Diari*, ed. R. Fulin et al., 58 vols (Venezia: Deputazione di storia patria, 1879–1903).

Sanz Ayán, C., *Los banqueros de Carlos II* (Valladolid: Universidad, 1988).

—, 'La estrategia de la Monarquía en la suspensión de pagos del 96 y su "Medio General"', in *Congreso Internacional Las Sociedades Ibéricas y el Mar a finales del siglo XVI*, 6 vols ([Madrid]: Sociedad Estatal Lisboa, 1998), vol. 2, pp. 81–95.

—, 'Financieros holandeses de Felipe V en la Guerra de Sucesión. Huberto Hubrecht', in A. Crespo Solana and M. Herrero Sánchez (eds), *España y las 18 provincias de los Países Bajos. Una revisión historiográfica* (Córdoba: Universidad de Córdoba, Ministerio de Asuntos Exteriores, Fundación Carlos de Amberes, 2002), pp. 563–81.

—, *Estado, Monarquía y Finanzas. Estudios de Historia financiera en tiempos de los Austrias* (Madrid: Centro de Estudios Políticos y Constitucionales, 2004).

—, 'Administration and Resources for the Mainland War in the First Phases of the War of the Spanish Succession', in H. V. Bowen and A. González Enciso, *Mobilising Resources for War: Britain and Spain at Work During the Early Modern Period* (Pamplona: EUNSA, 2006), pp. 135–58.

Sapori, A., *Studi di storia economica*, 3rd edn, 2 vols (Firenze: Sansoni, 1982).

Sargent, T. J., and F. R. Velde, *The Big Problem of Small Change* (Princeton, NJ: Princeton University Press, 2002).

Sarrazin, T., 'Die Finanzpolitik des Bundes 1970 bis 1982', *Finanzarchiv*, n.s. 41 (1983), pp. 373–87.

Scarmoncin, F. (ed.), *I documenti del Comune di Bassano dal 1259 al 1295* (Padova: Antenore, 1989).

Scherf, H., *Enttäuschte Hoffnungen – vergebene Chancen: Die Wirtschaftspolitik der sozialliberalen Koalition 1969–1982* (Göttingen: Vandenhoeck & Ruprecht, 1986).

Schildhauer, J. *Die Hanse. Geschichte und Kultur* (Stuttgart: Verlag Kohlhammer, 1984).

Schildt, A., D. Siegfried and K. C. Lammers (eds.), *Dynamische Zeiten: Die sechziger Jahre in beiden deutschen Gesellschaften* (Hamburg: Hans Christians Verlag, 2000).

Schimmelpfennig, B., 'Der Ämterhandel an der römischen Kurie von Pius II. bis zum Sacco di Roma (1458–1527)', in I. Mieck (ed.), *Ämterhandel im Spätmittelalter und im 16. Jahrhundert* (Berlin: Colloquium Verlag, 1984), pp. 3–41.

Schmidt, M. G., *Sozialpolitik in Deutschland: Historische Entwicklung und internationaler Vergleich*, 2nd edn (Opladen: Leske & Budrich Verlag, 1998).

— (ed.), *Geschichte der Sozialpolitik in Deutschland seit 1945*, vol. 7 (Baden-Baden: Nomos-Verlagsgesellschaft, 2005).

Schönberg, L., *Die Technik des Finanzhaushalts der deutschen Städte im Mittelalter* (Stuttgart and Berlin: J. G. Cotta'sche Buchhandlung Nachfolger, 1910).

Schorn-Schütte, L., 'Stadt und Staat. Zum Zusammenhang von Gegenwartsverständnis und historischer Erkenntnis in der Stadtgeschichtsschreibung der Jahrhundertwende', *Die alte Stadt* 10 (1983), pp. 228–66.

Schreiner, K., 'Die Stadt in Webers Analyse und Deutung des okzidentalen Rationalismus', in J. Kocka (ed.), *Max Weber, der Historiker*, Kritische Studien der Geschichtswissenschaft 73 (Göttingen: Verlag Vandenhoeck & Ruprecht Göttingen, 1986), pp. 119–50.

Schumpeter, J. A., 'The Crisis of the Tax State' (1918), in A. T. Peacock et al (eds), *International Economic Papers*, vol. 4 (London: Macmillan, 1954), pp. 5–38.

Sella, D., *L'economia lombarda durante la dominazione spagnola* (Bologna: Il Mulino, 1982).

Sieveking, H., *Studio sulle finanze genovesi nel medioevo e in particolare sulla Casa di S. Giorgio*, 2 vols (Genova: Società Ligure di Storia Patria, 1905–6).

Signorotto, G., 'Stabilità politica e trame antispagnole nella Milano del Seicento', in Y. M. Bercé and E. Fasano Guarini (eds), *Complots et conjurations dans l'Europe moderne: actes du colloque international organisé par l'École française de Rome, l'Institut de recherches sur les civilisations de l'occident moderne de l'Université de Paris-Sorbonne et le Dipartimento di storia moderna e contemporanea dell'Università degli studi di Pisa* (Rome: Ecole française de Rome, 1996), pp. 721–45.

Silver, F., *Observations on Vansittart's Plan of Finance* (London: n.p., 1813).

Silvestri, A., 'Sull'attività bancaria napoletana durante il periodo aragonese', *Bollettino dell'Archivio Storico del Banco di Napoli*, 6 (1953), pp. 3–57.

Simmert, D. B., and K. D. Wagner (eds), *Staatsverschuldung kontrovers* (Köln: Verlag Wissenschaft und Politik, 1981).

Sims, C. A., 'Fiscal Consequences for Mexico of Adopting the Dollar', *Journal of Money, Credit and Banking* 33:2 (2001), pp. 597–616.

Sinclair, J., *History of the Public Revenue of the British Empire*, 3rd edn, 3 vols (London: T. Cadell and W. Davies, 1803–4).

Skilling, D. G., *Policy Coordination, Political Structure and Public Debt: The Political Economy of Public Debt Accumulation in OECD Countries since 1960* (Ann Arbor, MI: University of Michigan Press, 2001).

Solinís Estalló, M A., *La alcabala del rey, 1474–1504. Fiscalidad en el partido de las Cuatro Villas cántabras y las merindades de Campoo y Campos con Palencia* (Santander: Universidad de Cantabria, 2003).

Sprandel, R., 'Der städtische Rentenmarkt in Nordwestdeutschland im Spätmittelalter', in H. Kellenbenz (ed.), *Öffentliche Finanzen und privates Kapital im späten Mittelalter und in der ersten Hälfte des 19. Jahrhunderts* (Stuttgart: G. Fischer, 1971), pp. 14–23.

Stabel, P., and J. Haemers, 'From Bruges to Antwerp. International Commercial Firms and Government's Credit in late 15th Century and early 16th Century', in C. Sanz and B. García (eds), *Banca, crédito y capital. La Monarquía Hispánica y los antiguos Países Bajos (1505–1700)* (Madrid: Fundación Carlos de Amberes, 2006), pp. 21–38.

Stasavage, D., *Public Debt and the Birth of the Democratic State. France and Great Britain, 1688–1789* (Cambridge: Cambridge University Press, 2003).

—, 'Cities, Constitutions and Sovereign Borrowing in Europe, 1274–1785', *International Organization*, 61 (2007), pp. 489–525.

—, 'Partisan Politics and Public Debt: The Importance of the Whig Supremacy for Britain's Financial Revolution', *European Review of Economic History*, 11 (2007), pp. 123–53.

Stone, L., *An Imperial State at War. Britain from 1689 to 1815*. (London: Routledge, 1994).

Strangio, D., *Il debito pubblico pontificio. Cambiamento e continuità nella finanza pontificia dal periodo francese alla restaurazione romana. 1798–1820* (Padova: Cedam, 2001).

—, '*Facilitare al Governo il mezzo di conoscere, e di soddisfare i veri bisogni del commercio, e delle arti*. La disciplina della Borsa di Roma nella prima metà del XIX secolo', *Studi Storici Luigi Simeoni*, 56 (2006), pp. 389–404

Stumpo, E., *Finanza e stato moderno nel Piemonte del Seicento* (Roma: Istituto storico per l'età moderna e contemporanea, 1979).

—, 'La distribuzione sociale degli acquirenti dei titoli del debito pubblico in Piemonte nella seconda metà del Seicento', in *La fiscalité et ses implications sociales en Italie et en France aux XVIIe et XVIIIe siècles* (Rome: École française de Rome, 1980), pp. 113–24.

—, *Il capitale finanziario a Roma fra Cinque e Seicento, contributo alla storia della fiscalità pontificia in età moderna (1570–1660)* (Milano: Giuffrè, 1985).

—, 'Città, stato e mercato finanziario: il diverso ruolo del debito pubblico in Piemonte e Toscana', in G. De Luca and A. Moioli (eds), *Debito pubblico e mercati finanziari in Italia. Secoli XIII–XX* (Milano: FrancoAngeli, 2007).

Sturm, R., *Staatsverschuldung* (Opladen: Leske & Budrich Verlag, 1993).

Sussman, N., and Y. Yafeh, 'Constitutions and Commitment: Evidence on the Relation Between Institutions and the Cost of Capital', *CEPR Discussion Papers* (June 2004), n. 4404.

Sylos Labini, P., *Torniamo ai classici. Produttività del lavoro, progresso tecnico e sviluppo economico* (Roma-Bari: Laterza, 2004).

Tabarrini, M. (ed.), 'Relazione inedita dello Stato di Milano di G.B. Guarini', *Archivio Storico Italiano*, 5:1 (1867), pp. 3–34.

Tanzi, V., and L. Schuknecht, *Public Spending in the 20th Century: A Global Perspective* (Cambridge: Cambridge University Press, 2000).

Terreni, A., '"Sogliono tutti i forastieri, i quali vanno a negotiare nelle città d'altri Dominii, essere favoriti et privilegiati". La concessione della "civilitas mediolanensis" ai mercanti-banchieri genovesi nel XVI secolo', in C. Donati (ed.), *Alle frontiere della Lombardia. Politica, guerra e religione nell'età moderna* (Milano: FrancoAngeli, 2006), pp. 105–22.

Thompson, I. A. A. 'Castile: Polity, Fiscality and Fiscal Crisis', in P. Hoffman and K. Norberg (eds), *Fiscal Crises, Liberty and Representative Government, 1450–1789* (Stanford, CA: Stanford University Press, 1994), pp. 140–81.

—, 'Money, Money and Yet More Money! Finance, the Fiscal-State and the Military Revolution', in C. J. Rogers (ed.), *The Military Revolution Debate: Readings on the Military Transformation of Early Modern Europe* (Boulder, CO: Westview Press, 1995), pp. 273–98.

Thornton, H., *An Inquiry into the Nature and Effects of the Paper Credit of Great Britain* (London: J. Hatchard, 1802).

Tilly, C., *Capital, Coercion and European States, 990–1990* (Oxford: Blackwell, 1990).

—, *L'oro e la spada. Capitale, guerra e potere nella formazione degli stati europei 990–1990* (Firenze: Ponte alle Grazie, 1991).

Toboso Sánchez, P., *La deuda pública castellana durante el Antiguo Régimen (juros) y su liquidación en el siglo XIX* (Madrid: Instituto de Estudios Fiscales, 1987).

Tognetti, S., *Il banco Cambini. Affari e mercati di una compagnia mercantile-bancaria nella Firenze del XV secolo* (Firenze: Olschki, 1999).

Torres Sánchez R., '"*Servir al rey*", más una comisión. El fortalecimiento de los asentistas en la corona española durante la segunda mitad del siglo XVIII', in P. F. Albaladejo (ed.), *Monarquía, imperio y pueblos en la España moderna. Actas de la IV Reunión Científica de la Asociación Española de Historia Moderna. Alicante, 27–30 de mayo de 1996* (Alicante: Caja de Ahorros del Mediterráneo, Universidad de Alicante, AEHM, 1997), pp. 149–67.

—, 'Cuando las reglas del juego cambian. Mercados y privilgio en el abastecimiento del ejército español en el siglo XVIII', *Revista de Historia Moderna*, 20 (2002), pp. 487–512.

Tracy, J. D., *A Financial Revolution in the Habsburg Netherlands. Renten and Renteniers in the County of Holland, 1515–1565* (Berkeley, CA: University of California Press, 1985).

—, *Holland under Habsburg Rule, 1506–1566. The Formation of a Body Politic* (Berkeley, CA: University of California Press, 1990).

—, *Emperor Charles V, Impresario of War. Campaign Strategy, International Finance and Domestic Politics* (Cambridge: Cambrige University Press, 2002).

—, 'On the Dual Origins of Long-Term Urban Debt in Medieval Europe', in M. Boone, K. Davids and P. Janssens (eds), *Urban Public Debts. Urban Government and the Market for Annuities in Western Europe (14th–18th centuries)* (Turnhout: Brepols, 2003), pp. 13–24.

Ullmann, H.-P., *Der deutsche Steuerstaat: Geschichte der öffentlichen Finanzen vom 18. Jahrhundert bis heute* (München: Verlag C. H. Beck, 2005).

Ulloa, M., *La Hacienda Real de Castilla en el reinado de Felipe II*, 3rd edn (Madrid: Fundacion Universitaria Española, 1986).

Vansittart, N., *An Inquiry into the State of the Finances of Great Britain* (London: J. Owen, 1796).

Velde, F. R., 'Government Equity and Money: John Law's System in 1720 France', working paper 31 (Chicago, IL: Federal Reserve Bank of Chicago, 2003).

—, 'Chronicle of a Deflation Unforetold', working paper 12 (Chicago, IL: Federal Reserve Bank of Chicago, 2006).

Velde, F. R., and D. R. Weir, 'The Financial Market and Government Debt Policy in France, 1746–1793', *Journal of Economic History*, 52:1 (1992), pp. 1–39.

Vicens Vives, J., *Aproximación a la historia de España* (Barcelona: Universidad de Barcelona, 1952).

Vigo, G., 'Manovre monetarie e crisi economica nello Stato di Milano (1619–1622)', *Studi storici*, 17:4 (1976), pp. 101–26.

—, *Fisco e società nella Lombardia del Cinquecento* (Bologna: Il Mulino, 1979).

Villari, R., *La rivolta antispagnola a Napoli. Le origini (1585–1647)* (Roma-Bari: Laterza, 1967).

Wagschal, U., *Staatsverschuldung* (Opladen: Leske & Budrich Verlag, 1996).

—, *Steuerpolitik und Steuerreformen im internationalen Vergleich* (Münster: Literatur-Verlag, 2005).

Wakefield, D., *Observations on the Credit and Finances of Great Britain* (London: F. and C. Rivington, 1797).

—, *Facts of Importance relative to the Present State of Great Britain* (London: F. and C. Rivington, J. Wright, and Bye and Law, 1800).

Wee, H. van der, 'Monetary, Credit and Banking Systems', in E. E. Rich and C. H. Wilson (eds), *The Cambridge Economic History of Europe, Vol. 5: The Economic Organization of Early Modern Europe* (Cambridge: Cambridge University Press, 1977), pp. 290–393.

—, *The Low Countries in the Early Modern World* (Aldershot: Variorum, 1993).

Wee, H. van der, and I. Blanchard, 'The Habsburgs and the Antwerp Money Market: the Exchange Crises of 1521 and 1522–1523', in I. Blanchard, A. Goodman and J. Newman (eds), *Industry and Finance in Early Modern History. Essays Presented to George Hammersley on the Occasion of his 74th Birthay* (Stuttgart: Franz Steiner Verlag, 1992), pp. 27–57.

Weingast, B. R., 'The Political Foundations of Limited Government: Parliament and Sovereign Debt in 17th and 18th Century England', in J. Drobak and J. Nye (eds), *The Frontiers of the New Institutional Economics* (San Diego, CA: Academic Press, 1997), pp. 213–46.

Weir, D. R., 'Tontines, Public Finance and Revolution in France and England, 1688–1789', *Journal of Economic History*, 49:1 (1989), pp. 95–124.

Wenner, H.-J., *Handelskonjunkturen und Rentenmarkt am Beispiel der Stadt Hamburg um die Mitte des 14. Jahrhunderts* (Hamburg: Christians, 1972).

White, E. N., 'From Privatized to Government-Administered Tax Collection: Tax Farming in Eighteenth-Century France', *Economic History Review*, 57:4 (2004), pp. 636–63.

Winter, G. (ed.), 'Die ältesten Lüneburger Kämmereirechnungen', in *Lüneburger Blätter*, 2 (1951), pp. 2–26

Witthöft, H., 'Struktur und Kapazität der Lüneburger Saline seit dem 12. Jahrhundert', *Vierteljahresschrift für Sozial und Wirtschaftsgeschichte*, 63 (1976), pp. 1–117.

Woods, E., *English Theories of Central Banking Control, 1819–58* (Cambridge, MA: Harvard University Press, 1939).

Woolf, S. J., 'Sviluppo economico e struttura sociale nel Piemonte da Emanuele Filiberto a Carlo Emanuele III', *Nuova Rivista Storica*, 46:3–4 (1962), pp. 1–57.

Yun Casalilla, B., *Marte contra Minerva. El precio del Imperio español c. 1450–1600* (Barcelona: Critica, 2004).

Zamagni, V., 'Il debito pubblico italiano 1861–1946: ricostruzione della serie storica', *Rivista di storia economica*, 14:3 (1998), pp. 207–42.

Zanden, J. L. van, and M. Prak, 'Towards an Economic Interpretation of Citizenship: The Dutch Republic between Medieval Communes and Modern-States', *European Review of Economic History*, 10 (2006), pp. 111–45.

Zaske, N., and Zaske, R., *Kunst in Hansestädten* (Leipzig: Verlag Koehler & Amelang Leipzig, 1985).

Zilli, I., *Carlo di Borbone e la rinascita del Regno di Napoli. Le finanze pubbliche, 1734–42* (Napoli: Edizioni Scientifiche Italiane, 1990).

—, *Imposta diretta e debito pubblico nel Regno di Napoli, 1669–1737* (Napoli: Edizioni Scientifiche Italiane, 1990).

—, *Lo Stato e i suoi creditori. Il debito pubblico del Regno di Napoli tra '600 e '700* (Napoli: Edizioni Scientifiche Italiane, 1997).

—, 'Il debito pubblico del Regno di Napoli fra '600 e '700: bilanci e prospettive', in G. De Luca and A. Moioli (eds), *Debito pubblico e mercati finanziari in Italia. Secoli XIII–XX* (Milano: FrancoAngeli, 2007).

Zimmermann, H., *Kommunalfinanzen: Eine Einführung in die finanzwissenschaftliche Analyse der kommunalen Finanzwirtschaft* (Baden-Baden: Nomos-Verlagsgesellschaft, 1999).

INDEX

For Product Safety Concerns and Information please contact our EU
representative GPSR@taylorandfrancis.com
Taylor & Francis Verlag GmbH, Kaufingerstraße 24, 80331 München, Germany